DOCUMENTS FROM THE LUCIFERIANS

WRITINGS FROM THE GRECO-ROMAN WORLD

General Editor
John T. Fitzgerald

Editorial Board
Christopher A. Baron
Andrew Cain
Margaret M. Mitchell
Teresa Morgan
Ilaria L. E. Ramelli
Clare K. Rothschild
David T. Runia
Karin Schlapbach
James C. VanderKam
L. Michael White

Number 43
Volume Editor
Andrew Cain

DOCUMENTS FROM THE LUCIFERIANS

In Defense of the Nicene Creed

Translated with Notes and Introduction by
Colin M. Whiting

Atlanta

Copyright © 2019 by SBL Press

All rights reserved. No part of this work may be reproduced or transmitted in any form or by any means, electronic or mechanical, including photocopying and recording, or by means of any information storage or retrieval system, except as may be expressly permitted by the 1976 Copyright Act or in writing from the publisher. Requests for permission should be addressed in writing to the Rights and Permissions Office, SBL Press, 825 Houston Mill Road, Atlanta, GA 30329 USA.

Library of Congress Cataloging-in-Publication Data

Names: Whiting, Colin M.
Title: Documents from the Luciferians : in defense of the Nicene Creed / by Colin M. Whiting.
Description: Atlanta : SBL Press, 2018. | Series: Writings from the Greco-Roman world ; Number 43 | Includes bibliographical references and index.
Identifiers: LCCN 2018020290 (print) | LCCN 2018037788 (ebook) | ISBN 9780884143284 (ebk.) | ISBN 9781628372229 (pbk. : alk. paper) | ISBN 9780884143277 (hbk. : alk. paper)
Subjects: LCSH: Luciferians (Christian heresy)—History—Sources. | Jesus Christ—Person and offices. | Nicene Creed. | Lucifer, Bishop of Cagliari, –approximately 370.
Classification: LCC BT1397 (ebook) | LCC BT1397 .D63 2018 (print) | DDC 273/.4—dc23
LC record available at https://lccn.loc.gov/2018020290

Printed on acid-free paper.

For Heather

Contents

Acknowledgements ix
Abbreviations xi
Map of Significant Locations xvi

Introduction 1
    Historical Background   3
    Lucifer and the Luciferians   10
    A Luciferian Theology?   14
    The Documents   23
    Texts and Editions   51

1. Faustinus, *Confessio fidei* 58

2. Faustinus (et Marcellinus), *Libellus precum* 62

3. Theodosius, *Lex Augusta* 170

4. Faustinus, *De Trinitate* 176

5. Pseudo-Athanasius, *Epistula 50* 316

6. Pseudo-Athanasius, *Epistula 51* 320

Bibliography 331
Scripture Index 345
General Index 349

Acknowledgements

I first and foremost owe an immense debt to Michele Salzman, who guided my course of studies at UC Riverside. She is a brilliant and meticulous scholar and a dear friend. I am proud to have been her student and hope that she finds some delight in this little book. Heather Van Mouwerik has been an unending source of love, comfort, and adventure. My parents have been generous and supportive beyond measure. Many beloved friends have kept me sane over long years spent in and around academia.

Numerous scholars contributed to this work in one way or another, and I wish to list a few here: Shane Bjornlie, Lucille Chia, Elizabeth De Palma Digeser, Piotr S. Gorecki, Denver Graninger, Randolph C. Head, Richard Janko, Jeremy McInerney, Georg Michels, Margaret M. Miles, Thomas F. Scanlon, and Thomas Sizgorich. Andrew Cain deserves special recognition for his many perceptive comments and suggestions. I also thank the members of the editorial board of Writings from the Greco-Roman World for their comments and the staff of SBL Press for shepherding this manuscript from its early stages to publication.

My professional and personal life has been deeply shaped by time spent at the American School of Classical Studies at Athens. The scholars I first encountered in Greece have become cherished friends, and it has been a true pleasure to work alongside my current colleagues. I also wish to thank the staff of the Department of History and the Interlibrary Loan office at UC Riverside.

It has become pro forma to state that any faults remaining in a book are one's own. It is nonetheless true.

Abbreviations

Primary Sources

Ab urbe cond.	Livy, *Ab urbe condita*
Abr.	Ambrose, *De Abraham*
Acta Callisti	Acta Sancti Callisti papae martyris Romae
Ad Const.	Hilary of Poitiers, *Ad Constantium*
Ad Eus.	Arius, *Epistula ad Eusebium Nicomediensem*
Agon.	Augustine, *De agone christiano*
An.	Tertullian, *De anima*
Anast.	Rufinus, *Apologia ad Anastasium papam*
Anc.	Epiphanius, *Ancoratus*
Apol. sec.	Athanasius, *Apologia contra Arianos*
Apoll.	Pseudo-Athanasius, *Contra Apollinarium*
Ar.	Phoebadius of Agen, *Contra Arianos*
C. Const.	Hilary of Poitiers, *Contra Constantium*
C. Jul.	Augustine, *Contra Julianum*
Cap. Franc.	Capitulare Francofurtense
Cap. Sanct. Aug.	Capitula Sancti Augustini
Catech. myst.	Cyril of Jerusalem, *Catecheses mystagogicae*
Cels.	Origen, *Contra Celsum*
Chron.	*Chronicon*
Cod. theod.	Codex Theodosianus
Coll. Ant. Par.	Collectanea Antiariana Parisina
Coll. Avell.	Collectio Avellana
Comm.	Commonitorium
Conc. Arel. prim.	Concilium Arelatense primum
Conf.	Augustine, *Confessiones*
Conf. fid.	Faustinus, *Confessio fidei*
Conf. fid. cath.	Damasus, *Confessio fidei catholicae*
Confid.	Damasus, *Confidimus*

Cor.	Tertullian, *De corona militis*
De rerum nat.	Lucretius, *De rerum natura*
Decr.	Athanasius, *De decretis*
Dial.	Origen, *Dialogus cum Heraclide*
Dig.	*Digesta*
Dion.	Athanasius, *De sententia Dionysii*
Ea grat.	Damasus, *Ea gratia*
Eccl. dogm.	Gennadius, *De ecclesiasticis dogmatibus*
Ennarat. Ps.	Augustine, *Ennarrationes in Psalmos*
Ep.	*Epistula*
Ep. Aeg. Lib.	Athanasius, *Epistula ad episcopos Aegypti et Libyae*
Ep. Afr.	Athanasius, *Epistula ad Afros episcopos*
Ep. can. Let.	Gregory of Nyssa, *Epistula canonica ad Letoium*
Ep. encycl.	Athanasius, *Epistula encyclica*
Ep. Eus.	Arius, *Epistula ad Eusebiam*
Ep. fest.	Athanasius, *Epistulae festales*
Ep. Rufin.	Athanasius, *Epistula ad Rufinianum*
Ep. Serap.	Athanasius, *Epistula ad Serapionem*
Epigr.	*Epigrammata*
Etym.	Isidore of Seville, *Etymologiae*
Eun.	*Contra Eunomium*
Exc.	Ambrose, *De excessu fratris sui Satyri*
Exp. Luc.	Ambrose, *Expositio Evangelii secundum Lucan*
Faust.	Augustine, *Contra Faustum*
Fid.	*De fide*
Gest. episc. Neapol.	*Gesta episcoporum Neapolitanorum*
H. Ar.	Athanasius, *Historia Arianorum*
Haer.	Augustine, *De haeresibus*
Hist. eccl.	*Historia ecclesiastica*
Hist. nova	Zosimus, *Historia nova*
Hist. rel.	Theodoret, *Historia religiosa*
Hom. Gen.	Origen, *Homiliae in Genesim*
Hymn.	Ambrose, *Hymni*
Incarn.	Ambrose, *De incarnationis dominicae sacramento*
Inst.	Quintilian, *Institutiones*
Inst. div.	Lactantius, *Institutiones divinae*
Jo. Hier.	Jerome, *Adversus Joannem Hierosolymitanum liber*
Jov.	Jerome, *Adversus Jovinianum*
Laud. Const.	Eusebius of Caesarea, *De laudibus Constantini*

Laude sanct.	Victricius of Rouen, *De laude sanctorum*
Lex Aug.	Theodosius, *Lex Augusta*
Lib. prec.	Faustinus and Marcellinus, *Libellus precum*
Lucif.	Jerome, *Altercatio luciferiani et orthodoxi seu dialogus contra Luciferianos*
LXX	Septuagint
Marc.	Tertullian, *Adversus Marcionem*
Maxim.	Augustine, *Contra Maximinum Arianum*
Metam.	Ovid, *Metamorphoses*
Mor. esse Dei Fil.	Lucifer of Cagliari, *Moriendum esse pro Dei Filio*
MT	Masoretic Text
Non conv. haer.	Lucifer of Cagliari, *De non conveniendo cum haereticis*
Or.	*Orationes*
Orat. fun. Flac.	Gregory of Nyssa, *Oratio funebris de Flacilla*
Pan.	Epiphanius, *Panarion*
Par.	Pacian, *Paraenesis*
Peristeph.	Prudentius, *Peristephanon*
Prax.	Tertullian, *Adversus Praxeam*
Psych.	Prudentius, *Psychomachia*
Quaest. Vet. Nov. Test.	Ambrosiaster, *Quaestiones Veteri et Novi Testamenti*
Res gest.	Ammianus Marcellinus, *Res gestae*
Rosc. com.	Cicero, *Pro Roscio comoedo*
Ruf.	Jerome, *Apologia contra Rufinum*
Sanct. Ath.	Lucifer of Cagliari, *Pro Sancto Athanasio*
Schism.	Optatus, *De schismate Donatistarum*
Serm.	*Sermones*
Sin. Vit. Boh.	Besa, *Sinuthii vita Boairice*
Spir.	Ambrose, *De Spiritu Sancto*
Syn.	*De synodis*
Tom.	Athanasius, *Tomus ad Antiochenos*
Trin.	*De Trinitate*
Trist.	Ovid, *Tristia*
Tusc.	Cicero, *Tusculanae disputationes*
Unic. bapt.	Augustine, *De unico baptismo*
Val. Urs.	Hilary of Poitiers, *Adversus Valentem et Ursacium*
Vir. ill.	*De viris illustribus*
Vit. Ant.	Athanasius, *Vita Antonii*

Vit. Aug.	Possidius, *Vita Augustini*
Vit. Hil.	Fortunatus, *Vita Hilarii*
Vit. Malch.	Jerome, *Vita Malchi*

Secondary Sources

ACCS	Ancient Christian Commentary on Scripture
AE	*L'Année épigraphique*
AW	Athanasius Werke
BHE	*Bulletin d'histoire ecclésiastique*
Bib	*Biblica*
CCSL	Corpus Christianorum: Series Latina
CF	*Classical Folia*
CH	*Church History*
CSCO	Corpus scriptorum christianorum orientalium
CSEL	Corpus scriptorum ecclesiasticorum latinorum
DACL	Cabrol, Fernand, Henri Leclercq, and Henri Irénée Marrou, eds. *Dictionnaire d'archéologie chrétienne et de liturgie*. 30 vols. Paris: 1907–1953.
DCA	Smith, William, and Samuel Cheetham, eds. *A Dictionary of Christian Antiquities*. Hartford, CT: Burr, 1880.
DHGE	*Dictionnaire d'histoire et de géographie ecclésiastiques*. 31 vols. Turnhout: Brepols, 1912–.
DOP	*Dumbarton Oaks Papers*
EME	*Early Medieval Europe*
GCS	Die griechischen christlichen Schriftsteller die ersten [drei] Jahrhunderte
HSCP	*Harvard Studies in Classical Philology*
HTR	*Harvard Theological Review*
JAAR	*Journal of the American Academy of Religion*
JECS	*Journal of Early Christian Studies*
JJP	*Journal of Juristic Papyrology*
JLAnt	*Journal of Late Antiquity*
JRS	*Journal of Roman Studies*
JTS	*Journal of Theological Studies*
LCL	Loeb Classical Library
MGH	*Monumenta Germaniae Historica*
MnemosyneSup	Mnemosyne Supplements

NPNF	Schaff, Philip, and Henry Wace, eds. *A Select Library of Nicene and Post-Nicene Fathers of the Christian Church*. 28 vols. in 2 series. 1886–1889. Repr., Peabody, MA: Hendrickson.
NRSV	New Revised Standard Version
NRTh	*La nouvelle révue theologique*
P.Oxy.	Grenfell, Bernard P., et al., eds. *The Oxyrhynchus Papyri*. London: Egypt Exploration Fund, 1898–.
PCBE	*Prosopographie chrétienne du Bas-Empire*. 4 vols. Paris: 1982–2013.
PG	Patrologia Graeca [= *Patrologiae Cursus Completus: Series Graeca*]. Edited by Jacques-Paul Migne. 161 vols. Paris: 1857–1866.
PL	Patrologia Latina [= *Patrologiae Cursus Completus: Series Latina*]. Edited by Jacques-Paul Migne. 217 vols. Paris: 1841–1855.
PLRE	Jones, A. H. M., J. R. Martindale, and John Morris, eds. *Prosopography of the Later Roman Empire*. 3 vols. Cambridge: Cambridge University Press, 1971–1992.
r.	reigned
REAug	*Revue d'études augustiniennes et patristiques*
RevScRel	*Revue des sciences religieuses*
SacEr	*Sacris Erudiri: Jaarboek voor Godsdienstwetenschappen*
SAW	*Sitzungsberichte der Kaiserlichen Akademie der Wissenschaften in Wien, Philosophisch-historische Klasse*
SC	Sources chrétiennes
SEAug	Studia Ephemeridis Augustinianum
StPatr	Studia patristica
TCH	Transformation of the Classical Heritage
ThH	Théologie historique
VC	*Vigiliae Christianae*
VCSup	Vigiliae Christianae Supplements
ZNW	*Zeitschrift für die neutestamentliche Wissenschaft und die Kunde der älteren Kirche*
ZPE	*Zeitschrift für Papyrologie und Epigraphik*

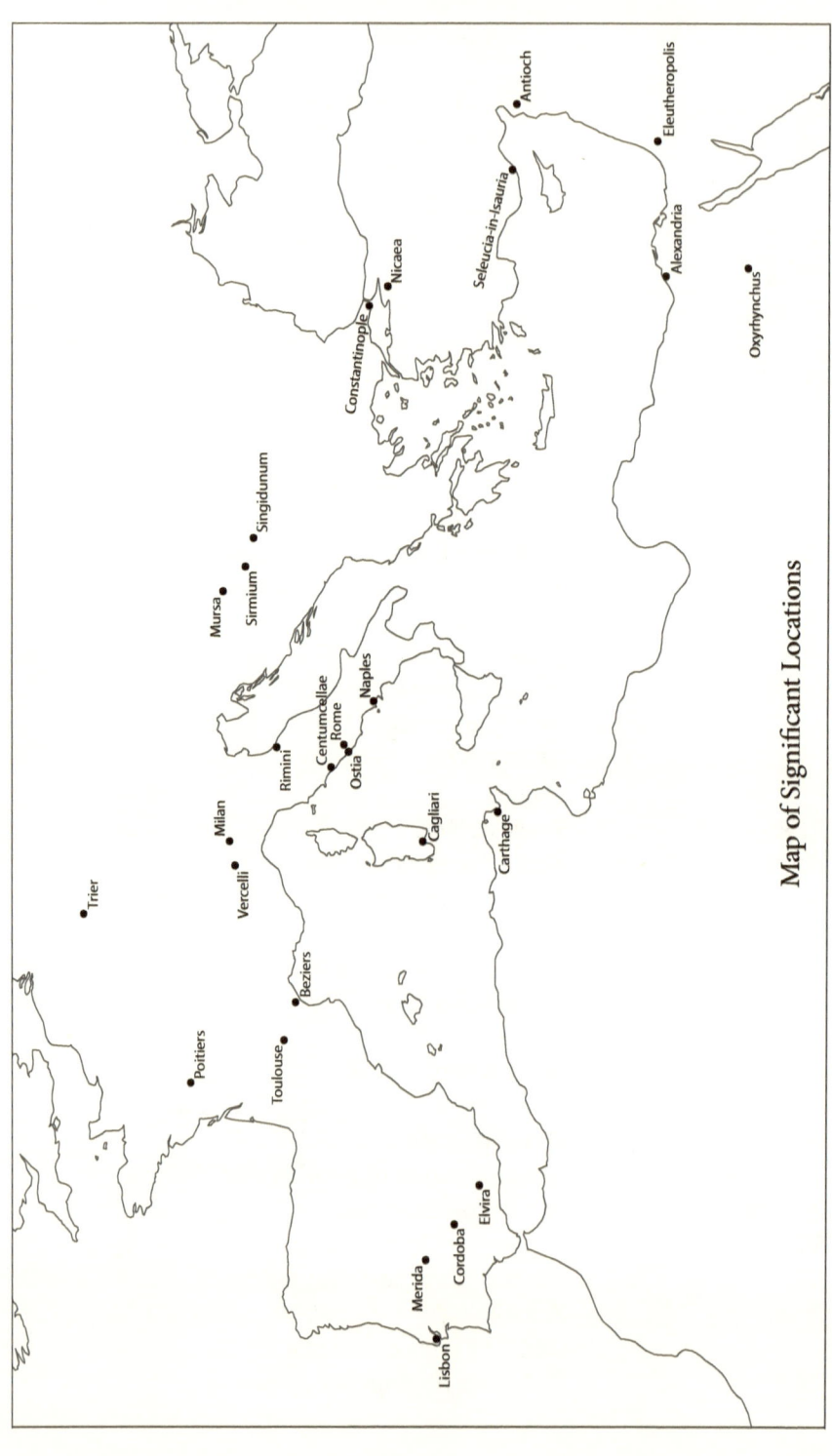

Map of Significant Locations

Introduction

Sometime in 383 or 384, two Christian presbyters named Faustinus and Marcellinus arrived in Constantinople to deliver a petition to Emperor Theodosius I. The two represented a handful of communities scattered across the Mediterranean, communities they described as the true Nicene Christian community/church (*ecclesia*) of the Roman Empire. Their members refused to hold communion with three groups: Arian Christians, any Nicene Christian clergyman who had agreed to Arian beliefs and later rejected them in favor of Nicene Christianity, and anyone who held communion with Arians or such clergymen. The second group was a particular target of their scorn, and they regularly called these individuals *praevaricatores*, translated throughout as "prevaricators."[1] In their petition, they requested that their community be recognized as the true Christian church of the Roman Empire—or, barring that, simply that other Nicene Christians cease persecuting them. The emperor may already have been aware of their intentions; he had probably earlier requested that one of the presbyters, Faustinus, draft a short confession of faith proving that he was a good Christian in the emperor's eyes, that is, that he adhered to the Nicene Creed.

The opponents of these presbyters and the communities they represented called them "Luciferians" after the fiery bishop Lucifer of Cagliari, who had vigorously supported the Nicene Creed and opposed Arians in the 350s.[2] Despite the anxiety that many other Nicene Christians seem

---

1. As in English, the word carries meanings akin to "liar" or "deceiver," but in a more oblique manner than straightforward lying, and with added connotations of both treachery and waffling (abuse against the inconstancy of these prevaricators appears throughout the *Libellus precum*). See Canellis (2006, 131n5) in her edition of Faustinus and Marcellinus, *Libellus precum*.

2. The name *Luciferians* is retained in this volume for clarity, but the reader should always be aware that the Luciferians themselves rejected this name and its

to have felt concerning these Luciferians, Theodosius granted the presbyters their wish in a rescript addressed to his Eastern prefect, Cynegius. By the year 400 or so, however, Rufinus described their community as a schism, "although only a few still circle around" (*Hist. eccl.* 1.28).[3] The latest documents we have from the Luciferians themselves come from the mid-380s. They appear in no further imperial legislation that is preserved. For authors of the fifth century, the Luciferians quickly became relegated to the past tense if they were mentioned at all.

We are fortunate to have on hand seven important documents concerning the Luciferians. The first is the *Confessio fidei*, a confession of faith written by Faustinus for the emperor Theodosius I. The second is the *Libellus precum*, a petition of requests by Faustinus and Marcellinus, also for Theodosius. The third is the *Lex Augusta*, Theodosius's imperial law written in reply. The fourth is a theological treatise on the Trinity, *De Trinitate*, written by Faustinus for Theodosius's wife, Flacilla. The fifth and sixth consist of two letters composed by Luciferians that purport to represent correspondence from Athanasius to Lucifer, included in the Athanasian corpus as *Ep.* 50 and 51. These six documents appear in this volume. The seventh document, though probably the first to be composed, is a *Dialogus adversus Luciferianos*, Dialogue against the Luciferians, an early work of the erudite Jerome.[4]

Together these documents give us a breadth and depth of knowledge concerning the history of the Luciferians, both from their own perspective and from that of their opponents, unparalleled in the early Christian world. Modern scholars, with a few exceptions, have shown very little interest in the Luciferians beyond occasional passages shorn of their context. It is hoped that this text, as an accessible translation including a detailed account of the historical and theological background relevant to study of the Luciferians, may go some way toward redressing this lack of attention.

---

implications (see Faustinus and Marcellinus, *Lib. prec.* 84, 86–91). There is of course a broader question of who exactly was a Luciferian, for which question in general see Perez Mas 2008.

3. "Schisma quod licet per paucos adhuc volvitur." All translations are mine, unless otherwise noted.

4. This work was translated into English by W. H. Fremantle, G. Lewis, and W. G. Martley in 1893 as part of the *Nicene and Post-Nicene Fathers* series. I have also benefited greatly from Aline Canellis's edition and French translation, published in 2003. The *Dialogus* deserves an updated English translation and commentary of its own.

Historical Background

To fully understand the Luciferians, it is necessary to start, as Faustinus and Marcellinus's *Libellus precum* does, with a historical and theological overview of the Arian controversy.[5] The Arian controversy was by far the predominant theological conflict of the fourth century and was essentially focused on the divine relationship between God as the Father and God as the Son, that is, Christ. In the years leading up to the Council of Nicaea in 325, Christians in Alexandria, Egypt, had been sharply divided over this question. The bishop Alexander of Alexandria and his fiery archdeacon Athanasius believed that the two were equal in all respects. In this view, which became more fully developed over the course of the century, the Son had always existed and was not created by the Father; the two were of the same substance (*ousia*); they had the same power and majesty. One of Alexander's presbyters, Arius, disagreed; he believed (we are told by his enemies) that the Son had been created by the Father and thus had not always existed; was of a similar, but not identical, substance; and was inferior to the Father in power and majesty. These views, too, became more nuanced, and variations developed over the course of the century. By the 320s, what began as a seemingly esoteric theological disagreement had devolved into chanting and riots in Alexandria; bishops throughout the Eastern Roman Empire had begun to take sides.

The emperor at the time, Constantine, had already seen the potential dangers of factionalism among his Christian subjects. Christians in North

---

5. A map is provided in the front matter of this volume (p. xvi) to help the reader navigate the numerous place names, particularly in the introduction and the *Libellus precum*, to make it easier to visualize the geographic extent of the Luciferian community, and to aid in seeing the close connections between various bishops, who tended to interact with their neighbors. For standard works on the Arian controversy, on which a large part of the following history relies, see Meslin 1968; Simonetti 1975; Hanson 1988; Ayres 2004; and for the years leading up to the rule of Julian, see Galvão-Sobrinho 2013. It must be stressed from the outset that there was no such thing as an "Arian" theology; the term was used by later authors to describe a variety of sometimes wildly differing beliefs, and the very definition of Arian beliefs changed over time, particularly as theological distinctions between the various beliefs concerning the Father and Son became more minute (see Ayres 2004, 105–10). The following is a highly simplified description of the differences between the two; many Western bishops were familiar with the differences between later variations of Arian thought but did not distinguish between them in their writings.

Africa had been split between the followers of the Carthaginian bishops Caecilian and Majorinus, whose successor was the very popular Donatus. In short, the Donatists claimed that the Caecilianists had handed over scriptures to pagans in the Great Persecution of 303–311 and refused to hold communion with them. Constantine had initially tried to create harmony among these Christian subjects by convening successive councils in Rome and Arles in 314.[6] Although both councils ruled against the Donatists, the Donatists refused to yield. Constantine, increasingly concerned about his divided subjects, decided to impose the council's decisions with legal coercion. But after a few years of ineffective persecution, Constantine threw up his hands in resignation and left North Africa's Christians to their own devices as he marched against his rival, Licinius, in the East.

The march, at least, was successful: in 324 Constantine defeated Licinius at Chrysopolis and made himself sole emperor over the Roman world. Just as he had tried to tamp down unrest and promote harmony among his Christian subjects in North Africa, Constantine attempted to quell the civic unrest in his new holdings caused by these theological disputes in Alexandria. Although he had not been able to establish religious harmony in North Africa, perhaps Constantine was more hopeful that a council could reach a satisfactory conclusion in the East because the question was one that in theory could be reasoned out. Thus Constantine convened a new council in 325 at Nicaea, a city in Asia Minor not far from the site of his future capital at Constantinople. Constantine does not seem to have cared much what the outcome of this council was, just that all of his bishops agreed with the result. Hundreds of bishops were invited to the Council of Nicaea, most but not all Eastern; the bishop of Cordoba, Hosius, led the proceedings, with Constantine himself present.

Although Arius and a handful of his supporters, who later were among those named Arians, argued tenaciously on behalf of their theological positions, the council sided with Alexander. The bishops present produced the Nicene Creed, which defined the Son as begotten, not created, and the Father and Son as equals, coeternal, and *homoousios*, "of the same substance." Constantine exiled six supporters of the opposition, including Arius, and ordered Arius's writings to be burned, and any who possessed them to be executed (Socrates, *Hist. eccl.* 1.9, quoting a letter

---

6. The Donatists had questioned the proceedings of the Roman council (the bishop of Rome had packed the court against them), so Constantine convened the second council in the hopes that the Gallic bishops would be more impartial.

of Constantine).⁷ Despite these legal threats, various Arians continued to spread their beliefs throughout various Eastern sees until Constantine died in 337.⁸

Following Constantine's death, however, supporters of the Nicene Creed found themselves in a delicate situation. They had indeed been the victors in 325, and Constantine's sons Constantine II and Constans (who ruled in the West) supported the Nicene Creed to the extent that they paid any attention at all to theology (Socrates, *Hist. eccl.* 3.18).⁹ However, Constantine's middle son, Constantius II (who ruled in the East), did not personally support the *homoousios* doctrine (Socrates, *Hist. eccl.* 2.2; Sozomen, *Hist. eccl.* 3.1, 18; Theodoret, *Hist. eccl.* 2.2).¹⁰ Under him, Arians could publicly argue for their beliefs, and the number of Christians who agreed with them continued to grow. Constantius also lent them the support of the state, eventually including the persecution of Nicene Christians, but his actions were limited to the Eastern half of the empire (Socrates, *Hist. eccl.* 2.7–8, 13; Sozomen, *Hist. eccl.* 3.7; Ammianus Marcellinus, *Res gest.* 14.10.2; Athanasius, *H. Ar.* 7.1; Barnes 1993, 212–13). Over time, Constantius and his allies were able to dramatically reduce the power of Nicene Christians in the East and either replace their bishops with Arians or compel Nicene bishops to swear to Arian creeds.

Constantine II died in 340; in 353, Constans was killed by an usurper. After swiftly defeating this usurper, Magnentius, Constantius II became sole ruler of the Roman Empire. Western supporters of the Nicene Creed suddenly found themselves facing persecution at the hands of the emperor, who immediately began to promote other Arianizing formulations of the relationship between the Father and Son. He did so by putting pressure on bishops who were attending a series of councils that Constantius convened to promote his own beliefs.

---

7. Ἐκεῖνο μέντοι προαγορεύω, ὡς εἴ τις σύγγραμμα ὑπὸ Ἀρείου συνταγὲν φωραθείη κρύψας, καὶ μὴ εὐθέως προσενεγκὼν πυρὶ καταναλώσῃ, τούτῳ θάνατος ἔσται ἡ ζημία· παραχρῆμα γὰρ ἁλοὺς ἐπὶ τούτῳ, κεφαλικὴν ὑποστήσεται τιμωρίαν.

8. Surely in part because of Constantine's later leniency toward Arius and his supporters, spurred on by Eusebius of Nicomedia: see Barnes 1993, 17–18.

9. Williams (2001) describes the general lack of attention paid to these disputes in the western half of the Roman Empire.

10. All blame an Arian presbyter who was in favor with Constantine and his half-sister Constantia for promoting Arian beliefs to Constantius; see also Williams 2002, 74–75; Hanson 1988, 264n103.

The first was in 353 or 354, when a council at Arles deposed and exiled Paulinus of Trier, a strong supporter of the *homoousios* formulation (Faustinus and Marcellinus, *Lib. prec.* 21).[11] Constantius then took advantage of a council convened at Milan in 355 at the request of the bishop of Rome, Liberius, to pressure bishops into deposing and exiling Athanasius, who had succeeded Alexander as bishop of Alexandria in 328.[12] Both supporters and opponents of the Nicene Creed knew that Athanasius was considered the leader of the faction supporting the *homoousios* doctrine. The scene at Milan was quite dramatic. Liberius himself was absent, represented instead by his appointed legates: the bishop Lucifer of Cagliari and two deacons, Hilarius and Pancratius. As the council began, the bishop Eusebius of Vercelli provided a copy of the Nicene Creed and asked Dionysius, the bishop of Milan, to sign it; a prominent Arian bishop, Valens of Mursa, violently slapped the stylus and parchment out of Dionysius's hand and cried out, "Nothing from that can be upheld!" (Hilary of Poitiers, *Ad. Const.* 1.8). Following the resulting tumult, the Arian bishops went to the imperial palace in Milan, where Constantius was staying. Constantius wasted no time and threatened the bishops at Milan with exile unless they would condemn Athanasius (*H. Ar.* 33). Many of the Western bishops, generally disinterested in what they viewed as Eastern quibbling, were convinced to sign. Three leading Nicene bishops instead chose exile and were led out from the church by imperial soldiers: Eusebius of Vercelli, Dionysius of Milan, and Lucifer of Cagliari. Lucifer, for his part, spent his exile in a number of cities writing vitriolic treatises directed at Constantius.[13]

Following Athanasius's condemnation at Milan, Constantius continued his policy of exiling other Western bishops who would not condemn Athanasius. The next victim was Hilary of Poitiers, deposed the next year

---

11. Constantius was present in Arles at the time and in all likelihood directed the bishops there to remove Paulinus. See Hilary of Poitiers, *Ad. Const.* 1.8; *C. Const.* 11; *Val. Urs.* preface 3.6; Athanasius, *Apol. sec.* 58.1; Rufinus, *Hist. eccl.* 10.21; Socrates, *Hist. eccl.* 2.36; Sozomen, *Hist. eccl.* 4.9; Brennecke 1984, 133–46; Gilliard 1984, 160, 163, 166; Barnes 1992b, 131; Beckwith 2005, 26.

12. For the Council of Milan, see Faustinus and Marcellinus, *Lib. prec.* 22; the following recounting of the events of the council and its aftermath incorporates the sources listed there.

13. The classic work on Lucifer (and the Luciferians) remains Krüger 1886. The best modern edition of Lucifer's writings is Diercks's *Luciferi Calaritani Opera quae Supersunt* (Lucifer of Cagliari 1978). See Pseudo-Athanasius, *Ep.* 50 and 51, which make reference to these treatises.

(356) by a council at Béziers (Faustinus and Marcellinus, *Lib. prec.* 24).[14] Like Lucifer, he spent his exile writing "venomous invective" against Constantius (Humphries 1997, 448).[15] Rhodanius of Toulouse was deposed and exiled, probably also at Béziers, even despite having condemned Athanasius, apparently because he was popular and a friend of Hilary (Faustinus and Marcellinus, *Lib. prec.* 24).[16] Next on Constantius's list was Liberius of Rome, a natural target given that his legate Lucifer was perhaps the most ardent supporter of the Nicene Creed in the West (Ammianus Marcellinus, *Res Gest.* 15.7.6–10; Sozomen, *Hist. eccl.* 4.11–12).

The situation looked, and indeed was, dire for the Nicene party. Constantius remained relentless. Having by 357 exiled nearly all the major supporters of the Nicene formula from their sees, he convened a council at Sirmium meant to come up with a new creed (Socrates, *Hist. eccl.* 2.30–31; Athanasius, *Syn.* 28; Hilary of Poitiers, *Syn.* 10–11). The creed published by this council, properly referred to as the Second Sirmian Creed, contained no mention of the word *substance* or *ousia* at all; Hilary refers to it as the *blasphemia* of Sirmium.[17] Reversals continued: Hosius of Cordoba, a staunch supporter of the Nicene formula and Constantine's close adviser at the Council of Nicaea, gave in to the Arian party and signed this *blasphemia* (Faustinus and Marcellinus, *Lib. prec.* 32). The Nicene party was nearly at its nadir, but one further insult remained: Liberius, the exiled bishop of Rome, conceded to Constantius's demands later in 357 and was

---

14. See also, e.g., Fortunatus, *Vit. Hil.* 5. For the date, see Barnes 1992a. The precise reasons for Hilary's exile are actually a matter of some scholarly debate. For a major overview of the arguments, see Barnes 1992b; Burns 1994; Beckwith 2005; Weedman 2007b, 10–13. The disagreement hinges on whether Hilary was exiled for consciously supporting Athanasius or merely because he composed a confession of faith that was sufficiently anti-Arian for Constantius to have him deposed, and then he later connected himself to the Athanasian party.

15. The example to which Humphries points is Hilary's *Contra Constantium* (not to be confused with his *Ad Constantium*).

16. See also, e.g., Hilary of Poitiers, *C. Const.* 11; Jerome, *Chron.* 283rd Olympiad (354–355); Rufinus, *Hist. eccl.* 10.21; Sozomen, *Hist. eccl.* 4.9 (not mentioned by Socrates); Sulpicius Severus, *Chron.* 2.39. Rhodanius had attended the Council of Milan and signed the condemnation of Athanasius (Beckwith 2008, 45). For Béziers as the council at which Rhodanius was exiled (not Milan or Arles, as some sources suggest), see Barnes 1992b, 134–35. According to Sulpicius, he was a staunch supporter of the Nicene Creed only because of his friendship with Hilary.

17. In addition to Socrates and Hilary, see also Meslin 1968, 276–81.

reinstated as the bishop of Rome (Athanasius, *Apol. sec.* 89.3; *H. Ar.* 41.2; Jerome, *Chron.* 284th Olympiad [359]; Socrates, *Hist. eccl.* 2.37; Sozomen, *Hist. eccl.* 4.15; Theodoret, *Hist eccl.* 2.17.1).

Still eager to produce a unified statement of faith for bishops in both halves of his empire, Constantius convened two major councils in 359, one at Rimini in the West and the other at Seleucia-in-Isauria in the East (Faustinus and Marcellinus, *Lib. prec.* 13–16). These councils were very well attended; their events and outcomes were very predictable. Nicene and Arian bishops found themselves at an impasse until the Arian bishops rushed to Constantius's palace, and at their instigation, Constantius compelled bishops at both councils, once more by threatening them with exile, to accept a variation of a formula devised earlier that year by Constantius and a small group of bishops at another council at Sirmium.[18] In this creed, rather than *homoousios* ("of the same substance") or even *homoiousios* ("of a similar substance"), the Father and Son were simply described as *homoios* ("similar"). Constantius's victory was, for all intents and purposes, complete by the year 360. "The whole world," as Jerome famously put it, "groaned and was shocked that it was Arian" (*Lucif.* 19).[19]

Shortly after this triumph, Constantius grew ill and died while marching against his rebellious cousin Julian. There being no real alternative, Julian took the throne in 361. The differences between the *homoousios*, *homoiousios*, and *homoios* formulas were academic to Julian, as he was a pagan; he allowed all Christian bishops to return to their sees and permitted anyone to worship in whatever way they pleased (Faustinus and Marcellinus, *Lib. prec.* 51). All the Nicene bishops Constantius had exiled to the East were free to return to their sees in the West.

Before these Western bishops returned, however, they and Athanasius (who had alternately been living in hiding or exile for many years) convened a council at Alexandria in 362. They did so to reaffirm the Nicene Creed, for which they had already endured so much, and to decide what should be done about the hundreds of bishops who had been compelled

---

18. A variant of the so-called Dated Creed, so called because its preamble claimed that "the catholic faith" was published on the eleventh of the calends of June in the consulate of Eusebius and Hypatius, i.e., 359. Nicene bishops quickly leapt on this gaffe as an example of Arian arrogance. The more proper name for the Dated Creed is the Fourth Sirmian Creed (the third is now lost). See Athanasius, *Syn.* 8; Hanson 1988, 363–64.

19. "Ingemuit totus orbis, et Arianum se esse miratus est."

Introduction 9

to sign Constantius's Arianizing creeds (Faustinus and Marcellinus, *Lib. prec.* 53). They had a simple choice: the clerics who had signed these creeds could undergo penance and be reduced to lay status, or they could undergo a laying-on of hands and be readmitted to Nicene communion as clerics. The council decided on the latter, more moderate approach, arguing (according to Jerome) "not that those who had been heretics could be bishops, but that it was clear that those who were being readmitted had not been heretics" (*Lucif.* 20).[20] Regional councils in Greece, Spain, and Gaul upheld this decision (Athanasius, *Epistula ad Rufinianum*; Barnes 1993, 158).

Many bishops and other individuals were irate at this leniency when the council's decision reached them (Jerome, *Lucif.* 19).[21] Lucifer of Cagliari in particular was incensed even though he had not been present (he had sent two deacons in his stead), having traveled from the Thebaid on to Antioch while the council gathered.[22] At Antioch, while the Council of Alexandria was deliberating, Lucifer found a number of Nicene Christians upset because an Arian had originally ordained their bishop Meletius, a Nicene Christian who had been exiled. Lucifer ordained Paulinus as the new Nicene bishop of Antioch while Meletius was still returning from exile (Rufinus, *Hist. eccl.* 1.30; Socrates, *Hist. eccl.* 3.9; 5.5; Sozomen, *Hist. eccl.* 5.12–13; 7.3; Theodoret, *Hist. eccl.* 3.5.1).[23] Some Nicene Christians in

---

20. "Non quo episcopi possint esse qui heretici fuerant, sed quod constaret eos qui reciperentur haereticos non fuisse." See Perez Mas 2008, 237–40. The problem of what to do with these bishops is only discussed by our earliest sources, Jerome and Rufinus; later sources only mention the reaffirmation of the Nicene Creed. It is worth noting that Jerome, our earliest source, mentions that the bishops attending the Council of Alexandria originally planned on stripping these bishops of their rank but were compelled to leniency by the threats made by supporters of these bishops (*Lucif.* 19). On the competing accounts of this council, see Duval 2001.

21. In the 380s, we still read Faustinus and Marcellinus describing these fair-weather bishops as prevaricators throughout the *Libellus precum*; it is unlikely they were the only ones who still harbored resentment.

22. Socrates states that Lucifer and Eusebius agreed that Lucifer would go to Antioch and Eusebius to Alexandria (*Hist. eccl.* 3.5); Theodoret claims that Eusebius begged Lucifer to go to Alexandria with him (*Hist. eccl.* 3.4.6). Hilary had already returned to his see and likewise was not present at the council; see Williams 1992, 8–14.

23. Jerome makes passing mention of the incident as well (*Lucif.* 20). According to Socrates, the Arian bishop of Antioch, Euzoïus, still controlled the actual church structures of Antioch (though he permitted Paulinus to use one for his Nicene congre-

Antioch followed Meletius, their original bishop, upon his return; some followed Paulinus because the unquestionably orthodox Lucifer had ordained him. Eusebius of Vercelli was distraught over the split at Antioch but took no action out of deference to his friend and ally Lucifer.

Lucifer and the Luciferians

After Lucifer learned of the Council of Alexandria's decision, he apparently remained apart from communion with the broader Nicene world until his death. In the *Dialogus adversus Luciferianos*, Jerome explicitly blames Lucifer for leading a schism, saying, "At such a turning point for the church, while the wolves were raging, he set a few sheep apart and deserted the rest of the flock" (*Lucif.* 20). Jerome never states that Lucifer returned to communion with the broader Nicene world, though he does mention his death in two other works without mentioning a schism at all (*Chron.* 287th Olympiad [370]; *Vir. ill.* 95). Rufinus, who was also a contemporary of the events in question and whose translation and addition to Eusebius of Caesarea's *Historia ecclesiastica* was composed around the year 400, explicitly states that Lucifer returned to Cagliari and never changed his mind about the Council of Alexandria. Rufinus writes:

> Thus Lucifer returned to Sardinia, and whether he was prevented by the suddenness of his death from having enough time to change his mind (for things begun rashly are often corrected with time) or whether he sat with an immoveable heart, I am not sure. Meanwhile, the schism of the Luciferians, which still exists (although only a few still circle around), took its beginning from him. (*Hist. eccl.* 1.30)[24]

It is not clear what relationship Lucifer had with the group associated with his name. Earlier scholars considered Lucifer the founder of the Luciferian community in the same way that Novatian was considered the founder of the Novatian community, Arius the founder of the Arian community, and so on (e.g., Krüger 1886). The explanation has simplic-

---

gation). When Meletius returned, he and his followers seized the largest basilica in the city for themselves. See Barnes 1993, 155–58; Shepardson 2014, 14–19.

24. "Ita regressus ad Sardiniae partes, sive quia cita morte praeventus, tempus sententiae mutandae non habuit (etenim temere coepta corrigi spacio solent) sive hoc animo immobiliter sederat, parum firmaverim. Ex ipso interim Luciferianorum schisma, quod licet per paucos adhuc volvitur, sumsit exordium."

ity in its favor: just as there was a man, Lucifer, there were those who followed his teachings, Luciferians. Such reasoning has many and early precedents.[25] Faustinus and Marcellinus understood this common line of argumentation and attack it: "It is also necessary that we dispel the malice of the false nickname, 'Luciferians,' that they call us. Who does not know that the name given to sectarians is that of the man whose new doctrines have been transmitted to his students on their teacher's authority?" (*Lib. prec.* 86).

More recent scholarship has vacillated on the question of whether or not Lucifer was the founder of some wide movement.[26] The language of Rufinus certainly suggests that while Lucifer was responsible for events on Sardinia, the broader Mediterranean community of Luciferians arose independently of him. Particularly important is his use of the word *meanwhile* (*interim*), which suggests that the beginning of the Luciferian schism occurred only concurrently with Lucifer's stubbornness in Sardinia, not that Lucifer personally led the schism.

In fact, two scholars recently working independently of each other have even cast doubts on whether a Luciferian community existed at all in the 360s. In their view, later persecutions of Nicene rigorists at Rome compelled these rigorists to reach out to other rigorists across the Mediterranean and form a unified community.[27] The issue is quite complex, and there is not enough space to fully treat the question here. In general, though, it is also possible that the Luciferians emerged when radical Nicene bishops in the 350s and 360s inspired similar radicalism within their original sees and within the communities where they spent their exiles, a radicalism which then coalesced as opposition to the decisions of the Council of Alexandria in the 360s.

It is worth noting here that there is some confusion in our sources about another community of rigorists that existed in Antioch also called

---

25. Vincent of Lérins, for example, writes, "And speak truly, what heresy ever bubbled up except under a specific name, at a specific place, in a specific time?" (*Comm.* 24.62: "Et revera, quae unquam haeresis nisi sub certo nomine, certo loco, certo tempore ebullivit?"). See also, e.g., Castelli 2004, 13.

26. For the question, see Krüger 1886, 55–56; Simonetti 1963a, 76; Simonetti 1998, 291–92; Figus 1973, 132–51; Diercks in Lucifer of Cagliari 1978, xxxii–xxxiii; Canellis 2003, 22–23; Corti 2004, 166–74; Perez Mas 2008, 8–13.

27. This is the general thesis of Perez Mas (2008, esp. 363) and appears in a slightly different form in Shuve 2014. See also Simonetti 1963a, 78.

Luciferians, which has led some scholars to identify the community at Antioch with the Luciferians of the *Libellus precum*.²⁸ The origin of this confusion comes from Socrates's *Historia ecclesiastica*. He relied heavily on Rufinus's translation and extension of Eusebius's *Historia ecclesiastica* but transformed it in many ways. For example, Rufinus writes this passage about the dissent at Antioch after Lucifer ordained Paulinus in the place of Meletius, as described above:

> The parties still dissented there, but they were nevertheless hopeful that it might be possible that they might be called back together, if such a bishop were chosen that both parties, not just one, would rejoice in him. [Lucifer] too hastily called on Paulinus for them, a catholic and holy man who was worthy of the priesthood in all things. But nevertheless both parties were unable to agree with the choice.²⁹ (*Hist. eccl.* 1.27)

Rufinus never describes the pro-Paulinus party at Antioch as "Luciferian," though he is given ample opportunity to do so later when he discusses the various attitudes toward Paulinus and Meletius (1.30).³⁰ Instead, he regularly refers to the supporters of Paulinus as Christians and his opponents as the "party of Meletius" (*partes Meletii*; 2.21).³¹ For Rufinus, the Luciferians had nothing to do with Antioch; they emerged instead as a reaction against the Council of Alexandria, as quoted above.

---

28. On this question, see Perez Mas 2008, 119–20, 130–32, 250–51.

29. "Ibique dissendentibus adhuc partibus, sed in unum tamen revocari posse sperantibus, si sibi talis eligeretur episcopus, erga quem non una plebs, sed utraque gauderet, praeproperus catholicum quidem et sanctum virum, ac per omnia dignum sacerdotio Paulinum episcopum collocavit, sed tamen in quem adquiescere plebs utraque non posset." See Perez Mas 2008, 119. Interestingly enough, Sulpicius Severus (*Chron.* 2.445.8) mentions Lucifer in Antioch withdrawing from communion with those who received former heretics into their communion, but not any resulting schism among Christians in Antioch.

30. Paulinus was in fact supported by Western bishops such as Damasus and other luminaries such as Jerome; his closeness to bishops whom Faustinus and Marcellinus loathed, such as Damasus, and the wholesale omission of any mention of Antioch or Paulinus in the *Libellus precum*, is another strong indication that the Luciferians did not consider these Antiochenes a part of their community.

31. E.g., concerning the factions at Tyre: "Diodorus, unus sane ex antiquis catholicis vir, et tentationem documentis probatus, Athanasii testimonio esset a confessoribus episcopus factus. modestia eius contemta, alius a Meletii partibus ordinatur."

Socrates, though he relied heavily on Rufinus, uses the term differently. Immediately after discussing the schism at Antioch, and Lucifer's role in it, he writes:[32]

> But Lucifer, perceiving that the ordination [of Paulinus] was not accepted by Eusebius, considered it an insult and was terribly irritated. In fact, he separated himself from communion with Eusebius, and wanted to reject the decisions of the council from his love of strife. These things, as they happened in a time of unhappiness, put many off of the church, and another heresy arose then: the Luciferians. But Lucifer did not let his anger fill him, for he had been bound by his own oaths in which he promised to be content with what had been decreed by the council, as he had sent his deacon. (*Hist. eccl.* 3.9.5–7)

Socrates here follows Rufinus in using *Luciferian* to describe rigorist Christians in the broader Christian world but connects it more directly to the Antioch narrative. Later in book 5, Socrates specifically refers to some of the supporters of Paulinus in Antioch as "Luciferians"; that is, Socrates uses *Luciferians* to describe a group of Christians that Rufinus expressly did *not* describe as "Luciferians" (5.5.7).[33] The confusion is easy enough to understand given Lucifer's role in ordaining Paulinus. Furthermore, at the time Socrates was writing, sometime between 438 and 449, the factions at Antioch were still active (and causing trouble!), whereas the disaffected communities across the Mediterranean following the Council

---

32. Λούκιφερ δὲ πυθόμενος μὴ δέχεσθαι ὑπὸ Εὐσεβίου τὴν χειροτονίαν αὐτοῦ ὕβριν ἡγεῖτο καὶ δεινῶς ἠγανάκτει· διεκρίνετο οὖν κοινωνεῖν Εὐσεβίῳ, καὶ τὰ τῇ συνόδῳ ἀρέσαντα ἀποδοκιμάζειν ἐκ φιλονεικίας ἐβούλετο. Ταῦτα ἐν καιρῷ λύπης γενόμενα πολλοὺς τῆς ἐκκλησίας ἀπέστησεν, καὶ γίνεται πάλιν Λουκιφεριανῶν ἑτέρα αἵρεσις. Ἀλλὰ Λούκιφερ τὴν ὀργὴν ἀποπληρῶσαι οὐκ ἴσχυσεν· ἐδέδετο γὰρ ταῖς ἑαυτοῦ ὁμολογίαις, δι' ὧν ἀποστείλας <αὐτοῦ> τὸν διάκονον στέρξειν τὰ ὑπὸ τῆς συνόδου τυπούμενα καθυπέσχετο.

33. οἱ δὲ Λουκίφερος διὰ τοῦτο διεκρίθησαν, ὅτι Μελέτιος ὑπὸ τῶν Ἀρειανῶν χειροτονηθεὶς εἰς τὴν ἐπισκοπὴν ἐδέχθη. Closely reading this passage could suggest that there were rigorist dissidents in Antioch, as the Luciferians in this passage are those who refused to agree to a settlement that other supporters of Paulinus were willing to accept. But Socrates could just as easily be referring to them as Luciferians for their staunch opposition to Meletius. Note, too, that Socrates refers to the "heresy of the Luciferians" (Λουκιφεριανῶν ... αἵρεσις) at 3.9.6, but "those of Lucifer" (οἱ δὲ Λουκίφερος) here in 5.5.7. Sozomen (*Hist. eccl.* 7.3.5), who relied heavily on Socrates's history, also identifies the supporters of Paulinus as "those of Lucifer," ὀλίγοι δὲ τῶν Λουκίφερος ἔτι διεφέροντο.

of Alexandria had apparently died away. Last, Eastern Christians were eager to blame Lucifer for the perpetual problems at Antioch, although it is interesting to note that Socrates also suggests that Lucifer did *not* separate himself from communion with other Nicene Christians, which our earlier sources (including Rufinus) state in no uncertain terms (Hanson 1988, 643–53). In any event, the supporters of Paulinus in Antioch play no real role in the history of the Luciferian community represented by Faustinus and Marcellinus.

A Luciferian Theology?

The obvious question is whether the Luciferians were orthodox or heretical, schismatic or catholic, but there is (of course) no easy answer. They naturally defined themselves as both orthodox and catholic, while other Christians (including Nicene Christians) varyingly defined them as orthodox or heretical, schismatic or catholic. It is also worth asking whether their separation from the broader Nicene community led the Luciferians to any differences in doctrinal beliefs or practices.[34] What follows is a brief survey of what the Luciferians said about their own beliefs and how their beliefs were portrayed by others.

A glance at any Luciferian writing confirms that they were doctrinally Nicene Christians: they proudly state as much, along with their hatred of the Arians, at every given opportunity. The *Confessio fidei* (§2) includes a recitation of the central tenets of Nicene Christianity. The arguments made in the *De Trinitate* concerning the Nicene Creed are too numerous to elaborate upon here; suffice to say that the document is a primer of Nicene thought (in part owing to Faustinus's liberal borrowing of ideas from other Nicene authors).

Although the Luciferians present themselves as ordinary Nicene Christians, many authors in the fourth and fifth centuries seem to have believed that they were not, accusing them of heresy in general and Sabellianism and a form of traducianism in particular. Socrates presents an oblique accusation of heresy in his depiction of Lucifer's anger at the decisions of the Council of Alexandria. As noted above, Socrates relied heavily on the *Historia ecclesiastica* of Rufinus, but one subtle change in Socrates's

---

34. See Tilley 2007 for a clear model with examples of how separation from communion might eventually lead to differences in doctrine.

account has major ramifications for understanding his narrative.³⁵ Both accounts present Lucifer as becoming angry following the decisions taken by the Council of Alexandria. But Rufinus carefully distinguishes the Council of Alexandria's decision to readmit the bishops who had sworn to Arian creeds from its reaffirmation of the Nicene formula, and he specifically notes that Lucifer was angry at the former. Socrates, on the other hand, entirely leaves the decision to readmit bishops out of his narrative.³⁶ Consequently, Lucifer's anger in Socrates's account appears to be directed at the council's reaffirmation of the Nicene Creed!³⁷ But this may in fact say less about Socrates's opinion of Lucifer and his followers and more about Socrates's casual handling of Rufinus instead. Generally speaking, Socrates tries to uphold Lucifer's ordination of Paulinus of Antioch against Meletius as valid (Allen 1990, 279). This would make little sense if Socrates believed that Lucifer was an anti-Nicene heretic. It is more likely that Socrates inattentively omitted a detail in Rufinus's account, and we should not read too much into it.

Theodoret, on the other hand, explicitly defines the Luciferians as heretics, even without using the word *hairesis*: "Lucifer, when he returned to Sardinia, added some other things to ecclesiastic teachings, and those who accepted these things also took the nickname 'Luciferians' from his name" (*Hist. eccl.* 3.5.3).³⁸ Suspiciously, Theodoret nowhere explains what doctrines Lucifer supposedly added. It seems more likely that Theodoret was

---

35. The accounts in question are in Rufinus, *Hist. eccl.* 1.28–30, and Socrates, *Hist. eccl.* 3.9. Sozomen follows Socrates here. That Socrates relied on Rufinus for this section of his account is clear. The order of events is almost identical, excepting that Socrates has added numerous quotations from Athanasius's *Apologia de fuga sua*. For a comparable analysis of how Socrates transforms Rufinus, see Lim 1995, 199–204, on their respective treatments of the Council of Nicaea.

36. What Lim (1995, 200) says of the Council of Nicaea might equally well apply to the Council of Alexandria: "Socrates' story also differs radically from Rufinus' in its treatment of details. His narrative is shorter and accords the debate less symbolic weight."

37. This accusation could be confirmed by Socrates's (*Hist. eccl.* 3.9.6) use of the word *hairesis* to describe the Luciferians themselves: καὶ γίνεται πάλιν Λουκιφεριανῶν ἑτέρα αἵρεσις). But in Socrates's *Historia ecclesiastica*, the word *hairesis* also signifies a "division" or "distinction" within Christendom with a much less moralizing significance than the modern word *heresy*. See Wallraff 1997, 256–57.

38. ὁ δὲ Λουκίφερ εἰς τὴν Σαρδὼ παραγενόμενος ἕτερά τινα τοῖς ἐκκλησιαστικοῖς προστέθεικε δόγμασιν. οἱ δὲ ταῦτα καταδεξάμενοι ἐκ τῆς τούτου προσηγορίας καὶ τὴν ἐπωνυμίαν ἐδέξαντο· Λουκιφεριανοί. See Faustinus and Marcellinus, *Lib. prec.* 87.

trying to find someone to blame for the divisions within Antioch caused by Lucifer's ordination of Paulinus; as Pauline Allen (1990, 279) argues, Theodoret was keenly embarrassed by the divisions still plaguing that city nearly a century after Lucifer's activity there. As a Westerner, Lucifer was an easy target (and to be fair, he did play a not-insignificant role in creating divisions among Antiochenes). Equally vague is an obscure text known as the *Adversus haereses* of Pseudo-Hegemonius, which compares the Luciferians to the Donatists, though offers no details as to why.[39]

Other authors level more substantial accusations at the Luciferians. In the beginning of the *Confessio fidei*, Faustinus states that his community has been accused of Sabellianism. Sabellianism was, in short, the belief that God had one person in one substance, that is, that the persons of the Father, the Son, and the Holy Spirit were the same, and not three different persons comprising one substance, as Nicene theologians had come to argue (e.g., Eusebius, *Hist. eccl.* 7.6, 26; Epiphanius, *Pan.* 62.1; Simonetti 1975, 8; Kelly 1978, 121–23).[40] Late antique authors often presented Sabellianism as anti-Arianism gone too far.[41] Faustinus also reports that the Luciferians were accused of Apollinarianism (*Conf. fid.* 3). Apollinaris argued that because the Son was one single person, and the Son's substance was the same as the Father's, the Son's mind had to be wholly divine, not both divine and human.[42] Apollinarianism was often seen as a radical rejection of Arianism, just as Sabellianism was; for Faustinus, it seems to be functionally very little different from accusations of Sabellianism, as his response to the charge addresses the number of persons and substances in the Godhead, not the mind of the Son. Indeed, Faustinus, as represented by the *De Trinitate*, seems like a perfectly Nicene Christian, certainly not Arian but not Sabellian either. There are three persons, namely, the Father, the Son, and the Holy Spirit, who differ from one another but are equal to

---

39. The very small amount of Pseudo-Hegemonius still extant was published in 1957 as part of CCSL 9 (Pseudo-Athanasius 1957).

40. Zahn (1867, 208) shows that Epiphanius's argument against Sabellius is really against Marcellus of Ancyra.

41. In more technical terms, Nicene theologians struggled to avoid modalism, the notion that all of the aspects of God were completely uniform; and subordinationism, the notion that God consisted of multiple persons who existed in some sort of hierarchy to one another (and thus differed in some way). This often found expression in reference to Sabellius as a modalist thinker and Arius as a subordinationist thinker; see Faustinus, *Trin.* 12.

42. An early form of monophysitism; see Kelly 1978, 289–95.

one another and of the same substance. Why were they accused of Sabellianism, then?

One possible reason is a transition in translations that occurred in the 370s and 380s. Faustinus, like many others, uses the Latin words *substantia* to refer to the "being" or "substance" of God and *persona* to refer to three "persons" of God, that is, the Father, the Son, and the Holy Spirit. In earlier Christian writings, the Latin word *substantia* was used to translate the Greek word *hypostasis*.[43] But at the same time as Faustinus was writing, Eastern Nicene Christians were beginning to describe God as three *hypostases* ("persons") in one *ousia* ("being" or "substance"), especially under the influence of Basil of Caesarea (Perez Mas 2008, 245–46, 350; Gregory of Nazianzus, *Or.* 31.30; Gregory of Nyssa, *Eun.* 1.34). A Latin author such as Faustinus would reject a description of God as having three *hypostases*, as he would equate this to God having three *substantiae*. Indeed, Faustinus does complain about those who assert a formulation of three *substantiae* in the *Confessio fidei*, and he and Marcellinus do the same in the *Libellus precum*.[44] They were not alone; Jerome, writing to Damasus in the 370s

---

43. Originally in Tertullian, according to Braun (1977, 176–94); for the fourth century, see Simonetti 1963a, 80–81. One prominent figure who equated *hypostases* with *substantiae* was Hilary of Poitiers, whose translation of the Nicene-accepted Council of Antioch's formulation in 341 was rejected by other Nicene rigorists such as Lucifer and the deacon Hilarius of Rome; see Hilary of Poitiers, *Syn.* 32; Perez Mas 2008, 348.

44. E.g., Faustinus and Marcellinus, *Lib. prec.* 114: "ipsi quoque, qui pie inter eos putantur credere, Patris et Filii et Spiritus Sancti tres esse substantias uindicantes uel respicientes." It is possible that, because of this confusion, Westerners had begun to avoid the term *hypostasis* when they were writing to Easterners (see Perez Mas 2008, 348–56). Damasus, bishop of Rome from 366–384, does use the term *substantia* in the same sense as the Greek *hypostasis* when reporting the history of the Council of Nicaea in his letter *Confidimus* to the Eastern bishops and in a report to Paulinus of Antioch (*Confid*. [PL 13:348]: "ut Patrem, Filium, Spiritumque Sanctum unius Deitatis, unius figurae, unius credere oporteret substantiae, contra sententientem alienum a nostro consortio iudicantes"; *Conf. fid. cath.* [PL 13:358]: "Anathematizamus eos qui non tota libertate proclamant cum Patre et Filio unius potestatis esse atque substantiae"). But he twice avoids the term directly, using the transliterated term *ousia* in a letter to the Eastern bishops and avoiding the issue entirely in another (*Ea grat.* [PL 13:351]: "quia omnes uno ore unius virtutis, unius maiestatis, unius divinitatis, unius usiae dicimus divinitatem"; *Non nobis* [PL 13:353]: "sed perfectum in omnibus virtute, honore, maiestate, deitate, cum Patre conveneramur et Filio" [this letter was signed by, among others, Meletius of Antioch, perhaps as a show of some reconciliation; see

after being accused of Sabellianism himself, was fiercely opposed to the three-*hypostases* formulation: "If you order it, a new creed is established beyond the Nicene, and let us orthodox confess along with the Arians using similar words.... Believe me, poison lurks under the honey" (*Ep.* 15.4).[45] Western opposition to the formulation was still well known in 380, according to an oration of Gregory of Nazianzus (*Or.* 21.35).

Even in the East, the three-*hypostases* formula was unpalatable among many prominent Nicene Christians. The most important of these was Athanasius, who in his early career was fiercely critical of the three-*hypostases* formula (Lienhard 1999, 37). In the *Tomus ad Antiochenos*, sent following the Council of Alexandria, Athanasius does say that the Council of Alexandria, which he led, decided that the three *hypostases* was a (not the) valid formulation (*Tom.* 5–6).[46] He seems to have come to accept its orthodoxy—but he never liked it. After the Council of Alexandria, sometime in the mid-360s, Athanasius writes, "*Hypostasis* is *ousia*, and holds no other meaning than 'that which is.'... For *hypostasis* and *ousia* are *existence* [*hyparxia*], for he *is* and he *exists*"[47] (*Ep. Afr.* 4). Nor was Athanasius a lone

---

Field 2004]). Similarly, Ambrose never uses the term *hypostasis* when writing to the Cappadocians (see Simonetti 1975, 524–25).

45. "Si iubetis, condatur post Nicaenam fides, et similibus verbis, cum Arianis confiteamur orthodoxi.... Sed mihi credite, venenum sub melle latet." See Phoebadius of Agen, *Ar.* 3.3, both perhaps referring to Lucretius, *De rerum nat.* 4.10–25. In the same passage, which is quite lengthy, Jerome calls the formulation sacrilegious and suggests that if he uses these words, Damasus should have to hold communion with Ursinus and Auxentius, Damasus's opponent in the battle for the episcopacy of Rome (who was also accused of Arianism) and the Arian bishop of Milan, respectively. It is interesting to note that the Luciferians were also accused of Apollinarianism (Faustinus, *Conf. fid.* 3) and that Jerome was a onetime student of Apollinaris (Jerome, *Ep.* 84); as noted above, Apollinaris's arguments were often conflated with those of Sabellianism.

46. See also Lienhard 1999, 200. For Athanasius as the author, see Tetz 1975, 207.

47. Ἡ δὲ ὑπόστασις οὐσία ἐστί, καὶ οὐδὲν ἄλλο σημαινόμενον ἔχει ἢ αὐτὸ τὸ ὄν.... Ἡ γὰρ ὑπόστασις καὶ ἡ οὐσία ὕπαρξίς ἐστιν. Ἔστι γὰρ καὶ ὑπάρχει. There are other Athanasian examples that also suggest he saw the terms as identical: see Prestige 1952, 167. Others knew of Athanasius's dissatisfaction as well: Basil of Caesarea (*Ep.* 69.2), writing to Athanasius in 371, substituted the term *hyparxis* for *hypostasis* in a conciliatory letter: Μαρκέλλῳ δέ, τῷ κατὰ διάμετρον ἐκείνῳ τὴν ἀσέβειαν ἐπιδειξαμένῳ καὶ εἰς αὐτὴν τὴν ὕπαρξιν τῆς τοῦ Μονογενοῦς θεότητος ἀσεβήσαντι καὶ κακῶς τὴν τοῦ Λόγου προσηγορίαν ἐκδεξαμένῳ, οὐδεμίαν μέμψιν ἐπενεγκόντες φαίνονται. Lienhard (1999, 160) draws attention to this substitution; see also Lienhard 1986, 386–88. Basil did apparently not convince Athanasius; the latter instead held communion with Marcellus of

Introduction 19

holdout. Epiphanius seems to waffle in the *Ancoratus* (§6) of the mid-370s, first describing *ousia* and *hypostasis* as representing the same thing (or at least that the Trinity had one *hypostasis*).[48] But he then separates the two terms in his *Panarion* (69.72) only a few years later, saying only that they are not equal (the exact distinction is left unclear).[49]

The charge of Sabellianism leveled against the Luciferians, then, was probably because they were Westerners who rejected the three-*hypostases* formulation of Nicene theology. Since the Luciferians believed three *hypostases* to be the equivalent of three *substantiae*, those who believed three *hypostases* to be the equivalent of three *personae* saw the Luciferian rejection of three *personae* as obvious evidence of Sabellianism. But this seems more a matter of translation and poor communication than of actual distinction in doctrine. In any event, this does not seem to have been a central issue for the Luciferians or their opponents. No extant authors themselves criticize Faustinus for opposing the three-*hypostases* formula; we have only Faustinus's testimony that the Luciferians were accused of Sabellianism.[50] Last, Theodosius apparently took no umbrage at their objections to the three-*hypostases* formula, given that his *Lex Augusta* (§8) states that Faustinus and Marcellinus's community was catholic.

A second specific accusation of heresy was raised against the Luciferians by the author of the Indiculus de haeresibus. The Indiculus is a heresiology of unknown provenance falsely associated with Jerome in the manuscript tradition and composed between 393 and 428.[51] Its unknown

---

Ancyra (whom Basil accused of Sabellianism) and never responded to Basil's letter (Epiphanius, *Pan.* 72.11.3; Lienhard 1989, 162).

48. ὅπου γὰρ ὁμοούσιον, μιᾶς ὑποστάσεώς ἐστι δηλωτικόν; 67.4: τριὰς αὕτη ἁγία καλεῖται, τρία ὄντα μία συμφωνία μία θεότης τῆς αὐτῆςοὐσίας τῆς αὐτῆς θεότητος τῆς αὐτῆς ὑποστάσεως; 81: ἀλλὰ καθ' ἑαυτὸ ἐσχηματίζετο, καθ' ἑαυτὸ ὑπόστασις ὄν, οὐκ ἀλλοία παρὰ τὴν τοῦ πατρὸς καὶ υἱοῦ, ἀλλὰ τῆς αὐτῆς οὐσίας, ὑπόστασις ἐξ ὑποστάσεως τῆς αὐτῆς πατρὸς καὶ υἱοῦ καὶ ἁγίου πνεύματος.

49. ποῖος τῶν ἀποστόλων οὐσίαν εἶπε θεοῦ; οὐκ ἴσασι δὲ ὅτι καὶ ὑπόστασις καὶ οὐσία ταὐτόν ἐστι τῷ λόγῳ. Hanson (1988, 666) writes, "He undoubtedly took the trouble to be well-informed; he understood pretty well the theology of Athanasius.... But he was of no great intellect."

50. Are these related to Jerome's accusers from *Ep.* 15? It is impossible to know. It is worth noting, however, that Gregory of Elvira, who plays an important role in the *Libellus precum* (§§33–40, 73, 77, 90, 98) and in the *Lex Augusta* (§8), says that he too was accused of Sabellianism *(De fide* preface 5–8).

51. For the Indiculus in general, see Bardy 1929; Chadwick 1976, 203.

author claims, "The Luciferians, although they hold the catholic truth in all things, were brought to this most foolish error: they say that the soul is generated from transfusion (*ex transfusione*); and they say this same soul is both from the flesh and from the substance of the flesh" (Indiculus 26.38 [PL 81:642]).[52] The distinction between "from the flesh" (*de carne*) and "from the substance of the flesh" (*de carnis … substantia*) seems to be minimal.[53] Gennadius of Marseille, a late fifth-century author, apparently read the Indiculus and believed that the Luciferians held this belief (*Eccl. dogm.* 14).[54] The description of this belief, including its attribution to the Luciferians, is copied word-for-word in other texts of the sixth and seventh centuries (see Cap. Sanct. Aug. [XIX] 18a (22a); Isidore, *Etym.* 8.5.54).[55] The basic criticism of the Luciferians seems to be that they believed the soul came from the flesh of the parents; the position of the author of the Indiculus is unclear.

A very similar belief existed in early Christian thought and is sometimes called traducianism (from *tradux*, "vine branch").[56] This is the belief that an individual's soul comes from his or her parents and is not created by God for each individual.[57] The earliest clear proponent of this view was Tertullian, who in the early third-century *De anima* writes, "How then is a living being conceived? Is the substance of both the body and the soul brought about together, or does one of these come first? No, we say that both are conceived, made, and completed at the same time, just as they are

---

52. "Luciferiani cum teneant in omnibus catholicam veritatem, in hunc errorem stultissimum prolabuntur, ut animam dicant ex transfusione generari; eamdemque dicunt, et de carne, et de carnis esse substantia."

53. See, e.g., Augustine, *Maxim.* 2.14.3 (PL 42:772), discussing how the Son was born from the Father: "Caro de carne nascitur, filius carnis de substantia carnis nascitur.… Credite creatorem, qui dedit carni carnem gignere, qui dedit parentibus veros carnis filios de carnis substantia generare."

54. "Animas hominum non esse … cum corporibus per coitum seminatas, sicut Luciferiani, Cyrillus, et aliqui Latinorum praesumptores affirmant, quasi naturae consequentiam servantes."

55. Capitula Sancti Augustini is a work of Roman origin sometimes attributed to Augustine and sometimes to John Maxentius, though neither wrote it.

56. On traducianism, see, e.g., Garrett 1990, 509–11.

57. A related belief is called generationism. The distinction between the two is not always clear in ancient texts, but in modern scholarship generationism refers to the creation of the soul from the parents' souls just as the body comes from their bodies, whereas traducianism directly links the creation of the soul to the creation of the body. See Garrett 1990, 509–11.

brought out together, and no moment separates their conception by which a ranking might be established"⁵⁸ (*An.* 27.1). The view has a certain logic to it, particularly when considering how the sin of Adam was supposed to spread to all of humanity (Beatrice 2013, 223–27). If God creates souls, the argument goes, then why are those souls laden with sins? Propagation of the soul through the souls of the parents provides a straightforward mechanism for understanding this transfer.⁵⁹

In the fourth century, the view remained popular, but some theologians were growing uneasy with it. Rufinus describes Tertullian, Lactantius, and others as holding this belief but refuses to pass judgment on which view of the soul is correct (*Anast.* 6). While lambasting Rufinus for misattributing the belief to Lactantius, Jerome asks whether or not the soul comes "from transference [lit. 'from a vine branch,' *ex traduce*], as Tertullian, Apollinaris, and the majority of Westerners assert"⁶⁰ (*Ep.* 126.1). But like Rufinus, Jerome does not clearly assert what he himself believes or whether or not he believes traducianism to be orthodox or heretical (*Ruf.* 2.8–10; *Ep.* 126.1). Augustine, on the other hand, does explicitly label this belief as heretical and ascribes it to Tertullian and the Manichaeans (*C. Jul.* 2.178).⁶¹

Did the Luciferians hold a view like this? It is difficult to say. The question of the generation of the soul never appears in the works Lucifer himself wrote or any of our extant Luciferian writings. Gennadius refers to the *Libellus precum* and the *De Trinitate* but does not seem aware of any other Luciferians texts (*Vir. ill.* 16). Nor does any discussion of the soul occur in Jerome's *Dialogus contra Luciferianos*, even though Jerome himself was interested in the question (Krüger 1886, 66).⁶² Furthermore,

---

58. "Quomodo igitur animal conceptum? Simulne conflata utriusque substantia corporis animaeque an altera earum praecedente? Immo simul ambas et concipi et confici, perfici dicimus, sicut et promi, nec ullum intervenire momentum in conceptu quo locus ordinetur." See also Rufinus, *Anast.* 6: "Legi quosdam dicentes quod pariter cum corpore per humani seminis traducem etiam anima defundatur.... Quod puto inter Latinos Tertullianum sensisse."

59. Tertullian, however, does not really discuss original sin in conjunction with this belief. See Beatrice 2013, 231–33.

60. "An certe ex traduce, ut Tertullianus, Apollinaris et maxima pars occidentalium autumat."

61. "Impietatem inquam, qua credis ita esse animarum traducem in Tertulliani olim et Manichaei profanitate damnatam, sicut est etiam corporum tradux."

62. For Jerome's interest, see the aforementioned *Ep.* 126 and *Ruf.* 2.8–10. Perez

Augustine read the Indiculus when he composed his own book *De haeresibus* (*Haer.* 81) and expresses serious doubts about this description of the Luciferians, making it a point to state that he could not find the name of the author of this text.[63]

It is interesting, however, to note the choice of words on the part of the author of the Indiculus: *ex transfusione*. No author in the fourth century (or the third, for that matter) wrote about traducianism as being *ex transfusione*; only the noun *tradux* appears in Rufinus and Jerome, and Julian of Eclanum claims that Augustine believes in the *animarum traducem*, which Augustine accepts as a fair definition of Tertullian's belief (though not his own) (*C. Jul.* 2.178). This apparently unique use of the word *transfusio* regarding the generation of the soul does suggest that the author of the Indiculus is not making a casual accusation, and that, if the Luciferians did believe in the *transfusio* of souls, they believed in a form of traducianism that was slightly different from what Rufinus, Jerome, and Augustine attribute to Tertullian in some technical way (perhaps in the emphasis on the transference from the flesh).

But if this wording was significant to the author of the Indiculus, it was not significant to any other ancient authors who write about the Luciferians or to the Luciferians themselves. Traducianism was not inherently at odds with orthodox Christian doctrines of the fourth century in the way its inclusion in the Indiculus implies it is. Jerome, though he is likely exaggerating, says that the "greatest part of Westerners" believed in this explanation for the generation of the soul.[64] Jerome was probably not suggesting that most Western bishops in the early years of the fifth century were heretical. In any case, traducianism was not a defining feature of the Luciferians that firmly distinguished them from other Nicene Christians of the fourth century.

Mas (2008, 201) concludes that it is "completely inadmissible to define the Luciferians as defenders of such a strange doctrine" ("todo inadmisible definir a los luciferianos como los defensores de tan extraña doctrina antropológica").

63. "Cuius nomen in eodem eius opusculo non inveni." Müller (1956, 28) argues that Augustine and the Indiculus both relied on an unknown source, but it seems simpler to imagine that Augustine had acquired a copy of the Indiculus at some point.

64. As cited immediately above, *Ep.* 126.1: "an certe ex traduce, ut Tertullianus, Apollinaris et maxima pars occidentalium autumat, ut, quomodo corpus ex corpore, sic anima nascatur ex anima et simili cum brutis animantibus condicione subsistat."

In fact, even their enemies seem to be at pains to find something wrong with them. Ambrose writes of his deceased brother Satyrus that

> He did not reckon that there was faith in schism. For even if they [the "heirs of Lucifer"] held faith in God, he did not reckon that they held faith in the church of God, as they suffered some of its joints to be divided and its limbs to be torn apart. Since Christ suffered for the church, and since the body of Christ is the church, it does not seem like those who make his suffering meaningless and drag apart his body show faith in Christ. (*Exc.* 1.47)[65]

Ambrose is probably blurring his definitions intentionally here: while the Luciferians hold faith in *God*, they do not hold faith in *Christ*. The implied question is, given that one cannot hold faith in God and not in Christ, do the Luciferians actually hold faith in God? But Ambrose points to no specific doctrinal reason why the Luciferians should be anathema. Augustine makes the problem explicit: "Whether … they are still heretics because they affirm their dissent with destructive vehemence is another question, and it does not seem to me that it should be dealt with in this place" (*Haer.* 81).[66] Is schism inherently heretical? Augustine penned these words only a year or two before he died, leaving the theological quandary unanswered.

The Documents

As noted above, the number of Luciferian texts that have survived makes us uniquely fortunate. We have documents written by Luciferians, a document written by the emperor in support of the Luciferians, and a document written in opposition to the Luciferians. There is also a small host of cita-

---

65. "Non putavit esse fidem in schismate, nam etsi fidem erga Deum tenerent, tamen erga Dei ecclesiam non tenere, cuius patiebantur velut quosdam artus dividi et membra lacerari, etenim cum propter ecclesiam Christus passus sit et Christi corpus ecclesia sit, non videtur ab his exhiberi Christo fides, a quibus evacuatur eius passio corpusque distrahitur."

66. "Sive … sint haeretici, quia dissensionem suam pertinaci animositate firmarunt, alia quaestio est, neque hoc loco mihi videtur esse tractanda." See also Augustine, *Agon.* 30.32: "Quod cum Luciferiani intelligunt, et non rebaptizent, non improbamus; sed quod etiam ipsi praecidi a radice voluerunt, quis non detestandum esse cognoscat?" Does *detestandum* mean they should be treated as heretics, even though they seem to hold the correct doctrinal positions? Augustine does not say.

tions in a great number of ancient sources, including the most prominent ecclesiastic historians of the fifth century.[67] The documents in this volume represent the complete collection of writings by Luciferians, as well as the emperor's response to the *Libellus precum*.

Confessio fidei

The *Confessio fidei* is a brief document written by Faustinus.[68] In the first section, he praises the Nicene Creed and defends himself against the charge of Sabellianism; the second section is a profession of the relationship between the Father, Son, and Holy Spirit in accordance with Nicene doctrines; the third is a rejection of Apollinarianism and any doctrine professing that the Father, Son, and Holy Spirit are of three *substantiae*. Faustinus ends his confession at this point.

Faustinus makes the purpose of the *Confessio fidei* explicit, stating that Theodosius ordered him to write it in the preface. The real question, of course, is why Theodosius ordered him to provide such a statement. One logical explanation is that prior to presenting the *Libellus precum* at court, Faustinus was asked by Theodosius to present a confession of faith proving that he was a properly Nicene Christian. The emperor would doubtless want to avoid wasting time arbitrating disputes between Christians he considered heretical. There are no independent markers by which to date the *Confessio fidei*, but if this proposed relationship to the *Libellus precum* is correct, it was probably also written in 383 or 384.

In its few, short lines, the *Confessio fidei* reveals the central concerns of Faustinus and his opponents: the proper relationship between the Father and Son (and to a noticeably lesser degree, their relationship to the Holy Spirit) and the proper treatment of clerics who swore to Arian creeds and then later returned to Nicene communion. As such, it serves as a fitting introduction to the *Libellus precum* proper.

Libellus precum

Unlike the *Confessio fidei*, the *Libellus precum* is a very lengthy document that pleads the case of the Luciferians to the emperor Theodosius. Its

---

67. For an excellent summation of all of the ancient sources related to the Luciferians, see Canellis 2006, 33–40.
68. For a discussion of the attribution to Faustinus, see Simonetti 1998, 292–98.

authors are Faustinus, the author of the *Confessio fidei*, and the otherwise unknown Marcellinus.[69] Faustinus is generally regarded as the primary author.[70] In the course of their pleading, the two describe the origins and fortunes of the Luciferians starting with the Arian controversy preceding the Council of Nicaea.

We are fortunate to be able to pinpoint the composition of the petition to either 383 or 384. The first indication derives from its addressees: Valentinian II, Theodosius, and Arcadius (Faustinus and Marcellinus, *Lib. prec.* 1). The absence of Gratian puts the *terminus post quem* in late 383, as Gratian was assassinated in August of that year. The text also treats Damasus as a living person (§§78–85). Damasus died in December of 384, thus providing the *terminus ante quem*.

While the *Libellus precum* is indeed addressed to Valentinian II, Theodosius, and Arcadius, the political situation at the time of its composition and elements within the text demonstrate that it was directed to Theodosius alone. First of all, absence of the Western usurper Magnus Maximus's name from the addressees serves as one indication that the Luciferians were attempting to gratify Theodosius, not the Western court. Furthermore, Valentinian II, who is addressed instead, was fourteen years old at the time; his mother, Justina, held Arian beliefs, and the vehemently anti-Arian tone of the *Libellus precum* would have done nothing to help the Luciferians achieve their goals if she were the intended recipient.[71] The inclusion of the young Valentinian II and Arcadius, Theodosius's very young child, is a formality—important, in that Faustinus and Marcellinus present themselves as good Roman citizens, but a formality nonetheless. Moreover, toward the end of the *Libellus precum*, the authors openly address Theodosius alone, and they even use the second-person singular

---

69. At §124, Marcellinus explicitly refers to himself as a presbyter; Faustinus claims that he is not worthy of the title, but as the preface to the *Confessio fidei* makes clear, this is just a bit of rhetorical humility. There is no evidence that Faustinus was later bishop of Rome (*pace* Ayres 2014, 98).

70. In his edition of Faustinus's (1978, 287n7) *De Trinitate*, Simonetti writes, "docti autem uiri consentiunt librum reuera a Faustino scriptum esse."

71. On Justina, see Theodoret, *Hist. eccl.* 5.13; Augustine, *Conf.* 9.7.15–16. Augustine describes Ambrose's discovery of the bodies of the martyrs Gervasius and Protasius as a blow "ad coercendem rabiem femineam sed regiam." See, too, McLynn 1994, 209–19, and on the revival of Western Arianism in the 380s in general, see Williams 1997, 185–210.

rather than plural in one instance.[72] Faustinus says that it is Theodosius who requested the *Confessio fidei*, and he wrote the *De Trinitate* at the request of Theodosius's wife, Flacilla; both suggest a closeness between Faustinus and the Eastern, not Western, court (*Conf. fid.* prologue; *Trin.* 1). Last, of course, it is Theodosius who wrote the response to the petition.

The petition is essentially chronological, divided into two parts. The first focuses on the indignities visited upon Nicene Christians by Arians under Constantius II and the second on more recent instances of other Nicene Christians persecuting the Luciferians. The petition is punctuated throughout by appeals to the emperor's sense of justice and piety. The main targets of the Luciferians are the aforementioned prevaricators, by which Faustinus and Marcellinus mean Nicene bishops who had sworn to Arian creeds when pressured by Constantius but then reverted back to the Nicene faith. The contents of the petition are described below, but an outline may also be useful for following the document:

Introduction
    §§1–4   Appeals to the emperor

Nicaea to Rimini
    §§5–11   Arius and the Arians
    §§12–20   Arianism triumphant; the Council of Rimini
    §§21–27   The exiles of Nicene bishops
    §§28–31   Constantius and the bishops
    §§32–47   Gregory of Elvira and events in Spain
    §§48–50   Events in the East

Interim
    §§51–52   Julian and Jovian
    §§53–61   Various arguments
    §§62–65   Zosimus and Lucifer at Naples
    §§66–68   Valens
    §§69–71   Various arguments

---

72. At §120 they use *sitis* to address all of the emperors, but at §123, just before their signatures, they make their case directly: "Maxime sub te, religiosissime Auguste Theodosi."

Recent events
§§72–76   Vincentius and events in Spain
§77   Bonosus of Trier and Aurelius of Rome
§§78–85   Macarius, Ephesius, and events in Rome
§§86–91   On the term *Luciferianus* and Lucifer
§§92–101   Heraclida and events in Oxyrhynchus
§§102–110   Hermione, Ephesius, Severus, and events in Eleutheropolis

Conclusion
§§110–121   Summation of argument
§§121–122   Request
§§123–124   Signatures

The beginning of the petition (Faustinus and Marcellinus, *Lib. prec.* 1–4) appeals to the emperor directly, positioning him as a pious ruler in contrast to previous rulers (Faustinus and Marcellinus are assuredly referring to Constantius, and probably to Valens as well). They also lay out the basic problem that the petition will focus on, namely, that bishops who formerly swore to Arian creeds now persecute Nicene Christians (the Luciferians) while deceitfully claiming to be Nicene Christians.

The narrative begins with a brief history of events concerning Arius (§§5–11), including a lurid and fantastical account of Arius's death that serves as an example of divine retribution. The struggles of the Arian and Nicene factions in the 340s and 350s are greatly abbreviated, culminating with the Council of Rimini (§§12–20); the parallel Council of Seleucia-in-Isauria is mentioned, but no details are provided. Faustinus and Marcellinus then backtrack a little (§§21–27) to describe the exiles of Paulinus of Trier, Lucifer of Cagliari, Eusebius of Vercelli, Dionysius of Milan, Rhodanius of Toulouse, Hilary of Poitiers (who is criticized for his later leniency toward former Arians), Maximus of Naples (whose death is reported), Rufininus (a man from Centumcellae whose grisly death is also recorded), and some unnamed Egyptian bishops. Before continuing the narrative, Faustinus and Marcellinus argue (§§28–31) that if the bishops at Rimini had shown similar backbone, Constantius would have backed down, that swearing to heresy is equivalent to participation in pagan sacrifices, and that the small number of Luciferians is irrelevant because they have proven their faith through their willingness to suffer torture and death.

Until this point, the narratives have been fairly abbreviated. But following their discussion of these exiles and persecutions, Faustinus and Marcellinus present a lengthy account (§§32–47) of events that supposedly occurred in Spain, all revolving around a set of bishops: Potamius of Lisbon, Gregory of Elvira, Hosius of Cordoba, and, at the end of the story, Florentius of Merida.[73] Faustinus and Marcellinus explain that this narrative, in which Gregory serves as hero and Hosius as archvillain, is a warning to others as an example of divine retribution. The fall of Hosius into Arianism was clearly a seminal event for the Nicene party, as Hosius was Constantine's adviser and one of the Nicene faction's most revered members. But most Nicene Christians (other than the Luciferians) were more interested in excusing Hosius than castigating him.[74] Faustinus and Marcellinus move from this long story to a brief discussion of events in the East (§§48–50), particularly the tendency of Arians there to reordain Nicene bishops who wished to swear to Arian creeds and remain bishops.

The intervening sections between the events before the Council of Rimini and the sufferings of the Luciferians alternate between narrative and argumentation. First, the narrative briefly resumes with the reigns of Julian and Jovian noted in turn (§§51–52). There follows a lengthy and at times meandering set of arguments (§§53–61) about holding communion with prevaricators and the value of martyrdom; peaceful coexistence with prevaricators is particularly singled out as a false peace. Faustinus and Marcellinus return to their narrative, now entering the phase in which the exiled bishops were returning to their sees (§§62–65). They tell how Lucifer encountered Zosimus, ordained as the Arian bishop of Naples in place of the Nicene Maximus; this Zosimus, like Potamius, Hosius, and Florentius, suffered gruesomely, which the Luciferians again interpret as a divine warning for his impiety. The narrative continues under Valens, with the Arians able to recover some of their former influence due to the unity among them and the divisions among Nicene Christians (§§66–68; Valentinian is ignored). The narrative is once again interrupted to recount two scriptural stories (Noah and the flood, and Jehu and Ahab), which Faustinus and Marcellinus interpret as proof of the virtue of purity of faith (§§69–71).

---

73. On the role of the well-known Hosius in the *Libellus precum*, see below.

74. De Clercq (1954, 507–9) provides no fewer than fourteen sources from the fourth to the sixth centuries that describe his change of allegiance. All of these accounts except that of the Luciferians emphasize that Hosius only changed allegiance under extreme duress.

The second half of the *Libellus precum* focuses on the events of more recent years and the persecution of Luciferians at the hands of other Nicene Christians. It begins by recounting the persecution suffered by Vincentius, a presbyter (not a bishop, significantly) in southern Spain (§§72–76). This repeated persecution came at the hands of a mob incited by two Spanish bishops, Luciosus and Hyginus, both described as prevaricators. In addition to their attacks on Vincentius and his congregation, they also persecuted local decurions, leading to one decurion's death.

By contrast, Faustinus and Marcellinus only very briefly describe the imprisonment and death of a presbyter named Bonosus in Trier and the persecution of a bishop named Aurelius in Rome (§77).[75] Retaining their focus on Rome, however, they detail the persecution and death suffered by an ascetic presbyter named Macarius, as well as his burial and reburial next to another martyr, and an additional courtroom scene in Rome involving a Luciferian bishop, Ephesius; these persecutions came at the hands of Damasus, who is depicted as a wrathful, evil man who unlawfully uses government agents and regularly drags his opponents to court (§§78–85).

Faustinus and Marcellinus interrupt the narrative to explain how the term *Luciferianus* is both inaccurate and malicious, while still heaping praise on Lucifer himself (§§86–91). The next portion of the narrative takes place in Oxyrhynchus, a city in southern Egypt, where the Luciferians and their bishop Heraclida faced persecution at the hands of prevaricators (§§92–101). The Luciferians repeatedly criticize another bishop in Oxyrhynchus, Theodore, who appears to have been ordained as a Nicene bishop, reordained as an Arian bishop, and then readmitted as a Nicene bishop.

The last narrative in the petition takes place in Eleutheropolis, a city in Palestine (§§102–110). Here, the Luciferians detail persecution suffered not by a bishop or a presbyter but by an ascetic woman, Hermione. The aforementioned Ephesius reappears, sent to Eleutheropolis in the place of Heraclida of Oxyrhynchus, whom Hermione had requested visit Eleutheropolis. Faustinus and Marcellinus also describe the conversion of a man named Severus to their community after he encountered Ephesius. After Ephesius sails away to North Africa at the request of other Luciferians, Hermione and other Luciferians in Eleutheropolis face persecution by the

---

75. The paucity of details about events in Trier suggests that they did not know much about the Luciferian community there.

bishop there, Turbo. The Luciferians in Eleutheropolis appear to have no bishop of their own.

The remainder of the petition sums up the case that Faustinus and Marcellinus are presenting to Theodosius (§§110–121). They ask whether he is willing to permit the injustices they detail and warn that permitting them so far has led to the disasters afflicting the Roman Empire, probably hinting at the military disaster at Adrianople in 378, the usurpation of Magnus Maximus in the West in 383, and major famines in Antioch in 382 and Rome and Antioch in 384. Peaceful coexistence with heretics and former heretics, as above, is denounced as a false peace; the emperor, as above, is pardoned due to his ignorance up to this point.

The Luciferians are very careful to include two requests in their petition, one quite large and one relatively small. This was a common tactic in antiquity as a way of avoiding the social humiliation that might come with the simple rejection of the former (Schor 2009, 292–94). In the case of the Luciferians, their desired outcome is clear: the emperor should recognize that they in fact represent the true "catholic church" of the Roman Empire, and all of the prevaricators and those who hold communion with them should be stripped off their clerical rank and reduced to lay status. This was, one might say, a big ask: Faustinus and Marcellinus were requesting that nearly all of the Nicene bishops in the Roman Empire be cast out of office at once. The two presbyters were not so simpleminded as to think that this request would be honored, of course, and near the end of their petition offer the emperor the second, more acceptable request (Faustinus and Marcellinus, *Lib. prec.* 121–122): let the prevaricators have their glory and wealth just so long as the Luciferians can rest in the mangers that, the authors add with a flourish, were good enough for Jesus. The *Libellus precum* ends with praise of Theodosius and personal signatures written by Marcellinus and Faustinus, respectively, both of whom express their best wishes to "the most pious" and "most glorious" emperors (§§123–124).

So runs the course of the *Libellus precum*. At a fundamental level, the narrative serves as a typical late antique petition.[76] It follows the normal Roman pattern for a petition with an exordium, an argument, and a peroration (Canellis 2006, 43–48). It is critically important to note that late antique petitions were not delivered with the intent of reforming laws in

---

76. The name even translates to "small book of requests." On petitions in late antiquity, see Harries 1999, 26–31.

general but rather to seek redress in specific circumstances. While Faustinus and Marcellinus may have hoped that the emperor would grant their communities state support, their core concern must have been a more immediate relief from the persecution they faced. Late antique petitions were also, by their nature, incredibly one-sided and prone to exaggeration or omission at their best—just as the *Libellus precum* clearly is. The rhetoric in use is quite normal as well. Ciceronian rhythms permeate the petition, particularly in the exordium and peroration, while the style of writing in the argument is much more distinct (and similar to the *De Trinitate*; Canellis 2006, 43–48). Simple plays on words are quite common.[77] In these ways, then, the *Libellus precum* is a perfectly normal petition.

In another sense, though, the *Libellus precum* is far more than just a petition: it is a collection of martyr stories, narrating accounts of various martyrs' deaths and other suffering at the hands of Arians and Nicene Christians alike. The Luciferians explicitly make the case that martyrdom is the best proof of orthodoxy (Faustinus and Marcellinus, *Lib. prec.* 10, 59, 72). Furthermore, by the early fourth century, the martyr-story genre was filled with very stereotypical motifs that continued to appear in martyr stories long after Christianity was granted legal toleration. One of the most common of these motifs was the image of a stalwart Christian facing a pagan Roman official in a courtroom scene, the Christian remaining calm while the persecutor grows increasingly angry (Shaw 2003). Such scenes occur twice in the *Libellus precum*, once when Gregory faces off against Hosius before the pagan official, Clementine, and once when Ephesius faces off against Damasus before the Christian official, Bassus. The latter example demonstrates how this narrative, born from experiences Christians recorded about martyrdom under pagans in earlier centuries, could be easily transferred to intra-Christian conflicts. The fact that both Gregory and Ephesius both end up victorious, rather than painfully executed, also demonstrates the ability of Faustinus and Marcellinus to play with a reader's expectations.[78]

---

77. As when (Faustinus and Marcellinus, *Lib prec.* 38) the pagan judge (*iudex*) fears being judged (*iudicaretur*) by God, or when Valens (§66) considers the actions of bishops in the reign of Constantius (*sub Constantio*) and compares the Arian constancy (*constantiam*) among them with the Nicene inconstancy (*cum inconstantia*). See Canellis 2001, 499.

78. On the role the martyr's death played in the typical story, see Grig 2004, 60–61.

One interesting pattern within the *Libellus precum* is how often its authors encourage the emperor to verify their claims. Faustinus and Marcellinus cite the people of Spain in general (Faustinus and Marcellinus, *Lib. prec.* 41), Merida (§44), and Naples (§65) as eyewitnesses, in the first case even explicitly stating that the emperor can confirm with the Spanish people that they are not making events up (all the more interesting given that Theodosius was from a prominent Spanish family). These instances all tellingly involve the more distant persecutions of the 350s and the return of the exiles in the early 360s, and in particular the divine punishments suffered by the persecutors, all of which have what modern readers would consider more fantastical or miraculous elements compared to the relatively straightforward accounts of the persecutions of the 380s. One cannot help but feel that the Luciferians knew how unbelievable their stories might sound and sought to preemptively deny that line of criticism.

Faustinus and Marcellinus also draw repeated connections between the persecution suffered by Nicene Christians in the 350s at the hands of Arians and the persecution suffered by Luciferians in the 370s and 380s at the hands of other Nicene Christians. One way they do this is by creating narrative parallels in the *Libellus precum* between the accounts set in the 350s and those set closer to 383/4. Several of these are clear in the account of Gregory and Hosius. Gregory and Hosius have a showdown in a court in front of a state official (§§35–40) just as some thirty years later Ephesius and Damasus also have a conflict in a court in front of a state official (§§84–85). The former persecutor was the archetypical traitor to the Nicene cause, a Nicene bishop who became an Arian, and the other was the prevaricator bishop of Rome himself, who had supported Constantius's Arian bishop of Rome in the 350s. Furthermore, as noted above, in both courtroom cases in the *Libellus precum* the judge unusually refuses to pass judgment on the upright man. The parallels between the two narratives become clear not only in how Faustinus and Marcellinus adhere to the same stock narrative but in how they play with it as well. There are other examples of parallels peppering the narratives in the *Libellus precum*, and not enough space to fully elaborate on all of them. One is particularly interesting: Faustinus and Marcellinus describe Nicene bishops swearing to an Arian creed as no less a sacrilege than sacrificing at a pagan idol (§29), and later describe prevaricator clerics taking a Luciferian altar and placing it at the feet of a pagan idol (§76).

Faustinus and Marcellinus connect past and present explicitly as well. Halfway through their narrative of Turbo's persecution of Hermione and

other Luciferians (§§102–110), they pause to recount Turbo's persecution of Lucifer (in exile) and other staunch Nicene Christians in Eleutheropolis in the 350s; here, nearing the end of the petition, they do not even expect readers to draw connections between past and present themselves. The irony that Turbo continued to persecute the same community, this time as a Nicene bishop persecuting Luciferians, is not lost on Faustinus and Marcellinus. Even outside the context of persecution these connections are evident, as when the Luciferians describe the exiled Nicene bishops of the 350s as maintaining their sense of community by shared letters (§50), the same way they describe their own disparate communities remaining in touch with one another (§§103, 107).

In a more abstract way, Faustinus and Marcellinus suggest a connection between the persecutions of the 350s and 380s by the geographical structure of the narratives (Canellis 2006, 51–53). The first half of the petition describes the bishops exiled in the 350s for defending the Nicene Creed; the exiles described, in order, are Paulinus from Trier, Lucifer from Sardinia, two bishops from northern Italy, two from Gaul, two from central Italy (one of whom died before he could be exiled), and then finally unnamed clerics from Egypt. In other words, the arrangement of their narrative begins in the West and ends up in the East. In the second half of the petition, Faustinus and Marcellinus describe persecutions against Luciferians in the 380s in the exact same geographical progression. They recount events in Spain, then Gaul, then Italy, and then turn to the East, describing events in Egypt and then Palestine. The literary route from West to East comes to an implied end with Faustinus and Marcellinus presenting their petition before Theodosius in Constantinople. Faustinus and Marcellinus thus "travel" the same route in the text when describing the persecutions of their communities in the 380s as they do in their narrative of the persecutions of the 350s. In this textual reflection, Faustinus and Marcellinus establish another link between the bishops exiled in the 350s and their own community in the 380s.

The result of connections both between specific narratives and in the structure of the petition itself is that the reader links the one with the other, connecting the persecutor of the 350s with the persecutor of the 380s, and the persecution of the 350s with the persecution of the 380s. It was important for the Luciferians to emphasize these connections in order to demonstrate that they were the true heirs of the Nicene tradition and not innovators in any respect (Castelli 2004, 13). Christians in antiquity believed that heresies arose in specific circumstances, while

orthodoxy formed an unbroken chain from Christ onward;[79] for the Luciferians, a direct connection to the unquestionably orthodox exiles of the 350s was proof of their own legitimacy and thus also of the illegitimacy of their opponents.[80]

The Luciferians also use these narratives to emphasize that they are good Christians. Luciferian individuals are generally described in glowing terms such as "holy" or "blessed." Some have powers granted by God: Macarius can exorcise demons (Faustinus and Marcellinus, *Lib. prec.* 78), Lucifer and Gregory work unspecified miracles (§§89–90), and Ephesius is accompanied by divine grace wherever he goes (§105). The Luciferians also emphasize the importance of asceticism. Macarius (§78), Heraclida (§§94, 98), and Hermione (§102) are specified as practicing ascetics, and there are other Luciferian ascetic women, some of whom live in Oxyrhynchus (§99) and some of whom who live in a monastery in Eleutheropolis with Hermione (§104).[81] Hermione is even called noble by birth but nobler in her ascetic practice, a description reflecting a growing trend among Christian authors such as Jerome to establish ascetic practice as complementary and superior to noble lineage (Salzman 2001). Luciferian communities in general are "uncontaminated" (Faustinus and Marcellinus, *Lib. prec.* 84) or "undiminished" (§104).

Faustinus and Marcellinus also emphasize that they are good Roman citizens. The introductory sections of the *Libellus precum* concern themselves with the importance of secular law and the emperor's role in defending the weak from the predation of the strong. Elsewhere, the Luciferians stress that the problem they face is a misapplication of just laws, *not* an application of unjust laws (§§49, 56, 83, 85, 97, 114). Particularly in regard to Bassus, who refused to judge Ephesius guilty of anything, the *Libellus precum* emphasizes that the fault here is not with the state and its officials but with prevaricating bishops—certainly a fine point to make

---

79. One of the clearest statements of this can be found in the fifth-century *Commonitorium* of Vincent of Lerins, particularly 24.62: "Et revera, quae unquam haeresis nisi sub certo nomine, certo loco, certo tempore ebullivit?"

80. Theodosius appears to have shared their view: see *Lex Aug.* 3.

81. Interestingly, despite these inclinations toward asceticism and the growing trend toward monasticism in general in the fourth century, Faustinus and Marcellinus describe no dedicated male ascetics. The large amount of travel that Ephesius undertakes in the course of the petition—from Rome to Oxyrhynchus to Eleutheropolis—suggests that the Luciferians did not have many clerics and possibly could not afford to have many or any dedicated ascetic men.

in a petition to an emperor. The state, they say, has already made the correct decision; Theodosius need only confirm what his representatives have already decided. Naturally, Theodosius is presumed ignorant of the plight of the Luciferians (§§49, 120) because he is so busy attending to affairs of state—no fault is found with him personally.

Luciferian opponents, by contrast, are generally described as irredeemably evil.[82] A few of the descriptions in the *Libellus precum* are worth special attention. Faustinus and Marcellinus's favored insult for their opponents is, of course, *praevaricator*, a slur not dissimilar from the word *traditor*, "traitor," or "one who hands over [scriptures to persecutors]," a term that Donatists used against other North African Christians. The perceived hypocrisy or treachery of these prevaricators is far and away the paramount concern for the authors. It is also interesting that the Luciferians seemed to have relied on the term *praevaricator* but never devised a term based on any person's name, as *Luciferiani* was used to describe them. Faustinus and Marcellinus also sarcastically refer to two persecuting bishops, Luciosus and Hyginus, as *egregii* (§§74, 75), a word normally meaning "outstanding" in a positive sense but here clearly used to indicate the opposite. They compare their opponents to pagans (as described above) and, according to Jerome (*Lucif.* 15), compared their opponents to Jews as well.[83]

Just as Faustinus and Marcellinus describe themselves as good Roman citizens, they describe their opponents as bad Roman citizens. The foremost way the authors make this point is by several times emphasizing the actions taken by these prevaricating bishops against Roman civic officials in particular. Their description of events in Spain is very telling (Faustinus and Marcellinus, *Lib. prec.* 74): after the bishops Luciosus and Hyginus have some Luciferian clergy beaten to death, they demand that the local decurions present themselves so that they can be jailed. This incarceration actually leads to the death of one. That Faustinus and Marcellinus's opponents would treat Luciferian clergy this way is almost taken for granted; the unthinkable crime here is that these bishops ordered around Roman officials and even caused one to die.[84] In this story we can see

---

82. On this standby in petitions, see Harries 1999, 185.

83. "Et ubi, quaeso, isti sunt nimium religiosi, immo nimium profani, qui plures synagogas asserunt esse quam ecclesias?" Comparing one's opponents to pagans and Jews was quite common in late antiquity; see, e.g., Shaw 2011, 195–306.

84. See also Faustinus and Marcellinus, *Lib prec.* 96, in which a bishop orders

the Luciferians playing not on the emperor's piety (which is addressed throughout the text) but on his role as the head of state.

One reason Faustinus and Marcellinus emphasize that their opponents are prevaricators, but do not use a term based in a person's name, may be that the *Libellus precum* is not so black-and-white as it first appears. While Faustinus and Marcellinus grouse about Hilary of Poitier's attempts at reconciliation with prevaricators. they are also quick to point out his good work in opposing heresy (§24). Praise is given to Athanasius (§88), who, the authors conveniently neglect to mention, led the Council of Alexandria that caused the rupture between their communities to begin with. Perhaps most telling is their emphasis on the actions of Florentius of Ostia, one of Damasus's allies, who provided a suitable burial place for the martyred Macarius and thus distanced himself from Damasus "inasmuch as he was able" (§82). While much of the petition is dedicated to lambasting their opponents, Faustinus and Marcellinus in these instances shed light on the much more variegated picture that must have existed for all communities of Christians in conflict in late antiquity.[85]

Despite the deference the Luciferians show to the emperor and his state, and their narrative emphasis on their opponents not showing the same deference, there are some ominous, threatening undertones to the Luciferian petition as well (Canellis 2006, 64–65). Persecutors are repeatedly cited as examples of divine judgment presaging the final judgment of God: Arius (Faustinus and Marcellinus, *Lib. prec.* 9–10, 20), Hosius (§§38–39), Potamius (§42), Florentius of Merida (§43), and Zosimus (§64) all suffer punishment in this life, which the Luciferians take as a divine warning; the point is made in a general sense repeatedly as well (§§4, 31, 46–47, 61).[86] These serve as ample evidence for an argument the Luciferians make a few other times in the text. At §83 they ask, con-

---

government troops to harass Heraclida until they finally refuse, and §§104, 108, in which a bishop harasses Severus, who is tellingly described as an ex-tribune who had served the state very well.

85. Consider, for example, the Donatists who attended Augustine's sermons (Possidius, *Vit. Aug.* 6–7) and other examples in North African literature of peaceful coexistence (even marriage!) between Donatists and other Christians in North Africa (Optatus, *Schism.* 4.2; Augustine, *Ep.* 33.5; 93.1; *Unic. bapt.* 2.7.10). It is altogether too easy, and dangerous, to take the rhetorical hostility in many late antique texts at face value.

86. The Luciferians do not address the apparent lack of divine judgment against their contemporary tormentors, i.e., Luciosus and Hyginus in Spain, Damasus in Rome, Theodore in Oxyrhynchus, and Turbo in Eleutheropolis.

cerning the actions of Damasus, whether the emperor is worried that permitting such actions will lead to calamities in the Roman Empire (the same point is made more generally at §§112, 122). The implication is clear: if the Roman Empire has been suffering because true Nicene Christians have been persecuted within it, Theodosius will bring further disaster on the Roman Empire if he does not accede to the Luciferian requests. Of course, the Luciferians emphasize that they are not personally bloodthirsty (see, e.g., §70).

The *Libellus precum* was probably not intended just for its imperial audience. If we examine the document as it might have been read by a Luciferian audience, we can see other elements of rhetoric within the text that, like many martyr stories, emphasize how Luciferians should act and who their true enemies are. Some of these points are simple—that constancy in faith is paramount, for instance, or that asceticism is an obvious virtue—but a few of the more interesting ones will be discussed below.

Returning to Hosius of Cordoba, Faustinus and Marcellinus dedicate a significant portion of the entire petition to describe Hosius's fall into Arianism. The Luciferians not only recount Hosius's fall but even include a story found nowhere else about the evil actions he took after swearing to an Arian creed. But why not emphasize the actions of Valens, Ursacius, Germinius, and other well-known Arian bishops who played a very active and well-documented role in opposing the Nicene faction in the 350s? Within the *Libellus precum*, these openly and even proudly Arian bishops receive only a brief mention as authors of the Fourth Sirmian Creed (§14). Using Hosius, however, emphasizes the Luciferian point that their true enemies are Nicene persecutors, not Arians or pagans. Hosius is not just an Arian persecutor but a Nicene bishop gone bad. In this way, he is a much more vivid figure for the Luciferian community members who would recount these stories while facing persecutors who were also seemingly good Nicene Christians. After all, everyone knows that Arians are bad; but Hosius? His fall exemplifies how even the staunchest of Nicene Christians could in fact become wicked. Given the temptation that must have existed for commingling between distinct Nicene communities, it makes sense that Faustinus and Marcellinus would want to emphasize to Luciferian readers the potential dangers of doing so.

Even in a general sense, the Luciferians use these stories to reinforce behaviors within their own communities. The most important of these was, not unexpectedly, that their members should be willing to suffer persecution, even death, in defense of their beliefs. This functions as something of

a spiritual test for the Luciferians. Faustinus and Marcellinus make their argument early on in the *Libellus precum* (§20), arguing that anyone who feared God's punishment would gladly suffer earthly evils rather than betray the faith. The point is reinforced a little further on down in the petition (§26), when the two define true catholics as those who suffered exile, punishments, or death on behalf of the faith.

One specific example concerns the burial of the martyred Macarius (§82). Macarius was originally buried in an unspecified tomb, but the sympathetic Florentius of Ostia moved his body to be buried next to the body of a third-century martyr, Asterius, in a basilica's presbyterium (the area at the rear of a basilica containing the altar, bishop's seat, and benches for the clergy). A reader familiar with the story of Asterius's death as related in the Gesta martyrum would see numerous resonances in the account of Macarius's death in the *Libellus precum*.[87] Asterius, for example, was left unburied only to be honorably reburied later by pious Christians, just as Macarius was improperly buried but then reburied by a pious Christian, Florentius. Thus the *Libellus precum* creates an equivalence between the holiness of the two in the reader's mind not only by the fact that Macarius was buried next to Asterius but in how both came to be buried in the same place the same way. Moreover, Faustinus and Marcellinus emphasize that Macarius was a presbyter. Given that the Luciferians put such great emphasis on the proper actions of clergy (rather than the laity), their emphasis on his martyr's burial as a cleric in the presbyterium, the central location where clergy performed their duties, further emphasizes that good clerics are those willing to suffer martyrdom.

Faustinus and Marcellinus routinely use biblical metaphors in the petition.[88] An interesting example is their reference to Noah, in which the

---

87. The main account of Asterius's death can be found in the Gesta martyrum, specifically Acta Callisti 9 (PG 10:120): "Post dies vero decem et septem venit presbyter eius, nomine Asterius cum clericis noctu, et levavit corpus Calixti episcopi et honorifice sepelivit in coemeterio Calepodii, Via Aurelia, pridie Idus Octobris. Post dies autem sex tenuit Alexander Asterium presbyterum: quem praecipit per pontem praecipitari. Cuius sanctum corpus inventum est in Ostia, et a quibusdam Christianis sepultum in eadem civitate sub die XII Kalendarum Novembris." The Gesta martyrum is a late antique collection of apocryphal accounts of the deaths of pre-Constantinian Christians in Rome. Despite questions concerning its date, some of the stories in the Gesta martyrum clearly came from the late fourth or early fifth century at the latest. On the Gesta martyrum, see Pilsworth 2000, 311, 314, and bibliography.

88. It is worth noting that nowhere in the *Libellus precum* do Faustinus and Mar-

authors paint the Luciferians as a small but righteous community faced with destruction at the hands of a seemingly more powerful force that can only be overcome with help from God (§69).[89] The image of Noah is particularly interesting because it also appears in Jerome's *Dialogus contra Luciferianos*. For Faustinus and Marcellinus, the ark was one of several images used to paint a picture of their isolated but virtuous community. For Jerome (*Lucif.* 22), the ark also depicted a Christian community ("Noah's ark was a prefiguration of the church [*ecclesiae*])," but he meant something much different by this.[90] In context, Jerome was justifying the inclusion of sinners and others into a broad *ecclesia*, essentially the complete opposite of the image of purity presented by the Luciferians (which one would expect in a dialogue written against Luciferians!). Faustinus and Marcellinus's need to reinforce the propriety of their community's isolation suggests that some of their own community's readers saw themselves as small, isolated, weak, and vulnerable by the 380s. But the framing of the same metaphor in Jerome's *Dialogus* also suggests that some of his non-Luciferian readers found the notion of a more pure community enticing as well.

The *Libellus precum*, in sum, is a fairly sophisticated document. Faustinus and Marcellinus crafted it as a petition that would both appeal to the emperor and reinforce behaviors in their own community. It includes a complex structure, plays with narrative expectations, and makes interesting uses of a number of metaphors. We are fortunate to have such a document available for study, as the number of documents that survive from minority Christian communities in late antiquity is paltry. Through the *Libellus precum* we have a window into the legal and social workings of a small rigorist Christian community about which we would know very little otherwise.

---

cellinus make any explicitly classical allusions. They do not outright reject them (as Faustinus does in the *De Trinitate*, discussed below), but the metaphoric language with which they make sense of their world is purely biblical.

89. It is also worth noting the flattery that Faustinus and Marcellinus offer to Theodosius here: if God is the only one who can help the beleaguered Noah, Lot, or Elijah, and Theodosius is the only one who can help the Luciferians, then there is some kind of an equivalence between God and Theodosius that the parallel structure provides.

90. "Arca Noe Ecclesiae typus fuit."

Lex Augusta

In response to the *Libellus precum*, the chancellery of Theodosius composed a document that has come down to us with the suitably generic title *Lex Augusta*. It is possible that Theodosius himself contributed to the language of the document rather than leaving it for his chancellery (Honoré 1998, 53); it is also possible that the work is a forgery, though no direct evidence suggests as much.[91] In accordance with normal Roman practice, the law was addressed not to the petitioners but to Theodosius's Eastern prefect, Cynegius (Theodosius had no jurisdiction over the western half of the empire, technically ruled by the young Valentinian II). The *Lex Augusta* must date between 384, when Cynegius was made Eastern prefect, and 388, when Cynegius died. The year 384 is most likely, seeing as the *Libellus precum* was written in 383 or 384.

Flavius Theodosius was a general from a military-aristocratic family. He had been elevated to the rank of Augustus by the emperor Gratian in 379 following the death of Valens at the Battle of Adrianople in late 378. He brought with him to Constantinople a number of other Spaniards, including Cynegius (Matthews 1967, 440). As noted above, Maternus Cynegius was Eastern prefect (*praefectus oriens*) for Theodosius from 384 to his death in 388, a most prestigious and influential government position second only to the emperor in late antiquity. Like Theodosius (and Theodosius's wife, Flacilla), he was an aristocrat from Spain. His long tenure as Eastern prefect is proof enough of how important his place was within Theodosius's government. Cynegius was apparently much more radically antipagan than Theodosius, who happily promoted certain pagans to high office (but did not interfere with Cynegius's activities either).[92] His religious zeal extended to antiheretical measures as well, and here he found Theodosius a much more eager partner.[93]

The form of the *Lex Augusta* is a rescript, by far the most common way by which emperors promulgated legislation.[94] A rescript functioned not as a planned piece of legislation meant to actively enact change within the empire, the way we conceive of modern legislation, but as a

---

91. See Harries 1999, 30, on false rescripts being common in late antiquity.
92. For Cynegius in general, see Libanius, *Or.* 30, 44–49; Zosimus, *Hist. nova* 4.39; Marique 1963; Matthews 1967; von Haehling 1978, 72–73; Olszaniec 2013, 100–107.
93. On Theodosius's increasingly intolerant legislation, see Rougé 1972.
94. On rescripts in general, see Harries 1999, 26–31.

specific response to a petition delivered by some complainant (as in the case of Faustinus and Marcellinus's petition) or to a letter sent by some bureaucrat seeking guidance about the proper course of action in a given situation. Although such rescripts could function as legal precedent for future decisions or be compiled by jurists into collections, they could also be ignored or languish in a drawer. Their purpose was to resolve an immediate problem, not to establish a legal norm. It is worth noting that rescripts were written based on the facts as presented but did not necessarily function to confirm that the facts as presented were actually factual.

Rescripts were generally fairly short, merely appended to the original text, making the length of the *Lex Augusta* somewhat unusual (Harries 1999, 21). One of the most valuable aspects of the *Lex Augusta* is that it provides us with an entire law. Generally speaking, the laws that have come down to us in the Codex Theodosianus and other collections were very heavily edited: they were, most notably, divided up and trimmed to avoid any supposedly unnecessary verbiage.[95] The *Lex Augusta*, however, is not included in the Codex Theodosianus.[96] It may be absent because it was a response to a specific petition, which the editors of the Codex Theodosianus were instructed to omit (Matthews 2000, 66–69), although it was addressed to the Eastern prefect and carried a fairly general force behind it. In any case, it provides an example of an imperial law *with* the kinds of rhetorical embellishments (such as Theodosius generously referring to Cynegius as a *parens carissime* in *Lex Aug.* 7) normally omitted from these laws. Reading this document demonstrates how many of the laws in the Codex Theodosianus sound much more formal and stilted than they probably were.

Turning to the content of the rescript, as noted above, the Luciferians made two alternative requests to Theodosius: that he recognize them as the true "catholic church" of the Roman Empire and strip nearly all of the Nicene bishops throughout the empire of their clerical standing, or, barring that, that he simply order these bishops to stop persecuting the Luciferians. It is not surprising that Theodosius did not acquiesce to their first request (it is not even mentioned); it is perhaps surprising that he did to their second,

---

95. On the formation of the Codex Theodosianus, see Cod. theod. 1.1.5: "ut constitutionum ipsa etiam verba, quae ad rem pertinent, reserventur, praetermissis illis, quae sanciendae rei non ex ipsa necessitate adiuncta sunt." See Matthews 2000, 55–71, esp. 57–59; Sirks 2007, 91.

96. For another, albeit much shorter, example, see Matthews 2010, 39–40.

particularly in light of his (and Cynegius's) general hostility to non-Nicene Christians. It seems likely that Theodosius was more concerned with those insufficiently Nicene in their doctrine than those who were perhaps overly zealous in their adherence to the Nicene Creed; he also, for example, treated the Novatians in Constantinople with unusual tolerance and even warmth (Socrates, *Hist. eccl.* 5.10). For Theodosius, doctrine seems to have taken precedence over unity, and the *Lex Augusta* thus provides a nice touch of nuance to our understanding of Theodosius's religious policies.

The rescript creates a definition to explain who exactly would be protected under its law: "Gregory and Heraclida, priests of the holy law, and the rest of the priests who are similar to these" (*Lex Aug.* 8). Cynegius was apparently granted total leeway in deciding who exactly were similar to Gregory and Heraclida. This form is not wholly dissimilar from another, more famous law (the so-called Edict of Thessalonica) Theodosius issued in 380, which declared proper Christian belief to be what was handed down from the apostles and defines this as whatever Damasus of Rome and Peter of Alexandria followed (*Cod. theod.* 16.1.2).[97] Together, these laws suggest that rather than defining the faith with a set of doctrinal statements (though not to the exclusion of them), Theodosius often found it easier or more effective to simply pick unquestionably orthodox individuals and define orthodoxy as shared communion with them.

The *Lex Augusta* completely sidesteps the question of schism, however, ignoring in its response the presence of Luciferian bishops of Rome (Aurelius and then Ephesius) alongside other orthodox bishops (namely, Damasus) despite the fact that Ephesius is one of the most prominent persons in the *Libellus precum*.[98] Given Theodosius's general support of

---

97. "Cunctos populos, quos clementiae nostrae regit temperamentum, in tali volumus religione versari, quam divinum Petrum apostolum tradidisse Romanis religio usque ad nunc ab ipso insinuata declarat quamque pontificem Damasum sequi claret et Petrum Aleksandriae episcopum virum apostolicae sanctitatis, hoc est, ut secundum apostolicam disciplinam evangelicamque doctrinam patris et filii et spiritus sancti unam deitatem sub pari maiestate et sub pia trinitate credamus. Hanc legem sequentes Christianorum catholicorum nomen iubemus amplecti, reliquos vero dementes vesanosque iudicantes haeretici dogmatis infamiam sustinere nec conciliabula eorum ecclesiarum nomen accipere, divina primum vindicta, post etiam motus nostri, quem ex caelesti arbitro sumpserimus, ultione plectendos."

98. Escribano (2005, 146–49) suggests that Theodosius's intent may have been to support bishops in communities such as the Luciferians to foment unrest in territories controlled by Magnus Maximus.

the Novatians in Constantinople alongside the broader Nicene community there, however, the problems arising from having too many Nicene bishops in one place seem not to have troubled Theodosius as much as the presence and activities of heretics.

Furthermore, just as the Luciferians had coded threats in their petition, so too did Theodosius include one in his response. The *Lex Augusta* (§2) opens with a statement agreeing with the petitioners but cautioning them against any innovations in Christian doctrine. For Theodosius, there must have been some lingering doubt, perhaps not that the Luciferians had developed any doctrines at variance with normal Nicene beliefs but that they would. Theodosius seems willing to support these Nicene Christians but also cognizant of the dangers in doing so.

Much like the *Libellus precum* and *De Trinitate*, the *Lex Augusta* provides us with an unusual glimpse into parts of late antiquity that usually remain closed to us. We can see the formulation of laws in relation to the petitions that prompted these laws and apart from their incarnations in the various compilations made in later centuries. We can also better appreciate the finesse that emperors such as Theodosius used to both support and warn potentially troublesome Christian communities without upending the religious landscape of the empire. In the *Libellus precum* and *Lex Augusta* we have a complex example how petitioner and respondent interacted with each other in late antiquity.

De Trinitate

While the *Libellus precum* represents the Luciferians as the persecuted victims of other Nicene Christians, the *De Trinitate* is Faustinus's attempt to situate his own theology squarely within the core of the Nicene tradition while replying to common Arian arguments about the nature of the Father and Son. Unlike the *Libellus precum*, the *De Trinitate* was written by Faustinus alone. He penned the treatise at the request of Theodosius's wife, Flacilla.[99] According to Faustinus (*Trin.* 1), Flacilla had received some Arian arguments that she asked Faustinus to refute; the author of these passages is unknown.

---

99. Sometimes erroneously given as Galla Placidia in the manuscript tradition; most manuscripts list Flacilla as the recipient, and Gennadius (*Vir. ill.* 16) says that the *De Trinitate* was written for Flacilla. Galla Placidia was Theodosius's daughter, born in 388.

Aelia Flavia Flacilla was from an aristocratic Spanish family and had married Theodosius before he became emperor.[100] When Theodosius promoted their son Arcadius to Augustus in 383, Flacilla also took the title Augusta, the first since Constantine elevated his mother, Helena, and wife, Fausta, to the rank in 324; Flacilla also appeared on imperial coinage in that guise (the first empress represented wearing a royal crown on a coin) and in official imperial portrait statues. The general impression is that Flacilla played a relatively active role in Theodosius's governance. She was apparently a staunch supporter of the Nicene Creed as well, in stark contrast with Justina, the Arian mother of the Western emperor Valentinian II.[101]

The dating of the *De Trinitate* is less secure than that of the *Libellus precum*, but it cannot have been much earlier or later. It must have been written after Theodosius made Flacilla Augusta in 383 and before Flacilla's death in 386, that is, within a few years of the *Libellus precum*. Unfortunately, we have no real indication as to which text was composed first, and thus no knowledge of whether Faustinus gained access to Theodosius through some preexisting relationship between himself and Flacilla or caught Flacilla's attention as an ardent supporter of the Nicene formula while he was at court presenting the petition. It would not be surprising if the *De Trinitate* was composed in 383 or 384, at roughly the same time as the *Libellus precum*: Faustinus repeatedly mentions that he is writing in a hurry (the text does show some signs of this; see *Trin.* 8, 19, 23, 30, 48, 50, 51), and he would naturally be rushing if he were composing the treatise while only visiting Constantinople to deliver his petition. That Gennadius of Marseilles encountered the *De Trinitate* in the late fifth century suggests that the text had spread out beyond the imperial court at Constantinople across the Roman Empire in the intervening century, though it is unclear how it did so.

It is also unclear why Marcellinus helped Faustinus author the *Libellus precum* but not the *De Trinitate*, or why there is no *Confessio fidei* of Marcellinus to match the one written by Faustinus. It is possible that Marcellinus was already known to the emperor or someone else at court, which would also explain how the Luciferians had access to the emperor

---

100. For what follows, see Gregory of Nyssa, *Oratio funebris de Flacilla*; Holum 1982, 21–44.

101. For Flacilla, see Sozomen, *Hist. eccl.* 7.6.3; for Justina, see, e.g., Theodoret, *Hist. eccl.* 5.13; Augustine, *Conf.* 9.7.15–16; McLynn 1994, 209–19.

(Harries 1999, 88). Perhaps Faustinus was the sole author of the *De Trinitate* because he was the theologian of the two, and he was introduced to the court to deliver their petition through Marcellinus, where he came into contact with Flacilla. Unfortunately, as attractive as this reconstruction is, it is speculative.

One purpose of the *De Trinitate* is quite simple, of course: if the empress of the Roman Empire requests one to answer some Arian arguments she has encountered,[102] it is in one's best interest (both as a Nicene Christian and as a Roman citizen) to answer. The *De Trinitate* is by no means the first work of its genre; significant Latin works on the Trinity had already been written by Phoebadius of Agen (*Contra Arianos*), Marius Victorinus (*Adversus Arium*), Hilary of Poitiers (*De Trinitate*), Gregory of Elvira (*De Fide*), and Ambrose of Milan (*De Fide*).[103]

This work had other rhetorical purposes as well. Although the vast bulk of the treatise is focused on the Arians, Faustinus (*Trin*. 7, 9, 12) does level criticism at Sabellius, whose beliefs are discussed above, and Photinus of Sirmium (§41), whose rejection of the divine in the incarnation of the human Christ Faustinus denies.[104] Another rhetorical element appears in the final section of the book, where Faustinus rails not against Arians but prevaricators, the main nemeses of the Luciferians in the *Libellus precum*. Last, the *De Trinitate* is also, as will be discussed below, steeped in the theology of fourth-century Nicene luminaries, particularly Athanasius and Hilary. One of the *Libellus precum*'s main arguments, discussed above, is that the Luciferians represented the true inheritors of the Nicene tradition. Reading the document, one certainly has the impression that the *Libellus precum* serves as the theological complement to the historical account of the *Libellus precum*: just as Luciferian communities are the true Nicene communities, emerging from the context of the 350s, so too does the Luciferian statement of Nicene theology emerge from that context.

---

102. The identity of the Arian who sent Flacilla must remain a mystery, though Faustinus's reference to his use of Aristotle suggests an Eastern author; see *Trin*. 11, esp. with n. 79.

103. For Phoebadius, see Weedman 2007b, 51–63; for Marius Victorinus, see Weedman 2007b, 63–73; for Hilary, see both Weedman 2007b and Beckwith 2008 (esp. 54–68, 99–100); for Gregory, see Buckley 1964; Brumback 2014; for Ambrose, see McLynn 1994, 98–119.

104. On Photinus, see below, *Trin*. 41 and n. 325.

A summary of the *De Trinitate* is made quite difficult by the sometimes rambling nature of the text. While there are some general categories that can be followed, Faustinus often uses the same scriptural passages to make multiple related, but not identical, points.

§1	Preface
§2	Statement of basic Arian beliefs
§§3–15	That the Son has always existed; basic refutations of Arian beliefs
§§16–29	That the Son was begotten, not made; that the Son was begotten, not adopted
§§30–34	That the Father and Son are both omnipotent and immutable; that the Son is also a man
§§35–37	Against Arian interpretations of John 14:28
§§38–42	Against Arian interpretations of Acts 2:36
§§43–47	Against Arian interpretations of Proverbs 8:22
§§48–50	On the Holy Spirit
§51	Conclusion

The *De Trinitate* (§§1–2) opens with a general address to Flacilla, who apparently sent him some Arian texts and requested a refutation. Before addressing these points, Faustinus explains that he must provide a general statement of Arian beliefs (from, one must always keep in mind, a staunch opponent of the Arians and one who saw no distinction between their variegated beliefs) to clarify what exactly it is Arians believe and why, and then dismantle these points, before he begins refuting the specific points Flacilla has raised (he does not address specific Arian creeds, as, for example, Hilary does in his *De Trinitate*, which was written in response to the "blasphemy" of Sirmium). Faustinus is appropriately deferential, highlighting the piety and wisdom of Flacilla's request and his own inability as a theologian and author to meet her high standards. The opening metaphor is militaristic: since Faustinus cannot turn his back to the enemy, he must meet them in battle.

The general thrust of the following argument (§§3–15) is that the Son has always existed. The argument begins, quite aptly, with an interpretation of John 1:1, "In the beginning was the Word" (NRSV). But as Faustinus's line of argument naturally bleeds into whether the Son was made or created and in what way the Father and the Son are both God, the result is a general, quite diffuse, refutation of Arian beliefs. The following

passages (§§16–29) focus on arguments over whether the Son was made or begotten and, relatedly, whether the Son was a begotten son or an adopted son. Likewise, the next major (though much shorter) section (§§30–34) concerns the basic problem of the person of Christ: in Nicene thought, he must be both perfectly God and also a man. Readers expecting something resembling the intricate theologies of the fifth century and beyond will be poorly rewarded, for Faustinus's theological discussion of this issue is rudimentary. Faustinus sometimes resorts to quoting long scriptural passages here with a minimum of interpretation.

The next three passages, however, are much more tightly focused. These attempt to refute, in turn, specific Arian interpretations of John 14:28 ("The Father is greater than me," *Trin.* §§35–37); Acts 2:36 ("God made him Lord and Christ," *Trin.* §§38–42); and Prov 8:22 ("The Lord created me," *Trin.* §§43–47).[105] Faustinus cites all three passages as among those that Flacilla specifically asked him about, and all three were commonly cited by Arians throughout the fourth century and discussed by Nicene theologians. The last interpretative passage (§§48–50) concerns the Holy Spirit, and just as the Holy Spirit receives very little attention in the Nicene Creed and in other Nicene theologians, it receives very little attention here.[106] The arguments of the fourth century predominantly concerned the Father and the Son, and the *De Trinitate* reflects this.

The closing of the document (§51) is quite interesting because Faustinus veers radically off topic. No longer content to refute and insult his Arian opponents, Faustinus lambasts "heretics and prevaricators" (more specific definitions are omitted in this document), explaining that he refuses to hold communion with anyone whose faith is suspect. While individuals may trust to their own conscience (a clearly deferential note, given his audience), Faustinus insists that he cannot risk the stain of association with these prevaricators and cites several scriptural passages to buttress his case. Based on what he says in the *Libellus precum*, it seems

---

105. Gregory Nazianzus lists these as among the most common Arian prooftexts: see *Or.* 29.18 with Hanson 1988, 107. Faustinus does not address John 17:3, which supporters of *homoios* formulas frequently cited.

106. This is not to say there were no controversies surrounding the Holy Spirit; so-called Pneumatomachians (sometimes erroneously called the Macedonians after Macedonius of Constantinople) believed either that the Father and Son were consubstantial but not the Holy Spirit, or that all three were not consubstantial. See Kelly 1978, 259–60.

more than likely that Faustinus here means that holding communion with clerics who formerly swore to Arian creeds is still a grave sin. Apparently, based on what Faustinus reports, he had been accused of superstition[107] for refusing to hold communion with these men; did Faustinus refuse to hold communion with some Nicene Christians in Constantinople and feel the need to defend himself to Flacilla? It is impossible to tell. Faustinus abruptly concludes the *De Trinitate* with a pleasant farewell to the empress.

Within the *Libellus precum* Faustinus speaks well of Gregory (Faustinus and Marcellinus, *Lib. prec.* 33–40, 90, 98) and Athanasius (§88), and if not well of Hilary, then well of his writings (§24), perhaps suggesting that his *De Trinitate* was in part dependent on their Trinitarian works. Many of the arguments in the *De Trinitate* remind one of the aforementioned Latin Nicene works on the Trinity, though quite a few are also reminiscent of Athanasius.[108] But it is difficult to know whether Faustinus had read or was working directly from copies of texts by these earlier theologians or whether he was simply making points common among Nicene theologians, though it seems fairly likely, on balance, that he was familiar with Hilary's *De Trinitate* and possibly Ambrose's *De Fide*. There are numerous arguments throughout the *De Trinitate* that appear in more obscure texts; it is possible that Faustinus knew these, though perhaps more likely that he knew of those arguments through some intermediary. If Faustinus did rely on his predecessors, he was doing nothing out of the norm; ancient authors borrowed ideas from one another shamelessly and generally without attribution. In fact, Faustinus's skill in synthesizing the arguments of these various authors into a single, cohesive work is appreciable.

At times, Faustinus's points are quite simple and straightforward. When arguing that the Son was begotten, not made, for instance, Faustinus (*Trin.* 20) repeatedly quotes John 1:18: "No one has ever seen God,

---

107. A technical Roman term; see Salzman 1987.

108. Again, it is unclear whether Faustinus knew of Athanasius's arguments directly or through some intermediary; he specifically discusses Greek only once, in an explanation of the etymology of *christus* (§39) that seems to be drawn directly from Athanasius. But it is also possible that Faustinus's knowledge of Eastern Trinitarian arguments came from reading Hilary, who spent extensive time in the East while developing his own understanding of the Trinity (see Simonetti 1986, esp. 37; Weedman 2007b, 113–15; Beckwith 2008, 54–68), or from Faustinus's own time in the East in Eleutheropolis and Constantinople. It is certainly telling that there are no direct references to any of the significant Nicene thinkers from the East other than Athanasius (Basil of Ancyra, Basil of Caesarea, Gregory Nazianzus, etc.) in any Luciferian texts.

except the only-begotten Son, who is in his Father's bosom." It is no great mark of theological brilliance for Faustinus to argue that when John calls Jesus the "only-begotten Son," he means that the Son is the only-begotten Son, not a created being or an adopted son. But when addressing Arian points, he is often less persuasive. One suspect argument is particularly illustrative, when he literally puts words in the mouth of Wisdom to make it "clear" what the text is saying (§44). Such tactics are unlikely to have seemed convincing to any Arian or even undecided reader. In general, we might say that Faustinus's rhetoric is oriented toward reaffirming the Nicene faith rather than convincing unbelievers.

Faustinus regularly describes the *De Trinitate* as akin to a debate or a sketch rather than a book, asking forgiveness for its shortness, hasty execution, and poor style.[109] In part, he is being honest. Throughout the *De Trinitate*, Faustinus often directly addresses his Arian opponent (presumably whoever had sent Flacilla these Arian arguments) as though he were participating in a dialogue. Faustinus also addresses Flacilla regularly throughout the text. He is, unsurprisingly, insulting toward his Arian addressee (e.g., §7) and flattering toward Flacilla (e.g., §1). But addressing them both occasionally leads to confusing moments, as at halfway through §16, when Faustinus addresses his Arian opponent and then Flacilla, one immediately after the other, using *tu* to address both. The effect is that Faustinus seems, at first, to be asking Flacilla a series of rather brazen questions about her faith. In general, though, Faustinus is participating in a very old tradition of rhetorical self-deprecation in which an author disparages his or her own talents. Superficially, this was a way of garnering sympathy and flattering one's recipients, regardless of the actual quality of the rhetoric; paradoxically, this rhetorical device became a tool used to assure one's audience that the author (or orator) was rhetorically competent enough to recognize that he should not claim to be too competent.[110] Faustinus plays the part well.

Another example of Faustinus's skill as an author comes in his use of metaphors. Faustinus occasionally makes use of biblical metaphors, sometimes quite vividly. The best begins at §16, when he creates an extensive metaphor filled with rich, bloody imagery, in which he plays the role of

---

109. There are numerous examples throughout the *De Trinitate*, but some of the more prominent are in §§1, 3, 8, 19, 23, 34, 38, 48, 50, 51.

110. This is explicitly stated by Quintilian at *Inst.* 4.1.8–9; see, e.g., Ober 1989, 174–77; Anderson 2001, 4–7.

David and his Arian opponents Goliath. This complex metaphor not only allows Faustinus to cast himself as the brave but unlikely warrior opposing a seemingly insurmountable force, but also gives him a means to perform a bit of self-deprecation and attribute his own victory not to his strength but to scriptural testimonies. Another section (§29) is comedic; Faustinus chastises his Arian opponent for pretending that "to make" and "to beget" mean the same thing by taking two phrases from Scripture and switching the two verbs.

Last, it is worth noting that classical literature is explicitly rejected by Faustinus, who describes his Arian opponent as "puffed up by secular literature" (§11). He also criticizes heretical reliance on the arguments of Aristotle, whom he calls a bishop of the heretics (§§11, 27). Rejection of classical learning (even while clearly participating in classical forms, using classical rhetoric) was certainly not unique to Faustinus.[111]

As a historical source, Faustinus provides a few examples of Nicene theology still in a state of development (§§23, 37). Significant additional value also comes particularly from the few hints we get of how imperial patronage of theologians might work. It was apparently (not unlike imperial lawmaking) very reactionary, as Flacilla only contacted Faustinus after she had received some troubling Arian writings (§1). We can also see how these theologians might rework their patrons' requests to better suit their own aims, as when Faustinus ends (§51) with the aforementioned condemnation of prevaricators. These are the same targets that Faustinus and Marcellinus attack in the *Libellus precum*, but there is nothing in this text that suggests Flacilla was at all interested in them. Faustinus may be obliging toward Flacilla, but he is still Faustinus.

The *De Trinitate* does not rank among the great theological treatises of late antiquity. Nevertheless, it represents an important document for understanding the development of Christian thought and late antique history. One often reads about disputation in late antiquity, whether in ancient texts or modern ones, but the *De Trinitate* provides a rare glimpse at that disputation in action. In it we have a synthesis of fourth-century Nicene Christian thought produced in the 380s, just as Nicene Christians were once more ascendant over their Arian adversaries, and composed at the behest of the imperial family.

---

111. On the tension between classical and Christian learning (and the dangers of overstating that tension), see, e.g., Cameron 1991; Rousseau 1999.

Pseudo-Athanasius, *Epistles* 50 and 51

Also included in this collection are two letters that have been transmitted to us as Athanasius, *Ep.* 50 and 51, both of which are almost certainly Luciferian forgeries (Saltet 1906).[112] These purport to be letters from Athanasius to Lucifer, the first praising Lucifer and requesting that he send copies of his books, the second thanking him for sending the aforementioned books and heaping more praise upon him. Faustinus and Marcellinus—whether or not they knew that these letters were forgeries—seem to reference them, as in the *Libellus precum* (§88) they remark that Athanasius received some of Lucifer's writings and translated them into Greek. These letters undoubtedly served as further proof for the Luciferians that Lucifer was undeniably orthodox and that he was closely allied with the leader of the Nicene party in the mid-fourth century. The two are connected by the final section of the first letter, where an interlocutor explains that Lucifer received the first letter and sent his books to Athanasius, thus motivating the second letter. Another letter by Eusebius of Vercelli is sometimes also called a Luciferian forgery, but it is probably authentic.[113]

Texts and Editions

The *Libellus precum*, *De Trinitate*, and especially the *Dialogus contra Luciferianos* were all known to authors in late antiquity and beyond.[114] At least two late antique authors, Gennadius of Marseilles and Isidore of Seville, were familiar with the *Libellus precum* and *De Trinitate*. It is curious that none of the Luciferian documents translated here seem to show any awareness of Jerome's *Dialogus contra Luciferianos*, and Jerome's work does not directly address any of the arguments that appear in these Luciferian texts.

---

112. Saltet also argues that Pseudo-Athanasius's *De Trinitate* is a Luciferian work, but this attribution is far less certain. The text is variously attributed to Athanasius, Eusebius of Vercelli, and Vigilius of Thapsus; Nicetas of Remesiana and Gregory of Elvira have also been suggested as authors. See Bulhart's remarks in Pseudo-Athanasius 1957, xxx–xxxi.

113. See Flower 2013, 249–51, for a discussion and translation of this letter.

114. Ayres (2014, 98–100), on the basis of linguistic similarities, believes that Augustine was also familiar with Faustinus's *Confessio fidei* and perhaps encountered it in a collection of short confessions.

Gennadius (*Vir. ill.* 16) writes that the petition proves that the authors were Luciferians, but aside from comparing them to the Novatians for their rigor, he offers no other criticism of them; in fact, he is fairly flattering toward Faustinus and the *De Trinitate*, stating that Faustinus "refutes" (*convincens*) the Arians in it.[115] As Canellis (2006, 67) points out, the details in Gennadius's descriptions of these works make it clear that he had personally read them and, therefore, that the texts had made their way from the court at Constantinople to southern Gaul by the late fifth century.[116]

Isidore shows some familiarity with the *Libellus precum* in two places in his *De viris illustribus*. In his notice on Hosius, Isidore (*Vir. ill.* 5.6–7) directly quotes the *Libellus precum* in describing Hosius's fall into Arianism (though, as is common in ancient texts, he does not say he is doing so).[117] Isidore also includes an entry on Marcellinus (14.16), briefly describing the petition but paying most of his attention, once again, to the Spaniards Hosius and Gregory.[118] Here Isidore quotes the *Libellus precum* again, this time for the words of the pagan official Clementine who refuses to send Gregory into exile.[119] Isidore's focus on events in Spanish Christian history is understandable given the ecclesiastic concerns he was engaged with as a Spanish cleric (Wood 2012, 623–28).

The attribution of the petition to Marcellinus and the complete absence of Faustinus's name give one pause, however. The name Faustinus

---

115. The *Libellus precum* does not have a true title in Gennadius but is referred to as a "librum … pro defensione suorum."

116. Canellis also suggests that Gennadius's comparison to the Novatians suggests that Gennadius was familiar with Jerome's *Dialogus contra Luciferianos* as well, since Jerome makes a similar comparison at §27; while certainly plausible, the comparison also seems natural enough that it could have occurred to Gennadius on his own.

117. Compare Isidore, *Vir. ill.* 5.7: "Nam accersitus a Constantio principe, minisque perterritus, metuens ne senex et dives damna rerum vel exsilium pateretur, illico Arianae impietati consensit"; and Faustinus and Marcellinus, *Lib. prec.* 32: "accersitus ad Constantium regem minisque perterritus et metuens ne senex et diues exilium proscriptionemue pateretur, dat manus impietate." See Codoñer Merino 1972, 56–57.

118. Interestingly enough, Isidore describes the addressees of the *Libellus precum* as Arcadius and Theodosius II; see Canellis 2006, 69.

119. Compare Isidore, *Vir. ill.* 14.16: "Non audeo episcopum in exsilium mittere, nisi prius eum ab episcopatu deieceris"; and Faustinus and Marcellinus, *Lib. prec.* 36: "Non audeo, inquiens, episcopum in exilium mittere, quamdiu adhuc in episcopale nomine perseverat."

appears in the *Libellus precum* itself at section 124, and Faustinus is identified as one of its authors in Gennadius's *De viris illustribus*, which Isidore's *De viris illustribus* was meant to continue just as Gennadius's continued Jerome's; Isidore must have known Faustinus was involved.[120] Isidore also nowhere mentions the *De Trinitate* of Faustinus, though it appeared in Gennadius's *De viris illustribus* by name. It is unclear why Isidore should show such a marked preference toward Marcellinus compared to Faustinus; perhaps he found something objectionable in Faustinus's *De Trinitate* that is not immediately apparent to us and wanted to dissociate himself from the work and its author as much as possible.

The *Confessio fidei* exists in an independent manuscript tradition that cannot be traced as early as the manuscript tradition of the *Libellus precum* and *Lex Augusta*; the earliest is of the eighth or ninth century.[121] The *Libellus precum* and *Lex Augusta* appear in earlier manuscripts, appearing together as part of the *Collectio Avellana* in manuscripts dating as early as the sixth or seventh century; dating to the time of Isidore of Seville, these manuscripts provide a remarkable degree of continuity from late antiquity to the present. The best manuscripts of the *Collectio Avellana* are of the ninth century, and two traditions, one with a fairly complete *Libellus precum* and one with significant portions missing, can be discerned. The *Collectio Avellana*, which contains the *Libellus precum* and *Lex Augusta*, is a collection of documents, mostly but not exclusively letters and laws. It is often stated that it was compiled sometime soon after the date of the last letter in the collection, that is, sometime not long after 14 May 553 (*Coll. Avell. Ep.* 83).[122] While Günther believes the collection was composed in the East, there is no explicit evidence of this.[123] The purpose of the *Collec-*

---

120. At *Etym.* 6.6, Isidore clearly names Jerome and Gennadius as the creators of lists of famous authors. See Wood 2012, 622, for a brief discussion and bibliography on the nature of Isidore's continuation.

121. For a more detailed look at the manuscript tradition and early editions of the *Confessio fidei, Libellus precum,* and *Lex Augusta*, see Canellis 2006, 70–83.

122. A letter of Vigilius of Rome to Justinian; see Günther's comments in Günther 1898, 1:ii. The earliest document is a letter from Valentinian, Valens, and Gratian to the urban prefect at Rome, Praetextatus, in 367 (*Coll. Avell. Ep.* 5).

123. The conclusion has also been questioned by speakers in two recent conferences held in Rome in 2011 and 2013, titled "Emperors, Bishops, Senators: The Significance of the Collectio Avellana, 367–553 A.D.," and "East and West, Constantinople and Rome: Empire and Church in the Collectio Avellana, 367–553 A.D.," respectively. That the documents are all in Latin, not Greek, is of little use in this argument, since

tio Avellana, and thus the exact relationship between the *Libellus precum*, *Lex Augusta*, and *Collectio Avellana*, remains unclear. As the letters and laws in the collection mostly involve bishops of Rome and emperors, it is often thought that these interactions lie behind the purpose of the collection; in this case, the sections of the *Libellus precum* concerning Damasus (Faustinus and Marcellinus, *Lib. prec.* 79–85) and the *Lex Augusta* in general would be the most relevant. It is perhaps worth noting here that in most manuscripts of the second tradition, in which significant portions of the *Libellus precum* are omitted, sections 76–97 (which includes the Damasus account) are retained (Canellis 2006, 74).

The first printed edition of the *Confessio fidei* was fairly late, appearing as an appendix to the collected works of Leo the Great published by Pasquier Quesnel in 1675. The *Libellus precum* and *Lex Augusta* were also printed late, their first publications prepared by Jacques Sirmond in 1650. The editions used for the translations of these three documents in this volume were prepared by Aline Canellis and published in 2006, and appear here courtesy of their publisher, Les Éditions du Cerf. There are few differences between her texts and those of Otto Günther, who published the *Collectio Avellana* in 1895, and Manlio Simonetti, who published the *Confessio fidei*, *Libellus precum* (based largely on Günther's text), and *Lex Augusta* (and *De Trinitate*) in CCSL 69 in 1967. The only passage where there are significant variations in readings between these three editions is at section 82 in the *Libellus precum*.

The *De Trinitate* comes to us in its complete form in only one manuscript, riddled with errors and lacunae, of the ninth century; this manuscript was the basis of the first printed edition, made in Basel in 1528 by Johann Faber, a bookmaker from Jülich (Ioannes Faber Iuliacensis, also known as Hans von Gülch).[124] Several other manuscripts containing only single chapters and dating back to the ninth century have helped fill in the gaps, as has a now-lost manuscript that the editor of an early printed version, Aquiles Estaço (Achilles Statius), used in Rome in 1575. The Latin version used for the following translation was admirably edited by Manlio

---

many bishops of Rome would naturally have written in Latin, and Latin was still the language used for legal purposes at court during most of the period covered by documents in the *Collectio Avellana*.

124. For the manuscript tradition and early editions of the *De Trinitate*, see Wilmart 1908, 24–33; Simonetti 1963b, 50–70; Simonetti in CCSL 69:291–92.

Simonetti from these various strands and published in CCSL 69 in 1967; it appears here courtesy of Brepols.

The *Confessio fidei* was translated into English in an early modern English text, discussed below. The *Confessio fidei* and the *Libellus precum* have only otherwise been translated in the French versions presented by Aline Canellis and in stilted, early drafts in English appearing in my graduate studies. The *Lex Augusta* was translated into English in 1966 (Coleman-Norton 1966, 2:390–92) as a very small part of a very large collection of documents relating to the legal standing of Christianity within the Roman Empire and into Spanish in 1997 (Fernández Ubiña 1997, 121–23).

There have been no modern translations of Faustinus's *De Trinitate* published in nearly three hundred years. The only exception is a small portion of the text from sections 39–40, which was incorporated into in the modern Catholic Church's Liturgy of the Hours (restructured under Pope Paul VI in the 1960s) as the second reading for Sunday in week 12 in ordinary time. The author is incorrectly given there as "Faustus Luciferanus, priest." This translation has been published three times in English (the original International Committee on English in the Liturgy translation of 1970; the Episcopal Conferences of Australia, England and Wales, Ireland, and Scotland translation of 1974; and the Paulines Publications Africa translation of 2009) and, naturally, has also been translated into the other languages in which the Catholic Church performs services using the Liturgy of the Hours. Beyond this brief passage, I can only explain the lack of modern interest in this text by pointing to the sometimes very dry nature of the subject and the relative obscurity of its author.

Oddly enough, however, the entirety of the *De Trinitate* has in fact been translated into English before, in a most curious edition that has generally escaped the notice of modern scholars.[125] In 1721 an English printer named George Mortlock published an anonymous translation of the *De Trinitate* as a little pamphlet.[126] The translator must have been well educated in both classical studies and theology, probably suggesting that he was a cleric. He probably used the 1678 edition of the Latin text published at Oxford under the direction of Bishop John Fell, which included the *Confessio fidei*, *Libellus precum*, and *Lex Augusta*, all three of which were certainly known to the translator based on the information in his preface.[127]

---

125. The one exception is Wilmart (1908, 29–30n1).
126. Faustinus 1721, 23–60.
127. Following Fell's publication of the text, Bishop Narcissus March, an English

The translator describes the *De Trinitate* as "A Treatise very necessary to be Read at this Time" on the title page, and it is clear that he did not intend his translation to be of interest for antiquarians alone. The preface opens by bewailing the fact that, as has been historically documented,[128] Arian beliefs had become increasingly popular throughout England in the late seventeenth and early eighteenth century:

> It is extremely sad and melancholy to observe, what amazing Inroads that dire Contagion, first raised and diffused in the Church of *Alexandria* by *Arius* an insolent assuming Presbyter, hath of late Years made on this Christian Nation: And what unwearied Pains in the wily Arts of Sophistry and Delusion are taken by false Brethren, of the same Complexion among our selves, to render it epidemical. (Faustinus 1721, iii)

The prefatory remarks continue for several pages, explaining the translator's main objections to Arianism and giving a brief explanation of who Faustinus was and why he wrote the treatise.

Why the author chose to remain anonymous is unclear. While Arian beliefs were increasingly popular in England at the time, they were by no means the dominant theology. Also curious is the choice of Faustinus's *De Trinitate* as the text set against these English Arians; while the translator perhaps goes too far in praising Faustinus as "a Man of Note and Consideration in the Western Church" (vii), he is also at pains to explain away Faustinus's Luciferianism: "I am not insensible, that an Objection lies in the Way of my Author, and expect, that *the Schismatick* will be thrown in his Teeth by our modern *Arians*, should he chance to be well received here, and on that Account only merit the Favour of their Notice" (viii). While the translator goes on to explain that Faustinus was simply quite passionate but deserves our charity, the question remains: why did this Englishman not simply rely on the same works that Faustinus followed,

---

cleric serving in Ireland, sent him various readings of the *Libellus precum* acquired through studying manuscripts in the library of Jacques Auguste de Thou, an early seventeenth-century book collector. March also sent him a copy of a letter from Faustinus to Paulinus, but this unfortunately is not another text by Faustinus the Luciferian to Paulinus of Antioch but instead by another, later author, Faustus of Riez (Rhegium), writing to Paulinus of Bordeaux (Burdigala). See Doble 1889, 30–31, for Fell and March's interactions, and Faustus, *Ep.* 5 (PL 58:845–50), for the correctly attributed letter of Faustus to Paulinus.

128. See, e.g., Wiles 1996, 62–164, for an overview of English Arianism.

that is, Athanasius, Hilary, and others? He spends as much time defending Faustinus as he does attacking the Arians the text is ostensibly about. This remarkable translation merits further study in its historical context.

In these translations I have consciously avoided introducing any new numbering systems, even where older section divisions sometimes result in awkward breaks in the text. The two forged letters are the sole exception, as Migne did not divide them into paragraphs. In preparing the *De Trinitate*, I have followed Simonetti, who presented his text with simple consecutive numbering of paragraphs but retained the earlier numbering system within parentheses (wherein the text is broken into seven "chapters," with section numbering starting over again with each new chapter). I have chosen to translate scriptural passages discussed by the authors myself because their arguments frequently rely on analyzing specific words that are not always present in more naturally rendered translations. Let that also serve as a warning that the translations of Faustinus and his scriptural sources may at times sound stilted. As an author, Faustinus is generally simple in style with occasional bouts of rhetorical flair; if he is not an exceptional author, he is still clearly an educated one, and I have tried to reflect this in the translations of the *Confessio fidei* and *Libellus precum*; the *De Trinitate*, by nature of its subject, is often much denser, and this, too, is reflected in its translation.

Faustinus, *Confessio fidei*

pr. Faustini presbyteri confessio verae fidei quam breuiter scribi et sibi trasmitti iussit Theodosius imperator.

1. Sufficiebat fides conscripta apud Nicaeam aduersus haeresim Arrianam; sed quia prauo ingenio quidam, sub illius fidei confessione, impia verba commendant, nobis inuidiam facientes quod uelut haeresim Sabellii tueamur, paucis, et contra Sabellium primae fidei confessione signamus, et contra hos qui, sub nomine catholicae fidei, impia verba defendunt, dicentes tres esse substantias, cum semper catholica fides unam substantiam Patris et Filii et Spiritus Sancti confessa sit.

2. Nos patrem credimus, qui non sit Filius, sed habeat Filium de se sine initio genitum, non factum; et Filium credimus, qui non sit Pater, sed habeat Patrem, de quo sit genitus, non factus; et Spiritum Sanctum credimus, qui sit uere Spiritus Dei. Vnde et diuinae Trinitatis unam substantiam confitemur; quia qualis est Pater secundum substantiam, talem

Faustinus, *Confession of Faith*

pr. The presbyter Faustinus's[1] confession of the true faith, which Emperor Theodosius ordered to be briefly written and sent to him.

1. The creed[2] composed at Nicaea used to be effective against the Arian heresy. But certain men, depraved in their disposition, endorse impious expressions while confessing that creed and cause ill will against us, as though we supported the heresy of Sabellius.[3] Because of this, we will show by confessing the principal creed in a few words that we are against both Sabellius and against those who defend their impious expressions under the name of the catholic faith. They say that there are three substances, though the catholic faith has always confessed that there is a single substance of the Father, the Son, and the Holy Spirit.[4]

2. We believe in the Father, who is not the Son, but has a Son begotten from him without a beginning, not made; and we believe in the Son, who is not the Father, but has a Father from whom he was begotten, not made; and we believe in the Holy Spirit, who is truly the Spirit of God. This is why we also confess that there is a single substance of the divine Trinity, because in regards to his substance, just as the Father is, so too did he beget

---

1. *PCBE* 2.1 (Faustinus 2).
2. The same word (*fides*) denotes the abstract concept of "faith" as well as specific formulas of faith. A ninth-century manuscript adds "Bithyniae" after Nicaea to distinguish the location of the Council of Nicaea from the Nicaea in Thrace (Canellis 2006, 101), where the Nicene delegates who traveled from Rimini in 359 to appeal to Constantius capitulated. For *sufficiebat*, see Phoebadius, *Trin.* 1.2, in which Phoebadius complains that one's conscience used to be sufficient to guard against heresy.
3. On these accusations, see above, pp. 16–19, and see Faustinus, *Trin.* 7, 9, 12.
4. These mutual accusations of heresy may derive from variations in translating the terms *ousia* and *hypostasis* into Latin in the mid-fourth century; see above, pp. 17–19.

genuit et Filium; et Spiritus Sanctus, non creatura existens sed Spiritus Dei, non est alienus a substantia Patris et Filii, sed est et ipse eiusdem substantiae cum Patre et Filio sicut eiusdem deitatis.

3. Nam qui nos putant esse Apollinaristas, sciant quod non minus Apollinaris haeresim execramur quam Arrianam. Miramur autem illos catholicos probari posse qui Patris et Filii et Spiritus Sancti tres substantias confitentur. Sed, etsi dicunt non se credere Filium Dei aut Spiritum Sanctum creaturam, tamen contra piam fidem sentiunt cum dicunt tres esse substantias. Consequens est enim ut tres deos confiteantur, qui tres substantias confitentur. Quam vocem catholici semper execrati sunt.

the Son;[5] and the Holy Spirit, which exists not as something created but as the Spirit of God, is not set apart from the substance of the Father and of the Son, but is itself of the same substance as the Father and Son just as it is of the same divinity.

3. As for those who think that we are Apollinarians, let them know that we denounce the heresy of Apollinaris no less than the Arian heresy.[6] However, we are amazed that those who swear that there are three substances—of the Father, of the Son, and of the Holy Spirit—can be judged to be "catholics." Even if they say that they do not believe that the Son of God or the Holy Spirit are created beings, they nevertheless hold opinions contrary to the pious faith when they say that there are three substances. For it follows that those who swear that there are three substances swear that there are three gods—a statement that catholics have always denounced.[7]

---

5. In other words, the Father begat the Son as identical to himself in regards to his substance, but not necessarily in regards to other properties of his being: a necessary delimitation to avoid charges of Sabellianism.

6. On these charges of Apollinarianism, see above, p. 16, and see Faustinus and Marcellinus, *Lib. prec.* 114.

7. Discussed at greater length in Faustinus and Marcellinus, *Lib. prec.* 114.

Faustinus (et Marcellinus), *Libellus precum*

1. Deprecamur mansuetudinem uestram, piissimi imperatores, Valentiniane, Theodosi et Arcadi, ut haec in contemplatione Christi Filii Dei qui vestrum iuuat imperium, infatigabiliter legere dignemini. Sublime regnum vestrum tunc ad sublimiora, Dei Patris omnipotentis et Christi unigeniti Filii eius opitulatione conscendit, cum nec in exiguis hominibus despicitis ueritatem, nec in multis uel potentibus mendacium roboratis. Hoc enim iustissimum est et saluberrimum apud regnum iustitiae, ut personae probentur ex merito ueritatis, non ueritas praesumatur ex potentia personarum; siquidem ius saeculi ideo scriptum est ne contra uerum aequumue potentia uel multitudo praeualeat, etiamsi ab exiguis uindicetur.

2. Quod si haec tanta cura etiam in rebus rei publicae a uestra tranquillitate et prouisione seruanda est, ut contra omnem uim potentiamue etiam in minimis ius veri obtineat, quo possit tradita uestro imperio Dei nutu florere res publica, quomodo, in negotiis divinis, sanctae fidei ueritas impiorum caterua et fraudulentissimis eorum circumuentionibus obfuscatur et premitur? Maxime cum uos, principes Romani imperii, piam Christianae religionis fidem puritatemque tot uestris constitutionibus uindicetis: totum quidem quia, uenerataores Christi Filii Dei, pro fide catholica

Faustinus and Marcellinus, *Petition of Requests*

1. We beseech Your Clemency, most pious Emperors Valentinian, Theodosius, and Arcadius,[1] to find it worthy to tirelessly read these things while contemplating Christ, the Son of God, who gives aid to your empire. Your lofty empire, with the assistance of God, the Father, and Christ, his only begotten Son, ascends even higher when you neither disregard truth among insignificant men nor affirm falsehood among the many or powerful. For this is the most just and salutary thing in an empire of justice: that people are judged by the merit of the truth, not that the truth is presumed from the power of the individuals, since secular law[2] is written so that the powerful or the many do not prevail even if the truth is upheld by the insignificant.[3]

2. Such a concern as this ought to be safeguarded by your tranquility and foresight even in affairs of state, so that even among the most insignificant, the law of truth may be paramount against every force and power; because of this, it is possible for the state, handed down to your rule by the will of God, to flourish. But if this is so, then why in divine affairs is the truth of the holy faith obscured and oppressed by a crowd of impious men and their most dishonest falsehoods? Especially since you, rulers of the Roman Empire, uphold the pious faith and purity of the Christian religion with so many of your laws, and because, being worshipers of Christ the Son of

---

1. This establishes the *terminus post quem* for the petition, as Gratian was assassinated by agents of Magnus Maximus on 25 August 383. Valentinian II and Arcadius were both very young when the petition was delivered to Theodosius, Valentinian having been born in 371 and Arcadius in 377.

2. Or the "law of this age"; *ius saeculi* refers to the laws of this world as opposed to those established in Scripture. Faustinus and Marcellinus frequently draw this distinction throughout the petition, particularly between divine and secular law, judges, and punishment.

3. This is a fairly common argument among Roman jurists: for examples, see *Dig.* 4.7.1.1 (Gaius); 1.16.9.5 (Ulpian); 1.18.6.2 (Pseudo-Ulpian).

decernitis et omni nisu contra haereticos et perfidos imperii uestri auctoritate conscribitis, non quasi aliqua propriae sententiae noua temptantes, sicut quidam anteriores principes in suam aliorumque perniciem conati sunt, sed ut ostendatis uestras sententias, uestramque fidem, cum sacris Scripturarum Diuinarum sententiis et piis confessionibus conuenire.

3. Sed hoc cum magis post atrocissimas prioris temporis persecutiones iuuare sanctam deberet ecclesiam, magis affligit, cum idem ipsi egregii episcopi, qui eam ante hoc sub adsertione uel adsensu haereseos persecuti sunt, nunc quoque sub auctoritate catholici nominis persequuntur et quanto nunc sub ementita piae fidei professione hoc fraudulentius agunt,

God, you decide everything for the benefit of the catholic faith[4] and arrange everything with all your effort against the heretics and the faithless by the authority of your sovereignty.[5] You do this not as though you were trying out some new matters of your own devising, as certain previous rulers[6] attempted to do (to the ruin of themselves and others), but so that you may demonstrate that your way of thinking and your faith are in harmony with the sacred expressions of divine scripture and with pious confessions.[7]

3. Although this should have helped the holy church[8], following the extremely fierce persecutions of the previous era,[9] it has instead hurt it all the more: those notorious[10] bishops, who prior to this persecuted the church while supporting or agreeing with heresy, now persecute the church under the authority of the catholic name.[11] Also, the more they deceptively do this nowadays under a false profession of pious faith, the more they plot danger-

---

4. *Catholicus* is used throughout the *Libellus precum* to refer abstractly to the community of Nicene Christians throughout the Roman world with whom they held communion; it does not refer to an organized entity like the Catholic Church. In some cases the term seems to refer to Nicene Christianity in general, but generally it does not even refer to all Nicene Christians, since the Luciferians would not hold communion with Nicene Christians who held communion with *praevaricatores*.

5. Perrin (2010, 213n37) provides other examples of Christians claiming that antiheretical legislation used against them is more properly used against their enemies (but is still inherently just legislation). For the link between God and emperor in late antiquity, see, e.g., Eusebius of Caesarea, *Laud. Const.*, esp. 3.5-8, and for a recent study of the evolution over the fourth century of Christian attitudes toward the role of the emperor, see Drake 2015, esp. 301–3.

6. Namely, Constantius (below, §§15–28) and Valens (below, §§66–67).

7. I.e., the Nicene Creed and any other profession of Nicene Christianity. This statement can be readily compared to Faustinus, *Trin.* 1, wherein Faustinus flatters Flacilla's intelligence and curiosity.

8. As with *catholicus* above (n. 4), *ecclesia*, meaning "church" or "community," is used throughout the *Libellus precum* to refer not to a formally organized group of Christians but rather to the abstract concept of the community of Nicene Christians throughout the Roman world.

9. As above, under Constantius and Valens; that Faustinus and Marcellinus do not here refer to the Great Persecution of 303–311 is made clear by the rest of the paragraph.

10. *Egregius* typically has the positive connotation of "outstanding" or "extraordinary" or "surpassing." It is used here and throughout the *Libellus precum* (§§52, 66, 74, 75, 79, 92, 96, 100, 107, 119) sarcastically, just as it is used by Jerome's mouthpiece "Orthodoxus" in *Lucif.* 19. See Canellis 2001, 500.

11. This is the central complaint of the *Libellus precum*: bishops who were compelled by Constantius to swear to Arian creeds, but then were granted clemency at the

tanto et perniciosius grassantur et dolentius aestuat ueritas, quod ei adhuc non licet nec sub uobis imperatoribus, qui piam fidem defenditis, respirare.

4. Sed ne hoc ad inuidiam sine rei probatione referre uideamur, causam ut possumus explicamus. Quaesumus autem, supplices quaesumus, ut regias aures uestras nobis exiguissimis commodetis, dum ostendimus non nos esse haereticos, et tamen quasi haereticos uehementer affligi, cum nec ipsi, qui nos uehementer affligunt, uel socii eorum, possint nunc dicere uel probare, quod simus haeretici; sed ne quidem de se negare, quod superiori tempore haeresim aut acerrime uindicauerint cum intolerablili supplicio fidelium aut certe ei manus dederint, damnata catholica fide, quam prius adserebant, dum metuunt pro Christo Filio Dei exilium perpeti, pro quo etiam laico fideli quaeuis mors atrocissima subeunda est, "quia nobis donatum est," ut ait Apostolus, "pro Christo, non tantum ut in eum credamus sed etiam pro illi patiamur"; talis enim mors uel passio beatae inmortalitatis occasio est.

5. Non latet mansuetudinem et deuotam Deo religionem uestram, quam impia quamue pestifera sit haeresis Arriana, contra quam a patribus nostris apud Nicaeam spiritali uigore conscriptum est, ita ut et apostolicae fidei pia confessio seruaretur atque ipsius haereseos perpetua damnatio seruaretur, ne quis falli posset in posteris.

6. Sed Arrius, ut cor Pharaonis, non credens diuinam in se tunc datam fuisse sententiam, nescio qua ratione subripuit apud Constantinum, sperans quod ipsius suffragio spiritalium sacerdotum sententia rescissa, recipi

2. Faustinus and Marcellinus, *Petition of Requests* 67

ously and the more the truth wavers grievously, because thus far it is not free to catch its breath—even under you, emperors, who defend the pious faith.

4. But, so that we do not seem to be reporting this out of malice without proof of the matter, we are explaining our reasoning as best we are able. However, we ask, we ask as suppliants, that you lend your royal ears to us, very insignificant though we are, while we show you that we are not heretics, and nevertheless we are violently assaulted as though we were heretics, while neither those who violently assault us nor their allies are at present able to say or to prove that we are heretics. Yet certain men among them cannot deny this about themselves: previously, they either most eagerly promoted heresy with unbearable torment against the faithful or at least put their hands to it,[12] and they condemned the catholic faith to which they previously swore while they were afraid to suffer exile on behalf of Christ, the Son of God, for whom even the faithful laity must submit to any sort of savage death. *Because it is given to us*, as the Apostle said, *not only that we believe in him, but also that we suffer for him.*[13] Such death or suffering is an opportunity for blessed immortality.

5. It is no secret to Your Clemency and Your Piety, since you are devoted to God, how impious and how pestilent the heresy of Arius is.[14] A creed was composed at Nicaea against it by our fathers with spiritual vigor to protect both the pious confession of the apostolic faith and the everlasting condemnation of heresy itself, ensuring that no one could be deceived later.[15]

6. But Arius, like the *heart of Pharaoh*,[16] did not believe that God's judgment had been given against him at that point, and somehow slipped back in[17] with Constantine. He hoped that by Constantine's adjudication, the decision of the devout priests would be annulled and he would be able

---

Council of Alexandria, are now unjustly persecuting Luciferians for refusing to hold communion with them.

12. A common metaphor taken from gladiatorial combat; see below, §§28, 32; Jerome, *Lucif.* 14; and see Canellis 2006, 113n1.

13. Phil 1:29.

14. Arius was the heretic par excellence for late antique authors. The theological underpinnings of his beliefs and those of his supporters and followers (to the extent we can understand them from the descriptions of their enemies) are discussed above, p. 3, and below in the *De Trinitate*. For a general overview of Arius and Arianism, see Wiles 1996.

15. In 325. See above, p. 4.

16. Exod 7:13.

17. Canellis (2006, 114–15n1) reads this use of *subripuit* as the perfect of *subrepo*

posset in Ecclesiam. Denique idem Constantinus iusserat ut ei sanctus ac beatae memoriae episcopus Alexander communicaret, non ille Alexander, qui fuit diuinae fidei episcopus in Alexandria (qui et plenus sapientia et spiritu sancto feruens eumdem Arrium primus et detexit et expulit et in perpetuum damnauit), sed iste Alexander, qui in hac Constantinopolitana urbe fuit et ipse admirabilis episcopus.

7. Qui, cum uideret quod Arrius saeculi istius rege niteretur, exclamauit ex imo pectoris dolore stans in loco sacrarii ad Christum uerum et sempiternum regem et dominum omnium regum, ne illam labem in Ecclesia pateretur intrare. Cuius oratio quam constans fuerit, quam fidelis, hinc probatum est quod idem Arrius, antequam intraret ecclesiam, dedit poenas nouas et grauissimas usque ad turpem interitum. Nam, cum pridie quam se putauit sanctam ecclesiam imperatoris auxilio homo impius intraturum, cum nihil languoris, nihil doloris in corpore pateretur sed, quod grauius est, solo animi morbo insanabiliter aegrotaret, humana con-

to be received back into the church. In the end, Constantine ordered that the bishop Alexander, holy and of blessed memory, hold communion with him.[18] This is not the Alexander who was bishop of the divine faith in Alexandria;[19] that one, both full of wisdom and *burning with the* Holy *Spirit*,[20] first exposed that same Arius, expelled him, and condemned him eternally. This instead is the Alexander who was in the city of Constantinople and was himself an admirable bishop.

7. When Alexander saw that Arius was relying on a king of this age, he stood in the place sacred to Christ,[21] true and eternal king and lord of all kings,[22] and cried out from the deepest pain in his heart that he would not suffer that fallen man to enter the church.[23] The following proves how fitting and faithful his speech was: the same Arius, before he entered the church, faced an unprecedented and most severe type of punishment that led to his shameful death. For the day before the impious man thought he was going to enter the holy church with the help of the emperor, although he suffered no weakness, no pain in his body (instead, he was incurably sick with a disease of the soul alone, which is more serious), he sought

---

rather than *subripio* ("steal"); she regards the use of *subripuit* rather than *subrepsit* as a mistake on Faustinus's part.

18. Alexander of Byzantion (later Constantinople), bishop from around 315 to 337. He was a very popular bishop for later Nicene authors, who saw him as a model of orthodoxy (Gregory of Nazianzus, *Or.* 27; Epiphanius, *Pan.* 69.10). See Socrates, *Hist. eccl.* 1.37, and Sozomen, *Hist. eccl.* 2.29, for Constantine's order and Alexander's refusal. Socrates specifically relates that Alexander was unafraid of losing his see (a risk Faustinus and Marcellinus explicitly address below in §§16, 49, 61, 117).

19. Bishop of Alexandria from 318–328 prior to Athanasius and first to denounce Arius's views. He made two great enemies for the Egyptian church, the first being Arius, the second being Meletius. Meletius was the bishop of Lycopolis, another Egyptian city, and refused to accept into communion those who had committed apostasy during the Great Persecution. His followers, the so-called Meletians, plagued the Egyptian church for over a century and frequently worked with Arians against the Nicene party. The Luciferians complain about a Meletian bishop, Apollonius, at §§100–101 below. In general, see above, pp. 3–4, and Barnes 1993, 10–18.

20. Rom 12:11.

21. Or more precisely, the sanctuary, that is, the place in which the altar of the church stood.

22. See Rev 1:5; 17:14; 19:16.

23. Faustinus and Marcellinus make this seem like a very public act, but Socrates (*Hist. eccl.* 1.37) reports that Alexander locked himself in the church without announcing his intentions to anyone and prayed in private that God punish Arius.

suetudine secessum petit atque illic cum sedit, grauissimo repente dolore cruciatus omnia sua uiscera et ipsum cor, quod erat thesaurum impietatis, effudit in stercora atque ita (mirabile dictu!) internis omnibus euacuatis attenuatus est uel ad momentum sicut luridati corporis tabe resolutus est, ut per angustias foraminis et sedilis totus ipse laberetur.

8. Digna haec poena impio, digna haec mors turpis pestifero haeretico atque de spiritu diaboli foetidissimis membris digna haec sepultura! Nouo enim exemplo et cruciari debuit et perire, qui nouas aduersus unigenitum Filium Dei commentatus fuerat impietates, dicens eum "non uere de Patre natum" et quia "erat quando non erat," et quia "ex nihilo substitutus est," ne eiusdem substantiae et diuinitatis et sempiternitatis et omnipotentiae cuius et Pater est, crederetur.

9. Hoc retulimus augustae mansuetudini uestrae ut uero intenta uestra prudentia animaduertat, quam uenerabilis fides sit conscripta apud Nicaeam aduersus Arrium, cui et Deus, non solum per auctorita-

2. Faustinus and Marcellinus, *Petition of Requests* 71

privacy in the human custom.[24] When he sat there, suddenly tortured by extremely severe pain,[25] he voided *all his intestines*[26] and his heart itself, which was the *treasure house of impiety*,[27] into his excrement. And thus (amazingly!) he was made so thin after all his innards were emptied out, or in just a moment became so softened like the decayed matter of a sallow corpse, that his whole body fell through[28] the narrow opening of the seat.[29]

8. This is a worthy punishment for an impious person, this is a worthy, shameful death for a pestilential heretic, and this is a worthy grave for his limbs, which were made most noxious from the devil's stench![30] For whoever produces unprecedented impieties against the only begotten Son of God should also suffer and die in an unprecedented way,[31] and Arius said that "he was not truly born from the Father," that "there was a time when he was not," and that "he was made from nothing," so that men would not believe that he was of the same substance, divinity, agelessness, and omnipotence of his Father.[32]

9. We recounted this for your revered clemency so that your good sense, because it is attentive to what is true, would give thought as to how venerable the creed composed at Nicaea against Arius is (to whom God

---

24. A euphemism; Arius, as the following description makes clear, was going to a latrine.

25. See 2 Macc 9:5.

26. Acts 1:18. Naturally the arch-heretic Arius is given a similar death to the arch-traitor Judas.

27. Prov 10:2; Mic 6:10.

28. The verb used here, *laberetur*, references the description of Arius as a *labem* above.

29. Leroy-Molinghen (1960, 107) describes this grotesque account of Arius's death as follows: "C'est le cas notamment de Faustin et Marcellin, auxquels nous accorderions volontiers la palme dans le domaine de l'imagination débridée." For the role that excrement played in late antique rhetoric, see, e.g., Leyerle 2009. For Arius's death in particular, see Ferrarini 1981; Martin 1989. Muehlberger (2015) discusses various other late antique accounts of Arius's death, focusing on the development of the narrative from the early accounts by Athanasius and Rufinus through the ecclesiastic historians of the fifth century.

30. For foul stench as reflective of Satan's foulness and foulness in general for late antique Christians, see, e.g., Harvey 2006, 99–134, 220–21. Of course, Satan could also give off a sweet and pleasing scent in order to deceive.

31. A common theme among early Christians; see Canellis 2006, 118–19n1.

32. See Faustinus, *Trin.* 2, for a longer basic explanation of Arian tenets as Faustinus understands them.

tem scripturarum diuinarum, sed etiam per sacratissimam orationem sancti quoque Alexandri testimonium dedit; et quam execrabilis est impia doctrina Arrii, quam in ipso Arrio nouo genere supplicii sententia diuina damnauit non expectans in illo diem iudicii, ut exemplo poenae eius ceteri perterriti praecauerent.

10. Quo utique exemplo nec illud dubitandum est, etiam doctrinam renouandam vel suscipiendam esse crediderunt. Quomodo enim eos perpetua poena disiungit, quos impia doctrina non separat? Pares reos etiam uestris legibus unus carcer includit atque una ferit sententia. Sed et illud ambigi non potest, hos esse uere catholicos, qui, per exilia, per genera suppliciorum, per atrocitatem mortis, illam fidem sine dolo uindicant quae apud Nicaeam euangelica atque apostolica ratione conscripta est, quam Deus apertissime probauit supplicio Arrii impugnantis eam.

11. Quod si haec apud uos uera sunt, quae apud scripturas diuinas uera roborantur, aduertite, piissimi et religiosissimi imperatores, in quo rei sint, qui sub his diuinis regulis et professionibus fidem suam ac deuotionem Christo Deo consecrauerunt nullum timorem diuino timori praeponentes.

12. Sed licet Arrius sit sepultus in stercoribus, reliquit tamen suae impietatis heredes; denique non defuerunt uermes, qui de eius putrido cadauere nascerentur. Per quos quae gesserit diabolus artifex erroris, longum est exsequi, etiamsi exsequi possemus; infinita sunt enim et incredibilia, non tamen falsa. Illud uero nunc, quod ad praesentem causam facit, exponimus, quod imperatorem Constantium per fraudulentam disputationem Arrianae impietatis participem fecerunt. Dedissent et isti in praesenti poenas, si non oporteret, secundum Apostoli sententiam, et haereses esse ut probati manifesti fierent.

gave evidence, not only through the authority of the divine scriptures, but also through the most devoted speech of holy Alexander) and how accursed the doctrine of Arius is (which God's judgment condemned by the unprecedented punishment against Arius, rather than waiting for the day of judgment, so that others might beware after being thoroughly terrified by the example set by his punishment).[33]

10. Certainly, because of this example, no one should doubt that those who believe that Arius's doctrine should be revived or taken up are damned before God. For how does eternal punishment distinguish between them when impious doctrine does not separate them?[34] Even in your laws, the same jail holds those convicted of the same thing and the same sentence falls on them. Yet it also cannot be doubted that the true catholics are those who—through exiles, through a variety of punishments, through the cruelty of death—upheld without deception that creed composed at Nicaea with evangelic and apostolic reasoning, which God quite openly proved good by punishing Arius when he was struggling against it.

11. Now, if these things, which are affirmed as true in divine scripture, are true in your view, give thought, most pious and religious emperors: how can those who consecrated their faith and devotion to Christ, our God, under these divine rules and declarations and who set no fear ahead of the *fear of God* be criminals?[35]

12. Although Arius was buried in excrement, he nevertheless left behind heirs to his impiety; from that point on, there was no lack of worms born from his rotting corpse.[36] It would take a long time to relate the sort of things that the devil, that craftsman of error, conducted through them, even if we could relate them; they are infinite and incredible, though not false. However, we will now explain what created the present situation. The Arians, through their deceptive argumentation, made the emperor Constantius a participant in the Arian impiety. Even those men would have paid the price in the present, if it was not necessary, according to the judgment of the Apostle, *that there be heresies so that men might become openly proven good*.[37]

---

33. See 2 Pet 2:6.
34. See below, §116.
35. Ps 13:3 LXX. See below, §118.
36. See 2 Macc 9:9; Isa 66:24; Acts 12:23; and see Faustinus, *Trin.* 23. Lucifer (*Mor. esse Dei Fil.* 4) calls Constantius a "worm of Arius," a likely origin for the phrase's use here.
37. 1 Cor 11:19.

13. Habentes ergo hi, quos diximus, uermes Arrii adsistentem sibi regiam potestatem primum quidem per singulos in euersionem catholicae fidei et in excidium sacrae religionis pro Arriana impietate contendunt, ita ut resistentes aut calumniis adpeterent uel poenis uel exilio cruciarent et necarent. Vbi tamen amplius per suam rabiem grassati sunt et fecerunt sui ubique terrorem, non iam contenti ire per singulos: postremo cogunt undique in unum episcopos conuenire. Et datur locus ad synodum Orientalibus quid Seleucia Isauriae, Occidentalibus uero ciuitas Ariminensis.

14. Atque illic primum quidem episcopi pro sancta fide uenientes confirmant illam expositionem, quae apud Nicaeam conscripta est, ita ut nihil inde minueretur, eo quod euangelicam fidem uerbis inexpugnabilibus explicaret et Arrii impiam doctrinam diuina auctoritate damnaret. Tunc demum oblatam ab Vrsacio, Valente, Germinio, et Gaio huiusmodi fidei conscriptionem, quae et fidem catholicam reprobaret et Arrium absolueret, immo et introduceret pestiferam eius doctrinam, execrantur et damnant tam impiam fidem eorum quam etiam ipsos, inexpiabile scelus esse iudicantes, qui patrum fidem uenerabilem uiolent, si hos tam impios atque impiam eorum conscriptionem pateretur Ecclesia.

15. Mittunt quoque decem legatos ad imperatorem Constantium scribentes quae gesta sunt et hortantes simul ut ipse quoque decreta

13. And so these worms of Arius that we mentioned had royal power assisting them. At first, naturally, they strove to overthrow the catholic faith and destroy the holy religion on behalf of the Arian impiety one at a time in this way: they attacked those who resisted with false accusations, or they tortured or killed them with either punishments or exile.[38] However, after they went further in their rage and made themselves universally feared, they were no longer content to go one by one. In the end, they forced bishops to gather from everywhere in one place. The location given for this synod in the East was Seleucia-in-Isauria, and in the West, the city of Rimini.[39]

14. Certainly at first, the bishops who came there on behalf of the holy faith affirmed the creed that was composed at Nicaea in such a way that nothing was taken away from it, since it explained the evangelic faith with unassailable words and condemned the impious doctrine of Arius with divine authority. Just then, they cursed a creed presented by Ursacius, Valens, Germinius, and Gaius of the kind that rejected the catholic faith and absolved Arius, and even introduced his pestilent doctrine.[40] They condemned such an impious creed as much as they condemned the very authors of it, judging that it would be an unforgivable crime if the church were patient with these men (who were so impious that they violated the venerable faith of the fathers) and their impious creed.

15. They also sent ten legates to the emperor Constantius, writing down the things that were done and urging at the same time that he

---

38. On exile as a form of imperial violence, see Fournier 2006; for Constantius in particular, see Stevenson 2014.

39. Frequently just described as the singular "Council of Rimini," these councils provoked a great deal of discussion in late antique sources: see above, p. 8, and Hilary of Poitiers, *C. Const.* 12–16; Athanasius, *Syn.* 10–12; Socrates, *Hist. eccl.* 2.37–40; Sozomen, *Hist. eccl.* 4.17–22; Theodoret, *Hist. eccl.* 2.16–22; Jerome, *Lucif.* 17–18; Sulpicius Severus, *Chron.* 2.41–45.

40. A variant on the Fourth Sirmian Creed (see above, p. 8). These were among the leading Western Arians in the decades following the Council of Nicaea and were responsible for most of the Arian creeds that were composed under Constantius. Ursacius was bishop of Singidunum (Belgrade); Valens was bishop of Mursa (Osijek); Germinius was bishop of Sirmium and is best known as the villain in the anti-Arian dialogue known as the *Altercatio Heracliani* (see Flower 2013, 1–6); Gaius's see is unknown. Ursacius and Valens were the leaders of the Arian faction at the Council of Milan in 355; they often appear together in late antique sources as a sort of exemplary heretical duo. They are also a kind of arch-*praevaricator*, as they were perfectly willing to recant their Arianism if the political winds shifted (see Socrates, *Hist. eccl.* 2.24). On these bishops, see Meslin 1968, 64–84.

patrum pro fide venerabili contra haereticos inuiolata seruaret.

16. Mittunt sane et haeretici legatos: quos tunc familiarissime et ut suos suscepit Constantius; eos uero legatos qui pro fide catholica contra haereticos uenerant, reprobat et per suos nunc gratia inuitat, nunc minis perterret; et interim sola dilatione discruciat, ut in ultimum, cum iram regis metuunt, cum non dignantur pro Christo Filio Dei exilium perpeti, cum propriis sedibus et ecclesiarum perniciosissimis possessionibus oblectantur, rescindant quod pie uindicauerant, et suscipiant quod ut impium damnauerant.

17. Liceat in hoc apud uos religiosos imperatores in causa Dei dolentius ingemiscere: episcopi plus iram regis terreni timuerunt quam Christum uerum Deum et sempiternum regem; grauius exilium temporale esse crediderunt quam perpetuam poenam secundum Esaiam indormitabilis uermis et ignis inextinguibilis; suauiora habuerunt propria domicilia et possessiones quam in regno Christi beatam et perpetuam habitationem!

18. Sed Constantius, non contentus ruina et labe decem legatorum, mittit Ariminum, ut omnes illic episcopi similiter uerterentur. Qui et ipsi, malo illo exemplo legatorum suorum, piam fidem patrum quam uindicauerant reprobant subscribentes in illa fide Arrianorum quam integro et libero iudicio damnauerant.

19. Aduertit sapientia uestra Ariminensem synodum piissime coeptam sed impiissime terminatam. Eadem autem et apud Seleuciam Isauriae ab episcopis impietas commissa est. Iudicate, piissime et religiosissimi imperatores, in quo rei sunt et in quo merentur affligi, qui nolunt cum tali-

2. Faustinus and Marcellinus, *Petition of Requests* 77

also keep inviolate what the fathers had decreed for the venerable faith against heretics.

16. Naturally, the heretics also sent legates, whom Constantius then received quite amiably as though they were his associates; he rejected those who had come on behalf of the catholic faith against the heretics. Through his associates, sometimes he enticed them with his charm, and sometimes he terrified them with threats; meanwhile, he would torment them by the delay alone[41] for one reason: so that when they feared the wrath of a king, when they did not think it worthwhile to suffer exile for Christ, the Son of God, when they took comfort in their own sees and in the pernicious possessions of their churches, they would repudiate what they had piously affirmed and take up what they had condemned as impious.[42]

17. On this point, let us lament before you religious emperors with even more grief for the sake of God. The bishops feared the wrath of an earthly king more than Christ, the true God and eternal King;[43] they believed that transitory exile was more serious than everlasting punishment (untiring worms and inextinguishable flames, according to Isaiah); they considered their own dwellings and possessions more sweet than the blessed and everlasting dwelling in the kingdom of Christ.[44]

18. But Constantius, not content with ruining and disgracing the ten legates, sent word to Rimini to likewise convert all the bishops there. And in that wicked pattern set by their own legates, they rejected the pious faith of the fathers that they had affirmed and swore to the faith of the Arians that they had condemned with sound and free judgment.

19. Your Wisdom notes that the synod at Rimini was so piously begun but so impiously concluded; moreover, this same impiety was also committed by the bishops at Seleucia-in-Isauria.[45] Judge, most pious and religious emperors, why those who do not wish to hold communion with such

---

41. In other words, he tormented them by making them remain at court. Faustinus and Marcellinus suggest that these weak-willed bishops missed the comforts of home, but more practically, it also would have been expensive for these delegates to maintain themselves for a lengthy period of time far from their sees.
42. See below, §§17, 32, 42, 49, 61, 117, 121.
43. See Rev 1:5; 17:14; 19:16.
44. See above, §16; below, §§32, 42, 49, 61, 117, 121.
45. The lack of details concerning the council at Seleucia compared to that at Rimini is interesting. Were they poorly informed about Eastern events? Or is their brevity an attempt at cutting down on repetition? They are also terse concerning Constantius's actions against Eastern bishops (below, §27) but are well informed about

bus episcopis conuenire, qui, cum primum fidem integram uindicarent et impiam fidem reprobarent, postea, cum metuunt exilium, cum rebus suis et sedibus oblectantur, uertunt sententias, damnantes, ad nutum haeretici imperatoris illam apostolicam quam uindicauerant fidem et suscipientes illam Arrii quam reprobauerant impietatem.

20. Nonne gratum habere debuerent, si tamen credebant futurum Dei iudicium, omnia mala perpeti quam esse uenerabilis fidei proditores, cuius uirtus sancti quoque Alexandri orationibus et Arrii supplicio fuerat adprobata? Maxime cum et gloriosae passionis praecessisset exemplum licet paucissimorum episcoporum, qui, ne euangelicam apostolicamque fidem uiolarent, ne impiis adquiescerent, non exilium, non supplicium nec aliquam atrocitatis mortem recusauerunt.

21. Denique, ante synodum Ariminensem, Paulinus de Triueris constantissimus episcopus datur in exilium piam fidem uindicans et execrans consortium Arrianorum.

22. Sed et apostolicus uir Lucifer de Sardinia Caralitanae ciuita-

bishops are guilty and worth being assaulted.[46] Those bishops, although at first they upheld the undiminished faith and rejected the impious creed, changed their minds later when they were afraid of exile, when they took comfort in their own property and sees. At the command of a heretical emperor, they condemned the apostolic faith that they had upheld and took up the impiety of Arius that they had rejected.

20. Yet, if they believed that the judgment of God was coming, shouldn't they have been glad to suffer all evils rather than betray the venerable faith, whose virtue had been proven by the speeches of holy Alexander and the punishment of Arius? Especially since there had been preceding examples of the glorious suffering of bishops, albeit only a very small number of them, who would not violate the evangelic and apostolic faith, who would not fall silent before the impious, who refused no exile, no punishment, nor any cruel sort of death.

21. In short: before the synod at Rimini, a most steadfast[47] bishop, Paulinus of Trier, was exiled after upholding the pious faith and cursing the company of Arians.[48]

22. The apostolic man Lucifer, bishop of Cagliari from Sardinia,[49] was

---

more recent events in Oxyrhynchus and even spent time in Eleutheropolis (§92–101, 102–110, respectively).

46. Refusing to hold communion with "heretics" was obviously not a peculiarly Luciferian belief; see Perrin 2010.

47. A pun on the name of Constantius; see below, §§25, 28.

48. At the Council of Arles in 353 or 354; for his exile, see above, p. 6. Note the relatively brief comments the Luciferians have to offer about events in Trier, and see below, §77. Paulinus is not very well known. He corresponded with Athanasius (*Apol. sec.* 58.1; *H. Ar.* 26.2) and sent him copies of letters written by Ursacius and Valens; Athanasius had previously spent time in Trier while in exile under Constantine and later visited during another exile in the 340s (see Hanson 1988, 264, 308), so it is possible that they made their acquaintance on one of these visits. Paulinus spent his exile in Phrygia and died there in 358 (Jerome, *Chron.* 284th Olympiad [358b]).

49. *PCBE* 2.2 (Lucifer 1). Lucifer was ordained bishop of Cagliari, presiding over the island of Sardinia, sometime before 355; Hanson (1988, 509) suggests that Lucifer was selected for this see by Liberius because he was not particularly intelligent. As one of the most prominent and vituperative opponents of Constantius and one of the staunchest supporters of the Nicene Creed, he was exiled at the Council of Milan in 355 and spent most of his exile in the East. He had a reputation throughout antiquity and beyond as a fierce and difficult person. He has been the subject of numerous modern studies; the first modern biography is Krüger 1886; other recent biographies include Figus 1973 and Corti 2004.

tis episcopus ob hoc, quod bene esset agnitus per contemptum saeculi, per studium sacrarum literrarum, per uitae puritatem, per constantiam fidei, per gratiam diuinam, a Romana ecclesia missus est legatus ad Constantium et, ob hoc quod fidem uenerabilem uindicauit, quod detexit et conuicit haereticos, ductus est in exilium cum omni atrocitate iniuriarum.

23. Similiter Eusebius a Vercellis nec non et Dionysius Mediolanensium, Constantio regi primum familiaris, cum adhuc ignoraret eum fautorem esse haereticorum; postea tamen quam ei cognitum est et pro-

sent by the Roman church as a legate to Constantius[50] because he was well known for his contempt for this age, his fervor for holy scripture, his purity of life, his steadfastness of faith, and his divine grace.[51] Because he upheld the venerable faith and exposed and refuted heretics, he was led into exile with every sort of cruel injustice.[52]

23. It went the same way for Eusebius of Vercelli[53] and for Dionysius of Milan,[54] who was at first an associate of King Constantius[55] while still unaware that he was the patron of heretics; but after it was made known

---

50. Lucifer was specifically sent to the Council of Milan in 355; Faustinus and Marcellinus appear to be embellishing the truth, as Liberius of Rome sent Lucifer as his delegate to the Council of Milan, at which Constantius had him (and others) exiled, but he was not sent directly to Constantius himself. The council plays a prominent role in a number of ancient sources: Hilary of Poitiers, *Ad Const.* 1.8; Athanasius *H. Ar.* 31–34; Jerome, *Chron.* 284th Olympiad (359); Rufinus, *Hist. eccl.* 1.20; Socrates, *Hist. eccl.* 2.36; Sozomen, *Hist. eccl.* 4.8–11; Theodoret, *Hist. eccl.* 2.12; Sulpicius Severus, *Chron.* 2.39. See also Barnes 1993, 116–18. Note how the authors refuse to name Liberius, who eventually did acquiesce to Constantius's demands.

51. See below, §88, and the praise of Lucifer in Pseudo-Athanasius, *Ep.* 51.

52. At the Council of Milan in 355; see above, p. 6.

53. *PCBE* 2.1 (Eusebius 1); in general, see de Clercq, "Eusèbe de Verceil," *DHGE* cols. 1477–83. Despite this being the only mention of him in the *Libellus precum*, Eusebius was one of the leading Nicene figures of the mid-fourth century. He went with Lucifer to the Council of Milan in 355 as representatives of Liberius of Rome, where he and Lucifer and Dionysius were exiled. Eusebius and Lucifer spent some time exiled together in the Thebaid, from which Eusebius went to the Council of Alexandria and Lucifer went to settle matters in Antioch (see above, p. 9). He died sometime around 370, the same period in which Hilary and Lucifer died (Jerome, *Chron.* 286th–287th Olympiads). Three short letters of his are extant, addressed to Constantius, his congregation, and Gregory. The earliest Latin copy of the gospels, the Codex Vercellensis, is sometimes said to have been composed in Vercelli while he was bishop (see Levine 1955 for discussion). Eusebius was born in Sardinia (see Hanson 1988, 507); for how long had he known Lucifer?

54. *PCBE* 2.1 (Dionysius 1). Dionysius was the host of the council at Milan in 355. He appears to have had little interest in the theological minutiae of the disputes over the Nicene Creed in the 350s and was even willing to sign an Arian creed but then sided with Eusebius for reasons that are unclear. McLynn (1994, 17) treats Dionysius's reversal as an intentionally dramatic, even scripted, event. It is also possible, though, that Dionysius was simply influenced by the personalities involved (see the relationship between Hilary and Rhodanius, below, n. 57). Dionysius of Milan's successor in Milan following his exile was the Arian Auxentius; under the Nicene emperor Valentinian I, there were several attempts to drive him from his see, including a major push by Hilary of Poitiers in 364, but he remained bishop until his death in 374 (perhaps

batum quod haereticos uindicaret, respuit regis impiam familiaritatem, malens exilium, ne Christi Dei amicitiam perderet, ne sanctorum consortium non haberet.

24. Sed et Rodanius mittitur in exilium nec non et Hilarius, qui etiam

to him, and proven that Constantius supported heretics, he spat back the impious association of the king. He preferred exile[56] so that he would not lose the friendship of Christ, our God, and so that he would keep the company of holy men.

24. Rhodanius, too, was sent into exile,[57] as well as Hilary,[58] who also

---

in part through the help of Valentinian's wife, the Arian Justina). On Auxentius, see Meslin 1968, 41–44; McLynn 1994, 20–31.

55. Faustinus and Marcellinus explicitly use the word *rex* here instead of *imperator* to emphasize the unlawfulness of Constantius's actions (see below, §116).

56. Like Lucifer, both Eusebius and Dionysius were exiled at the Council of Milan in 355; see above, p. 6.

57. On Rhodanius's exile, see above, p. 7. For Rhodanius in general, see Crouzel 1976. Not much is known about Rhodanius; he was the bishop of Toulouse, not far from Hilary's see in Poitiers, and Beckwith (2008, 45–46) suggests that Rhodanius may have been Hilary's source for information about the events at the Council of Milan, which he attended.

58. On Hilary's exile, see above, pp. 6–7; for his life and works, see Simonetti 1975, 298–312; Hanson 1988, 459–71, with extensive bibliography. Hilary was one of, if not the, most prominent Western bishops of the 350s and 360s, part of a generation that included Eusebius of Vercelli, Lucifer of Cagliari, and Gregory of Elvira. The date of his birth and his early years are unclear, though he seems to have been well educated in secular literature. This might lend some credence to his statements about his relatively late education in Christianity given in his quasi-autobiography found in Hilary of Poitiers, *Trin.* 1.1–5. He was made bishop of Poitiers (ancient Pictavium) around 353, where he quickly became drawn into the Arian controversy. After being exiled at Béziers for refusing to condemn Athanasius (and having drawn the ire of the Arian Saturninus of Arles), Hilary spent years in exile in the East, mostly in Phrygia, where he appears to have become familiar with the works of Gregory of Nyssa. This was also his most prolific period of writing, including several treatises against Constantius, Ursacius, and Valens, his important history of the Christian councils of the period titled *De Synodis*, and his substantial *De Trinitate*. At the time, he faced accusations of swearing to an Arian creed from another Hilarius, this one a deacon of Lucifer, to which he angrily replied to Lucifer and explained that he had torn up Constantius's condemnation of Lucifer when it was offered to him (see Smulders 1978). He returned to Gaul sometime before the Council of Alexandria in 362 (Jerome [*Chron.* 284th Olympiad (359g)] puts his return in 359, even before Constantius's death), but eagerly set about the process of reconciliation with those who returned to Nicene communion (see esp. the letter in *Coll. Ant. Par.* B 4.2). He, with Eusebius of Vercelli, also unsuccessfully tried to have Auxentius of Milan (Ambrose's Arian predecessor) deposed. Hilary worked with Liberius on reconciling returning clergy after the Council of Alexandria, while the Luciferians seem to have ordained their own bishops of Rome (see below, §77); Hilary worked against Auxentius with Eusebius of Vercelli, while Lucifer

scripta contra haereticos et praeuaricatores edidit, licet postea uero interruperit fauens praeuaricatoribus, ut non dicamus interim, quia fauit <et> haereticis, in quos eloquentiae suae uiribus perorauerat.

25. Maximus quoque de Neapoli Campaniae, eo quod esset inhabili stomacho et corpore delicatior, primum quidem, ut cederet, diu afflictus iniuriis; deinde, ubi ob constantiam animi fideique uirtutem carnis infirmitate non uincitur, ductus est in exilium atque illic martyr in Domini pace requieuit.

26. Sed et Rufininus, mirae quidem simplicitatis sed admirabilior in tuenda fide, effusione sui sanguinis praeuenit exilium. Denique, cum pro fidei integritate persistit, hunc Epictetus atrox ille et dirus de Centumcel-

published writings against heretics and prevaricators—though in truth, he later stopped that and befriended prevaricators. We are not saying, however, that he also[59] befriended heretics, against whom he spoke at length using the powers of his eloquence.

25. Also Maximus of Naples, in Campania.[60] Because he had a disagreeable stomach and was more delicate in body, he was naturally first unjustly assaulted so that he would withdraw. Then, when he was not overcome by the weakness of his flesh because of the steadfastness[61] of his soul and the virtue of his faith, he was led into exile and there rests, a martyr in the peace of the Lord.

26. Rufininus,[62] a man of marvelous simplicity but even more admirable in how he protected the faith, pre-empted his exile by shedding his own blood. In the end, when he persisted on behalf of the undiminished faith, that fierce and horrible Epictetus, bishop of Centumcellae,[63] forced

---

and Eusebius had a falling out over the Council of Alexandria and Lucifer's ordination of Paulinus in Antioch; Hilary had previously been criticized by Lucifer's deacon Hilarius, and Faustinus and Marcellinus criticize him as well. These instances all suggest that the experiences they faced from 355–362 split this generation of Westerners into two irreconcilable parties. According to Jerome (*Chron.* 286th Olympiad [367e]), Hilary died in 367.

59. The text is corrupt, but the meaning is clear; Mazochi proposes *et*, which Canellis accepts.

60. *PCBE* 2.2 (Maximus 4); although he apparently died in exile, he is said to have been buried in Naples next to his predecessor, Fortunatus (Gest. episc. Neapol. 9), and the epitaph of a Maximus called a *confessor* has been discovered (see Canellis 2006, 132n1). See below, §§62–65, for the successor of Maximus, Zosimus. The ninth-century Gesta episcoporum Neapolitanorum also conveniently lists a Maximus as bishop of Naples followed by a Zosimus; however, it places Maximus in the reigns of Diocletian and Maximian, and Zosimus in the reign of Constantine. The Gesta are surely in error here but might be taken as some confirmation that Zosimus was Maximus's direct successor (Desmulliez 2015, 139–40).

61. Another pun on Constantius; see above, §21; below, §28.

62. Otherwise unknown.

63. On Epictetus, see Meslin 1968, 37–39. Lucifer (*Non conv. haer.* 7.18; *Mor. esse. Dei Fil.* 7) twice lambasts Epictetus in his tracts. Epictetus was apparently a close ally of Constantius and staunch opponent of Liberius of Rome before Liberius swore to an Arian creed. He was present when Constantius first exiled Liberius and spoke a few words against him (Theodoret, *Hist. eccl.* 2.13), and then participated in the ordination of Felix in his stead (Athanasius, *H. Ar.* 8.75; see also Athanasius, *Ep. Aeg. Lib.*1.7). Epictetus later appears in a letter sent by Liberius to Ursacius, Valens, and Germinius (*Coll. Ant. Par.* 7.10), in which Liberius claims that since he is now in communion

lis episcopus ante raedam suam currere coegit et, cum diu currit, sic in via ruptis vitalibus sanguinem fundens expirauit. Sciunt hoc Neapolitani in Campania, ubi reliquiae cruoris eius in obsessis corporibus daemonia affligunt, pro gratia utique fidei illius pro qua et sanguinem fudit.

27. Fuerunt et alii episcopi de Aegypto, licet pauculi, quorum alii in fugam uersi sunt, alii uero in exilium dati eo quod nollent cum episcopis impiis et crudelibus conuenire.

Quam utique salubre fuerat, quam pulchrum quamue gloriosum, si omnes illi episcopi pari uirtute et simili conspiratione fidem, quam recte semper uindicauerant, in finem usque seruassent, non exilia neque supplicia pertimescentes, ad capiendam utique futuram in Dei Christi regno perpetuam beatitudinem!

28. Et tacemus quod fortassis ipsum illum Constantium, quamuis regni potestate terribilem, tantorum tamen episcoporum unita constantia confutasset et frangeret, fortassis etiam et intellegere fecisset magnum pretium esse istius fidei, pro qua nullus episcoporum exilium, proscriptiones, tormenta mortemque recusaret. Sed, paululum territus, tantus episcoporum numerus cateruatim dederunt manus impietati et ad maiorem iam uesaniam incalluit impietas tam facile strage multitudinis.

29. Non hoc minus sacrilegium est, non haec minor impietas, quam

him to run in front of his carriage. After he ran a long ways, he died in the road, spilling out blood because his vital organs had been ruptured. The Neapolitans in Campania know this, where the remains of his gore assault demons in possessed bodies, surely from the grace of the faith for which he also spilled his blood.[64]

27. There were also some bishops from Egypt, though very few; some turned to flight,[65] while others were given to exile because they did not wish to hold communion with impious and cruel bishops.[66]

In any case, how salutary, how beautiful, how glorious it would have been if all those bishops had protected the faith that they had always rightly upheld, with equal virtue and similar unanimity, terrified of neither exile nor punishment, in order to assuredly grasp the everlasting blessedness to come in the kingdom of Christ, our God!

28. We are staying silent about how perhaps the united constancy of so many bishops might have checked and subdued Constantius,[67] however dreadful he was in his regal power. Perhaps he would have even understood the great worth of that faith for which no bishops refused exile, proscriptions, torments, and death. But, because they were frightened just a little, a great number of bishops gave their hands en masse to impiety, and their impiety hardened[68] to an even greater madness after the multitude was overthrown so easily.

29. No less a sacrilege is this, no less an impiety, than if under a pagan

---

with Epictetus, the three Arians should intercede with Constantius so that he might return to Rome. Constantius may also have sent Epictetus as an ambassador to Julian (see Ricciotti 1960, 137).

64. Faustinus and Marcellinus elsewhere highlight the miraculous powers of living ascetics (below, §§78, 89–90, 105) but here give a glimpse into the growing cult of the martyrs as it existed in the late fourth century. See, e.g., Grig 2004, 86–94.

65. Most famously, Athanasius, who penned his treatise *Apologia de fuga sua* to defend his going into hiding.

66. See Athanasius, *Apologia de fuga sua*. See above, §19, and note how little information is provided concerning Eastern bishops under Constantius.

67. Faustinus here makes the play on words between *constantia* and *Constantium* much more clearly; see above, §§21, 25.

68. Accepting the reading in the manuscripts, *incalluit*, despite the fact that this perfect of *incallesco* is otherwise unattested. Also possible is *incaluit*, the perfect of *incalesco* (to be warm, to be inflamed): "and their impiety inflamed them to an even greater madness."

si sub persecutore gentili idolo sacrificatum est, quia et in haeresi perterritum subscribere daemoniis sacrificare est, siquidem docentibus Scripturis Diuinis doctrina daemoniorum est haeresis, sicut et idolatria.

30. Interea, quia apud quosdam multitudo praeponitur ueritati eo quod paeculos habeat sectatores, et ob hoc affligimur quod in paucis sequimur inuiolabilem fidem et multos uitamus propter impias haereses et sacrilegas praeuaricatorum subscriptiones, quid censetis in hac causa, o iustissimi imperatores et catholicae fidei uindices? De his duabus partibus cui calculum datis? Vna est pars, in qua multi sunt episcopi; sed ubi multi sunt, illic per praeuaricationem sacra Christi fides uiolata est semper ante defensa, illic metu regis Arrii suscepta impietas est semper ante damnata. Vbi uero paucissimi sunt, illic per exilia, per cruciatus, per effusionem sanguinis, per ipsam mortem fides Christi uindicatur et Arrii impietas atque omnis haeresis ut summum malum execrabiles sunt.

31. Sed etsi non est dubitandum paucos episcopos esse pretiosos de merito confessionis et inuiolabilis fidei, multos uero nullificare merito haereseos uel praeuaricationis, quia in causa ueri, maxime in causa religionis et sacrae fidei, non numerus numero comparandus est sed pura illa apostolica fides probata exiliis, probata cruciatibus licet unius, multorum infidelitatibus praeponenda est, tamen necessarium est damnatae praeuaricationis diuinum quoque praesens proferre documentum, ut sicut in Arrio impia secta eius diuina animaduersione punita praeiudicat et de sectatoribus eius, quod eadem illos poena maneat qua torquetur et Arrius, ita et de praeuaricatoribus sacrae fidei nihil aliud sentiendum sit quam

persecution they sacrificed to an idol[69]—because to swear to heresy out of fear is the same as sacrificing to demons,[70] if indeed, as the holy scripture teaches, heresy is the *doctrine of demons*,[71] like idolatry.

30. Meanwhile, in the view of certain men, a multitude is better than the truth, because the truth has few followers. We are assaulted because we follow the inviolable faith among the few and we shun the many on account of their impious heresies and the sacrilegious signatures of prevaricators. Because of this, what is your opinion in this case, most just emperors and supporters of the catholic faith? Out of these two parties, whom do you support? One is the party in which there are many bishops; but where there are many, there the sacred faith of Christ is always violated before it is defended, due to their prevarication. There, because they are afraid of a king,[72] the impiety of Arius is always taken up before it is condemned. But where the fewest are, there the faith of Christ is upheld through exiles, through torture, through the spilling of blood, and through death itself—and Arius's impiety and every heresy are cursed as the highest wickedness.

31. It should not be doubted that a small number of bishops may be greatly esteemed by virtue of their confession and inviolable faith but a large number may be despised by virtue of their heresy or prevarication, since in a case of what is true (especially in a case of religion and the sacred faith) number ought not be compared to number; instead, the pure apostolic faith that is proven by exile and torture (even if just the torture of one) ought to be preferred to the infidelities of many. But even so, it is now nevertheless also necessary to present proof of God's condemnation of their prevarication for this reason: just as judgment against Arius's followers was made in advance when his impious sect was punished by God's chastisement against Arius himself, since the same punishment that torments Arius awaits them as well, so too should no one expect anything other than what has been established by God's judgment in present-day

---

69. See below, §76, and Faustinus, *Trin.* 1.

70. The Luciferians were far from alone in identifying heresy as a form of apostasy; see, e.g., Gregory of Nyssa, *Ep. can. Let.* 2–4; Basil of Caesarea, *Ep.* 188; Pacian, *Par.* 11; Optatus, *Schism.* 1.22; Augustine, *Serm.* 352.8.

71. 1 Tim 4:1.

72. Here meaning an emperor. The play between the earthly and heavenly kings is apparent throughout the text (see above, e.g., §§7, 17). The authors also refer to Constantius (but not Theodosius, Valentinian II, or Arcadius) as *rex* (§§23, 32, 33, 35, 116).

quod in uno uel duobus praeuaricatoribus poenis praesentibus diuino iudicio determinatum est.

32. Potamius, Odyssiponae ciuitatis episcopus, primum quidem fidem catholicam uindicans, postea uero, praemio fundi fiscalis quem habere concupiuerat, fidem praeuaricatus est. Hunc Osius de Corduba apud ecclesias Hispaniarum et detexit et reppulit ut impium haereticum.

Sed et ipse Osius Potami querela accersitus ad Constantium regem minisque perterritus et metuens ne senex et diues exilium proscriptionemue pateretur, dat manus impietati et post tot annos praeuaricatur in fidem. Et regreditur ad Hispanias maiore cum auctoritate, habens regis terribilem iussionem, ut si quis eidem episcopus iam facto praeuaricatori minime uelit communicare, in exilium mitteretur.

33. Sed ad sanctum Gregorium, Eliberitanae ciuitatis constantissimum episcopum, fidelis nuntius detulit impiam Osii praeuaricationem;

2. Faustinus and Marcellinus, *Petition of Requests* 91

punishments against one or two prevaricators for those who prevaricated concerning the sacred faith.

32. Potamius, bishop of the city of Lisbon, certainly upheld the catholic faith at first.[73] But later, he prevaricated about the faith to be rewarded with a government-owned estate that he had longed to possess.[74] Hosius exposed this man in the churches of Spain and rejected him as an impious heretic.

But even Hosius, summoned to King Constantius by a complaint of Potamius, was terrified by his threats.[75] Fearing that he would suffer exile or proscription as an old and wealthy man, he gave his hands to impiety, and after so many years, prevaricated about the faith. He returned to Spain with greater authority, because he had a terrible order: if any bishop did not wish to hold communion with him at all, now that he had become a prevaricator, he would be sent into exile.

33. But a faithful messenger reported the impious prevarication of Hosius to holy Gregory, most steadfast bishop of the city of Elvira.[76] From

---

73. Potamius wrote several commentaries that survive to the present; see Conti 1998 in general, and pp. 23–26 in particular for a discussion of the various interpretations of his career. Conti, contra others who dismiss Potamius's apostasy as a Luciferian invention and the Luciferians' own discussion of Potamius's death, argues that Potamius swore to an Arian creed and then returned to Nicene communion later. But the Luciferians so vehemently denounce other bishops who swore to Arian creeds under Constantius but then returned to Nicene communion under Valentinian that it seems unlikely that in this case they would have omitted such a history.

74. See above, §§16, 17; below, §§42, 49, 61, 117, 121. Simonetti (1975, 131n16) argues that Potamius was more interested in gaining political influence from Constantius than material rewards.

75. Hosius's capitulation was a major event among Christians in late antiquity; for a full discussion of the event, see de Clerq 1954, 459–530. Hosius had previously written very harsh words against Constantius (see Athanasius, *H. Ar.* 44.7–8). Fernández (1993) argues that Hosius was actually trying to garner influence with Constantius in opposition to Potamius of Lisbon (see n. 73, above).

76. See *Lex Aug.* 8. Gregory of Elvira's exact relationship to the Luciferians is a matter of some debate. From the outset, it is very important to note that there are no affirmative statements in any source as to whether Gregory accepted the decision of the Council of Alexandria (a letter attributed to Eusebius of Vercelli suggests that Gregory refused to hold communion "cum ypocritis," but probably dates to 360: see Flower 2013, 249–51). The inclusion of the following narrative within the *Libellus precum* is the strongest evidence that Gregory was associated with the community represented by the petition's authors in some way; Jerome's (*Chron.* 287th Olympiad [370a]) identification of Gregory and Lucifer (and Philo of Libya, otherwise unknown)

unde et non adquiescit, memor sacrae fidei ac diuini iudicii, in eius nefariam communionem. Sed Osius, qui hinc plus torqueretur si quis ipso iam lapso staret integram fidem uindicans inlapsa firmitate uestigii, exhiberi facit per publicam potestatem strenuissimae mentis Gregorium, sperans quod eodem terrore quo ipse cesserat hunc quoque posse cedere.

Erat autem tunc temporis Clementinus uicarius. Qui, ex conuentione Osii et generali praecepto regis, sanctum Gregorium per officium Cordubam iussit exhiberi.

then on, Gregory would take no comfort in his unholy communion, as he was mindful of the sacred faith and God's judgment. But Hosius henceforth was tormented all the more if anyone who upheld the undiminished faith with a firmness that had not lapsed one bit[77] stood against him now that he himself had lapsed.[78] Through his civic power, he made Gregory, a man with a most vigorous mind, appear before him, in the hope that Gregory might also relent because of the same terror that caused him to relent.

Now, Clementine was *vicarius* at that time.[79] Due to Hosius's indictment and the general order of the king, he ordered holy Gregory to present himself at Cordoba through his office.

---

as three opponents of Arianism is also suggestive but by no means conclusive. Jerome (*Dialogus contra Luciferianos* 15) also tantalizingly refers to a "Spanish serpent" (Hiberam excetram); a reference to a still-intransigent Gregory? Simonetti (1975, 444–45) identifies Gregory as a leader of the Luciferians on the basis of these points. Perez Mas (2008, 320–30) summarizes later arguments against any real connection between Gregory and these later Luciferians and refutes them. More recently, Brumback (2014, 61–66) argues that Gregory was not a Luciferian because he used the *Contra Arianos* of Phoebadius, who was in favor of reconciliation, in composing his own *De fide*, but Faustinus's apparent use of the works of Hilary and Ambrose (and others) throughout his *De Trinitate* suggests that, perhaps unsurprisingly, anti-Arian arguments were considered valuable no matter who authored them. Brumback also suggests that Theodosius was willing to support Gregory and the Luciferians were attempting to take advantage of Gregory of Elvira's reputation (66–69). The argument is reminiscent of Shuve (2014, 258–61), who argues that Faustinus and Marcellinus, facing persecution in Rome, attempted to "claim the mantles" of Gregory of Elvira and Heraclida. The lengthy narration later in the *Libellus precum* (see below, §§73–76) concerning the intransigent presbyter Vincentius in southern Spain, but no intransigent bishop, perhaps suggests that while some rigorists persisted in refusing to hold communion with *praevaricatores* in Spain, Gregory was perhaps only tangentially related to them. On the other hand, Faustinus and Marcellinus explicitly state that Vincentius was persecuted for holding communion with Gregory; perhaps this presbyter was persecuted for holding communion with Gregory but Gregory's reputation was such that he could not be persecuted directly. See below, §73.

77. See Wis 5:1.
78. Note the play on words between *lapso* and *inlapsa*.
79. *PLRE* 1 (Clementinus 1). Otherwise unknown. The *vicarius* was the Roman official in charge of a diocese, in this case Diocesis Hispaniarum, which included several provinces in Spain: Tarraconensis, Carthaginensis, Baetica, Lusitania, Gallaecia, and Mauritania Tingitana. Canellis (2006, 141) believes that his seat may have been in Merida, not Cordoba, as the *Libellus precum* implies.

34. Interea, fama in cognitionem rei cunctos inquietat et frequens sermo populorum est: "Quinam est ille Gregorius, qui audet Osio resistere?" Plurimi enim et Osii praeuaricationem adhuc ignorabant; quinam esset sanctus Gregorius nondum bene compertum habebant! Erat enim etiam apud eos, qui illum forte nouerant, rudis adhuc episcopus, licet apud Christum non rudis uindex fidei pro merito sanctitatis.

35. Sed ecce uentum est ad uicarium et multi ex administratoribus intersunt et Osius sedet iudex, immo et supra iudicem, fretus regali imperio. Et sanctus Gregorius, exemplo Domini sui, ut reus adsistit, non de praua conscientia sed pro conditione praesentis iudicii, ceterum fide liber, et est magna expectatio singulorum ad quam partem uictoria declinet. Et Osius quidem auctoritate nititur suae aetatis, Gregorius vero auctoritate nititur veritatis; ille quidem fiducia regis terreni, iste autem fiducia regis sempiterni. Et Osius scripto imperatoris utitur, sed Gregorius scripto diuinae uocis obtinet.

36. Et cum per omnia Osius confutatur, ita ut suis uocibus, quas pro fide et ueritate prius scripserat, uindicaretur, commotus ad Clementinum uicarium: "Non," inquit, "cognitio tibi mandata est, sed exsecutio. Vides ut resistit praeceptis regalibus: exsequere ergo quod mandatum est, mittens eum in exilium." Sed Clementinus, licet non esset Christianus, tamen exhibens reuerentiam nomini episcopatus in eo maxime homine quem uidebat rationabiliter et fideliter obtinere, respondit Osio: "Non audeo," inquiens, "episcopum in exilium mittere, quamdiu adhuc in episcopale nomine perseuerat. Sed da, tu, prior sententiam eum de episcopatus honore deiciens et tunc demum exequar in eum quasi in priuatum quod ex praecepto imperatoris fieri desideras."

37. Vt autem uidit sanctus Gregorius quod Osius uellet dare sententiam ut quasi deiectus uideretur, appellat ad uerum et potentem iudicum

34. Meanwhile, rumor disturbed everyone's understanding of the matter, and the common talk of the people was, "Who is this Gregory that dares to stand up to Hosius?" Many were still ignorant of Hosius's prevarication; they had not yet fully ascertained that it was Gregory who was holy! For in the view of those who happened to have known him, he was still an inexperienced bishop. In the view of Christ, however, he was no inexperienced supporter of the faith, by virtue of his holiness.

35. But look! He came to the *vicarius*, and many of his administrators were present, and Hosius was sitting like judge, no, beyond even a judge, since he was relying on royal authority. Holy Gregory, in imitation of his Lord,[80] was sitting like a criminal, not because he had an evil conscience, but in light of the circumstance of the present judgment;[81] otherwise, he was free in his faith. There was great anticipation among all as to which party would turn out victorious.[82] Hosius, naturally, leaned on the authority of his age, but Gregory leaned on the authority of the truth; the former, indeed, leaned on the assurance of an earthly king, but the latter on the assurance of the eternal King;[83] and Hosius used the writings of an emperor, but Gregory held fast to the writings of God's voice.

36. When Hosius was checked in all respects, vanquished by his own statements that he had previously written on behalf of the faith and the truth, he moved to the *vicarius* Clementine and said, "Understanding is not your responsibility, but taking action. You see that he stands up against royal commands: do your duty, then, and send him into exile." But Clementine, although he was not Christian, nevertheless showed reverence for the title of the episcopate in this great man whom he saw prevailing reasonably and faithfully. He responded to Hosius, saying, "I do not dare send a bishop into exile, as long as he still continues to have his episcopal title. First pass judgment casting him out from the honor of the episcopate, and then, and only then, will I do to him what you wish to happen in accordance with the order of the emperor, as though I were acting against a private citizen."[84]

37. But when holy Gregory saw that Hosius wished to pass judgment so that it would seem like he were cast out, he appealed to the true and

---

80. See Matt 27:11–26; John 18:28–40.
81. See Wis 4:20–5:1.
82. See Exod 17:11–12.
83. See Rev 1:5; 17:14; 19:16.
84. Bishops had to be deprived of their office before they were liable to government punishment. See Girardet 1974, 63–91; Canellis 2006, 145n1.

Christum totis fidei suae uiribus exclamans: "Christe Deus, qui uenturus es iudicare uiuos et mortuos, ne patiaris hodie humanam proferri sententiam aduersus me minimum seruum tuum, qui pro fide tui nominis ut reus adsistens spectaculum praebeo. Sed tu ipse, quaeso, in causa tua hodie iudica! Ipse sententiam proferre dignaberis per ultionem! Non hoc ego quasi metuens exilium fieri cupio, cum mihi pro tuo nomine nullum supplicium non suaue sit, sed ut multi praeuaricationis errore liberentur cum praesentem et momentaneam uiderint ultionem."

38. Et cum multo inuidiosius et sanctius Deum uerbis fidelibus interpellat, ecce repente Osius, cum sententiam conatus exprimere, os uertit, distorquens pariter et ceruicem de sessu in terram eliditur atque illic expirat uel, ut quidam uolunt, obmutuit; inde tamen effertur ut mortuus. Tunc admirantibus cunctis etiam Clementinus ille gentilis expauit et, licet esset iudex, timens ne de se quoque simili supplicio iudicaretur, prostrauit se ad pedes tanti viri, obsecrans eum ut sibi parceret qui in eum diuinae legis ignoratione peccasset, et non tam proprio arbitrio quam mandantis imperio.

39. Erat tunc stupor in omnibus ac diuinae uirtutis admiratio, quod in illo spectaculum totum nouum uisum est: nam qui proferre uoluit humanam sententiam, mox diuinam perpessus est grauiorem, et iudex, qui iudicare uenerat, iam pallens ut reus timebat iudicare, et qui quasi reus in exilium mittendus adstiterat, a iudice prostrato rogabatur ut parceret quasi iudex!

40. Inde est quod solus Gregorius ex numero uindicantium integram fidem, nec in fugam uersus, nec passus exilium, cum unusquisque timuit de illo ulterius iudicare.

41. Videtisne damnatae a Deo praeuaricationis mira documenta? Scit melius omnis Hispania, quod ista non fingimus.

powerful judge, Christ,[85] crying out with the powers of his entire faith, "Christ, our God, you who *are going to come to judge the living and the dead*,[86] suffer not today that human judgment be brought out against me, the least of your servants, who offers himself like a criminal standing at a public spectacle on behalf of the faith of your name. Instead, I beg you to pass judgment in this case today! Find it worthwhile to carry out judgment in vengeance yourself! I do not want this to happen as though I were afraid of exile,[87] since no punishment on behalf of your name is not sweet to me, but so that many might be freed from the error of prevarication when they see your present and instantaneous vengeance."

38. When Gregory appealed to God with his faithful words, more zealous and holy [than Hosius] by far—look!—suddenly, when Hosius attempted to pass judgment, his face turned, his neck likewise twisting. He was thrown out from where he was sitting onto the ground and died there, or, as some like it, he "became silent." From there, at any rate, he was carried out as a dead man. Then, as everyone was marveling, even that pagan Clementine became terrified, and though he was the judge, fearing that judgment with a similar punishment might also be passed against him, he prostrated himself at the feet of so great a man. He begged him to spare one who had sinned against him in ignorance of divine law, and not by his own opinion so much as by the command of someone ordering him.

39. Then everyone was astonished and had admiration for divine law, because an entirely unprecedented spectacle was seen in this way: the one who wished to pass human judgment now endured the more serious judgment of God, the judge who had come to judge, now growing pale, was afraid of being judged as guilty, and the one who had stood like a criminal about to be sent into exile was being begged by a prostrate judge to spare him as though he were a judge!

40. For this reason, Gregory alone, out of the company of those who upheld the undiminished faith, neither turned to flight nor suffered exile, since everyone was afraid to judge him further.[88]

41. Do you not see the amazing proof of how prevarication is condemned by God? All Spain knows quite well that we are not making these

---

85. See Acts 19:11.
86. 1 Pet 4:5; 2 Tim 4:1.
87. See below, §122.
88. Although the details of this story might well be doubted, Gregory never appears to have fled his see or suffered exile.

Sed et Potamio non fuit inulta sacrae fidei praeuaricatio. Denique, cum ad fundum properat quem pro impia fidei subscriptione ab imperatore meruerat impetrare, dans nouas poenas linguae per quam blasphemauerat, in uia moritur, nullus fructus fundi uel uisione percipiens.

42. Non fuit auari hoc tormentem leue: moritur, qui propter concupiscentiam fundi fiscalis fidem sacram uiolauerat et, cum ad fundum properat, poenali morte praeuenitur ne uel visionis solatio potiretur. In sacro Euangelio legimus uerba improperantis ad diuitem qui sibi de conditis uanissime gloriabatur: "Stulte," inquit, "hac nocte anima tua abs te augeretur; quae praeparasti, cuius erunt?" Si quis hoc scriptum et de Potamio conuenire consideret, intelleget in eum non leuiter iudicatum, maxime passum linguae supplicium in qua et diues ille apud inferos uehementius cruciatur.

43. Sed et Florentius, qui Osio et Potamio iam praeuaricatoribus sciens in loco quodam communicauit, dedit et ipse noua supplicia. Nam cum in conuentu plebis sedet in throno suo, repente eliditur et palpitat atque foras sublatus uires resumpsit. Et iterum et alia uice cum ingressus sedisset, similiter patitur, nec adhuc intellegens poenas suae maculatae communionis. Nihilominus postea cum intrare perseuerasset, ita tertia uice de

2. Faustinus and Marcellinus, *Petition of Requests* 99

things up.[89] Yet Potamius's prevarication about the sacred faith was also not left unpunished. In fact, when he was hastening on to the estate that he had earned from the emperor for his impious subscription of faith, he was punished in an unprecedented manner by the tongue through which he had blasphemed.[90] He died in the road, receiving no delight from his estate, not even in seeing it.

42. This is no light torment for a greedy man: he, who violated the sacred faith because he longed for an estate from the treasury, died, and when he was hastening to his domain, he came first to a punitive death that did not even give him the comfort of seeing it.[91] In the holy gospel we read words reproaching a rich man who was glorifying himself in vain about his preparations:[92] *Fool, it says, your soul will be carried away from you this night; the things you have prepared, whose will they be?*[93] If anyone considers how this text is suitable regarding Potamius, he would understand that it was not light judgment that was passed against him, especially as the punishment he suffered was of his tongue, by which that rich man is also tortured violently in hell.[94]

43. Even Florentius,[95] who held communion in some place with Hosius and Potamius while knowing at the time that they were prevaricators, was also punished in an unprecedented manner. For when he sat on his throne in an assembly of the people, he was suddenly forced off it and trembled; after he was brought outside, he recovered his strength. A second time in turn, when he had sat down after he entered, he likewise suffered, not yet understanding that these were punishments for his polluted communion. Nevertheless, afterwards, when he had kept trying to

---

89. See below, §§44, 65, 93.

90. Potamius's death is also referenced in the next section, but it is hard to tell what exactly is supposed to have happened. For another death involving the tongue, see below, §§64–65. Heretics and traitors suffering punishment through their tongues carries obvious symbolic significance.

91. See above, §§16, 17, 32; below, §§49, 61, 117, 121.

92. See Luke 12:16–19.

93. Luke 12:20, 43.

94. See Luke 16:19–26; above, §41.

95. Florentius is a very common name, but we may have earlier notices about this particular Florentius. In 314, at the Council of Arles, a certain deacon named Florentius accompanied Liberius of Merida (*Conc. Arel. prim.* 22). Florentius of Merida attended the Council of Sardica with Hosius and several other Spanish bishops in 343 (see Hefele 1871, 97).

throno excutitur, ut quasi indignus throno repelli uideretur, atque elisus in terram ita palpitans torquebatur, ut cum quadam duritia et magnis cruciatibus eidem spiritus extorqueretur, et inde iam tollitur non ex more resumendus sed sepeliendus.

44. Scit hoc quod referimus magna ciuitas Emerita, cuius in ecclesia plebs hoc ipsum suis uidit obtutibus. Sed et hoc considerandum est, quia Florentius haec passus est, qui nondum subscripserat impietati, sed tantum quod communicauit praeuaricatoribus fidei, non ignorans eorum praeuaricationem.

45. Hoc ideo intulimus ut uideant illi quid sibi agendum sit, qui, cum non subscripserint ut praeuaricatores, tamen per communionem praeuaricatoribus sibi cognitis copulati sunt. Et puto quod intellegant quid, exemplo Florentii, timere debeant.

46. Sed longum est referre alia quoque documenta poenis praesentibus damnatae praeuaricationis, quae diuinum iudicium uariis in locis exercuit, ad hoc scilicet ut qui Scripturas Diuinas quadam ratione non respicit, uel praesenti ultionis diuinae animaduersione intellegat quid sibi sectandum sit quidue uitandum. Vindicare uoluit Deus uel in paucos sine dubio et illa ratione ne, quae per Scripturam Diuinam de praeuaricatorum futuris suppliciis minitatur, uelut fabula putaretur si nunc in hoc saeculo in neminem uindicaret.

47. Intellegant nunc omnes episcopi praeuaricatores fidei quam grauissimis suppliciis reseruati sunt, quando in suos socios in hoc quoque saeculo ad stuporem omnium uindicatum est. Ad hoc enim etiam praesentes poenas praeuaricationis exposuimus ut, quod in paucos uindicatum est, credatur et in omnes eorum similes uindicari, maxime cum et Scriptura

enter the church, he was forced off his throne a third time in a way that made it seem like he was being driven back as though he were unworthy of the throne. Forced onto the ground trembling, he was tortured in such a way that his breath was forced out of him with some severity and great torment. From there he was again lifted, not soon to recover, as was customary, but soon to be buried.[96]

44. The great city of Merida knows what we are referring to.[97] The people saw this very thing with their own eyes in their church. But you should also consider that Florentius, who had not yet sworn to impiety, suffered these things only because he held communion with those who prevaricated about the faith while not being ignorant of their prevarication.

45. We mentioned this so that they might see what should be done by men who—although they did not sign like the prevaricators did—are nevertheless joined through communion to those whom they know are prevaricators. And I think that they should understand why, given the example of Florentius, they should be afraid.[98]

46. Now, it would take a long time to report other proofs of prevarication being condemned by present-day punishments. God obviously carried these out as judgment in various places so that whoever is not mindful of divine scripture (for whatever reason) would understand by observing God's vengeance in the present either what he should follow or what he should shun. Without a doubt, God wished to take vengeance against a few so that whatever divine scripture threatens concerning future punishments against prevaricators is not considered a myth, even if he does not now take vengeance against someone in the present.

47. All the bishops who betray the faith should now understand what very serious punishments are reserved for them, seeing as vengeance has come against their own allies in the present, to everyone's amazement. To this end we have related contemporary punishments of their treachery so that, because vengeance has come against a few, they believe that vengeance will come against all of those who are like them—especially

---

96. The text is vague as to whether these events occurred on the same day or over a course of several days.

97. See above, §41; below, §§65, 93. Sometime after Florentius was bishop, the church at Merida was led by Hydatius, a fifth-century continuator of Jerome's *Chronicon*. See below, §75.

98. The authors here switch to the singular (*puto*), possibly suggesting that the *Libellus precum* features a principal author (probably Faustinus).

Diuina hoc ipsum adseueret quod et per praesentia documenta monstratum est, et hoc consideretur, piissimi imperatores, in quo rei sunt, qui cum talibus diuina sacramenta non copulant, quorum et perpetua supplicia sacris leguntur in libris et suppliciorum exempla uidentur in saeculo.

48. Sed quaesumus miram beniuolentiam vestram, ut adhuc nobis pro contemplatione Christi Dei infatigabilem audiendi patientiam commodetis, dum adhuc, summatim licet, exponimus in quantum creuit impietas. Execrabiles enim Arriani, in partibus Orientis et maxime in Aegypto, non fuerunt hoc solo contenti ut episcopi damnata fide integra in eorum impiam sententiam declinarent, sed hos ipsos, qui primum fuerant per catholicos episcopos ordinati, ubi pro eorum desideriis subscripserunt, in laicorum numerum exigebant et postea iterum eos idem haeretici episcopos ordinabant, ut non solum fidem catholicam damnare uiderentur, sed etiam ordinationem factam per catholicos episcopos.

49. Intendite in hoc aduersus catholicos quasi quemdam triumphum haereticorum et miseram et quasi ultimam et foedissimam captiuitatem in his episcopis, qua, damnata pia fide et catholicis episcopis, in eorum se dominium delusionemque tradiderunt metu exilii et ut episcopale nomen apud homines retinere uiderentur, quod utique iam apud Deum post subscriptiones impias non habebant. Sed ideo nominis istius etiam cum omni dedecore quaerebatur auctoritas, ne illis possessiones Ecclesiae tollerentur, quas utinam numquam possedisset Ecclesia ut, apostolico more uiuens, fidem integram inuiolabiliter possideret. Et nunc his talibus non

since divine scripture affirms what is also demonstrated through these contemporary proofs. We have also done this so that you consider this, most pious emperors: how are men guilty if they do not join in the divine sacraments with men such as these, whose everlasting punishments are described in the holy books and whose exemplary punishments are seen in this era?

48. But we ask your admirable benevolence to grant us, in the contemplation of Christ, our God, your tireless patience in listening while we explain, albeit briefly, to what extent impiety has grown.[99] For in the eastern regions and especially in Egypt, the accursed Arians were not content with bishops only falling in with their impious way of thinking and condemning the undiminished faith. When these bishops gave their signatures for the sake of their desires, the Arians expelled them, though they were originally ordained by catholic bishops, into the body of the laity. Afterwards, these same heretics ordained them again as bishops, so that not only did they appear to condemn the catholic faith, but even ordination performed by catholic bishops.[100]

49. Turn your attention to this so-called triumph of the heretics against the catholics, and to the wretched, supposedly final and most abominable captivity of those bishops.[101] After they condemned the pious faith and catholic bishops, they handed themselves over to the dominion and delusion of these men because they were afraid of exile, and so that they might seemingly retain their episcopal title in the view of men. In any case, they no longer had that title in the view of God after they gave their signatures. Yet the authority of that title is sought, even with every disgrace, so that the possessions of the church are not taken from them. Would that the church had never possessed these things, so that living in the apostolic custom it might have inviolably possessed undiminished faith![102] Now it is called

---

99. See above, §§1, 4.

100. See below, §96. Reordination was always anathema in late antiquity, but there was constant tension as to whether sacraments performed by those considered heretics (especially baptism and ordination) were valid to begin with. For example, if an Arian did not consider a Nicene ordination to be valid, then ordaining the cleric in question would be considered his first real ordination, not a reordination. See, e.g., Tilley 2001 for a nuanced view of how attitudes toward this question might shift over a long period of time in North Africa.

101. An allusion to the Old Testament accounts of the Hebrews in Egypt and Babylon, in which the captive Hebrews fell into impious ways (e.g., worshiping idols).

102. See above, §§16, 17, 32, 42; below, §§61, 117, 121.

communicare summa impietas dicitur et hoc sub uobis imperatoribus qui, ut uestrae constitutiones eloquunter, uenerabilis Ecclesiae diuinam sanctimoniam uindicatis (non est autem mirum, si haec tam atrocia eorum commissa, occupati rei publicae prouisionibus, ignoratis).

50. Has eorum impietates execrantes episcopi, qui pro fide poenas exilii perpetiebantur uel qui se in fugam dederunt, licet essent corpore discreti per interualla regionum, tamen spiritu in unum positi per mutuas litteras apostolico uigore decernunt nullo genere talibus episcopis posse communicari, qui fidem illo modo, quo supra retulimus, prodiderunt, nisi si laicam postulauerint communionem, dolentes suis impietatibus.

51. Sed mortuo Constantio patrono haereticorum, Iulianus solus tenuit imperium, ex cuius praecepto omnes episcopi catholici de exiliis

the highest impiety *not* to hold communion with men such as these—and this is said under you emperors who, as your laws proclaim, uphold the divine sanctity of the venerable church! It is, however, no wonder that you do not know such terrible things are committed, since you are occupied with matters of state.

50. The bishops who cursed their impieties and suffered the punishment of exile for the faith, or those who gave themselves to flight, though they were separate in body because of the distances between their locations, nevertheless were arranged in spirit into one body through shared letters.[103] They decided with apostolic force that in no respect was it possible to hold communion with such bishops who betrayed the faith in the way we related above, unless they requested communion as laymen and suffered penance for their impieties.[104]

51. When Constantius, the patron of heretics, died, though, Julian held the empire alone.[105] By his command, all catholic bishops were freed from

---

103. See Col 2:5; Jerome, *Ep.* 5.1; 7.2; 8.1. A few of these letters survive. For example, Liberius of Rome wrote to Lucifer of Cagliari, Eusebius of Vercelli, and Dionysius of Milan while they were in exile (see Hilary of Poitiers, *Adv. Val. Urs.* B 7.2). Eusebius of Vercelli also wrote Gregory of Elvira a very intransigent letter in 360 or 361, which was later quoted in a fragment of Hilary of Poitiers (*Coll. Ant. Par.* A 2.1); for this letter, see Hanson 1988, 508; Flower 2013, 249–50.

104. A common late antique policy, despite the decision of the Council of Alexandria to the contrary. See Tilley 2001; Carola 2005, 73–77. The general reasoning behind this position was that if a layman sinned, a clergyman prayed for him; if a clergyman sinned, there was no one of sufficient authority to pray on his behalf, so he had to be reduced in status. The common argument was taken from 1 Sam 2:25.

105. In late antiquity, starting in the reign of Diocletian (r. 284–305), the Roman Empire frequently had multiple emperors reigning alongside one another. There was often an Augustus or several Augusti, who ruled as emperor, and a Caesar or Caesars, a kind of vice-emperor. Constantius, as Augustus, named his cousin Julian as Caesar in 355 (Ammianus Marcellinus, *Res gest.* 15.8). After successful campaigns in Gaul, Julian took the title Augustus for himself in 360 (20.4) and marched against Constantius (21.5). By 361, Julian had reached Constantinople; Constantius was preparing for war with Persia, but turned his army westward (21.13). He then grew ill and died in Mopsuestia (21.15), a city in southern Anatolia near Tarsus. Julian is best known as the last pagan emperor, who (briefly) ended state sponsorship of Christianity in favor of traditional pagan cults, thus making him an archvillain among late antique Christians. Faustinus and Marcellinus are writing to an audience that was obviously very familiar with Julian's history and reputation and so devote practically no time at all to what was usually a topic of much discussion for late antique Christians.

relaxantur. Solet hoc facere Diuinitas, ut etiam per aduersarios Christianae religioni suae consulat, ut tanto magis, qui cultores sunt Christi, pro fidelibus elaborent.

52. Sed non multo post, Iuliano intercepto, Iouianus efficitur imperator, qui uindicans fidem catholicam dedit calculum episcopis catholicis. Sed illi egregii episcopi, quamquam sub Constantio integram quam uindicauerant fidem haeretica subscriptione damnauerant, uidentes quod imperator pro catholicis episcopis interuenit, iterum se ad confessionem fidei catholicam transtulerunt. Et ubi iam fides et ueneratio Christi est quando, pro terreni imperatoris arbitrio, episcopi nunc ex catholicis fiunt haeretici et idem ipsi ex haereticis ad fidem catholicam reuertuntur?

53. Sed etsi quidam confessores fatigati in ultimo talium se communioni iungendos esse crediderunt, euertentes illa statuta quae prius aduersus eos prophetica et euangelica atque apostolica auctoritate

their exiles.[106] God is accustomed to act this way, so that even through the adversaries of his Christian religion, he sees to it that worshipers of Christ exert themselves for the faithful all the more.[107]

52. Not much later, after Julian was killed, Jovian was made emperor.[108] He upheld the catholic faith and gave his support to catholic bishops. But those notorious bishops, even though[109] under Constantius they had condemned with their heretical signatures the undiminished faith that they had upheld, transferred themselves back to the catholic confession of faith when they saw that the emperor was interceding on behalf of catholic bishops. Now where is the faith and veneration of Christ, when bishops go from being catholics to being heretics and those same bishops turn back from being heretics towards the catholic faith, siding with the judgment of an earthly emperor?

53. Even if certain exhausted confessors[110] believed in the end that they should join themselves in communion with such men, and overturned the decisions against them that they had previously reached with prophetic, evangelic, and apostolic authority,[111] is it not possible that they covered up the truth?[112] Is it not possible that they passed judgment that

---

106. Ammianus Marcellinus, *Res gest.* 22.5.3–4; Rufinus, *Hist. eccl.* 1.27; Socrates, *Hist. eccl.* 3.4; Sozomen, *Hist. eccl.* 5.5; Theodoret, *Hist. eccl.* 3.2. Ammianus claims that Julian's intention was to sow disorder among Christians. Faustinus and Marcellinus do not mention here or elsewhere Lucifer's ordination of Paulinus at Antioch during his exile.

107. That is, since even pagan emperors such as Julian have helped the church, catholic emperors are expected to help the church all the more.

108. Julian died on campaign in Persia in 363 and was replaced by Jovian, a general in the army (Ammianus Marcellinus, *Res gest.* 25.3, 5). Jovian was an important figure among late antique Christians for restoring state sponsorship to Christianity, but he died less than a year later, in 364 (25.10), and was replaced by Valentinian and Valens, two generals and brothers with the army (26.1–2, 4). For Valens, see below, §§66–67.

109. Günther, Simonetti, and Canellis all accept the reading *quamquam* for the *quam* present in the manuscripts.

110. Such as Hilary of Poitiers and Eusebius of Vercelli, who willingly held communion with bishops who had sworn to Arian creeds and then renounced them later.

111. This is the closest Faustinus and Marcellinus come to making reference to the Council of Alexandria in 362 (see above, pp. 8–9).

112. Modern scholars would generally agree with Faustinus and Marcellinus. Most agree that the bishops who swore to Arian creeds knew what they were doing, but a pleasant fiction was adopted at the Council of Alexandria in which they were said to have been deceived (see esp. Battifol 1920, 108–9; Duval 2001, 290–91). Consider,

decreuerant, numquid hoc potest diuinam obruere ueritatem? Numquid hoc potest euangelicis praeiudicare doctrinis? Numquid apostolicas labefactare sententias et illam praesertim Dei uocem dicentis, "Qui perseuerauerit usque in finem, hic saluus erit"?

54. Sed et apostoli Pauli, uasis electionis, a Christo Domino pronuntiati, cuius ad Galatas scribentis haec uerba sunt: "Sed etsi nos aut angelus de caelo euangelizauerit praeterquam euangelizauimus uobis, anathema sit!" Vnde et idem ipse inferius in eadem epistola prosequitur dicens, "Si enim, quae destruxi, haec iterum aedifico, praeuaricatorum me constituo." Confessor utique factus est de Euangeliis, de uocibus prophetarum, de doctrinis apostolorum: quis fidelium dubitet hunc confessionis meritum non habere, si Scripturarum Diuinarum iura subuertens incipiat aedificare quae destruunt Euangelia?

55. An non Scripturae Diuinae impugnantur, quando cum episcopis Filii Dei negatoribus pax ecclesiastica copulatur? Quis est enim qui considerans uim diuinae religionis pacem perfidorum Deo placere confidat, nisi si, ut a patribus decretum est, in laicorum se numerum tradant suae perfidiae dolentes?

56. Sed esto habeant pacem cum infidelibus! In quo tamen offendunt, in quo laedunt imperatores, in quo rem publicam uexant, qui, diuini contemplatione iudicii, huiusmodi pacem respuunt quae sacrilegos recipit, praeuaricatores fidei honorat, fauet hypocritis, despicit ueritatem, Christi

went beyond evangelic doctrines? That they weakened the apostolic decisions, and especially that statement of God, who said, *He who persists up to the end, this man will be saved*?[113]

54. The apostle Paul, too, whose words these are, was declared the *chosen vessel*[114] by Christ, our God; he wrote to the Galatians, *But even if an angel from heaven preaches beyond what we preach to you, let him be anathema.*[115] Furthermore, he follows up on this later in the same letter, saying, *For if I rebuild these things that I have destroyed, I confirm that I am a prevaricator.*[116] At any rate, a confessor is made from the gospels, the voices of the prophets, and the doctrines of the apostles. Who among the faithful would doubt that someone is unworthy of being a confessor, if he should begin to undermine the laws of the divine scriptures and *build* that which the gospels *destroyed*?

55. Are not the divine scriptures assaulted when the church's peace is joined together with bishops who deny the Son of God? For who is there who, when he considers the strength of God's religion, trusts that the peace of liars *is pleasing to God*,[117] unless (as was decided by the fathers) they hand themselves over into the body of laymen, undergoing penance for their deception?

56. But let them have peace with the unfaithful! In what way do they cause offense when in contemplation of God's judgment they spit back peace of this sort? In what way do they harm the emperors? In what way do they trouble the state? This peace that receives the sacrilegious, honors those who prevaricate about the faith, shows favor to hypocrites, looks down on the truth, and establishes the deniers of Christ, the true Son of

---

e.g., Jerome's (*Lucif.* 19) description of how the confessors at the Council of Alexandria first *did* try to remove these bishops from their sees, or how Sulpicius Severus (*Chron.* 2.41–44) states both that the bishops involved were steadfast supporters of the Nicene Creed at Rimini until they were threatened *and* that they were deceived (2.45). On the other hand, Hilary of Poitiers (*Syn.* 91) said that he did not even know what the Nicene Creed was in 356; we should perhaps not take him at his word, though, since he was willing to suffer exile for it only four months later, the gospels alone having explained to him the distinction between *homoousios* and *homoiousios*.

113. Matt 10:22.
114. Acts 9:15.
115. Gal 1:8.
116. Gal 2:18.
117. Rom 8:8.

Dei ueri Filii negatores tamquam dominos Ecclesiae constituit, populum perfidiae labe contaminat, euertit Euangelia?

Hinc rei sumus, hinc, sub nominis uestri auctoritate, patimur persecutiones ab his episcopis qui, pro nutu prioris imperatoris, haeresim uindicantes contra fidem catholicam perorabant. Heu gemitus! Idem episcopi aduersus fideles et catholicae fidei defensores haeretici prius imperatoris decreta praeferebant! Idem et nunc episcopi aduersus fideles et catholicae fidei defensores catholicorum imperatorum iura proponunt!

57. Haec cum dolore omnium uiscerum loquimur deflentes, non quod non sit fidelibus gloriosum sub quolibet pro vero perpeti, sed quia tantus est stupor in saeculo, ut haec illorum tantis inuoluta perfidiis non agnoscatur impietas, ut nemo intellegat quomodo etiam reges aures semper inludunt in uexationem Christianorum et fidelium sacerdotum. Sed, sub uocabulo pacis, impietas tegitur et speciosum nomem unitatis opponitur ad patrocinium perfidorum.

58. Sed bene quod ipse Saluator uirtutem suae pacis exposuit, ne quis simplici pacis uocabulo caperetur et eam quibuscumque saeculi impietatibus copularet, dicens: "Pacem meam relinquo uobis, pacem meam do uobis; non sicut hic mundus dat, ego do uobis." "Pacem suam" a "mundi pace" discreuit. Nam si haec pax Deo grata est quae in Ecclesiam recepit episcopos infideles, quid ergo opus est in persecutionibus aestus perpeti, carcerem sustinere, ire obuiam gladiis atque omnia genera suppliciorum mortisque tolerare, quando quidem post negationem, post perfidiae sacrilegia propter pacem hanc quam Deo placere confidant, securus unusquisque infidelium tamquam inlibatus saluo episcopali honore suscipitur?

59. Vani iam secundum hanc adsertionem et martyres iudicandi sunt! Ad quos enim fructus poenas mortemque ferre maluerunt? Si enim qui metu persecutionis negauerunt Filium Dei non habent poenam, immo potius honorantur, nec martyres coronam passionis sperare debuerunt! Immo potius pendunt supplicia suae temeritatis! Hoc enim necesse est

God, as the lords of the church, contaminates the people with the disgrace of faithlessness and overturns the gospels!

For this we are considered guilty. For this, under the authority of your name, we suffer persecution from these bishops. At the nod of a previous emperor, these bishops spoke at length in affirming heresy against the catholic faith. Alas! Woe! The same bishops earlier preferred the decrees of a heretical emperor[118] against the faithful and the defenders of the catholic faith, and now the same bishops put forth the laws of catholic emperors against the faithful and the defenders of the catholic faith!

57. We say these things with pain in all our heart. We are weeping not because it is inglorious for the faithful to suffer whatever one may for the truth, but because the stupidity in this age is so great that this impiety of theirs, enveloped by so many lies, is not known, and because no one understands how they always toy with even royal ears to vex Christians and faithful priests. Yet their impiety is hidden under the label of "peace," and the specious name of "unity" is set up to protect traitors.

58. It is good, though, that the Savior himself explained the virtue of his peace, lest anyone be taken in by the simple label of "peace" and apply it to any impieties of this era. He says, *I leave behind my peace with you, I give my peace to you; I give it to you not in the way this world gives it.*[119] He distinguishes "his peace" from "the peace of the world." For if this peace that has received unfaithful bishops into the Church is gratifying to God, then what need is there to suffer troubles in persecution, to undergo incarceration, to advance in the way of swords, and to endure all types of punishments and death, when indeed after their denial, after the sacrileges of their treachery on account of this peace that they trust *is pleasing to God*,[120] any of these unfaithful men is received free from care as though he is untarnished and with his episcopal honor preserved?

59. According to this argument, even martyrs should be judged as worthless! I mean, what good did it do them to choose to bear punishments and death? For if those who denied the Son of God because they were afraid of persecution are not punished, then they are instead honored even more, and the martyrs should not have hoped for the crown of suffering. Instead, they are weighing out punishments for their reckless-

---

118. Constantius; Valens may also be meant, although he plays a very small role in the *Libellus precum*.
119. John 14:27.
120. Rom 8:8.

consequatur. Non enim fieri potest ut non, ubi contraria iudicentur. Nonne manifestum est ad quam uocem coartantur uocabulo pacis istius uel quod pronuntiare cogantur, ut si negatores Filii Dei recte in honore corroborantur, credamus martyres tamquam pro sua temeritate puniri?

60. Sed absit! Absit ut hoc admittat conscientia Christiana! Credimus enim Filio Dei pronuntianti: "Qui me negauerit coram hominibus, et ego negabo eum coram Patre meo," et "Qui me confessus fuerit coram hominibus, et ego confitebor eum coram Patre meo."

61. Verumtamen, et in hac causa diuinum iudicium cognoscite prolatum praesentibus documentis, ne quis putaret acceptandam pacem talium episcoporum, etiamsi ad uerae fidei confessionem reuerterentur post subscriptiones impias uel nefarias haereticorum communiones, quibus scientes subcubuerunt, ne aut possessiones Ecclesiae perderent aut honores.

62. Sanctus uir Maximus episcopus, cuius supra meminimus, fidem uindicans rectam consortiumque reprobans haereticorum, ductus est in exilium. In loco eius praeuaricatores ordinant nomine Zosimum, qui et ipse prius quidem catholica uindicabat. Res ista in Neapoli ciuitate Campaniae acta est. Cognoscit hoc sanctus Maximus et, de exilio scribens, dat in eum sententiam non solum episcopali auctoritate sed etiam aemulatione ac uirtute martyrii feruens in gloriam diuinam.

63. Sed post aliquot annos beatus Lucifer, de quarto exilio Romam

ness all the more! For it cannot be that this is not so whenever opposites are considered.[121] Is it not obvious that they are held to this argument in the name of that peace, or that they are compelled to proclaim that if the deniers of Christ, our God, are rightfully made greater in honor, then we should believe that the martyrs are punished as though for their own recklessness?

60. Begone with it! Begone with it, that Christian conscience would accept this! For we believe in the Son of God, who proclaims, *He who denies me in the presence of men, I also shall deny him in my Father's presence,*[122] and *He who has acknowledged me in the presence of men, I also shall acknowledge him in the presence of my father.*[123]

61. Nevertheless, even in this case, recognize God's punishment revealed in contemporary proofs, lest anyone think that the peace of such bishops ought to be accepted—even if those bishops turn back to the confession of the true faith after their impious signatures or unholy communions with the heretics to whom they consciously surrendered, so that they would lose neither the possessions of the church nor their honors.[124]

62. The holy man Bishop Maximus, whom we mentioned above,[125] affirmed the upright faith, rejected the company of heretics, and was exiled. In his place, the prevaricators ordained a man named Zosimus.[126] Indeed, he himself also previously upheld catholic interests. This affair took place in Naples, a city of Campania. Holy Maximus knew this and wrote from exile. He passed judgment against him not only by his episcopal authority but also burning with the zeal and virtue of a martyr.[127]

63. Now, after a few years, blessed Lucifer proceeded toward Rome

---

121. Previous scholars have considered this passage to be corrupted, but Canellis retains the manuscript reading. The sense is obscure, but it seems to mean that if those who avoided martyrdom are praised all the more, then it should logically follow (according to Faustinus and Marcellinus) that those who suffered martyrdom (i.e., their "recklessness") are punished all the more. The phrase "whenever opposites are considered" suggests that if two opposites are compared, anything said about one implies the opposite about the other.

122. Matt 10:33.

123. Matt 10:32.

124. See above, §§16, 17, 32, 42, 49; below, §§117, 121.

125. See above, §25.

126. *PCBE* 2.2 (Zosimus 2). See above, §25 and n. 60, for the appearance of these two bishops in the Gesta episcoporum Neapolitanorum.

127. See Rom 12:11.

pergens, ingressus est Neapolim, Campaniae, ut diximus, ciuitatem; ad quem Zosimus uenire temptauit illa forte fiducia qua scilicet iam de impietate correxisse uidebatur. Sed hunc confessor Lucifer suscipere noluit non ignorans quae gesserat, immo et Sancti Spiritus feruore episcopi et martyris Maximi sententiam robustius exequitur dicens quod episcopatum ipsum quem sibi ut adulter uindicat spiritalis, animaduertentis Dei iudicio non habebit, hic quoque sentiet poenam suae impietatis.

64. Sed non post multum temporis idem Zosimus cum in coetu plebis uult exsequi sacerdotis officia, inter ipsa uerba sacerdotalia eius lingua protenditur nec ualet eam reuocare intra oris capacitatem, eo quod contra modum naturae extra os penderet ut boui anhelo. Sed ut uidit se linguae officium perdidisse egreditur basilica et, res mira!, foris iterum in officium lingua reuocata est. Et primum quidem non intelligitur compleri in eum sententiam martyris et confessoris; sed, cum hoc totiens patitur quotiens et basilicam diuersis diebus temptauit intrare, ipse postremo recognouit ob hoc sibi linguam inter pontificii sollemnia uerba denegari ut sanctorum episcoporum in eum rite prolata sententia probaretur. Denique cessit episcopatum ut ei lingua quae cesserat redderetur.

65. Non res antiquas referimus, quae solent quadam ratione in dubium uenire: uiuunt adhuc praesentia ista documenta! Nam et Zosimus hodi-

from his fourth exile.[128] He entered Naples, a city of Campania, as we said. Zosimus tried to approach him, perhaps with some assurance that he certainly by then appeared to have corrected his impiety. But the confessor Lucifer did not wish to receive him, as he was not ignorant of what he had done. Rather, with the fervor of the Holy Spirit, he firmly followed the judgment of the bishop and martyr Maximus and said that in the judgment of the watchful God, Zosimus would not have that episcopate which he claimed as a spiritual adulterer. This man would also know the punishment for his impiety.

64. Not much later, when that same Zosimus wished to carry out a priest's duties in a gathering of the people, in the course of his priestly remarks his tongue stretched out and he lost the ability to call it back into his mouth.[129] So it hung outside his mouth in an unnatural manner, like a panting cow's. Now, as he saw that he had lost the use of his tongue, he went out from the basilica, and once he was outside—how astonishing!—his tongue was called back into service. At first, certainly, he did not understand that the judgment of the martyr and of the confessor[130] was being fulfilled against him. But when he suffered this on various days whenever he tried to enter the basilica, he finally recognized from this that his tongue was being denied to him during his solemn remarks as a high priest so that the judgment of the holy bishops (which was rightfully brought forth against him) would be proven. In the end, he left the episcopate, with the result that his tongue, which had left him, was returned to him.[131]

65. We are not reporting bygone matters, which customarily come into doubt for whatever reason; these present-day proofs still live![132] For

---

128. Shuve (2014, 257) suggests that Lucifer may have been trying to convince Liberius to reconsider his support of the clemency offered at the Council of Alexandria, but Liberius's own capitulation to Constantius makes it unlikely that Lucifer had much interest in Liberius, or that Liberius had much interest in anything but clemency; Shuve's second suggestion, that Lucifer was heading to Rome to explicitly condemn Liberius, is much more likely, particularly given Lucifer's prickly personality.

129. See above, §§41–42. Canellis (2006, 169n3) points out that without the use of his tongue, Zosimus would be unable to perform his priestly duties and in effect would no longer be a priest.

130. Maximus and Lucifer, respectively.

131. Note the twin uses of *cessit* and *cesserat*.

132. See above, §§41, 44; below, §93. Interestingly, however, Faustinus and Marcellinus report no Luciferian communities in Naples or Campania; see Perez Mas

eque in corpore est, usum iam linguae non amittens, posteaquam maluit cum amissione episcopatus uiuere dolens suis impietatibus. Nonne etiam de similibus praeiudicatum est nihil illis prodesse, quod quasi sub correctione episcopi esse perseuerant? Non enim correctio est ista, sed inlusio prout sunt imperatorum tempora fidem uertere.

66. Haec, haec res decepit et Valentem imperatorem, cum in haereticis uidet constantiam defensionis, in istis autem egregiis catholicis inconstantiam fidei. Nam utique probatur illi quod hi qui se catholicos adserebant subscripsissent prius cum haereticis, damnantes quam primum defenderant fidem. Et dicebant haeretici: "Si nostra fides mala est, quare sub Constantio pro ipsa subscriptum est ab his, qui nunc se catholicos dicunt hanc fidem uindicantes, quam cum primum defenderent conuicti rationibus sub Constantio damnauerunt?" His rebus Valens motus, ignorans uirtutem uerae fidei et constantiam cum inconstantia conferens, impietatem haereticorum cum quadam iustitia uindicabat.

67. Et tacemus quod, etiam sub Valente, iterum se quidam haereticis tradiderunt, quos nunc nihilominus uidemus inter catholicos nominari. Inde est unde etiam plebes haereticorum ad fidem impiam roboratae sunt, dum haeretici in malo perseuerant et, qui putantur catholici, de bono rece-

Zosimus is even alive today and no longer lacks the use of his tongue, after he chose to live with the loss of the episcopate[133] and do penance for his impieties. Concerning bishops like him, was it not previously judged that it does them no good to persist in being bishops as though they were rehabilitated? For it is not rehabilitation, but mockery, to change their faith in accordance with the reigns of the emperors.

66. *This* matter deceived the emperor Valens as well, when he saw the constancy of defense among the heretics but the inconstancy of faith among those notorious "catholics."[134] For surely it was proven to him that those who asserted they were catholics had previously signed along with the heretics and cursed that faith which they had at first defended. And the heretics said, "If our faith is wicked, why did these men sign on behalf of it under Constantius? They now say that they are catholics and affirm this faith which—though they defended it at first—they condemned under Constantius when they were refuted by our arguments." Valens, stirred by these things, did not know the virtue of the true faith. He compared constancy with inconstancy[135] and protected the impiety of the heretics with some justification.

67. We are saying nothing as to how, even under Valens, certain men handed themselves over the heretics again, men whom we nevertheless now see named among the catholics. This is the reason that even commoners under heretics are fortified in their impious faith while the heretics persevere in evil, and those who are considered catholics fall back from

---

2008, 336. It is possible that the Luciferians that Ambrose (*Exc.* 1.27, 47) reports his brother Satyrus encountering following a shipwreck somewhere between North Africa and Milan were in Campania, but this is just one of many possible locations for the shipwreck (McLynn [1994, 70], for example, assumes that Satytus shipwrecked on Sardinia itself).

133. Note the parallel use of *amittens* and *amissione*.

134. Valens ruled as Augustus from 364–378 in the East alongside his older brother Valentinian, who ruled as Augustus from 364–375 in the West. When Valens died in battle in 378 (Ammianus Marcellinus, *Res gest.* 31.13), Valentinian's successor (his son Gratian) made Theodosius, the addressee of the *Libellus precum*, Augustus in the East. Valentinian supported the Nicene party, and he does not appear in any Luciferian writing. Valens supported the Arian party, but with less vigor and success than Constantius did, and plays a relatively minor role in the *Libellus precum* as an Arian persecutor when compared to Constantius.

135. The play on words in this passage resumes in earnest with *Constantio*, *constantiam*, and *inconstantiam*.

dunt aliquotiens subcumbentes haereticis. Qua enim auctoritate hi tales episcopi contra haeresum praedicant cui se subscripsisse negare non possunt? Et qua fiducia catholicam fidem plebi suadere nitantur, cum constet quod eam impiis subscriptionibus reprobauerint?

68. Videtisne etiam uestris temporibus, sed, ut credimus, ignorantibus uobis, fidem quidem piam, atque utinam uel uere, sed etsi uere cum quadam tamen iniustitia uindicari, cum per indignos episcopos uindicatur in afflictionem piam fidem defendentium sacerdotum et in perniciem fidelium laicorum? Sed nefas putatur tot praeuaricatores deicere et conscientem ad iniustitiam turbam reprobare. Et ubi est iustitia uerae religionis, si addicenda est impiae multitudini et hoc sub piissimis et religiosissimis imperatoribus?

69. Non sic in diluuio iudicatum est ut turba uinceret infidelium, sed et Noe ille iustissimus ideo magis Deo placuit quod, in illo excidio mundi, solus iustus inuentus est. Nihilominus et in Sodoma et Gomorra graues poenas dedit impia multitudo, unde hospitalissimus Loth ob iustitiam liberatus est cum duabus tantummodo filiabus. Sed nec Dei aemulator Helias, qui fuit singularis, obtritus est, cum aduersus illum quadringenti quinquaginta falsi sacerdotes niterentur, sed omnis turba illa impia sacerdotum luit poenas sub unius fidelis manu et hoc spectante rege Achab, qui falsos sacerdotes impie uindicabat.

70. Sed nec Iehu rex Israhel detulit impiae multitudini sacerdotum; denique omnes falsos sacerdotes, qui sub rege Achab fuerant in culmine, cum religiosa fraude in domum religionis impiae conuocasset quasi eos post ritus religionis remuneraturus, iussit occidi, ita ut nemo de his super-

good, time and again yielding to the heretics. For by what authority do bishops like these warn against a heresy to which they cannot deny that they themselves subscribed? With what trust do they strive to promote the catholic faith to the people, when it so happens that they rejected it with their impious signatures?

68. Do you see? Even in your own times (although we believe that you are unaware of this), the pious faith indeed is supported (and would that it were actually truly supported!)—but even if it is truly supported, it is nevertheless supported with a certain injustice, since it is supported through unworthy bishops, by the suffering of those priests who defend the pious faith, and by the ruin of faithful laymen. But it is considered unholy to cast out so many prevaricators and to reject a host of men conscious of their injustice. Where is the justice of true religion if it must be yielded to an impious multitude—and this under the most pious and most religious emperors?

69. Thus it was not judged in the case of the flood that the host of unfaithful men would be victorious. Instead, that exceedingly just man, Noah, was more pleasing to God, because in that destruction of the world he was the only just man found.[136] Nevertheless, the impious multitude in Sodom and Gomorrah also faced serious punishments, whereas the most hospitable Lot, on account of his justice, was spared with only two of his daughters.[137] The emulator of God, Elijah,[138] who was by himself, was also not overwhelmed when 450 false priests strove against him. Instead, that whole impious host of priests faced its punishment under the hand of one faithful man while King Ahab was watching, a man who was impiously protecting the false priests.[139]

70. Nor did the king of Israel, Jehu, give in to the impious multitude of priests. In short, he gathered all the false priests who had been elevated under King Ahab into the house of their impious religion by religious deception, acting like he was going to reward them following their religion's rites. Then he ordered them to be cut down so that not one of them would survive.[140]

---

136. See Gen 6–9. This interpretation of Noah's ark flatly contradicts that of Jerome (*Lucif.* 22) but closely matches the interpretation offered by Gregory of Elvira; see above, pp. 38–39.
137. See Gen 18:16–19:29.
138. See Pseudo-Athanasius, *Ep.* 51.6.
139. See 1 Kgs 18:16–46.
140. See 2 Kgs 10:18–28.

esset. Et legimus quia ob hoc factum ita placuit Domino ut "filii eiusdem regis quarta progenie sederent in throno Israel." Sunt et alia multa simillima exempla.

71. Quae quidem nos non ideo dicimus quasi qui uelimus alicuius sanguinem fundi: absit hoc a uotis nostris! Hoc enim qui nunc fieri cupit, exorbitat a legibus Christianis. Factum est quidem tunc, quia et illo tempore id ipsum diuinia lege fieri licebat, quando adhuc totum corporaliter agebatur, donec cresceret instructio spiritalis. Sed non, quia quidem nunc non licet bonis et fidelibus falsorum sacerdotum sanguinem cupere, idcirco fideles falsis sacerdotibus addicendi sunt, ita ut grauissimis eorum persecutionibus affligantur.

72. Falsum videatur quod dicimus, si non, uariis in locis, ecclesiae fidelium sacerdotum alibi inuasae et alibi destructae sunt, si non interpellationibus illorum, sancti quique comprehensi et diu ad iniurias inclusi et postremo missi sunt in exilium, si non etiam et ceteri quidam in carcere, alii autem tractu et caede mulcati animas reddiderunt, ob nullam aliam causam quam quia, metu diuini iudicii, nolebant communicare cum perfidis uel sociiss perfidorum.

73. In Hispania, Vincentius presbyter, uerae fidei antistes, quas non atrocitates praeuaricatorum passus est eo quod nollet esse socius impiae praeuaricationis illorum, eo quod beatissimo Gregorio communicaret, illi Gregorio, cuius supra, ut potuimus, fidem uirtutemque retulimus? Contra quem, primum, interpellauerunt Baeticae prouinciae consularem tunc demum sub specie intercessionis postulatae ex aliis locis plebeia colligitur

And we read that because of this deed, he was pleasing to God in such a way that *the sons* of this same king, *to the fourth generation,* were seated *on the throne of Israel.*[141] There are also many other very similar examples.

71. Naturally, we are not saying these things because we are the sort of men who want anyone's blood to be spilled; let that be far from our prayers! For whoever wishes this to occur has deviated from Christian laws. It happened back then, naturally, because at that time it was also allowed under divine law. That was when everything was still done according to the body, while spiritual instruction was developing.[142] But certainly the faithful should not be condemned by false priests in such a way that they are assaulted by their severest persecution just because it is not now permitted for the good and faithful to wish for the blood of false priests.[143]

72. What we say would seem false if certain churches of faithful priests were not attacked in some places and destroyed in others; if due to the appeals of those men, certain holy men were not arrested and confined unjustly for a long time and later sent into exile; and if, too, some were not imprisoned and others did not give up their lives, wounded by being dragged and cut— for no other reason than because they were afraid of God's judgment and did not wish to hold communion with traitors or their allies.

73. In Spain, what cruelties did the presbyter Vincentius,[144] a priest of the true faith, not suffer at the hands of prevaricators because he did not wish to be an ally of their impious prevarication? Because he held communion with the most blessed Gregory, that Gregory whose faith and virtue we related above to the best of our ability?[145]

First, they appealed against him to the consular of the province of Baetica.[146] Then, under the pretense that mediation had been requested, a

---

141. 2 Kgs 10:30.

142. See Rom 7:7, 14.

143. In other words, bloodshed in the name of God was permitted under the Old Testament, but not following the coming of Christ; now the Luciferians are being punished for their pious unwillingness to draw blood.

144. Otherwise unknown.

145. See above, §§33–40, esp. §33. If this statement is true, it is possible that Vincentius faced persecution for holding communion with Gregory while Gregory himself escaped similar persecution because of his reputation. It is also possible— though more speculative—that Vincentius was persecuted for holding communion with Gregory and *not*, by implication, with other bishops (perhaps even his own?).

146. Canellis (2006, 176–77) suggests that this may be Caelestinus, who was Consularis Baeticae in 357, but the internal chronology of the document suggests that the

multitudo et irruunt die dominica in ecclesia et Vincentium quidem non inueniunt, eo quod ipse, praemonitus, etiam populo praedixerat ne illo die procederent quando cum caede ueniebant. Hoc enim putauit fieri melius, si irae locum daret.

74. Sed illi, qui ad caedem parati uenerant, ne sine causa furor illorum uenisse putaretur, certa Christo Deo deuota ministeria quae illic inuenta sunt ita fustibus eliserunt, ut non multo post expirarent. Sed, quia plebs sancta Vincentii presbyteri magis eos execrabantur post illas eorum caedes quae in dominico factae sunt, egregii episcopi, ut plebs uniuersa terreretur, ab ipsis principalibus incipiunt. Denique postulant exhibitionem decurionum ciuitatis illius et ut includantur in carcerem. Ex quibus unus principalis patriae suae, eo quod fidem firmiter ut fidelis in Deo retineret execrans labem praeuaricationis, inter eos et ipse catenatus fame frigore necatus est, cum fletu et gemitu illius prouinciae quae honestam uitam eius optime nouerat.

75. Egregii et catholici episcopi Luciosus et Hyginus huius crudelitatis auctores sunt!

multitude of commoners was gathered from various places. On the Lord's day they rushed into the church, yet they did not find Vincentius, because he had been forewarned. He had also told the people beforehand that they should not come out on that day since others were coming intent on violence, and he thought it would be better if he let them have the place in their anger.

74. But those who had come prepared for violence, so that no one would think that their fury had come without reason, used clubs to strike some attendants devoted to Christ, our God, whom they found there; not much later, the attendants died died. Yet because the holy people of the presbyter Vincentius cursed them even more after these violent acts of theirs—which were done in a church[147]—the notorious bishops, in order to frighten all the people, started with their leaders. Accordingly, they demanded that the decurions of that city make an appearance so that they might confine them in jail.[148] Because one of these, a leader of his country, firmly kept the faith like one faithful to God and cursed the disgrace of prevarication, he was put in chains in their midst and died from hunger and the cold. The province that had known his upright life best wept and lamented this.

75. The notorious "catholic" bishops Luciosus and Hyginus are the authors of this cruelty![149]

---

consular in question was in office sometime after 357. Hosius, further, would still be bishop of Cordoba in 357, not Hyginus (see below, §75). The only other known consular governor of Baetica from the period is Taunacius Isfalangius (Ammianus Marcellinus, *Res gest.* 28.1.26), but he is probably too early, as he served under Valentinian I.

147. For a contemporary use of *dominicum* as "church," see, e.g., Rufinus, *Hist. eccl.* 1.3.

148. Every Roman city was led by a council composed of decurions, a sort of petty nobility who were responsible for maintaining their cities, constructing civic buildings, etc. In late antiquity, being a decurion became more and more of a financial burden, and many consciously avoided the "honor"; bishops were exempt from being made decurions, and as such some men actively sought the episcopacy for the financial relief it afforded. See Loseby 2009, 141–48.

149. Now the sarcastic *egregii* is matched with a sarcastic *catholici*. Luciosus and Hyginus provide an interesting link between the earlier persecutions of Nicene Christians and the later persecution of Luciferians. Faustinus and Marcellinus do not explicitly state that Vincentius preached in Baetica, but Luciosus and Hyginus appealed to the governor of that province above (above, §73), so it is likely the case. In the late fourth century, Luciosos was bishop of an unknown see, but Hyginus was the bishop of Cordoba—Hosius's see in the 350s—and eventually a staunch opponent of Priscillian and his followers Instantius and Salvianus (Chadwick 1976, 6, 25; Van Dam

Et interea inuaserunt quidem basilicam, sed fidem plebis inuadere non potuerunt. Denique, alibi in agello eadem plebs basilicam sibi ecclesiae fabricauit, ad quam cum sancto Vincentio conueniret. Sed Satanas, qui nusquam patitur Christum pie coli, inflammat eos et iterum deposita postulatione ex diuersis urbibus decurionum ac plebeia multitudo colligitur.

76. Simul etiam et presbyteri eius ad locum ueniunt, ecclesiae illius ianuas confringunt diripientes inde quicquid ad sacra ecclesiae ministeria pertinebat, et postremo, quod horroris est dicere, ad cumulum perpetrati sacrilegii, ipsum altare Dei de dominico sublatum in templo sub pedibus idoli posuerunt!

Haec utique illi faciunt qui, paenitentes de impia subscriptione, suscepti sunt ad catholicam disciplinam propter bonum pacis et unitatis! Quid grauius gentilis cultor idolorum faceret, si haberet licentiam Ecclesiam persequendi?

77. Sed apud Triueros, Bonosus presbyter inclusus intestatus ac diu

2. Faustinus and Marcellinus, *Petition of Requests* — 125

Meanwhile, they took hold of the basilica, but they were not able to take hold of the faith of the people. Then these same people built a basilica for a church for themselves in some other little field, where they assembled together with holy Vincentius. But Satan, who does not allow Christ to be worshiped reverently anywhere, fired the others up. Again, after a request was delivered, a multitude of decurions and common people were gathered from various cities.

76. At the same time, Satan's presbyters came to the place. They broke apart the doors of that church and seized from it whatever pertained to the church's holy ministry.[150] In the end—something which is horrifying to say—at the height of the sacrileges which they perpetrated, they took the altar of God from the church[151] and placed it at the feet of an idol in a temple![152]

Those men surely did these things, those men who, after they showed repentance for their impious signatures, were admitted to the catholic denomination for the sake of peace and unity. What more grievous thing would a pagan worshiper of idols do, if he could freely persecute the church?

77. Now, in Trier the presbyter Bonosus,[153] an old man, was locked up

---

1992, 94; Escribano 2005, 139). Both Cordoba and Gregory's see of Elvira were within Baetica. Furthermore, Luciosus was likewise known as an opponent of Priscillianism; he read the charges against Priscillian and his associates at the Council of Zaragoza in 379 or 380 (Chadwick 1976, 13). Priscillian's other major opponent at the council was Hydatius of Merida, who succeeded Florentius as bishop there (see above, §44). Moreover, the first charge against Priscillian and his associates was that of Sabellianism, an accusation made against Gregory of Elvira and the Luciferians as well (Escribano 2005, 142–46; see above, pp. 16–19). The parallels between these sees and these allied bishops make it likely that the circle of bishops including Hosius of Cordoba and Florentius of Merida evolved into a circle of bishops that included Hyginus of Cordoba, Hydatius of Merida, and Luciosus, who set themselves in opposition to Priscillian and his associates *and* the Luciferians. (See Escribano 2005, 142, for a possible connection between another strident anti-Priscillianist, Ithacius, and Lisbon.) It remains unclear, however, why Gregory is absent from this narrative; Vincentius is clearly meant to parallel the role of Gregory in this later narrative, but the Luciferians never explain or even note Gregory's death (if he was dead; Jerome [*Vir. ill.* 105] speaks of Gregory as though he were alive in the early 390s).

150. In other words, the Eucharist.
151. For this use of *dominicum* as "church," see above, n. 147.
152. See above, §29, in which the Luciferians compare Nicene bishops swearing to Arian creeds to sacrificing before an idol, and Faustinus, *Trin.* 1.
153. Otherwise unknown. Perez Mas (2008, 334–35) suggests that this Bonosus is to be identified with the presbyter of Paulinus, Bonosus, who was bishop of

poenas senex dedit propter obseruantiam intaminatae fidei illius pro qua et inclytus Paulinus eiusdem ciuitatis episcopus in exilio martyr animam dedit.

In ipsa quoque urbe Roma quam graues persecutiones fidelibus inlatae sunt! Vbi et beatus Aurelius episcopus communicans beatissimo Gregorio, aliquotiens afflictus est; sed hic uir sanctus, licet sit saepenumero afflictus, tamen propria accersione requieuit.

78. In Macarium uero presbyterum multa impiorum commissa sunt. Hic erat in eadem urbe Roma presbyter mirae continentiae, non uino stomachum releuans, non carnis esculentia corpus curans, sed oleo solo escas asperiores mitigans, ieiuniis et orationibus uacans. Sane, pro merito fidei et abstinentia, habebat gratiam sancti Spiritus in hoc ut de obsessis corporibus eiceret daemonia. Ideo uitam eius meritumque memorauimus ut tanto magis impii iudicentur hi qui tales uiuere non sinunt in Romano imperio.

even though he had not been convicted of anything, and for a long time he was punished for heeding that uncontaminated faith for which the famous Paulinus, bishop of the same city, gave his life as a martyr in exile.[154]

In the very city of Rome as well, what severe persecution was brought against the faithful! It was here that even the blessed bishop Aurelius, who held communion with the most blessed Gregory, was assaulted several times![155] But this holy man, though he was assaulted again and again, nevertheless went to his rest by his own summons.

78. Many impious acts indeed were committed against the presbyter Macarius.[156] He was a presbyter of remarkable ascetic self-discipline in the same city, Rome. He did not comfort his stomach with wine, nor nourish his body by eating meat, but mellowed his coarser dishes with oil alone and devoted himself to fasting and prayer.[157] Because of the worthiness of his faith and his abstention, he certainly had the grace of the Holy Spirit: he would throw demons out of possessed bodies. For this reason, we commemorate his life and his worthiness, so that those who do not permit such men to live in the Roman Empire will be considered all the more impious.

Trier from 360–373 and a staunch Nicene supporter; the Luciferians fictitiously connect themselves to this Bonosus in order to seem more connected to other Nicene Christians, thus explaining their vagueness about Bonosus. This identification seems unlikely, however. The Luciferians describe Bonosus as a presbyter, never as a bishop, and state that he died as "an old man" while rhetorically emphasizing his age by placing it between the words *poenas* and *dedit*. It furthermore seems unlikely that the bishop of Trier (an imperial capital) would have died of persecution in 373, when the Nicene faction was ascendant and supported by the Western emperor Valentinian. It seems more likely that a rigorist Nicene community led by a presbyter refused to hold communion with the bishop of Trier (perhaps Bonosus the bishop's successor, Veteranius/Britonius) because that bishop would have been in communion with a variety of other bishops such as Hilary of Poitiers whose communion the Luciferians considered stained by their leniency toward prevaricators. See above, §73, in which the Luciferians are also led by a presbyter and not a bishop, and below, §103, where their community at Eleutheropolis has no clergy mentioned.

154. On Paulinus, see above, n. 48, and once again note how brief the Luciferian comments on events at Trier are. The Luciferians here draw a direct connection between the exile of Paulinus under Constantius and the persecution of Bonosus.

155. *PCBE* 2.1 (Aurelius 1); otherwise unknown. Shuve (2014, 257) suggests that he could have been ordained by Lucifer (see above, §66), and this is not unlikely.

156. *PCBE* 2.2 (Macarius 1); otherwise unknown.

157. See below, §94.

79. Eodem tempore grauis aduersum nostros persecutio inhorruerat, infestante Damaso egregio archiepiscopo, ita ut fidelibus sacerdotibus per diem sacros plebis coetus ad deseruiendum Christo Deo conuocare libere non liceret. Sed quia pro conditione rerum quolibet tempore uel clam salutis nostrae sacramenta facienda sunt, idem sanctus presbyter Macarius dat uigilias, in quadam domo conuocans fraternitatem, ut, uel noctu, diuinis lectionibus fidem plebs sancta roboraret.

80. Sed diabolus, qui fauet impiis, quia et impii fauent diabolo, nec in occulto patitur diuina sacramenta celebrari. Denique tendunt insidias clerici Damasi et, ubi cognouerunt quod sacras uigilias celebrat cum plebe

79. At that time, a severe persecution had risen up against us. Damasus, the notorious archbishop, was plaguing us.[158] It was not permitted for faithful priests to freely call together holy gatherings of the people during the day in devotion to Christ, our God. But since the sacraments of our salvation had to be done at any time whatsoever,[159] even in secret, owing to the state of affairs, the presbyter Macarius set up vigils by calling together the brotherhood in a certain house, so that even at night the holy people might strengthen their faith with divine readings.[160]

80. But the devil, who favors the impious (because the impious also favor the devil), did not let the divine sacraments be celebrated even in secret.[161] In the end, the clerics of Damasus laid an ambush.[162] When

---

158. *PCBE* 2.1 (Damasus); in general, Trout (2015) offers translations of Damasus's poetry and commentary. Damasus had been a deacon of his predecessor, Liberius of Rome, but when Liberius was exiled, Damasus remained in Rome and was loyal to Felix, Liberius's Arian replacement, until Liberius's return. In 366, upon Liberius's death, this unhappy memory remained and prompted bitter, bloody struggles between partisans of Damasus and those of another, Ursinus. A tendentious account entitled Quae gesta sunt inter Liberium et Felicem episcopos (the first document in the *Collectio Avellana*) recounts the events from the perspective of a supporter of Ursinus. It was not penned by the Luciferians (contra Green 1971; Brent 1995, 382; McLynn 1994, 56): its account of Liberius's return to Rome is quite positive (while Faustinus and Marcellinus omit Liberius's name from their accounts entirely), including Liberius's leniency toward *periuri* (in stark contrast to the Luciferians's hard line against *praevaricatores*), and the Luciferians mention two bishops of Rome of their own, Aurelius (§77 above) and Ephesius (§84 below) while Ursinus was alive into the 370s. The Quae gesta sunt also includes sixth-century material (see Blair-Dixon 2007, 71–72). During Damasus's contentious episcopacy, he was frequently in conflict with followers of Ursinus as well as others; one of his most prominent supporters was a young Jerome, who was probably forced by opponents of Damasus to leave Rome following Damasus's death (see Kelly 1975, 111–15). This reference to Damasus establishes the *terminus ante quem* for the petition; Damasus died in December 384 but is here treated as though he were alive. The first-person voice used in this narrative suggests that Faustinus and/or Marcellinus may be Roman or at least have been in Rome at the time. See below, §107, which suggests that one or both of them accompanied Ephesius from Rome to Eleutheropolis.

159. That is, it did not matter to the Luciferians whether their services were held by day or night.

160. See Maier 2005 on the various methods that different minority Christian communities used to avoid persecution, including secret meetings in households.

161. The Luciferians here draw a very close equivalence between Damasus and Satan without explicitly stating such.

162. Trout (2015, 8) writes that Macarius was "presumably earmarked as a

presbyter Macarius, irruunt cum officialibus in illam domum et plebem dissipant non resistentem ipsumque presbyterum comprehensum non iam ducere dignantur sed per silices trahunt, ita ut in coxa eius perniciosum uulnus fieret, atque alio die sistunt eum ante iudicem ut magni criminis reum.

81. Cui quidem iudex, ueluti sub imperiali rescripto et minis extorquere contendit ut cum Damaso conueniat. Sed presbyter, memor diuini iudicii, praesentem iudicem non timens reppulit perfidi communionem atque ideo datur in exilium et, cum est apud Ostiam, atrocitate illius uulneris moritur.

82. Cuius quidem tanta fuit sanctitas ut eum etiam episcopus loci illius nomine Florentius, communicans Damaso, cum quadam ueneratione suspexerit. Namque cum in quodam uetusto monumento eum fratres sepelissent, non est passus idem Florentius iacere eum illic ubi indigna sepultura uideretur, sed transfert eum inde et sepelit in basilica martyris Asterii, ubi in loco presbyterii qui [est] iuxta sepulturam. Hoc pio

they knew that the presbyter Macarius was celebrating holy vigils with the people, they rushed into that house with officials[163] and scattered the people, who were not resisting. At that point, they did not think it was fitting to arrest and lead away the presbyter; instead, they dragged him through the rocks, causing a very serious wound to his hip, and on another day, they made him stand before a judge as though he were guilty of a great crime.

81. Indeed, the judge, as though under an imperial rescript, tried threatening him to make him hold communion with Damasus.[164] But the presbyter, mindful of God's judgment and unafraid of a judge in the present,[165] rejected communion with a traitor and for that reason was sent into exile. When he was at Ostia, he was killed by the severity of his wound.

82. His holiness was in fact so great that even the bishop of that place, a man named Florentius[166] who held communion with Damasus, looked up to him with a certain veneration. For after the brethren had buried Macarius in some ancient monument,[167] that same Florentius did not allow him to lie there, where his burial seemed unworthy. Instead, he relocated him from there and buried him in the basilica of the martyr Asterius, where he is in a spot of the presbyterium next to the grave [of Asterius].[168]

Ursinian," but it may be better to simply see Damasus's activities in Rome as a reaction against a wide variety of Christian communities outside his sphere of influence (Luciferians, Ursinians, Novatians, Donatists, Montanists, etc.) than to assume he conflated the Luciferians with others among his enemies (see Sághy 2000 and above, n. 158).

163. Specifically, Damasus had the support of the civic officials in Rome. See below, §96.

164. Other courtroom scenes occur above, §§33–39, and below, §§84–85.

165. See above, §38.

166. *PCBE* 2.1 (Florentius 3). He had been ordained by Damasus.

167. Late antique funerary inscriptions forbidding the reuse of tombs demonstrate that the practice must have been somewhat common; doubtless this is why Faustinus and Marcellinus specify that the tomb was *vetusto*. See Rebillard 2009, 35–56.

168. See above, p. 38. The manuscript tradition here is very corrupt; see Canellis 2006, 186–87n1. Günther and Simonetti have "ubi in loco presbyterii quiescit iusta sepultura," "where in a place of the presbyterium, he lies in a just grave." In any case, the connection to Asterius is paramount. Asterius was a third-century martyr who, like Macarius, was given an improper burial that was later rectified by pious Christians; his account appears in the Acta Sancti Callisti papae martyris Romae. The identification of the basilica of Asterius at Ostia is unknown. For burials in basilicas at Ostia in general, see Luiz Torres 2008, 92. Sághy (2012, 253) connects this passage to

suo obsequio, in quantum poterat, Damasi scelus a se facere contendebat alienum.

83. Aduertat tranquillitas uestra: si haec fieri uultis in Romano imperio aduersus sanctos et fideles ab his qui praeuaricatores sunt, nonne metus est ne sanguis fidelium Romanum grauet imperium? Nam idem Damasus accepta auctoritate regali etiam alios catholicos presbyteros nec non et laicos insecutus misit in exilium, perorans hoc ipsum per gentiles scolasticos, fauentibus sibi iudicibus, cum utique uestrae constitutiones aduersus haereticos decretae sint, non aduersus catholicos, et tales catholicos, qui fidem integram nec sub haereticis imperatoribus reliquerunt, et quidem grauia multa perpessi!

84. Sed et nuper temptauit grauiter persequi beatissimum Ephesium episcopum sanctae fidei aemulatione feruentem, ordinatum intaminatae plebi Romanae a constantissimo episcopo Taorgio et ipso inlibatae fidei uiro, sub inuidia falsi impositi cognomenti per suos defensores interpellans iudicem Bassum quasi aduersum "Luciferianos."

85. Sed Bassus, olim catholicam fidem uenerans, sciebat in Lucifero nullam haereseos fuisse prauitatem, quippe quem et bene nouerat pro fide catholica decem annos exilia fuisse perpessum et pro constantia suae

By this pious favor of his, he strove to distance himself from Damasus's crime inasmuch as he was able.

83. Let your tranquility give thought to this: if you want these things to be done in the Roman Empire against the holy and faithful by prevaricators, aren't you afraid that the blood of the faithful might burden the Roman Empire? In fact, that same Damasus, once he received royal authority,[169] persecuted other catholic presbyters and laymen and sent them into exile. He pled this very matter through pagan lawyers to judges favorable to him. Surely, though, your laws were decreed against heretics, not against catholics—especially catholics who did not relinquish the undiminished faith under the heretic emperors, and who indeed have endured many enormities!

84. Damasus also recently attempted to cruelly persecute the most blessed Ephesius, a bishop burning with zeal for the holy faith.[170] He was ordained for the uncontaminated Roman people by the most constant bishop, Taorgius,[171] himself also a man of undiminished faith. Through his officials, Damasus appealed to the judge, Bassus,[172] as though against "Luciferians"—with malice intended by this falsely imposed nickname.[173]

85. But Bassus, who had long respected the catholic faith, knew that there had been no depravity of heresy in Lucifer. Naturally, he had known well that Lucifer had suffered exiles for ten years on behalf of the catholic faith.[174] In accordance with the constancy of his own integrity, he rejected

---

other examples of a growing general fourth-century practice of relocating bodies of saints to new cult sites within churches.

169. It is clear from what follows that Faustinus and Marcellinus mean that Damasus began acting like a tyrant in enforcing laws of Theodosius against Nicene Christians rather than against heretics. The use of *regali* carries connotations of tyranny not immediately apparent in English, but the point should not be made too strongly; above, at §4, e.g., Faustinus and Marcellinus refer to Theodosius's *regias aures*.

170. See Rom 12:11. *PCBE* 2.1 (Ephesius); otherwise unknown.

171. Taorgius is otherwise unknown, as is the location of his see. The name is almost certainly Germanic. The previous Luciferian bishop in Rome was Aurelius, as noted above in §77.

172. This is the well-known Anicius Auchenius Bassus, *praefectus urbi* from 382–383 (*PLRE* 1 [Bassus 11]).

173. For *sub invidia*, compare, e.g., Livy, *Ab urbe cond.* 9.19.15: "absit invidia verbo."

174. An exaggeration; Lucifer was exiled in 355 at the Council of Milan, and the exiles were rescinded by Julian in 362. He appears to have spent time in Germanicia in

integritatis reppulit accusationes Damasi negans se facturum ut homines catholicos et integrae fidei uiros insequeretur, dicens maxime quod ipsae constitutiones imperatorum contra haereticos solummodo promulgatae uideantur, non contra hos qui sanctissimam fidem sine saeculi ambitione conseruant. Et tunc primum erubuit Damasus quod inuentus est iudex qui solus imperialia scripta piissime interpretans tueretur.

86. Nam et hoc ipsum necessarium est ut falsi cognomenti discutiamus inuidiam qua nos iactant esse "Luciferianos." Quis nesciat illius cognomentum tribui sectatoribus cuius et noua aliqua doctrina transmissa est ad discipulos ex auctoritate magisterii? Sed nobis, Christus magister est; illius doctrinam sequimur atque ideo cognomenti illius sacra appellatione censemur, ut non aliud iure dici debeamus quam Christiani, quia nec aliud sequimur quam quod Christus per apostolos docuit. Haereses autem ideo hominum appellationibus denotatae sunt, quia et hominum commenta tradiderunt. Perdit enim in se Christiani nominis appellationem, qui Christi non sequitur disciplinam.

87. Dicant nunc quid Lucifer nouum docuerit quod non ex Christi magisterio traditum est, quod non ab apostolis discipulis Saluatoris transmissum est in posteros. Et bene quod libros scripsit ad Constantium, non, ut plerique, gloriam captans ingenii sed diuina testimonia aptissime

Damasus's accusations. He said that he would not cause himself to persecute catholic men and men of undiminished faith, and he said especially that those laws of the emperors appeared to have been promulgated against heretics and heretics alone, not against those who maintained the holiest faith without ambitions in this age.[175] Then, for the first time, Damasus grew red because a solitary judge was found who appeared to be interpreting imperial decrees most piously.

86. Now, it is also necessary that we dispel the malice of the false nickname, "Luciferians," that they call us.[176] Who does not know that the name given to sectarians is that of the man whose new doctrines have been transmitted to his students on their teacher's authority?[177] But Christ is our teacher.[178] We follow the teaching of that man, and for that reason we are known by his name; by law we should not be called anything other than Christians, since we follow nothing other than what Christ taught through his apostles.[179] But heresies are denoted by the names of men because they also transmit the inventions of men. He who does not follow the teaching of Christ loses the name "Christian" for himself.

87. Now let them say that Lucifer taught something new that was not handed down from the teaching of Christ and was not transmitted by the apostles, the students of the Savior. It is good that he wrote books to Constantius not, as many others did,[180] in order to capture the glory of his talent, but in order to collect divine testimonies very appropriately against

---

Commagene, Eleutheropolis, and the Thebaid; the fourth location is unknown (if this is not a further exaggeration). See Krüger 1886, 20–23.

175. In other words, those who were eager for heavenly rewards, not earthly ones. This is another clear dig against Damasus, who was accused of being overly ambitious not only in the *Libellus precum* but also throughout the Quae gesta sunt and in Ammianus Marcellinus (*Res gest.* 27.3.12). For another complaint about government agents who did not properly enforce religious laws, see, e.g., Maximus Taurinensis, *Serm.* 82 (PL 57:698): "Principes quidem tam boni Christiani leges pro religione promulgant, sed eas exsecutores non exerunt competenter."

176. See Humfress 2007, 239–41.

177. E.g., *Arians* from Arius, *Donatists* from Donatus, and so on. See Jerome, *Lucif.* 28.

178. Matt 23:10. Christ is frequently described or represented as a philosophical *magister* in late antiquity; see, e.g., Zanker 1995, 289–97; Urbano 2013, esp. 28, 152. See below, §116, and Faustinus, *Trin.* 11, 27.

179. See Acts 11:26; 1 Tim 6:3.

180. Probably a reference to Hilary of Poitiers, who also penned several treatises to Constantius while in exile.

congerens contra haereticos et contra ipsum patronum haereticorum, ad diuinam aemulationem pro Filii Dei amore succensus. Denotent, quid illic contrarium Scripturis, quid nouum quasi haereticus scripsit.

88. Quos quidem libros, cum per omnia ex integro ageret, suspexit et Athanasius ut ueri uindicis, atque in Graecum stilum transtulit, ne tantum boni Graeca lingua non haberet. Parum est: quin etiam propriis litteris idem Athanasius eosdem libros praedicat ut prophetarum et Euangeliorum atque apostolorum doctrinis et pia confessione contextos. Et quamuis plurimis in eum laudibus erigatur, tamen non aequat ad meriti eius praeconium, et quidem cum amplius laudare non posset. Ita, rerum eius supereminentia quaeuis laudans lingua superatur!

89. Sed Lucifer, ignarus licet artificiosae eloquentiae tamen ut prophetico et euangelico atque apostolico more scriberet, quod super omnem humanam eloquentiam est, habuit gratiam sancti Spiritus ex merito rectae fidei et sincerissimae conscientiae. Per quem etiam diuinas uirtutes operatus est, non solum in Sardinia, sed in ipsis quoque quator exiliis usque adeo ut eum aduersarii magum dicerent, cum apostolicas virtutes per eum fieri negare non possent.

90. Venit ad hunc et sanctus Gregorius et admiratus est in illo tantam

heretics and that patron of heretics,[181] as he was inflamed with divine zeal for the love of the Son of God. Let them point out what is contrary to scripture there, what new thing he wrote as though he were a heretic.

88. Indeed, Athanasius also accepted these books as the books of a true defender [of the faith] when he was going through all of them anew. He translated them into Greek, for fear that the Greek language would not have such a good thing.[182] This is not enough; even in his own letters, that same Athanasius mentioned that those same books were woven together with the doctrines and pious confession of the prophets, gospels, and apostles.[183] However much Lucifer is elevated by the greatest amount of praise,[184] no accolades are equal to what he deserves, even when it is impossible to praise him further. The preeminence of his deeds surpasses whatever language[185] praises him.

89. But Lucifer, although ignorant of artificial eloquence, nevertheless wrote in the prophetic, evangelic, and apostolic custom, which is beyond all human eloquence.[186] He did this because he had the grace of the Holy Spirit from the merit of his upright faith and his most sincere conscience. Through this grace he even worked divine miracles,[187] not only in Sardinia, but during those four exiles, too, up to the point where his enemies said that he was a sorcerer, since they could not deny that apostolic miracles were done through him.

90. Holy Gregory also came to this man[188] and marveled at his great

---

181. Constantius. For less-flattering appraisals of Lucifer's prose, see n. 6 in Pseudo-Athanasius, *Ep.* 50.4. Only one of Lucifer's treatises, *Moriundum esse pro Dei Filio*, has appeared in translation (Flower 2016, 141–86).

182. No such translations survive, and it is unlikely that Athanasius translated Lucifer's writings. But Lucifer did spend time in exile in Egypt, and there were Luciferian communities in Egypt, so it is not out of the question that other Greek translations of Lucifer's works once existed.

183. This is probably a reference to the two letters appearing in translation at the end of this volume.

184. See, e.g., Pseudo-Athanasius, *Ep.* 51, which is particularly lavish in its praise.

185. With two meanings: Faustinus and Marcellinus use *lingua* here to refer both to Greek and to the "language" of praise.

186. See Faustinus, *Trin.* 1.

187. See above, §78, and below, §§90, 105. On the interplay between ascetic practice and the capacity to perform miracles, see Rapp 2005, 17–18.

188. Gregory of Elvira, a central figure in §§33–41 above, which took place prior to the Council of Alexandria. There is no mention of such a visit in any other extant source; Perez Mas (2008, 97) convincingly argues that this visit was improbable.

doctrinam Scripturarum Diuinarum et ipsam uitam eius uere quasi in caelis constitutam. Iam quantus uir Lucifer fuerit, cum illum admiretur et Gregorius, qui apud cunctos admirabilis est non solum ex conlisione illa Osii sed etiam ex diunis uirtitibus quas habens in se gratiam Sancti Spiritus exsequitur?

91. Quid ergo? Et in hoc impii sunt, [quod] cum Lucifer secundum Scripturas Diuinas et crediderit et docuerit et uixerit et in nomine Christi sit uirtutes operatus, ad opprimendos uerae fidei uindices Luciferi nomen imponant nescientes miseri summum se committere sacrilegium, cum doctrinam Christi sub hominis appellatione designant, sicut et in hoc impii sunt, quando sacrilegas institutiones pro arbitrio hominum editas sub Christiani nominis auctoritate defendunt! An non summa impietas est iniquitates suas et sacrilegia sub Christi nomine uindicare? An non summa impietas est piam doctrinam sub Christi nomine consecratam humanis apellationibus denotare? Sed haec fraus, haec atrocitas aduersus fideles in Hispania et apud Triueros et Romae agitur et in diuersis Italiae regionibus.

92. Adserendum nunc necessario est quod in his partibus gestum est, ubi egregii episcopi, non fidei ueritate sed sola catholici nominis appellatione uestiti, non solum per iudices neque tantummodo per manum militarem fideles et ueros catholicos dissipant, sed etiam interdum per suos clericos, ignorantibus iudicibus uel etiam dissimulantibus, atrocia exercent. Et qui finis erit, si cuncta referamus, quae singuli quoque fidelium passi sunt atque patiuntur? Vnum tamen atrox persecutionis facinus ad compendium referendum est quod in Aegypto apud Oxyrhynchum commissum est sub totius testimonio ciuitatis.

93. Certa pars est apud Oxyrhynchum sanctae plebis in cuius sacro numero plerique, quanto intentius ad res diuinas studium curamue posuerunt, tanto sollicitius diligentiusque fidem catholicam inuiolabiliter seruare contendunt, ita ut se nullis haereticis nullisque praeuaricatoribus per diuina commisceant sacramenta. Ad hanc obseruantiam plerique eorum eruditi sunt exemplo et motu beatissimi Pauli, qui isdem fuit tem-

learning concerning divine scripture and at how his life was truly like one established in heaven.[189] Now, how great a man was Lucifer, seeing as even Gregory marveled at him—Gregory, admired by all not only from that demolishment of Hosius but also from the divine miracles that he performed, having the grace of the Holy Spirit within himself?

91. What, then? Even in this they are impious, because although Lucifer believed, taught, and lived according to divine scripture and worked miracles in the name of Christ, they impose the name of Lucifer to oppress the defenders of the true faith. They do not understand that they are wretches committing the highest sacrilege when they classify the doctrine of Christ under the name of a man, just as they are also impious in defending their sacrilegious teachings which they published under the authority of the Christian name instead of being published as the opinion of men! Is it not the highest impiety to affirm their injustices and sacrileges under the name of Christ? Is it not the highest impiety to associate pious doctrine, consecrated under the name of Christ, with the names of men? But this fraud, this cruelty against the faithful in Spain, Trier, and Rome, is also done in various regions of Italy.

92. We must now declare what was done in places where notorious bishops, not clad in the truth of the faith but only under the label of the catholic name, scattered the faithful and true catholics. They carried out these cruelties not only through judges, nor only through military power, but occasionally even through their own clerics while judges were ignorant or pretended not to know about them. And if we related everything that individuals of the faithful suffered or are suffering, would there be an end to it? Nevertheless, one cruel criminal act of persecution must be presented in order to comprehend what was committed in Egypt at Oxyrhynchus, which the whole city would swear to.

93. There is a certain group of holy people at Oxyrhynchus.[190] Most of this sacred number directed their eagerness or attention intently towards divine matters, and even more anxiously and carefully strove to inviolably protect the catholic faith. Thus they did not associate with heretics and prevaricators in their divine sacraments. Most of them learned to observe this by the example and inspiration of the most blessed Paul, who lived at

---

189. See Phil 3:20; and in this volume, see Pseudo-Athanasius, *Ep.* 51.6. Shuve (2014, 260) rightly points out that Gregory's orthodoxy is here used to emphasize Lucifer's.

190. On the size and importance of Oxyrhynchus in late antiquity, see, e.g., Turner 1952; 1975; Bagnall 1993, 45–54.

poribus quibus et famosissimus ille Antonius, non minori uita neque studio neque diunia gratia quam fuit sanctus Antonius. Nouit hoc et ipsa ciuitas Oxyrynchus, quae hodieque sanctam Pauli memoriam deuotissime celebrat.

94. Sed haec ipsa pars plebis, ubi uidit episcopum illius ciuitatis nomine Theodorum in impiam praeuaricationem fuisse conlapsum ita ut, non solum fidem integram condemnaret neque ut tantummodo impie subscriberet, sed ut etiam laicum se fiere ab impio Georgio pateretur et denuo ab ipso haeretico episcopum ordinari, execrata est eius communionem, habens secum presbyteros et diacones illibatae fidei, per quos fruebatur diuinis sacramentis una cum supra memorato beatissimo Paulo.

Sed postea etiam episcopum sibi per tunc temporis episcopos catholi-

the same time as that very famous Antony.[191] He had no less life, nor zeal, nor divine grace than holy Antony. That city Oxyrhynchus also knows this, as it celebrates the holy memory of Paul to this day with great devotion.[192]

94. Now, this same group of people saw that the bishop of that city, who was named Theodore, had fallen into impious prevarication: not only did he condemn the undiminished faith and impiously give his signature, he even permitted himself to be made a layman by the impious George and then once again be ordained as a bishop by that very heretic.[193] After this, the group cursed his communion, since they had presbyters and deacons of the unbroken faith with them, and with these they enjoyed the divine sacraments together with the most blessed Paul (who was mentioned above).[194]

Later, through the catholic bishops of that time,[195] they even ordained

---

191. Antony was perhaps the most famous ascetic, subject of Athanasius's *Vita Antonii*. He was one of the earliest ascetics to retreat to the desert, and his life and the legends surrounding him (aided by Athanasius's promotion) became the model for Christian ascetics throughout late antiquity and beyond. The identity of this Paul has never been satisfactorily explained. Blumell (2012, 152) identifies him with Paul the Simple, a disciple of Antony; Cavallera (1926) identifies him with Paul of Thebes, who is described in Jerome's hagiography. Blumell also makes the point that Paul was a common name in Egypt at the time, especially for monks, and we might well be encountering an otherwise-unknown Paul here.

192. See above, §§41, 44, 65.

193. Theodore was ordained in 347 (Athanasius, *Ep. fest.* 19.10); by 351/2, a certain Dionysius was the Nicene bishop of Oxyrhynchus (P.Oxy. 23.2344; see Gonis 2006; Blumell 2012, 150). The natural inference is that by 351/2, Athanasius had ordained a replacement for the now-Arian Theodore (but see Perez Mas 2008, 309). George of Cappadocia was the Arian bishop of Alexandria from 356 until his murder at the hands of a pagan mob in 361, thus providing a range of dates in which Theodore might have been reordained by him (see Socrates, *Hist. eccl.* 3.2).

194. That is, they did not rely on Theodore to celebrate the sacraments since they had clergy of their own.

195. The Luciferians seem reluctant to name these bishops. Undoubtedly, whatever influence the hermit Paul had in the creation of this rigorist Nicene community in Oxyrhynchus, the bishops Lucifer of Cagliari and Eusebius of Vercelli must have played some part; Oxyrhynchus was a major city in the Thebaid, where they spent part of their exile living together (Socrates, *Hist. eccl.* 3.5), and it seems likely that if they were living in the Thebaid they were living in Oxyrhynchus. Just as Shuve (2014, 257) argues that Lucifer's time in Rome may well have inspired a rigorist community there, so too might Lucifer's (and Eusebius's) time near Oxyrhynchus have inspired a rigorist community there. But it is not clear whether or not Lucifer and Eusebius

cos ordinauit sanctum Heraclidam, tanto magis idoneum quanto et firmius contra haereticos et praeuaricatores debuit ordinari, qui in uita esset perspicuus, a prima aetate Deo deseruiens contemptis bonis saecularibus et in fide et doctrina perfectus existens. Vnde et pro apostolica fide, pro doctrina euangelica, pro conuersatione caelesti apud cunctos illic uenerabilis

2. Faustinus and Marcellinus, *Petition of Requests*   143

a bishop for themselves, holy Heraclida.[196] The more suitable he was to be ordained, the more firmly he needed to be ordained against both heretics and prevaricators.[197] He was a man plain in life, devoted to God from the earliest age, who held worldly goods in contempt and lived as a man perfect in faith and doctrine.[198] Because of this, he was he was also respected by all the people there for his apostolic faith, his evangelic doctrine, and his

---

directly ordained Heraclida; if Lucifer was involved, it might suggest that the Luciferians were wary of appearing *too* closely tied to Lucifer (despite their extravagant praise in §§87–91 above).

196. See Theodosius, *Lex Aug.* 8; otherwise unknown. A *tabula ansata* (votive tablet) from an unspecified location in the catacombs in Rome carries the inscription "Heraclida epis(copus) | servus Dei fec(it)" (de Rossi 1871, 65 and plate 5; *DACL* 1, col. 1987, fig. 543 [H. Leclercq]). Another, this one from the catacombs outside Rome near the basilica of Hippolytus in Portus, carries a similar inscription: "Heraclida epis(copus) servus | [Dei] basil[icam] Yppolito | [beatissimo martyri | fecit]" (Testini 1979, 35–46; *AE* 1982 [1984], 38, no. 135; Brent 1995, 384–85). This second inscription dates to the late fourth or early fifth century. Testini and Brent believe it to be connected to the Heraclida of the *Libellus precum*. They argue that Heraclida and Damasus were establishing rival cults of Hippolytus; by the fourth century the rigorist and independent third-century bishop of Rome, Hippolytus, had been conflated with a supposed third-century Novatian martyr at Portus also named Hippolytus (see Prudentius, *Peristeph.* 11; Damasus, *Epigr.* 35). Brent (1995, 368–88) does an excellent job working out how these legends became conflated into the same person, though *caveat lector*, he treats the Quae gesta sunt as a Luciferian document and the Luciferians as supporters of Damasus's rival Ursinus (see above, n. 158). Trout (2015, 8–9n35, 192) rightly remains more skeptical, as it is unlikely that this Heraclida is the same as the Luciferian one. This inscription is the only evidence of any connection between a Heraclida in Oxyrhynchus and a Heraclida in Rome. The theory requires Heraclida to have lived, probably in exile, in Ostia or Portus, and to have had enough resources to construct a basilica there. Brent (1995, 384) takes §§98–99 below as suggesting that Heraclida was exiled from Oxyrhynchus, and thus perhaps to Portus or Ostia, but the context of those sections makes it clear that the quotation about Heraclida as an "indigent" is about his simple lifestyle, not his exile; §§103–104 instead strongly suggest that Heraclida remained in Oxyrhynchus while Ephesius traveled to Eleutheropolis in his stead. The Luciferians discuss events in Rome at length (above, §§77–85) but do not mention Heraclida traveling there following the events they relate in Oxyrhynchus. Last, nowhere in their writings do the Luciferians show sympathy to (or even mention) any Novatians, who by way of contrast to the Luciferians were quite friendly with other Nicene Christians.

197. That is, against Arians and against those who professed to be Arians for imperial support but later reversed their position.

198. See below, §102.

est, solis tantummodo haereticis et praeuaricatoribus displicens! Vnde et magis Deo placet cum talibus displicit!

95. Sed hic tantus ac talis ita coepit exercere pontificium ut ad opinionem fidei eius et doctrinae atque ipsius sanctissimae conuersationis plerique etiam de longissimis regionibus aduenirent, execrantes nefariam praeuaricatorum societatem eiusque sacrosanctum consortium desiderantes!

96. Sed ille egregius bis episcopus hoc non patitur! Et primum quidem uexat per publicas potestates, ita ut aliquotiens solum intempesta nocte raptum per lancearios de urbe sustulerit. Sed cum eaedem potestates non in hoc perseuerant in quo temerarie coeperant (quod enim ius habere poterant contra episcopum catholicum? Vnde et merito a coepta persecutione cessarunt, maxime unus ex ipsis etiam diuina plaga admonitus!), tunc egregius iste bis episcopus iam propriis uiribus nititur et mittit turbam clericorum ad ecclesiam beati Heraclidae catholici episcopi eamque euertit destruens undique parietes, ita ut ipsum altare Dei securibus dissiparet, cum horrore totius ciuitatis et gemitu, quod illa ecclesia euerteretur cuius episcopum etiam diuersae partis homines rectae et illibatae fidei confitentur.

97. Aduertite, quaesumus, piissimi imperatores et rectae fidei uindices! Numquid pro tam impiis episcopis edicta proponitis? Ut hi affligantur qui ob meritum fidei et sanctissimae uitae mundo ipso pretiosiores sunt? Credite, religiosissimi imperatores, beatum Heraclidam unum esse de illo numero sanctorum de quibis refert Scriptura Diuina dicens, "Circuierunt in melotis et caprinis pellibus indigentes, in tribulationibus et doloribus afflicti, quorum non erat dignus mundus."

2. Faustinus and Marcellinus, *Petition of Requests*　　　145

heavenly conduct; he was displeasing only to heretics and prevaricators, while he was even more *pleasing to God*[199] since he displeased such men.

95. Such a man as this, with such qualities, began to exercise his priestly duty in such a way that many men from faraway places came to the point of view of his faith, his teaching, and his most holy way of life. They cursed the unspeakable society of prevaricators and longed for his sacrosanct company.

96. But that notorious "twice-bishop"[200] did not put up with this! Naturally, at first he caused trouble through his public powers: several times in the middle of the night he had guards seize Heraclida and took him alone from the city.[201] But these same forces would not continue to do what they had recklessly begun. For what law could they have against a catholic bishop? After this, they also justifiably ceased the persecution they had begun, particularly after one of them was even warned by a blow from God! So then that notorious twice-bishop strove with his own forces and sent a crowd of clerics to the church of blessed Heraclida, the catholic bishop. They completely destroyed the walls and overturned the church to the point that they broke up the very altar of God with axes.[202] The city felt horror and lamentation because the church was overthrown, and even men of the opposite faction confessed that its bishop was of upright and unbroken faith.

97. Give thought, we ask, most pious emperors and defenders of the upright faith! Do you really proclaim your edicts for the benefit of such impious bishops? So that these men, who are more valuable than the world itself because of the merit of their faith and their holiest way of life, might be assaulted? Most religious emperors, believe us: blessed Heraclida was one of that body of saints whom divine scripture means when it says, *They have walked around as indigents in sheepskin and goatskin garments, assaulted by troubles and pains, of whom the world was not worthy.*[203]

---

199. Rom 8:8.

200. The term *bis episcopus* refers to his two ordinations, once by the catholic faction and again by George of Cappadocia; being ordained twice was anathema to the Luciferians and most other Christians.

201. *Lancearii* (or *lanciarii*) are somewhat obscure, but seem to be, among other things, soldiers who served as bodyguards for eminent persons, often though not always serving within legions. See, e.g., Strobel 2007, 274.

202. Christian altars were made of wood in antiquity; see, e.g., Augustine, *Ep.* 185.7.27, in which he accuses Donatists of beating a catholic bishop with boards ripped from the altar of his own church, and *DCA*, s.v. "altar," III, for further sources.

203. Heb 11:37–38.

98. Quomodo enim beatus Heraclida non talis est, qui omnia saecularia respuens oblectamenta, per ipsas amaritudines confragosae uitae istius, aemulans dominica uestigia, nudus expeditusque uirtutum iter salutare sectatur, qui sic pro diuiniae fidei amore conspirat sicuti et sanctos legimus conspirasse, nihil habens de saeculo quam pro fide "tribulationes et dolores," sic uiuens, sic incedens, sicuti et illi sancti de quibus supra positum est testimonium? Merito ergo et beatus Gregorius ceterique sancti episcopi sanctimoniae istius uenerabili consortio in tot malis afflictae Ecclesiae uelut diuinis solatiis releuantur.

99. Non solum autem in tam uenerabilem episcopum grassatus est Theodorus sed et in ipsam sanctissimam plebem eius, quae pro sincerrissimi et fidelissimi sacerdotis doctrina et moribus instituta est. Et longum est referri quae contra pudorem propositumue sacrarum uirginum molitus est, quarum monasteria pro merito sanctimoniae earum ciuitas ipsa ueneratur. Sed et ipsos seruos Dei aliquotiens atrocibus afflixit iniuriis quos magis probauerat sanctiores! Sed quid mirum si oues ut lupus affligeret, quarum bonum pastorum frequenter affligit?

100. Ecce qui sub uobis piis imperatoribus et pro fide catholica uenientibus iactat se esse catholicum euertens Ecclesiam catholicorum, persequens catholicos sacerdotes et seruos Christi nec non et sacras eius uirgines impie affligens! Hic est egregius et sanctissimus illi episcopus, qui, cum fuisset primum a catholicis episcopis episcopus ordinatus, postea, ab impio Georgio in laicorum numerum redactus, nihilominus ab ipso Georgio episcopus ordinatus est in uexationem fidelium, sedens

98. For how is Heraclida not such a man? He rejects all the delights of this age, and through the very bitterness of his difficult life, he strives to proceed along the Lord's footprints, simple and unencumbered, and follow the *salutary road*[204] of virtues. He lives in harmony with his love of the divine faith just as we read that the saints lived in harmony. He has nothing from this age other than *troubles and pains*[205] for the faith. Thus he lives, thus he progresses, just like those holy men in the passage cited above. Therefore both blessed Gregory and the other holy bishops are deservedly comforted among the many evils that assault the church in the venerable company of his sanctity as though by God's consolation.

99. Moreover, Theodore moved against not only such a venerable bishop but also his most holy people, who were organized according to the teaching and customs of that most sincere and faithful priest. It would take a long time to report the things he worked against the modesty and intention of the holy virgins,[206] whose cells[207] that city justifiably venerated on account of their sanctity. Several times he also afflicted with unjust cruelty the servants of God whom he had commended as being quite holy. But what wonder is it if he should assault sheep like a wolf, when he so often assaults their good shepherd?

100. Look at who claims that he is a catholic under you pious emperors, who come forth for the catholic faith, and overturns the community of catholics, persecutes catholic priests and servants of Christ, and even impiously assaults Christ's holy virgins! This is that notorious and oh-so-holy[208] bishop who, although he had first been ordained a bishop by catholic bishops, was nevertheless later led back into the body of laymen by the impious George and then was ordained as a bishop by that very George, which disturbed the faithful. George was seated and held com-

---

204. Ps 49:22 LXX.
205. Heb 11:37.
206. See below, §108. Whether or not Theodore did anything of the sort, this makes for excellent rhetoric in a petition: not only are Faustinus and Marcellinus's enemies heretical persecutors, they even attack innocent, virginal women. On the importance of virginity for ascetics, see §102.
207. In the fourth century, the word *monasterium* could mean an organized community or an individual ascetic's dwelling (even in the same work; see, e.g., Jerome, *Vit. Malch.* 17.3; 19.1; see below, §104). Here it seems to refer to individual cells, not multiple monasteries.
208. The sarcastic *egregius* is now joined by the sarcastic epithet *sanctissimus*.

et communicans in una eademque ciuitate cum Apollonio Melitianorum episcopo consentienti impietatibus Georgii et cum ipso item Apollonio idem Theodorus persequens beatum Heraclidam catholicae fidei uindicem!

101. Ecce cui, quasi catholico, basilica nunc tradita est Apollonii ex generalis edicti uestri auctoritate, cum utique idem Theodorus, qui quasi catholicus haeretici Apollonii basilicam accepit, similiter impie gessit ut gessit et Apollonius, nisi quia atrocius gessit Theodorus, cum de episcopo catholico fit laicus, damnans piam fidem et subscribens Arrianae impietati ut ab haeretico iterum episcopus ordinetur! Sane hinc se uult catholicum uideri quod et ipse nunc quosdam presbyteros seu diacones Apollonii facit suasu quodam laicos et eos iterum ordinat, ut uideatur turpissimae istius ordinationis uicem referre quam passus est. Numquid non excedit omne sacrilegium haec ludibria sub nomine catholico uindicare in afflictionem fidelium sacerdotum atque laicorum?

102. Sed et apud Palaestinam in Eleutheropoli est sacra uirgo Christi nomine Hermione generosis quidem edita natalibus, sed fide et sanctimo-

2. Faustinus and Marcellinus, *Petition of Requests* 149

munion in the same city with Apollonius, bishop of the Meletians, who approved of George's impieties;[209] that same Theodore along with Apollonius likewise persecuted blessed Heraclida, defender of the catholic faith.

101. Look at how on the authority of your general edict the basilica of Apollonius was just now handed over to Theodore as though to a catholic, even though without a doubt that same Theodore, who received the basilica of Apollonius like a catholic receives that of a heretic, likewise acted just as impiously as Apollonius acted—except that Theodore acted more dreadfully, since he was made a layman from a catholic bishop, condemned the pious faith, and subscribed to the Arian impiety, so that he might again be ordained as a bishop by a heretic! He clearly wants to appear to be catholic these days,[210] since even now (with some coaxing) he makes certain presbyters or deacons of Apollonius laymen and ordains them again, so he seems to be reciprocating that extremely shameful ordination that he underwent. Does it not go beyond every sacrilege to defend these mockeries that are done under the catholic name to assault faithful priests and laymen?

102. Now there is also a holy virgin of Christ named Hermione at Eleutheropolis in Palestine.[211] She was certainly born noble in her lineage, but

---

209. Epiphanius (*Pan.* 73.26.4) describes him as a Meletian bishop who signed to an Arian creed in 359; he is otherwise unknown. For the Meletians, see above, n. 19.

210. This presents a bit of a chronological conundrum, since Theodore was made bishop for the first time in 351/2 and reordained as an Arian between 356 and 361 (see above, n. 193). If these events are meant to be taking place in the 380s, this would make Theodore quite an old man at the time the *Libellus precum* was written. Furthermore, Dorotheus was bishop of Oxyrhynchus by 381 (when he was a signatory to the Council of Constantinople). Blumell (2012, 150–53) takes this as evidence that the persecution the Luciferians describe must have occurred in the 360s, while emphasizing that the account is confused. But the account is not so confused as it looks. The basilica could only have been given to a Nicene bishop following Theodosius's accession in 378, since Valens was a supporter of the Arian party. That Theodore would change his allegiance *back* to the Nicene party is no surprise, and they explicitly accuse him of switching sides here and in §100 above (it is also the sort of political maneuvering that the Luciferians complain about throughout the *Libellus precum*, e.g., §§65, 67). The word *nunc* in the Luciferian account implies that this handover occurred very recently. As for Dorotheus, the name is likely a textual corruption (Lequien 1740, 2:578–79; Papaconstantinou 1996, 173). Papaconstantinou also points out that another document from 371 lists the bishop of Oxyrhynchos as "Theodoulos."

211. The following narrative is presented in the present tense in the *Libellus precum*, lending it a sense of immediacy, but it has been translated into the past tense

nia multum facta generosior, ipsam uirginitatem condecorans contemptu rerum saecularium et humanae gloriae, ad quam plerique affectant, etiam qui se saeculo et concupiscentiae carnis adrenuntiasse gloriantur.

103. Haec, in quantum castimoniam corporis sacro rigore custodit, in tantum animae puritatem casta piae fidei obseruatione conseruat, non haereticis, non praeuaricatoribus communicans, eo quod intellegat uirginitatem corporis nihil prodesse nisi et integritatem animae sacra confessione tueatur, labem adulterinae communionis effugiens et sectans salutaria sacramenta fidelium sacerdotum.

Denique, suppliciat religiosis litteris apud beatum Heraclidam ut eius sacris uisitationibus iuuaretur.

104. Sed, pro beato Heraclida, sanctus Ephesius uisitat, qui id temporis, ob utilitates ecclesiasticas, ad episcopum Heraclidam de urbe Roma

2. Faustinus and Marcellinus, *Petition of Requests*   151

was made more noble by her faith and sanctity.[212] She carefully adorned her virginity with contempt for matters of this age[213] and for human glory, which many pursue, even those who glory in their renunciation of this age and of carnal desire.[214]

103. This woman protected the purity of her soul by chaste observation of the pious faith just as she guarded the chastity of her body with holy rigor. She did not hold communion with heretics, nor with prevaricators, because she knew that the virginity of her body would in no way benefit her unless she also defended the integrity of her soul by her holy confession, fled from the disgrace of adulterous communion, and followed the salutary sacraments of faithful priests.[215]

Eventually, in religious letters to blessed Heraclida, she begged him to give her the pleasure of his holy presence.[216]

104. Instead, holy Ephesius visited on behalf of blessed Heraclida. At the time, he had come to the bishop Heraclida from the city of Rome for

---

for a more natural read. Hermione is otherwise unknown. She may have been named for one of the prophesying daughters of the apostle Philip mentioned in Acts 21:8–9, as in the medieval period a martyred Hermione said to be Philip's daughter was venerated at Ephesus (*Menologion*, 4 September), but the name was not uncommon, as a simple derivation from Greek myth (Hermione was Menelaus and Helen's daughter, betrothed to Orestes but ultimately married to Achilles's son Neoptolemus). Of course, the name has also gained great significance in modern literature.

212. See above, p. 34.
213. See above, §94.
214. See Jerome, *Ep.* 22.13, 27.
215. Physical and spiritual virginity were closely connected in antiquity, and ascetic women who lost their physical virginity could be denied communion sometimes even on their deathbeds (Council of Elvira, canon 13; see Hefele 1871, 151). Basil (*Ep.* 199.18) recommends fifteen years' excommunication for ascetic women who broke their vows in this way. Nor are the Luciferians unique in emphasizing the greater importance of her spiritual "virginity"; Jerome (*Ep.* 22.38) calls heretical ascetic women prostitutes, and Basil (*Ep.* 199.20) does *not* recommend fifteen years' excommunication for lapsed ascetic women from heretical communities, because their vows were never valid in the first place. See Jerome, *Ep.* 48.6; *Jov.* 1.11; Augustine, *Faust.* 20.21; and see Elm 1994, 145–48; Kelly 2000, 4.
216. See above, §50. It could be quite difficult for private citizens to send letters to each other between cities in antiquity; typically, one had to find a traveler willing to carry the letter who was also heading toward the intended recipient and hope that the letter (and the traveler, for that matter) arrived in one piece. See, e.g., Augustine, *Ep.* 71.2; Casson 1974, 220.

uenerat. Hic est Ephesius quem supra diximus illibatae plebi Romanae episcopum a constantissimo Taorgio episcopo ordinatum. Sed cum uenisset Eleutheropolim, non solum Hermione cum suo sacro monasterio releuatur, sed et quidam fidelissimi serui Dei; inter quos etiam nobilis domus religiosi ad catholicam fidem Seueri ex tribunis. Diu quidem non communicans haereticis et praeuaricatioribus; sed nondum qui inuenisset catholicorum sacram communionem.

105. Vbi autem uidit sanctum Ephesium, post multas examinationes probans eum catholicum, traditit se ei in sacram communionem, beatum se iudicans quod domum suam ex insperato diuina misericordia uisitasset tam sancti sacerdotis aduentu, ductus in eius admirationem non solum uitae eius puritate sed et quibusdam caelestibus documentis: est enim tantae fidei et sanctimoniae beatus Ephesius ut, quocumque perrexerit, eum gratia diuina comitetur. Probauit hoc et plebs sancta apud Oxyrynchum beato Heraclidae communicans: quae illum ob meritum diuinae gratiae pia eius dilectione constricta ut quondam Asiani apostolum Paulum cum magno fletu deduxit proficiscentem.

106. Non haec laudandi studio loquimur, sed ut scire possitis quam sanctae et fideles animae sub uestri nominis auctoritate grauissimis perse-

ecclesiastical services.[217] This is the Ephesius whom we discussed above, the bishop of the undiminished people at Rome who was ordained by a very constant bishop, Taorgius.[218] After he had come to Eleutheropolis, not only was Hermione comforted along with her holy monastery,[219] but also some very faithful servants of God. Among these was even the noble house of Severus, a former tribune who was devoted to the catholic faith.[220] Indeed, he had not held communion with the heretics and prevaricators for a long while, but he had still not found the holy communion of catholics.[221]

105. However, when he saw holy Ephesius, he determined that Ephesius was catholic after many examinations and handed himself over to Ephesius in holy communion. He judged himself to be blessed because God's mercy had visited his house unexpectedly by the arrival of such a holy priest. He was led to admire Ephesius not only by the purity of his life but also by certain divine proofs: for blessed Ephesius is of such great faith and sanctity that, wherever he presented himself, divine grace accompanied him. The holy people at Oxyrhynchus who held communion with blessed Heraclida also approved of him. They were so attached to him by pious love, because of that divine grace, that as he was setting out they led the way with much weeping, as the people of Asia once did for the apostle Paul.[222]

106. We do not say these things because we are eager for praise but so that you may be able to understand how holy and faithful souls are assaulted

---

217. The phrase is quite vague; parallels occur in Gregory the Great (*Ep.* 78) and the *acta* of the Council of Frankfurt in 794 (*Cap. Franc.* 55). In both cases, however, it seems to refer to the management of church affairs and suggests that Ephesius and Heraclida had a preexisting relationship (contra Perez Mas 2008, 317).

218. See above, §84.

219. As noted above (n. 207), the word *monasterium* could mean an organized community or an individual ascetic's dwelling. It seems clear that Faustinus and Marcellinus are here referring to an organized community. For other communities of ascetic women in Eleutheropolis (albeit in the fifth century), see Schwartz 1939, 13–14; Binns 1994, 187, 190.

220. *PLRE* 1 (Severus 11); otherwise unknown.

221. This suggests that Luciferian efforts at proselytizing were minimal, as Severus—for decades?—had apparently no knowledge of the Luciferian community in his own city, even despite the fact that Hermione and Severus, as a noblewoman and a former tribune, might be expected to move in the same social circles.

222. See Acts 20:37–38.

cutionibus affliguntur ab his quos constat, ignorantibus uobis, etiam nunc usque aut haereticos esse, aut praeuaricatores, aut socios talium.

107. Sed aduersus sanctum Ephesium modicum quid conati in Palaestina hi quibus sacra ueritas onerosa est; postea destiterunt metuentes in illo et fidei libertatem et constantiam animi et hoc ipsum cogitantes quod magis haeresis eorum et impietas prodi poterat, si sub uobis catholicis imperatoribus integrae et constantis fidei episcopum acrius inquietassent. Vbi autem idem beatus Ephesius, inuitatus fidelium litteris, in Africam nauigauit, nobis apostolico more dans praeceptum ut circa sanctam fraternitatem diuinis et ecclesiasticis officiis incubaremus, id ipsum sancta illic fraternitate poscente, egregius Turbo Eleutheropolitanae episcopus ciuitatis, nostram exiguitatem despiciens, in nos coepit uelle consummare quod in sanctum Ephesium consummare non ausus est, nesciens quod Christi Dei gratia etiam minimissimis seruulis eius patrocinetur, maxime pro causa rectae fidei laborantibus.

108. Namque hic Turbo, posteaquam audiuit quosdam se integrae fidei copulare et per Dei gratiam rem ueri crescere, nobis exitia minitatur et turbas. Sed et Seueri domui incendium minitatum ueritati, qui tanto magis fidem Dei uindicat quanto et Romano imperio fideliter militauit.

by very harsh persecution under the authority of your name—persecution done by those who (it is generally agreed, though you remain unaware) are still, even now, either heretics, prevaricators, or allies of such men.

107. For some, the holy truth is burdensome; but what they attempted in Palestine against holy Ephesius was slight. In the end, they ceased, because they were afraid of both the boldness of his faith and the constancy of his soul. They thought that their heresy and impiety might instead be revealed if they forcefully harassed a bishop of undiminished and constant faith under you catholic emperors. Then, however, blessed Ephesius sailed to Africa after he was invited there by letters of the faithful, and in the apostolic custom he ordered us to watch over the holy brotherhood in our divine and ecclesiastic offices (which the holy brotherhood there requested).[223] That notorious Turbo, bishop of the city of Eleutheropolis,[224] looked down on our insignificant size[225] and began to desire carrying out against us that which he did not dare to carry out against holy Ephesius. He did not know that the grace of Christ, our God, gives protection to even his smallest servants, especially those who toil away for the upright faith.

108. For example, after he heard that certain men were joining the undiminished faith and that truth's party was growing through the grace of God, this Turbo threatened to disturb and ruin us.[226] His fire was also threatening the truth at Severus's house. Severus, as much as he had faithfully served in the government of the Roman Empire, defended the faith of God all the more. Turbo even tried to pursue the holy virgin

---

223. See Acts 20:13–37. Nothing else is known of the Luciferian community in North Africa. Perez Mas (2008, 317) suggests that Ephesius was traveling to North Africa in order to proselytize there, but the text makes it clear that Ephesius was summoned by a preexisting community for some unknown reason. Note that Faustinus and Marcellinus are priests (see below, §124). The text here takes on an autobiographical tone, suggesting that Faustinus and/or Marcellinus were in Eleutheropolis, perhaps having accompanied Ephesius from Rome to Eleutheropolis (see above, §79). That they were not from Eleutheropolis originally seems clear from the parenthetical statement. It seems likely that the people there wanted Faustinus and Marcellinus to stay because there were no clergy in Eleutheropolis to administer the sacraments, or at least, we hear of no clergy there. Presumably they then traveled from Eleutheropolis to Constantinople, perhaps spurred to seek imperial support by the actions of Turbo described in the following paragraphs.

224. Otherwise unknown.

225. See above, §1.

226. There is a play on words between *Turbo* and *turbas*.

Temptat quoque et sacram uirginem Hermionem insequi, illam feminam quam quicumque didicit, ut aliquam de euangelicis feminis admiratus est. Sed et singulis quibusque tendit insidias qui nobiscum sacrae communionis consortio copulantur, ueluti nefas obiciens, ex lege illa Babyloniae, quod intra nostra domicilia, sine labe haeresos et sine communione perfidiae, secundum euangelicas et apostolicas traditiones desiderantibus fidelibus diuina sacramenta celebremus. Simili enim furore et quondam Babyloniae sanctum Danihelum hostilibus odiis insecuti sunt quod in sua domo Deum obseruantia diuinae legis adoraret.

109. Hic est Turbo qui diaconus fuit Eutychi haeretici, sub quo beatus

Hermione, too.[227] Anyone who knew this woman admired her for being like the women in the gospels.[228] And he also plotted against any individuals who joined in the company of holy communion with us as though he were exposing unholiness in accordance with that law of Babylon,[229] because we celebrate the divine sacraments for the desirous faithful within our dwellings without the disgrace of heresy and the communion of treachery, in accordance with the gospels and apostolic traditions. For at Babylon they also went after holy Daniel in a similar fury, filled with malicious hatred because he worshiped God in observance of divine law.[230]

109. This is the Turbo who was a deacon of Eutychius the heretic,[231]

---

227. Faustinus and Marcellinus do not directly accuse Turbo of sexual misconduct as they do Theodore (see above, §99), but the verb *insequor* does have classical antecedents as meaning sexual pursuit (Ovid, *Metam.* 1.504; Martial, *Epigr.* 5.83). Turbo must have felt very confident that he would not face repercussions for his persecution, as Hermione is described as a noblewoman and Severus as a former tribune, both individuals of social importance.

228. Canellis (2006, 219n2) suggests that she resembles Elizabeth, mother of John the Baptist, and the Virgin Mary, as well as a number of Old Testament figures. The vague description, however, also permits one to think of other kindly women in the gospels, such as the Mary whom Jesus met at a house with her sister Martha (Luke 10:38–42).

229. See Dan 3.

230. See Dan 6.

231. Eutychius (Eutychus in the *Libellus precum*) was a prominent Arian who supported the *homoios* formula; see Epiphanius, *Pan.* 73.23–26, 37; Jerome, *Jo. Hier.* 4; Socrates, *Hist. eccl.* 2.40–41; 3.25; Nautin, "Épiphane," *DHGE* cols. 15.617–31; Nautin, "Eutychius, évêque d'Éleuthéropolis," *DHGE*, cols. 95–97; Kim 2015, 142–45; Jacobs 2016, 10. According to Epiphanius, he allied himself to Acacius of Caesarea because he personally disliked Cyril of Jerusalem (Kim suggests this dislike may have come about as Cyril tried to impose his authority on other sees around Jerusalem). Cyril and other supporters of the *homoiousios* formula excommunicated Acacius, Eutychius, and others; this prompted them to travel to Constantinople to petition Constantius, where they also created a new creed (which the bishop Ulfilas then spread to the Goths). Following Julian's death, Eutychius was among the signatories at a council in Antioch that affirmed a qualified version of the Nicene Creed, and Kim (2015, 143) thus calls him a "pragmatist and perhaps a bit of an opportunist," the exact kind of bishop that Faustinus and Marcellinus despise. In a passage of Epiphanius's *Panarion* (73.37.5–6), Nautin ("Eutychius, évêque d'Éleuthéropolis," *DHGE* col. 97) reads a parallel construction using the names Euzoïus and the otherwise unknown Gemellinus as suggesting that Gemellinus was ordained as bishop of Eleutheropolis following Eutychius; if Nautin's interpretation is correct, Turbo may have then succeeded Gemellinus. Epiphanius was a native of the area around Eleutheropolis (Sozomen,

Lucifer Eleutheropolitanae ciuitatis patiebatur exilium, qui et ipsum Luciferum fidem libere uindicantem atrocitatibus uehementer afflixit. Sunt adhuc hodie in Palaestina qui illo tempore, istis insequentibus, poenas grauissimas dederunt eo quod cum catholicae fidei episcopo Lucifero conuenirent. Negent, si non inter cetera sua atrocia ianuam clausam securibus effregerunt, si non irruentes in Luciferum fidelissimum sacerdotem diuina quoque sacramenta euerterunt, unumquemque illic de his gratribus qui conuenerant impia caede mulcantes! Negent, si non hodieque apud se mystica uasa, quae tunc impie Lucifero diripuerunt, cum sacris codicibus possident!

110. Tunc utique Turbo cum Eutychio haeretico uersabatur. Extunc, se catholicum dicens, catholicos persequitur sub auctoritate uestri nominis! Auctoritatis piae contemplatione fidem catholicam uindicatis. Permittetis, piissimi imperatores, ut sub uestri nominis auctoritate aduersus fideles diu ubique dominetur impietas? Expedit enim hoc Romano imperio (quod tamen affectu et fide eius quam Christo Deo exhibetis obseruantiae dicimus), ut qui Christum pie praedicant persecutiones mortesque patiantur, ita ut nusquam liceat Deo pia altaria conlocare aut certe, cum conlocata fuerint, destruantur?

111. Sub impio Achab, rege Israel, occisis prophetis altariisque destructis, interpellat Helias Deum aduersum Israel in libro Regnorum dicens: "Domine, prophetas tuos occiderunt, altaria tua destruxerunt et ego relictus sum solus et quaerunt animam meam." Hanc inuidiosam interpellationem etiam uestris temporibus sinitis ad Deum fieri a singulis quibusque fidelibus sacerdotibus?

112. Si enim et taceant, numquid Deus haec ipsa fieri ignorat? Quid? Putamus quod sine offensione Dei haec in ueros catholicos et in ueram

under whom blessed Lucifer suffered exile in the city of Eleutheropolis.[232] He also violently assaulted Lucifer himself, who was boldly defending the faith, with numerous atrocities. Today, there are still those in Palestine who paid a very harsh price back when those men were coming after them because they gathered together with Lucifer, a bishop of the catholic faith. Let them deny that among their other cruelties they broke open the closed door with axes, overturned the divine sacraments, rushed in at Lucifer, the most faithful priest, and wounded anyone who had gathered together there with an impious blow! Let them deny that to this very day they possess for themselves the ritual vessels that they impiously plundered from Lucifer at the time, along with the sacred codices!

110. At that time, at any rate, Turbo used to consort with the heretic Eutychius. Now he says that he is catholic and persecutes catholics under the authority of your name! You defend the catholic faith in consideration of the pious authority [of God]. Will you, most pious emperors, allow impiety to have dominion against the faithful everywhere and at length under the authority of your name? We say this, now, with goodwill and faith in the respect that you show to Christ, our God: is it good for the Roman Empire that those who profess Christ piously suffer persecution and death in such a way that pious altars to God are not allowed to be set up anywhere? Or of course, after they have been set up, that they be destroyed?

111. Under the impious Ahab, king of Israel, after the prophets were killed and the altars destroyed, Elijah[233] appealed to God against Israel in the book of Kings, saying, *Lord, they killed your prophets, they destroyed your altars, and I am left alone and they want my life.*[234] In your own times, are you letting each and every faithful priest make this anger-inducing appeal to God?

112. For if they remain silent, will God not know that these things were done? What? Do we think that these things are perpetrated against

---

Hist. eccl. 6.32.1) and thus probably knew Eutychius personally. Nautin also suggests that Epiphanius moved to Cyprus when Eutychius chose Gemellinus instead of him to succeed him in the bishopric of Eleutheropolis; Kim (2015, 144–45) instead suggests that Epiphanius was simply unwilling to shift his doctrinal positions in order to garner the necessary patronage.

232. Eusebius of Vercelli had also spent time in exile in Palestine, but in the northern city of Scythopolis rather than in the more southerly Eleutheropolis: Eusebius of Vercelli, *Ep.* 2.1.

233. See above, §69; Pseudo-Athanasius, *Ep.* 51.6.

234. 1 Kgs 19:10–14. See above, §§76, 96, 110.

eius Ecclesiam perpetrentur, quae olim aduersus seruos Dei perpetrata grauissime diuinis animaduersionibus uindicata sunt? Et unde sunt tot plagae quibus orbis Romanus quatitur et urguetur?

113. Non opus est nunc nos singula quaeque plagarum recensere, quae tranquillitas uestra recognoscit cum aestu et sollicitudine imperii sui. Communem istum dolorem uel tacendo mitigemus, ne non tam compati quam exulcerare uideamur. Sed hoc, quaesumus, piissimi imperatores, cogitare dignemini quibus ex causis ista proueniunt: utrum quia fideles serui Christi metuentes leges diuinas nolunt cum infidelibus conuenire an quia ueri catholici a falsis sacerdotibus obteruntur?

114. Quomodo enim non falsi sacerdotes sunt qui iam, non solum ob causam praeuaricationis supra expositam deuitandi sunt sed etiam quod plurimi quique eorum proprias etiam nunc haereses uindicant sub ementita apud uos catholici nominis professione? Quis enim iam timeat episcoporum impia praedicare quando totiens commissa impietas honorata est, cum minime deicitur sacerdotio? Denique, cum sint alii eorum Origenistae, alii anthropmorphitae, alii autem Apollinaris impii sectam tuentes, triplici cuneo alii aduersum Sanctum Spiritum diuersis studiis

2. Faustinus and Marcellinus, *Petition of Requests* 161

true catholics and God's true church without offending him, when they were perpetrated long ago against servants of God and were avenged very harshly by God's punishment? Why is the Roman world shaken and beset by so many misfortunes?[235]

113. There is no need at present to recount individual misfortunes, which your tranquility recognizes in the agitation and anxiety of your empire. We might even ease our shared pain by remaining silent, so that we would appear to be suffering alongside you rather than making things worse. But we ask for this, most pious emperors: find it worthwhile to consider the reasons these things come to pass, whether it is because faithful servants of Christ do not wish to hold communion with the unfaithful because they are afraid of divine law, or because true catholics are being trampled on by false priests.

114. For how are they not false priests who should now be shunned, not only because of the prevarication explained above, but also because many of them even now defend their own heresies to you under a deceptive profession of the catholic faith? What bishop would now fear to proclaim impieties when impiety is honored as often as it is committed, seeing as it is not driven out of the priesthood in any way? In fact, while some of them are Origenists,[236] others are anthropomorphites,[237] others the impious overseers of the sect of Apollinaris,[238] and others blaspheme with a triple wedge against the Holy Spirit in various independent

---

235. Possibly referring to, among other things, a major famine in Antioch in 382, Gratian's assassination in 383, and famines at Antioch and Rome in 384. See above, pp. 36–37.

236. Origen was the leading Christian intellectual of the third century, but by the late fourth century, opinion had begun to turn against him. Still, he was not universally condemned in the fourth century, and it is interesting that Faustinus and Marcellinus take such a strong stand against him without further elaboration. See Clark 1992.

237. Prior to Canellis, editors corrected this to *anthropomorphistae*, but Canellis retains the manuscript readings of manuscripts D and E. According to their opponents (who were obviously biased against them), anthropomorphites offered a relatively literal reading of Gen 1:27 and argued that when God created man "in his own image," God must therefore have had a corporeal form. It was apparently a fairly common belief among desert ascetics; see Socrates, *Hist. eccl.* 6.7.

238. Apollinaris argued that the Son's mind was wholly divine, but Faustinus and Marcellinus treat his beliefs as a variation of Sabellianism; see above, p. 16, and see Faustinus, *Conf. fid.* 3.

solis blasphemantes, sed et ipsi quoque, qui pie inter eos putantur credere, Patris et Filii et Spiritus Sancti tres esse substantias uindicantes uel respicientes: nihilominus hi omnes de uestris gloriantur edictis et sibi ecclesias uindicant, cum has impias sectas patres nostri apostolica semper et euangelica auctoritate damnauerint.

115. Quas quidem nunc discutere non est praesentis opusculi; sed tamen quod moueat ad horrorem intentum uerae fidei animum uestrum dicimus.

116. Vna, ut opinamur, haeresis apud Ariminum sub haeretico rege suscepta est et nunc sub uobis piis catholicis imperatoribus tot haereses uindicantur, non minus impiae quam est Arrii impietas! Et cum aduersus se libros uel epistolas singuli quique conscribant, tamen sibi omnes uel ex directo uel ex obliqua concatenatione communicant, inani studio philosophorum solis disputationibus litigantes, non etiam ut Christiani ex deuotione sacramenti alter alterum uelut impium deuitantes, ut iam, sicut in scolis, ingenii uideatur inter eos esse certamen, non autem sacra defensio uerae religionis, quandoquidem inter se sacramenta non separant, cum impiis sententiis ab inuicem separentur.

117. Hoc autem ideo faciunt quia quidam eorum gloriae humanae, quidam uero auaritiae student; et inde est quod sibi inuicem sub impia dissimulatione conludunt ut, nec possessiones perdant ecclesiae, nec honores. Et interea, ut tot suas uelent impietates, ad inlusionem singulorum ueluti benignissimae mentis indicia praeferentes, aiunt ideo se etiam

studies,[239] but even these, who think among themselves that their beliefs are pious, affirm or consider that there are three substances of the Father, the Son, and the Holy Spirit. Nonetheless, all of these glory in your laws and lay claim to churches for themselves, although our fathers always condemned these impious sects with apostolic and evangelic authority.

115. Certainly, it is not for this present little work to dispel these sects; but nevertheless, we are saying something which may move your soul to horror, intent as it is on the true faith.

116. One heresy, in our opinion, was taken up at Rimini under the heretic king,[240] and now under you pious catholic emperors so many heresies are defended that are no less impious than the impiety of Arius! Although these individuals each compose books or letters against one another, they nevertheless all join in communion with each other, whether through a direct connection or an oblique one. They disagree in debates alone, with the empty zeal of philosophers, and not even as Christians. The one shuns the other as an impious man because of his devotion to the sacraments, but just like in schools nowadays, in such a way that it looks like a contest of talent between them instead of the holy defense of the true religion,[241] seeing as they are not different from one another in their sacraments even though they are different in their impious way of thinking.

117. Now, they do this because some are zealous for human glory and others for material gain; this is the reason they secretly collude with each other under an impious disguise, so that they lose neither the possessions of the church nor their honors.[242] Meanwhile, as they cover up their many impieties, they offer evidence of their supposedly great benevolence (in order to lie to everyone) and say that they are joined in the association of ecclesiastic communion even with those whose opinions are contrary

---

239. Meaning here among others the Macedonians or *pneumatomachi*, who denied the divinity of the Holy Spirit or at least diminished its importance compared to the Father and Son. See Kelly 1978, 259–60.

240. Constantius (see above, §§13–19). Note the contrast between the vocabulary used to describe the heretical *rex* and the pious *imperatores;* but see above, §§4, 7, 17, and n. 169.

241. The trope of Christianity versus traditional philosophy was a common rhetorical trope used by many Christians. See above, §86, and Faustinus, *Trin.* 27; see Jerome, *Lucif.* 11, 14.

242. See above, §§16, 17, 32, 42, 49, 61; below, §121.

contraria sentientibus ecclesiasticae communionis consortio copulari ne bonum pacis in Ecclesia pereat, quasi uero huiusmodi pax Christo Deo placeat quae in eius Ecclesiam tantas recipit impietates!

118. Sed hoc qui ita putant, audiant de se scriptum: "Et uiam pacis non agnouerunt; non est timor Dei ante oculos eorum." Sed apertius quoque et apud Hieremiam legimus de ea pace impia et iniqua, sicut exequitur subiectum testimonium: "A pusillo eorum usque ad magnum cuncti perpetrauerunt iniqua. A sacerdote usque ad pseudoprophetam uniuersi operati sunt falsa; et meditabantur obtritioni populi mei pro nihilo constituentes et dicentes 'Pax, pax!' Et ubi est pax?" Et intendendum est quam atrocia de illis prosequatur qui hac uanissima pace gloriantur. Sequitur enim: "Confusi sunt, quoniam defecerunt et nec sic quidem confusionem sustinentes erubuerunt et ignominiam suam non cognouerunt. Propterea cadent in ruina sua et in tempore visitationis infirmabuntur."

119. Quid mali committimus, quid impie facimus, si seruantes fidem Christo, huiusmodi pacem respuamus, cuius tanta confusio et ignominia grauissimique exitus describuntur? Sed isti egregii pacis amatores fidelibus sacerdotibus bellum exagitant. Quid enim uult diabolus, quam ut impii et praeuaricatores saeculi pace glorientur? Quid enim uult diabolus, quam ut hi qui pii sunt et fideles infestantium persecutione uexentur?

120. Haec ideo prosecuti sumus ne per uestri ignorantiam diu fundatur sanguis Christianorum piissimam fidem defendentium. Quid enim prodest si sitis catholicae fidei uindices et patiamini catholicae fidei sectatores ubique cruciari, ubique effugari, nusquam libere piam fidem praedicare?

121. Habeant illi basilicas auro coruscantes pretiosorumque marmorum ambitione uestitas uel erectas magnificentia columnarum! Habeant

to theirs so that the benefit of peace does not perish in the church.[243] As if a peace of this sort, which accepts such great impieties into his church, would truly be *pleasing to* Christ, our *God!*[244]

118. But those who think this way should hear what is written about them: *They did not know the way of peace; the fear of God is not before their eyes.*[245] We also read about that impious and sacrilegious peace even more clearly in Jeremiah, as the following testimony relates: *From the smallest of them up to the greatest of all, they perpetrated sacrileges. From the priest up to the pseudo-prophet, they all created falsehoods, and they considered the destruction of my people, reckoned it to be nothing, and said, "Peace, peace!" And where is there peace?*[246] It should be noted what cruelties he describes for those who glory in this vainest peace. For he goes on, *They have been confused, because they fell away, and they neither blushed at thus maintaining their confusion nor understood their own disgrace. Therefore, they will fall into ruin and grow weak in the time of my visitation.*[247]

119. What evil do we commit, what do we do impiously, if serving the faith for Christ we spit back peace of this sort, which is described as such a great confusion and disgrace with a very harsh end? But these notorious lovers of peace stir up war against faithful priests. For what does the devil want other than impious men and prevaricators to glory in the peace of this age? What does the devil want other than these men who are pious and faithful to be troubled by the persecution of their attackers?

120. We have presented these things to you so that the blood of Christians who defend the most pious faith will not be spilled at length because you were not informed. For what good is it if you are the protectors of the catholic faith but you allow the followers of the catholic faith to be tortured everywhere, to be put to flight everywhere, and to nowhere proclaim the pious faith freely?

121. Let them have their basilicas glittering with gold, ostentatiously adorned with costly marbles or pompously supported by columns![248] Let

---

243. See John 14:27, as in §58 above.
244. Rom 8:8.
245. Ps 13:3 LXX.
246. Jer 6:13–14.
247. Jer 6:15. The first part of the passage is somewhat garbled; the LXX reads "confusi sunt quia abominationem fecerunt quin potius confusione non sunt confusi et erubescere nescierunt."
248. The entire text up to this point has presented the emperor with little choice

quoque porrectas in longum possessiones, ob quas et fides integra periclitata est! Quid etiam suis impietatibus uindicant communes Romanis omnibus ciuitates ut neminem in his pie uiuere permittant, in quibus a plurimis etiam uana superstitio sine periculo colitur et sine illorum inuidia uindicatur? Liceat saltem ueritati, uel inter ipsa uilissima et abiecta praesepia, Christum Deum pie colere ac fideliter adorare, ubi et aliquando natus secundum carnem idem Christus infans iacere dignatus est.

122. Hoc quod petimus, non ideo petimus quasi expauescamus pro uero interfici: Deus testis est, qui uerus speculator est cordis, quia per Dei gratiam nobis ut summum refrigerium est et certa spes futurae beatitudinis si pro hac fideli adsertione iugulemur. Non ergo quasi qui timeamus perpeti, ideo sumus ista prosecuti, sed ne aliorum impietatibus et crudelitatibus sanguis effusus fidelium Christianorum diu piissimum uestrae principalitatis grauet imperium.

123. Maxime sub te, religiosissime Auguste Theodosi, qui mira deuotione contra omnes haereticos Christianae religionis pia confessione conspiras, magnum nobis apud Deum fore supplicium credidimus, si apud te tam religiosum, tam piissimum imperatorem et Christo Deo diuino ac plenissimo timore consecratum quem uere ad imperium Deus Chris-

them also have their possessions, spread far and wide, for which even the undiminished faith is endangered!²⁴⁹ Why do they claim cities common to all Romans for their impieties so that no one is permitted to live piously within them? Even vain superstition is worshiped in them without danger by the majority and without those men being hated.²⁵⁰ At least let it be permitted to piously worship Christ, our God, in truth and to adore him faithfully, even among those most worthless and abject mangers where that same Christ, born in the flesh as an infant, once deemed it worthy to lie down.²⁵¹

122. What we ask for, we do not ask for because we are terrified of being killed for what is true. *God is our witness, who is the true examiner of the heart,*²⁵² because through the grace of God the highest consolation is possible,²⁵³ and there is sure hope for future blessedness²⁵⁴ if our throats are cut for our faithful declaration.²⁵⁵ We do not present these things, then, as though we were the sort of people who would be afraid to suffer, but so that the blood of faithful Christians, which has been spilled for a long time due to the impieties and cruelties of others, does not burden the most pious dominion of your empire.

123. We believed that God would punish us severely if we stayed silent with you about things that concern the true faith and the true church—especially under you,²⁵⁶ most religious Theodosius Augustus, who with admirable devotion act with your pious confession of the Christian religion against all heretics, a very religious, very pious emperor, and one dedicated to Christ, our God, with divine and most complete reverence,²⁵⁷ whom

---

but to either throw his full support behind the Luciferians or the *egregii episcopi*; here, the Luciferians present a more practical alternative. See above, p. 30.

249. See above, §§16, 17, 32, 42, 49, 61, 117.

250. That is, if even pagans may worship openly, then the Luciferians should be able to as well. While there were growing restrictions on pagan worship in the Roman Empire, it was still not forbidden in the 380s.

251. See Luke 2:7–13.

252. Wis 1:6.

253. See Wis 4:7. Canellis (2006, 233n3) suggests Tertullian as the antecedent for this specific verbiage.

254. See Wis 3:4.

255. See 1 Pet 4:12–19.

256. Note that the authors switch from the plural form of address used throughout the text to the singular.

257. See Ps 13:3 LXX.

tus elegit, quae sunt uerae fidei ac uerae Ecclesiae taceremus. Post haec non ambigimus quo sollicitus agas qua pater imperii, ne in orbe Romano professae fidei communionisque sinceritas affligatur. Quicquid in causa sacrae fidei ac professae ueritatis sanctius gesseritis, tanto gloriosius et hic et in perpetuum Christi fauore regnabitis!

124. Ego Marcellinus presbyter, optans felicissimo imperio uestro securam quietam et in regno Christi et Dei perpetuam beatitudinem, piissimi imperatores.

Ego Faustinus, qui non possum dignus uocari presbyter Dei, optans ut et hic multos annos clementissimae diuinitatis auxilio feliciter imperetis et in futuro Christi Filii Dei regno perpetuam cum sanctis beatitudinem consequamini gloriosissimi imperatores.

truly Christ, our God, chose for the empire. After this, we do not doubt that because you have been made anxious, you will act like the father of the empire so that the purity of the professed faith and communion in the Roman world is not ruined. The more you do blessedly in the cause of the holy faith and the professed truth, the more you will reign gloriously both here and in eternity by the favor of Christ.

124. I, the presbyter Marcellinus,[258] hope for untroubled calm in your most felicitous empire and for everlasting blessedness in the kingdom of Christ and of God, most pious emperors.

I, Faustinus, who could not be worthy of being called a presbyter of God,[259] hope both that you rule felicitously here for many years with the help of the most merciful divinity and that you attain everlasting blessedness with the saints in the future kingdom of Christ, the Son of God, most glorious emperors.

---

258. *PCBE* 2.2 (Marcellinus 3).
259. *PCBE* 2.1 (Faustinus 2). This statement is simply rhetorical humility. He calls himself a presbyter in the preface of the *Confessio fidei*.

Theodosius, *Lex Augusta*

Ad has preces ita lex augusta respondit:

1. Salue, Cynegi carissime nobis! Etsi nulla humanis pectoribus maior quam diuinae legis debet esse reuerentia nec adici quicquam ad eam possit, cuius ambitiosa praestantia, mundi terraeque moderatrix omne, quod sub nobis esse uoluit fauor omnipotentis Dei, propitiata custodit,

2. tamen, quia per Faustinum atque Marcellinum, plenissimos fidei sacerdotes, interpellata clementia nostra, ueriti sumus ne, si per nos nihil fuisset responsum petentibus, nos uideremur annuere his qui diuinae legi cui seruimus contra propositum nostrum aliquid addidissent. Atque ideo ita utrumque moderamur ut petitionem quae est oblata ueneremur, fidei autem nihil ex nostro arbitrio optemus uel iubeamus adiungi. Nemo enim umquam tam profanae mentis fuit qui, cum sequi catholicos doctores debeat, quid sequendum sit doctoribus ipse constituat!

3. Et sane probabilis et iusta illatio precum est, quae omnem prope seriem haereticae superstitionis, quae contraria est fidei catholicae,

Theodosius, *Augustan Law*

The Augustan law in response to these requests:

1. Greetings, Cynegius,[1] most dear to us.

No law ought to be revered in human hearts more than divine law, and even if it is not possible to add anything to it, as its all-encompassing superiority, which is the director of all of the world and the earth, keeps guard over everything that the favor of omnipotent God wished to be subject to us,[2]

2. Nevertheless, priests completely filled with faith, Faustinus and Marcellinus, have appealed to our clemency. Because of this, we were afraid that if we made no response to the petitioners, we would appear to give approval to those who have added something against our intent to the divine law that we serve. So, for this reason, we decide to honor the petition that has been presented, and also wish—or order, rather—that nothing be added to the faith on our own authority.[3] For there was never anyone with such a profane mind that he thought that while he ought to follow catholic teachers, he himself should establish what these teachers should follow!

3. The presentation[4] of their requests, which covers nearly the whole range of heretical superstition contrary to the catholic faith,[5] is certainly

---

1. *PLRE* 1:235 (Maternus Cynegius 3).

2. Theodosius's language is markedly more ornate than that of Faustinus and Marcellinus.

3. Though Theodosius accepts their petition, he includes this clear warning to the Luciferians as well.

4. Canellis corrects the text to read *illatio* instead of *laudatio*, which fits the text better and anticipates the use of *illatio* in §6 below.

5. While the bulk of the Luciferians' ire is directed toward Arius and his followers, Faustinus and Marcellinus do offer criticisms of a wide variety of heresies at *Lib. prec.* 114. Sabellius and Apollinaris are both additionally mentioned in Faustinus's *Confessio fidei*, and at *Trin.* 41 Faustinus also castigates Photinus.

ordinemque complexa est. Nam et unde exorta et quo prouecta auctore fuisset aperuit, quippe cum persuasu quorumdam totius saeculi antiquitate mutata acti pro fide in exilium innocentes uitam cum summa laude posuerunt.

4. Sed circa eos non est dilata ultio qui insidiati bonis moribus et caelestibus institutis paulisper ex contentione non fide sed factione multorum mentes detestanda insinuatione peruerterent. Nam usque adeo omnipotentis Dei mota patientia est, ut poenam, quae criminosis post fata debetur, in exemplo omnium ante fata sentirent.

5. Sed ne hoc quidem facto conuerti ad praeceptum Dei flectique potuerunt: catholicos occultis molitionibus urguent, insequuntur, oppugnant. Tanta perseuerantia erroris est ut cum aliis diuersae obseruantiae sectatoribus cottidie peccare malint quam cum catholicis recta sentire.

6. In quo petentum laudanda illatio est qui, communicantes Gregorio Hispaniensi et Heraclidae Orientali, sanctis sane et laudabilis episcopis, optant in fide catholica sine oppugnatione alicuius ac molestia uiuere nul-

just and worthy of praise. For it made clear both whence heretical superstition had arisen and what instigator had carried it forward,[6] since, in fact, the ancient tradition of the entire world[7] was changed by the persuasiveness of certain men,[8] and the innocent, driven into exile for the faith, laid down their lives with the highest praise.[9]

4. But revenge has not been delayed against those who prepared an ambush against good morals and heaven's ordinances, and who, acting not out of faith but out of factionalism,[10] little by little perverted the minds of many by ingratiation that ought to be detested. For the patience of omnipotent God was so moved at this point that, as an example for all, they experienced before their fates the punishment owed to criminals after their fates.[11]

5. Yet not even once this was done could they be turned round and bent to the command of God. They bore down on catholics with secret designs, they pursued them, they assaulted them! So great is the persistence of their error that they would rather sin daily with the other followers of a deviant religion than think rightly with catholics.

6. In this, the presentation of the petitioners should be praised: they hold communion with Gregory of Spain and Heraclida of the East,[12] clearly holy and praiseworthy bishops, and wish to live within the catholic faith

---

6. It is unclear whether Arius or Constantius is meant here.

7. The ancient tradition here must refer to the Scriptures and apostles; referring to the world as the *totius saeculi* is an interesting departure from Faustinus and Marcellinus's use of *saeculum* to refer to the secular world in contrast to the envisioned divine era following the return of Christ (see, e.g., Faustinus and Marcellinus, *Lib. prec.* 7, 22, 47, 57, 85, 98, 102, 119).

8. Probably a reference to Arius and his later "heirs"; see Faustinus and Marcellinus, *Lib. prec.* 12, 14.

9. As described throughout the first third of the *Libellus precum*.

10. See Faustinus and Marcellinus, *Lib. prec.* 12, 116.

11. Thus referencing both general arguments and numerous stories of divine punishments found in the *Libellus precum* (see Faustinus and Marcellinus, *Lib. prec.* 9, 31, 38–39, 46, 65).

12. For Gregory (of Elvira), see Faustinus and Marcellinus, *Lib. prec.* 33–40, 73, 77, 90, 98; for Heraclida (of Oxyrhynchus), see §§94–105. Brent (1995, 384) suggests that Heraclida may have been living in exile at Ostia or Portus at the time this rescript was sent; this seems unlikely in part because Theodosius never says as much and in part because Theodosius surely would have wanted to specify at least one Luciferian bishop living within his half of the empire. See also the comments at Faustinus and Marcellinus, *Lib. prec.* 97, on the speculation of Heraclida in exile.

lisque appententum insidiis conuentionibusque pulsari, quippe quibus placeat susceptam semel fidem omni in aeuum religione seruare.

7. Sit itaque inuiolatum quicquid esse meruit aeternum. Non conuentio aliquid, non appetitio, non fraus attemptet aliena. Vtantur quo in loco uoluerint proposito suo! Vtantur ad catholicam fidem amore diuino!

Cynegi, parens carissime atque amantissime,

8. Sublimitas tua praeceptum nostrae serenitatis, quo catholicam fidem omni fauore ueneramur, sine qua salui esse non possumus, ita iubeat custodiri ut Gregorium et Heraclidam, sacrae legis antistites, ceterosque eorum consimiles sacerdotes qui se parili obseruantiae dederunt ab improborum hominum atque haereticorum tueatur et defendat iniuriis sciantque cuncti id sedere animis nostris ut cultores omnipotentis Dei non aliud nisi catholicos esse credamus.

without anyone's aggression and without trouble. They also wish to be disturbed by no ambushes and mobs of attackers, and in fact it would please them to preserve with continual devotion the faith that that they took up only once, with all religious conscience.

7. Thus, let whatever has been deemed worthy of being eternal be inviolable. Let not any mob, let not any assault, let not any other's fraud assail it. Let them practice their own way of life in whatever place they wish. Let them enjoy divine love in the catholic faith.

Cynegius, dearest and most beloved kinsman,[13]

8. By Our Serenity's command, we venerate with full support the catholic faith, without which we cannot be saved. Let your loftiness order that command to be observed in such a way that it protects and defends Gregory and Heraclida, priests of the holy law, and the rest of the priests who are similar to these and have given themselves over in equal reverence,[14] from the violence of vile men and heretics. And let all know that this occupies our mind: we believe that worshipers of omnipotent God are none other than catholics.

---

13. *Parens* here does not necessarily refer to a parent, or even a blood relative, but rather reinforces the closeness between Theodosius and Cynegius (see above, p. 40). Dunn (2007) discusses the use of familial terms among late antique clergy, and many of the same terms were used to describe relationships between laity as well. Günther and Simonetti both take this second personal address to go with the preceding phrase, but it makes more sense to follow Canellis and assume that the address is directed toward what follows, namely, Theodosius's summation of his decision and his actual command to Cynegius.

14. This clause is quite similar to Cod. theod. 16.1.2 (*Cunctos populos*); see above, p. 42.

Faustinus, *De Trinitate*

1. Faustinus Augustae Flaccillae.

Reginam te orbis Romanus suspicit; et quia iam nihil est, quo amplius crescere debeas in rebus humanis, sublimitatibus non contenta terrenis, sacra in Deum fide caelestia desideras possidere, quae uerus Filius Dei in se pie credentibus pollicetur. Et hoc quasi una de sapientissimis elaboras, intellegens omnem hanc regni sublimitatem nihil profuturam, si non ad caelestem gloriam consequendam uerae fidei cognitione et defensione contendas. Et tamen apparet quam grata sis in Christo Deo et Domino nostro, qui uobis hoc regnum tribuit, cum sollicita interrogatione perquiris quomodo capitula illa soluantur, quae ab Arrianis aduersus catholicos sacrilegis interpretationibus opponuntur. Habens affectum uerae fidei, cupis, prout possibile est, intellegere quod fideliter credis, quia et tunc magis anima religiosa uelut diuinis epulis pascitur, si quod credit intellegit. Sed et cum exsecraris impias uoces haereticorum, tamen religioso

Faustinus, *On the Trinity*

1. Faustinus, to Flacilla Augusta.[1]

The Roman world welcomes you as empress, and because there is no longer anything in human matters to which you may aspire, you, not being content with earthly pinnacles, long through your holy faith in God to master the heavenly matters that the true Son of God promises to those who piously believe in him.[2] You work at this like a sage,[3] understanding that all the loftiness of your reign will be of no value to you if you do not struggle to pursue heavenly glory by understanding and defending the true faith. It nevertheless is apparent how pleasing you are to Christ, our God and Lord, who conferred this reign on you,[4] when you diligently inquire with anxious questioning as to how those chapters, composed against catholics by Arians with their sacrilegious interpretations, may be refuted. Possessing true faith, you desire (as much as possible) to understand what you faithfully believe, because if a religious soul understands what it believes, then it is fed even more, as if by divine feasts.[5] But also, though you curse the impious expressions of the heretics, you nevertheless desire to be

---

1. *PLRE* 1 (Flavia Aelia Flacilla). Her name sometimes appears as Placilla. A Spaniard, she was Theodosius's first wife and mother of his sons Arcadius and Honorius. Theodoret (*Hist. eccl.* 5.19) specifically mentions that she had devoted herself to religious education.

2. For the language, see Ovid, *Trist.* 4.10.19: "At mihi iam parvo caelestia sacra placebant"; for the sentiment, see Theodoret, *Hist. eccl.* 5.18: Οὐ γὰρ ἐπῆρεν αὐτὴν τῆς βασιλείας ἡ δυναστεία, αλλὰ τὸν θεῖον πλέον ἐπυρσευσε πόθον.

3. See below, §19.

4. See Faustinus and Marcellinus, *Lib. prec.* 2, 123.

5. This also appears as a term apparently meaning the emperor's table, though of course it has a different meaning here. See Cod. theod. 6.13.1: "Praepositos ac tribunos scholarum, qui et divinis epulis adhibentur et adorandi principis facultatem antiquitus meruerunt."

studio instrui aduersus eos desideras, ut et rationem iam respuas, ne hoc quod exsecraris, quasi ex regni potentia, praesumptionis uideatur esse, non probationis. Sed huic tam pio tam necessario et pulcherrimo desiderio tuo, etsi me inparem uideo, tamen ut resistens obuiam uenire non audeo. Confiteor enim quod hac me inhabilis conscientia et inperitia squalidi sermonis suffundit, ut taceam; hac feruor fidei periculum credit esse, si taceam: quomodo enim periculum non uidetur, si aduersus hostem impium prouocati, conscientia eloquendique uerecundia quasi terga uertamus? Maxime cum in causa fidei non sermonum sublimitas requirenda est, quando ipsa sola testimonia diuina sufficiant, quae potentius operantur quam quaeuis facundi oris eloquentia. Sed nec uitiorum conscientia cogitanda est, quando potius releuatur, si primo Deum non trepidet confiteri, exemplo illius euangelici latronis, qui quo die confessus est Deum, ipso die meruit in paradiso cum eo, quem confessus fuerat, inueniri. Incipiamus ergo, oboedientes religiosissimis praeceptis tuis, collidere cum aduersario, non quidem de nostris uiribus praesumentes, sed

instructed in religious study against them so that you might also spit back reason at the same time, for fear that your curses would appear to be presumed, not proven, as though they depended on the power of your reign.

But even though I regard myself as unequal to this desire of yours—which is so pious, so necessary and becoming—I nevertheless do not dare obstruct you by holding back. For on the one hand, I confess that I am filled with poor understanding and have an awkward, rough way of speaking; I should stay silent.[6] On the other hand, the fervor of my faith believes that it would be dangerous if I remain silent. How would it not seem dangerous, if we acted like we were turning our backs when we were called forth against an impious enemy because we understood and were ashamed of our eloquence?[7] Especially since in furthering the faith, loftiness of speech should not be required. Divine testimonies, which are used with more force than the eloquence of an articulate mouth, should be enough on their own.[8] But neither should one consider one's knowledge of his own sins, since he is comforted all the more if he does not fear acknowledging God right away. This is like the example of that robber in the gospels who, on the same day he acknowledged God, earned entry into paradise along with the one whom he had acknowledged.[9]

Being obedient to your most religious commands, let us begin to collide with the adversary.[10] Of course we do not trust in our own strength but have confidence in the patronage of our Savior, against whom the

---

6. See below, §§48, 51. A conventional rhetorical tactic in antiquity was to emphatically deny, in a bout of modesty, that one was capable of doing exactly what one then goes on to do. See, e.g., Jerome, *Ep.* 1.1–2, which also begins by expressing Jerome's doubts about his abilities to complete a requested literary task, the argument that piety and the Word supersede any deficiencies in his style, and an agreement to fulfill the request because he does not "dare" to refuse: "Cumque ego id verecunde et vere, ut nunc experior, negarem, meque assequi posse diffiderem; sive quia omnis sermo humanus inferior est laude coelesti: sive quia otium quasi quaedam ingenii rubigo, parvulam licet facultatem pristini siccasset eloquii: tu e contrario asserebas, in divinis rebus non possibilitatem inspici debere, sed animum; neque posse eum verba deficere, qui credidisset in Verbum. Quid igitur faciam? quod implere non possum, negare non audio."

7. The military metaphor reappears in §§2, 3, 12 below.

8. See Faustinus and Marcellinus, *Lib. prec.* 89.

9. See Luke 23:43.

10. One manuscript tradition begins with this sentence. Are there shades of the famous epitaph for the Spartans at Thermopylae here? Cicero (*Tusc.* 1.101) translates it thus: "Dic, hospes, Spartae, nos te hic vidisse iacentes / dum sanctis patriae legibus obsequimur." The vocabulary Faustinus uses is much different—*oboedientes* rather

habentes fiduciam de patrocinio Saluatoris, aduersus quem more gentilium et furore Iudaeorum bellum exagitat impietas haereticorum. Sed quia in his quae scribere dignata es ex persona haereticorum, uidi plurima esse confusa ita ut uidereris mihi non plenius nosse quae adserant Arriani, melius opinatus sum si primum liquido palam facerem quomodo credant et quomodo sub anabiguitate sermonis simplices animas capiant, et tunc maxime, cum sub communi confessione impia sua uerba commendant: quia et tunc demum absolutionum fidelis responsio manifesta est, si prius sacrilegae sectae impia tergiuersatio propaletur.

2. (I, 1) De professione impia Arrianorum.

Arriana impietas adserit multa quidem nobiscum iisdem sermonibus, sed non iisdem sensibus, cum ad diuinae fidei confessionem uocatur. Nam iisdem quibus et nos uocibus personat Deum Patrem et Deum Filium, et omnia a Deo Patre per Filium facta, et Filium ante saecula genitum. Sed cum nobiscum per haec uerba concordet, nihilominus sacrilegis uerborum interpretationibus a piis ecclesiae catholicae sensibus abrumpit, ita dicens Patrem, ut non uere genuerit; ita Filium quoque pronuntians, ut

impiety of the heretics wages war in the custom of the pagans and with the fury of the Jews.[11] But I have seen that among the characteristically heretical things that you found worth relating, most are confused. To me, this means that you do not seem to fully know what the Arians assert. For this reason, I think it is better if I first make it loud and clear what they believe and how they seize simple souls under the ambiguity of their speech—especially when they make their own impious words sound acceptable under a shared confession.[12] If the impious deception of their sacrilegious sect is revealed first, the faithful refutation from our answers will also be made clear at the exact same time.

2. (I, 1) On the impious profession of the Arians.

The impious Arians[13] indeed assert many things with the very same words as ours, but not with the same sentiments, when they are called to confess the divine faith.[14] For in the same language as ours, they call out that God is the Father and God is the Son, and that all things from God the Father were made through the Son, and that the Son predates the time of creation. But although they agree with us in these words, they nonetheless separate themselves from the pious sentiments of the catholic church with their sacrilegious interpretations of these words.[15] Thus they say about the Father that he did not truly beget the Son, and proclaim about the Son, too, that he was not his natural son but was with him by adoption—that

---

than *obsequimur, praeceptis tuis* instead of *patriae legibus*—but the use of *religiosissimis* interestingly parallels Cicero's addition of *sanctis* to the original.

11. See Faustinus and Marcellinus, *Lib. prec.* 29, 76, wherein they compare their adversaries to pagans, and Jerome, *Lucif.* 15, wherein Jerome suggests that Luciferians describe other Nicene communities as synagogues. Jews also appear as a target for Faustinus in §10 below.

12. That Arians intentionally kept their creeds vague was a common enough complaint: Phoebadius of Agen, *Ar.* 1.3; Gregory of Elvira, *Fid.* 18; Hilary of Poitiers, *Trin.* 10.70; Jerome, *Ep.* 15.4. Hilary of Poitiers (*Syn.* 40, 68, 89) writes that the Arians made the same complaint about Nicene terms such as *homoousios*.

13. Faustinus refers to the "Arrian impiety" (*Arriana impietas*) throughout the text, but it is more natural in English to render this as "impious Arians."

14. See Athanasius, *Ep. encycl.* 7; *Apol. sec.* 1.9; *Syn.* 15; Hilary of Poitiers, *Trin.* 4.3; Ambrose, *Fid.* 1.5.34.

15. On the basic tenets of Arianism, which was never a single set of defined religious beliefs as it is presented here, see above, p. 2. See Faustinus and Marcellinus, *Lib. prec.* 8, for another Luciferian presentation of these beliefs.

apud eum adoptione non natura sit filius, id est: ut aliunde ad filii nomen adsumptus, non uere de Deo Patre sit genitus. Nam licet et ante saecula Filium natum esse fateatur, tamen ei initium tribuit dicendo: Erat quando non erat. Sed et sic quoque per eum facta dicit uniuersa, ut eum adserat ex nullis exstantibus substitutum, quia praesumpsit non uere de Deo Patre genitum. Et inde est quod ita uult haberi persuasum, Christum Deum quidem esse, sed non uerum, cui initium deputetur; et Filium quidem ita, ut factus intellegatur esse, non natus. Si quidem non uere de Patre natus est, sed de nihilo substitutus, ob hoc quoque et mutabilem credit, quia in fide eius non uere Deus neque uere Filius est. Et ut hos impios sensus apud ignaros uel simplices commendet, adhibet quoque, ut sibi uidetur, Scripturarum diuinarum testimonia, dicens ex persona sapientiae prolatum: *Dominus creauit me initium uiarum suarum in opera sua*. Christum autem sapientiam esse apostolus quoque confirmat dicendo: *Christum Dei uirtutem et Dei sapientiam*. Constat ergo Christum, qui est—apostolo interprete—sapientia, esse creaturam: et iam, inquit, consequens est ut non sit uere Deus, qui sit creatura; iam nec uere Filius, qui non sit a Deo genitus, sed creatus et si creatus est, erat ergo quando non erat.

3. (I, 2) Haec sunt nequitiae arma proposita, aduersus quae ire prouocamur, ut adsertionis aduersae propaletur impietas, non quidem nostro, ut diximus, ingenio, sed gratia Dei adiuuante semper pios conatus. Tu modo, quaeso ne squalido sermone fatigeris, sed rerum intenta uirtutibus da

is, he was elevated to the name of the Son and was not truly begotten from God the Father.[16] Although they also confess that the Son was born before time had begun, they nevertheless assign a beginning to him, saying, "There was a time when he was not." They also say that everything was done through him. Thus they assert that he was constituted from nothing that had existed, since they suppose that he was not truly begotten from God the Father. This is why they wish it to be considered settled that Christ indeed is God, but not truly, as they ascribe a beginning to him; and that Christ indeed is the Son, in such a way that he is understood to have been made, not born. Indeed, if he were constituted from nothing, and not truly born from the Father, they believe based on this that he is changeable, because in their faith he is neither truly God nor truly the Son.

To make these impious sentiments more acceptable among the ignorant or simpleminded,[17] they also employ the testimonies of divine scripture (as it seems to them), relating something uttered by the person of Wisdom: *The Lord created me as the beginning of his ways for his work.*[18] Moreover, the Apostle affirms that Christ is Wisdom, saying *Christ, the Power of God and the Wisdom of God.*[19] Thus it stands that Christ, who is Wisdom (as the Apostle explains), is a created being; and then, they say, it follows that one who is a created being is not truly God; and then, one who was not begotten by the Father, but created, is not truly the Son; and then, if he were created, there was therefore a time when he was not.

3. (I, 2) These are the weapons of their wickedness which have been brandished.[20] We are provoked to move against them so that the impiety of our opponent's assertion may be revealed. As we said, we certainly are not attempting to do this by our own wits but by the grace of God, which always helps the pious. Now, I ask you, do not grow weary of our rough way of speaking, but stay mindful of the importance of these matters and

---

16. Adoptionism long predated Arianism; see Kelly 1978, 115–19.

17. See Hilary of Poitiers, *Trin.* 5.32: "Haec si stultitia atque impietas haeretica, ad fallendum ignorantes simplicioresque, dicta esse ex persona Dei patris mentietur."

18. Prov 8:22. This theme will be fully treated in §43 below. In this treatise, Wisdom is generally referred to as the *persona Sapientiae*, one of the guises of the Son, as the next sentence makes clear.

19. 1 Cor 1:24.

20. The return here to the military theme pervasive in §1 above indicates that §2 serves as a brief summation of Arian thought (as Faustinus represents it). See §12 below as well.

calculum ueritati. Hoc autem non ut librum scribimus, sed quasi cum praesente aduersario certis disputationibus dimicamus. Et in primis contra hoc quod dicunt: Erat quando non erat, occurrendum est quod semper fuerit, et opponendum de Euangelio testimonium, dicente Iohanne: *In principio erat Verbum.* Sicut enim Christus Dei sapientia et Dei uirtus est, ita et Dei Verbum est. Cum ergo ait: *In principio erat Verbum,* quomodo Arriana impietas dicit: Erat quando non erat? *In principio*—inquit—*erat Verbum*; non dixit: In principio factum est Verbum: et utique quod in principio erat, semper fuisse credendum est. Si enim, ut putat impietas, factura est Filius, sine dubio Scriptura diuina hoc ipsum quod factus est in principio prodidisset, ex illa utique institutione, qua et Moyses locutus est dicendo *In principio fecit Deus caelum et terram.* Si enim et Filius Dei factura esset, dixisset Iohannes: In principio factum est Verbum. Sed praeuidens euangelista, magis autem Spiritus Sanctus per euangelistam, futuros impiae mentis homines, qui dicerent de Filio: Erat quando non erat, ideo sic coepit: *In principio erat Verbum*: nihil enim illo anterius est, qui inuenitur ante principium. Scripturae diuinae ob hoc editae sunt, ut secundum illarum sensum nostram fidem dirigamus, non ut nostros sensus illarum sacris dictionibus inseramus. Viderit, si sunt quaedam capitula, quae sui obscuritate dare putantur occasionem ambiguitatibus: certe in hoc capitulo nulla ambiguitatis occasio est. Non licet interpreti aliter sentire, quam scriptum est, nec opus est ut nunc nostros sensus ingeramus: sufficit ad plenam percipiendae fidei notitiam, ut diuina uerba recitemus: *In prin-*

cast your vote for the truth.[21] Moreover, we are writing this not like a book, but as though we were contending against an adversary present in an actual dispute.[22]

First, when they say, "There was a time when he was not," we must counter: "He has always been." Testimony from the gospel should be set against them.[23] John says, *In the beginning was the Word*.[24] For just as Christ is the Wisdom of God and the Power of God,[25] so too is he the Word of God. When, therefore, he says, *In the beginning was the Word*, how can the Arians say, "There was a time when he was not"? *In the beginning*, he says, *was the Word*. He did not say, "In the beginning the Word was made."[26] Surely we must believe that whatever *was* in the beginning has always existed. For if, as the Arians reckon, the Son were something made, undoubtedly the divine scriptures would have related that he was made in the beginning, just like when Moses said *In the beginning, God made heaven and the earth*.[27] For if the Son of God were also something made, John would have said, "In the beginning, the Word was made." But the Evangelist—or rather, the Holy Spirit through the Evangelist—foresaw that impious-minded men would come and say about the Son, "There was a time when he was not," and began thus: *In the beginning was the Word*. For there is nothing earlier than that which is found before the beginning.

The divine scriptures were revealed so that we could direct our faith in accordance with their meaning, not so that we might insert our own meanings into their sacred expressions. Let them see if there are any chapters that they think cause ambiguity by virtue of their obscurity; certainly in this chapter there is no cause for ambiguity. Nor is an interpreter allowed to consider anything other than what has been written, and there is no need now for us to heap up our own meanings on top.[28] To fully conceive of the faith that we must observe, it is enough to recite these divine words:

---

21. See below, §§28, 30, 42.
22. In other words, the style will be colloquial, not polished for publication; the treatise is not written as a traditional dialogue. See below, §§8, 19, 48.
23. See Athanasius, *Apol. sec.* 1.11; Hilary of Poitiers, *Trin.* 2.13.
24. John 1:1.
25. See 1 Cor 1:24. This returns to the statements that Faustinus takes as foundations for the entire discussion immediately above in §2.
26. See Gregory of Elvira, *Fid.* 25: "Non enim dixit, In principio factum est verbum, sed in principio, inquit, erat verbum."
27. Gen 1:1. See Athanasius, *Apol. sec.* 2.57.
28. See below, §44, where Faustinus essentially does do this.

cipio—inquit—*erat Verbum*. Numquid aliqua hic est opinio temporis, numquid aliqua suspicio saeculorum uel aliquod interuallum puncti aut momenti alicuius, ut dicere audeas: Erat quando non erat?

4. (I, 3) *In principio*—inquit—*erat Verbum*, et ne forte uerbum intellegas, quod est loquentis officium, sequitur: *Et Verbum erat apud Deum*: non dixit: Et uerbum quod locutus est Deus, sed: *Et Verbum erat apud Deum*. Ipse postremo interpretatus est quid sit Verbum, dicens: *Et Deus erat Verbum*. Si in principio erat Verbum et hoc ipsum Verbum apud Deum erat et Deus erat Verbum, confusa est impietatis intentio. Probatur enim de hoc capitulo Christum Filium Dei et semper fuisse et semper inseparabilem a Patre et semper Deum. Sicut enim sine initio est, cum dicitur: *In principio erat*, sic et cum dicitur: *apud Deum erat*, inseparabilitas eius a Patre sine initio declaratur. Sed et cum hoc Verbum Deus esse definitur, non est ambiguum quod sine initio Deus creditur. Hoc enim quod praemisit dicens: In principio, ad omnia referendum est, id est: *In principio erat Verbum*; et cum sequitur: *Et Verbum erat apud Deum et Deus erat Verbum*, sine dubio In principio subaudiendum est. Denique et ipse ita concludit dicens: *Hoc erat in principio apud Deum*. Quomodo ergo erat quando non erat, qui semper est? quomodo ex nullis exstantibus est, qui semper apud Patrem est? quomodo creatura, qui semper Deus, immo et per quem uniuersa creatura est? Sequitur enim: *Omnia per ipsum facta sunt*. Quomodo ergo ex nullis exstantibus factus est, per quem omnia facta sunt? Si enim et ipse factus est, quomodo per ipsum omnia facta sunt? Non enim cum fieret, potest sui auctor esse, qui non fuit: atque ideo infectus esse

In the beginning, he says, *was the Word.* Is there any supposed time here, is there any indication of some age, or even some interval of an instant or of some moment, so that you might dare say, "There was a time when he was not"?

4. (I, 3) *In the beginning,* he says, *was the Word.*[29] If you should happen to understand the "word" as the one that functions in speech, there follows *and the Word was with God.*[30] He did not say "and the word which God spoke" but *and the Word was with God.* At the end, he explained what the word was, saying, *and the Word was God.*[31] If in the beginning was the Word, and this same Word was with God, and God was the Word, then the strategy behind their impiety is confounded. For this chapter proves that Christ is the Son of God, that he always existed, that he was always inseparable from the Father, and that he was always God.[32] For just as he is without a beginning, when it says *In the beginning was,* so, too, is his inseparability from the Father, without a beginning, declared when it says *was with God.* But even when this Word is being defined as God, there is no ambiguity when we believe that God is without a beginning. For what it says first, *In the beginning,* must be ascribed to all the parts—that is, it says, *In the beginning was the Word*; and when there follows, *and the Word was with God, and the Word was God,* without a doubt *In the beginning* must still be understood. Finally, it concludes this way: *This was in the beginning with God.*[33] How then was there a time when he, who always is, was not? How is he, who is always with the Father, from nothing that exists? How is he, who is always God, and likewise through whom everything was created, a created being? For there follows, *All things were made through him.*[34] How then was he, through whom all things were made, made from nothing that existed? For if he himself were also made, how were all things made through him? After all, when he was being made, he who did not exist could not have been his own originator. This is why we must believe that he, through whom all things were made, was not made, because it is

---

29. See Hilary of Poitiers, *Trin.* 2.14; 7.9–11; Athanasius, *Apol. sec.* 1.11.
30. John 1:1.
31. John 1:1.
32. See Gregory of Elvira, *Fid.* 27. On this point, Hilary (*Trin.* 2.14) uniquely coins a Latin imperfect participle: "Est ergo erans apud Deum." On this phrase, see Smulders 1988; Beckwith 2008, 119.
33. John 1:2.
34. John 1:3. See Hilary of Poitiers, *Trin.* 2.18; Ambrose, *Fid.* 1.14.88.

credendus est, per quem omnia facta sunt; quia uanum est et absurdum, ut et ipse, cum non exstaret, factus per se esse dicatur.

5. (I, 4) Similiter et Paulus docet Christum semper fuisse et Deum esse et aequalem Patri. Tunc enim uere Deus est, cum aequalis est Patri: quia nec aequalis diceretur, si non uere Deus haberetur. Iniuria est enim Dei ueri, si ei non Deus uerus dicatur aequalis. Ponit itaque in epistula sua: *Hoc enim existimate in uobis, quod in Christo Iesu: qui cum in forma Dei esset constitutus, non rapinam arbitratus est esse se aequalem Deo, sed semetipsum exinaniuit, formam serui accipiens.* Si uere homo est Christus, cum formam serui accipit, uere quoque Deus est, cum in forma Dei esse perhibetur; nec alia ratione aequalem diceret Deo, nisi in forma Dei esse uerum Deum esse uoluisset intellegi. Et qui uerus Deus est, utique semper Deus est, et qui semper Deus est, non potest dici de eo: Erat quando non erat. Sed et per ipsum omnia facta ait apostolus Paulus scribens: *Quia in ipso creata sunt omnia, siue quae in caelis siue quae in terris, inuisibilia et uisibilia, siue throni siue dominationes siue principatus siue potestates: omnia per ipsum et in ipso creata sunt, et ipse est ante omnes.* Ergo ipse semper est, per quem et in quo omnia facta sunt. Sed et hymnidicus cantans ait: *Omnia in sapientia fecisti.* Non tamen ipsam dixit factam esse sapientiam, quia et apostolus, cum dicit: *Et ipse est ante omnes*, factum negauit. Si enim eum qui non erat, factum credi uoluisset, ita posuisset: Et ipse factus est ante omnes; at cum dicit *Et ipse est ante omnes*, omnibus dedit initium, quorum anterior, immo et factor est; ipse uero sine initio

meaningless and absurd to say that he was made through himself when he did not exist.

5. (I, 4) Similarly, Paul also teaches that Christ always existed, and that he is God and equal to the Father. For he is truly God only when he is equal to the Father. He would not be called equal if he were not truly considered God, since it would be unjust to God if one who is not the true God were called equal to him.[35] So, Paul puts in his epistle, *Consider among yourselves that which was also in Jesus Christ, who, though he was constituted in the form of God, did not regard equality with God as a boon, but diminished himself by taking the form of a servant.*[36] If Christ were truly a man because he took the form of a servant, then truly he is God as well, since he is said to be in the form of God. Paul would only call him equal to God if he had wanted *in the form of God* to be understood as *to be the true God*. Whoever is the true God is certainly always God, and one cannot say about one who is always God that "there was a time when he was not."

The apostle Paul also says that all things were made through him.[37] He writes, *Since all things are created in him, whether in heaven or on earth, invisible and visible things, whether thrones or dominions or sovereigns or powers—all things are created through him and in him, and he is prior to all.*[38] Therefore he, through whom and in whom all things are done, always exists. The psalmist also sings, *In Wisdom you have made all things.*[39] He did not say that Wisdom itself was made, because the Apostle also denies that it was made when he says, *And he is prior to all*. For if he wanted us to believe that he who was not made was made, he would have put it thus: "And he was made prior to all." But when he says, *And he is prior to all*, he gives a beginning to "all," and the Son is instead the preceding maker of all. He is truly without a beginning, since he is not spoken of as made but

---

35. See Hilary of Poitiers, *Trin.* 8.45; 12.6.

36. Phil 2:5–7. See below, §§17, 20, 23, 32, 34, 36–38. This passage is a constant thread throughout Faustinus's *De Trinitate*. On this passage in patristic authors in general, see Grelot 1971. See also Phoebadius of Agen, *Ar.* 16.3; 26.1–2; Hilary of Poitiers, *Trin.* 9.14–15; Lucifer of Caligari, *Mor. esse Dei Fil.* 10; Ambrose, *Fid.* 2.8.62–65. Hilary (Weedman 2007b, 131–32, 157–66) goes on to examine a number of scriptural passages using this *servus/Deus* terminology as his touchstone. *Servus* can be translated "servant" or "slave"; here I have retained the more common English translation of "servant," although at §20 below the word is used more in the sense of "slave."

37. See Hilary of Poitiers, *Trin.* 2.19; Athanasius, *Decr.* 17.

38. Col 1:16–17.

39. Ps 103:24 LXX. See Athanasius, *Apol. sec.* 1.19; 2.51; Ambrose, *Fid.* 1.14.88.

est, qui ante omnes non factus sed esse memoratur. Item apostolus: *Vnus*—inquit—*Deus Pater, ex quo omnia et nos in ipso, et unus Dominus noster Iesus Christus, per quem omnia et nos per ipsum*: et hic cum dicit per Christum esse omnia, apertissime factorem discreuit a factis, nec posse intellegi naturam facturae in eo qui fecit omnia.

6. (I, 5) Sed uideamus si et Moyses hoc idem docuit, quod apostoli adnuntiauerunt, id est, omnia ex Deo facta esse per Filium. Inter cetera, cum fabricam mundi refert ait: *Et dixit Deus: Fiat firmamentum in medio aquae, et sit diuidens inter aquam et aquam, et factum est sic. Et fecit Deus firmamentum, et diuisit Deus per medium aquae.* Cum dicit: *Et dixit Deus: Fiat firmamentum,* in dicente Patris intellegenda persona est; cum autem dicit: *Et fecit Deus,* in faciente Filii intellegenda persona est. Nam si non putas ita intellegendum, apostolica periclitabitur adsertio, dicens: *Vnus Deus Pater, ex quo omnia et nos in ipso, et unus Dominus noster Iesus Christus, per quem omnia et nos per ipsum.* Nisi enim totam fabricam mundi per Filium factam esse credideris, immo et omnia inuisibilia siui et uisibilia, quemadmodum in fidem recipis uocem apostoli dicentis: *Vnus Dominus noster Iesus Christus, per quem omnia,* et illud quoque quod supra retulimus: *Quia in ipso creata sun omnia,* nec non et illud: *Omnia in sapienta fecisti?* Sed et hoc quod Iohannes prosecutus est: *Omnia per ipsum facta sunt,* quomodo omnia, si negas de Filio Dei dictum: *Et fecit Deus firmamentum, et diuisit Deus per medium aquae*? Ergo et Moyses factorem Filium induct, non factum. Si enim factum, Sancto Spiritu reuelante, didicisset, inter cetera quae facta describebat, ipsum quoque prius factum esse memorasset.

as existing prior to all. Moreover, the Apostle says, *There is one God, the Father, by whom all things exist, and for whom we exist. And there is one Lord, our Jesus Christ, through whom all things exist and through whom we exist.*[40] When he says that all things exist through Christ, he quite clearly separates the maker from the made. One cannot perceive the nature of something made within the one who made all things.

6. (I, 5) Now, let us see if Moses teaches the same thing that the apostles proclaim, that is, that all things were made by God through the Son.[41] When he refers to the creation of the world, he says, among other things, *And God said: Let there be a firmament in the middle of the water, and let it divide water and water, and so it was made. And God made the firmament, and God made a division through the middle of the water.*[42] When he says, *And God spoke: Let there be a firmament,* the person of the Father should be understood in the speaking; but when he says, *And God made,* the person of the Son should be understood in the making.

If you do not think we should understand it this way, the apostolic assertion that *There is one God, the Father, by whom all things exist, and for whom we exist. And there is one Lord, our Jesus Christ, through whom all things exist and through whom we exist* is put to the test.[43] Unless you believe that the entire creation of the world was made through the Son, that is to say, all things, whether invisible or visible, how do you faithfully accept what the Apostle expresses when he says, *one Lord, our Jesus Christ, through whom all things exist*? What we brought up above, too: *Since ... all things are created ... in him*,[44] and also this: *In wisdom you have made all things*?[45] John also followed this with *All things were made through him.*[46] So how is it "all things" if you deny that this was said about the Son of God: *And God made the firmament, and God made a division through the middle of the water*? Thus even Moses represents the Son as the maker, not the made. If he had known by the Holy Spirit's revelation that the Son was made, Moses would have also recounted earlier that the Son was made among the other things that he described as being made.

---

40. 1 Cor 8:6. See Hilary of Poitiers, *Trin.* 4.16.
41. See Hilary of Poitiers, *Trin.* 4.16.
42. Gen 1:6–7.
43. 1 Cor 8:6, referring to §5 above.
44. Col 1:16, referring to §5 above.
45. Ps 103:24 LXX.
46. John 1:3.

7. (I, 6) Sed absolutius inferius prosequitur, ubi iam fabricati mundi incola faciendus est: *Et dixit Deus: Faciamus hominem ad imaginem et similitudinem nostram.* Non est enim unius personae dicere: *Faciamus ad imaginem et similitudinem nostram,* sed neque diuersae deitatis. Nam pluralitas horum uerborum, id est, "faciamus" et "nostram," Patris et Filii personas significat. Quod autem singulariter "imaginem" dicit, una deitas una uirtus utriusque personae manifestatur. Si creatura est Christus, quomodo in opere Deo consors adhibetur? ad ipsum enim dicitur: Faciamus. Si non est uerus filius, quomodo una illi cum Patre imago est? Adoptiuus filius non habet imaginem adoptantls: potest quidem habere munificentiam, non autem potest imaginis habere naturam. Scio quidem esse discretiones imaginum, quas nunc exsequi longum est et non necessarium. Sed quod facit ad causam, uindico dicens: Hoc in loco nulla discretio est imaginis, ubi et Patris et Filii una imago perhibetur. Non enim dixit: Faciamus ad imagines nostras, sed, ad imaginem nostram. Et ne forte stupida mente, o quisquis ille es haereticus, usurpares etiam de una persona dici potuisse: Faciamus, ut sit scilicet apud se cogitantis affectio, non designatio personarum, subsequitur: *Et fecit Deus hominem, ad imaginem Dei*

7. (I, 6) He continues more explicitly further below, when an inhabitant of the created world[47] was going to be made: *And God said, Let us make man in our appearance and likeness.*[48] Now, a single person would not say, *Let us make man in our appearance and likeness*, but neither would a divided deity. For the plural nature of the words, that is, *Let us make* and *our*, signify the persons of the Father and the Son. Yet because he says *appearance* in the singular, he clearly indicates a single deity, and the single power of both persons. If Christ is a created being, why is he brought up as a partner of God in his work? For on this subject, he says, *Let us make*. If he is not the true Son, how is his appearance one with the Father?[49] An adopted son does not have the appearance of the one who adopts him; he can have his generosity, of course, but he cannot have the natural characteristics of his appearance.[50]

Of course, I know that there are differences in their appearances which are long and unnecessary to elaborate on now.[51] But I insist upon what matters in this case: in this passage, where the appearance of the Father and the Son is asserted to be one, there is no difference in their appearance. For he did not say, "Let us make in our appearances" but *in our appearance*. You, heretic, whoever you are, in case with your dull mind you should happen to assume that one person might say, *Let us make*, so that there is no doubt it reflects the mindset of one thinking to himself and does not indicate several persons, there follows *And God made man, he made him in the appearance of God.*[52] These things are openly brought to light; if anyone does not see, he is blind. *God*, he says, *made man, he made*

---

47. See Cicero, *Tusc.* 5.37.108: "Socrates quidem cum rogaretur, civitatem se esse diceret, 'mundanum' inquit; totius enim mundi se incolam et civem arbitrabatur."

48. Gen 1:26. See below, §§15, 36; Hilary of Poitiers, *Trin.* 3.23; 4.17–18; Boersma 2016, 46–50.

49. *Appearance*, a synonym here of "likeness" or "image," in this passage reflects more than just a physical resemblance, even though Faustinus immediately below uses physical characteristics as a key analogy.

50. Hilary (*Trin.* 2.2.3–9) discusses this point at much greater length; see Beckwith 2008, 101–2.

51. Faustinus is here sidestepping one of the fundamental arguments made by the firmly anti-Arian Marcellus of Ancyra (who was often accused of Sabellianism), namely, that an image of God cannot be God, and thus if Christ and the Father made man in *their* image, then Christ must be God; see Lienhard 1999, 182–86.

52. Gen 1:27. Faustinus does not address the natural interpretation of the first-person plural as a "royal we."

fecit eum. Quae coram in luce posita sunt, si quis non uidet, caecus est: *Deus*—inquit—*fecit, ad imaginem Dei fecit.* Nonne apertissimum est quod iam tunc Spiritus Sanctus per Moysen euangelica sacramenta tractabat, dicens: Deum et Deum, non tamen duos deos, quia una imago est Patris et Filii? Et, o quam omnia prospecte edita sunt! Deum et Deum sacra Scriptura pronuntiat, ut Sabellium excluderet defendentem Patris et Filii unam esse personam. Sed ne iterum Arrius sub occasione personarum duos deos introduceret, inter uerba quibus pluralis significatio personarum est, unam imaginem inseruit. Hoc ita esse inuenies, intendens testimonio dicenti: *Faciamus hominem ad imaginem et similitudinem nostram.* Quid agis, impietas Arriana? Si creatura Christus est, quomodo creaturae et creatori una imago est? Diuersitas naturae non admittit unius formae communionem.

8. (I, 7) Multae sunt uoces in libris Moysi, quibus redargui possint impii in Filium, immo et in Patrem: nam quomodo non et in Patrem haec tendit impietas, quae profano spiritu exercetur in Filium, cum Patri adimunt quod uere patris est, auferentes Filio quod uere filii est? quomodo enim uere Pater est, qui secundum ipsos non genuit? quomodo Christus uere Filius eius est, quem negant uere de ipso Patre generatum? Sed, ut dixi, multae sunt uoces in libris Moysi, quibus redargui haec eorum possit impietas; sed quia haec ipsa non studio librum scribentis exsequimur, sed ueluti in scida certas summas quasi properantes deliniamus, ut tuo qualitercumque uideamur oboedisse praecepto, ceterae uoces praetereundae sunt, maxime quia et in diuinis uocibus non numerus testimoniorum sed auctoritas requirenda est, quae idonea est etiam si una uoce proferatur. Sufficit interim de hoc uno capitulo Moysen concordasse cum Euangeliis et apostolis. Deum et Deum praedicat Moyses, sicut superius de Genesi

him in the appearance of God. Is it not exceedingly clear at this point, then, that the Holy Spirit was discussing the revelations of the gospels through Moses by saying God and God, but not two gods, because the appearance of the Father and the Son is the same?

How providently they are all put forth! God and God, the holy scripture pronounces, so that it might shut out Sabellius, who defends the unity of the person of the Father and the Son.[53] But just in case on the pretext of the persons Arius might once more introduce two gods by using the words that indicate a plural number of persons, Moses puts in a singular appearance. You will find this to be so if you consider the testimony that says, *Let us make man in our appearance and likeness.* What do you make of that, impious Arians? If Christ is a created being, how is the appearance of the created and the creator the same? A difference in nature does not allow a singular form to be shared.

8. (I, 7) There are many expressions in the books of Moses with which those who are impious regarding the Son, or rather, the Father, might be refuted.[54] Do not the Arians also direct against the Father with a profane spirit whatever they work against the Son when they deprive the Father of that which truly belongs to a father and take away from the Son that which truly belongs to a son? For how is he truly the Father, if according to them he did not truly beget? How is Christ truly a Son, if they deny that he was truly begotten from the Father?[55]

As I said, there are many verses in the books of Moses by which this impiety of theirs might be refuted, but we are not following up on them. We are not intent on writing a book; we are just sketching out some highlights onto a sheet in a hurry so that we might appear obedient to your command in some way.[56] Thus we must pass over certain verses, particularly because in regards to divine verses, it is not the number of witnesses but their authority that is required, and their authority is sufficient even if only one verse is brought out. For the moment, let it suffice to have brought Moses into agreement with the gospels and the apostles from this one chapter. God and God, Moses proclaims, just as his testimony from

---

53. The Luciferians elsewhere complain about being accused of Sabellianism; see above, pp. 16–19, and see below, §§9, 12. Gregory of Elvira (*Fid.* 9) makes a similar point but without reference to Gen 1:26.

54. See Hilary of Poitiers, *Trin.* 2.1–3, 23.

55. See below, §25.

56. See above, §3; below, §§19, 48.

testimonium loquitur. Ita et Iohannes Deum et Deum adnuntiauit dicens: *In principio erat Verbum, et Verbum erat apud Deum, et Deus erat Verbum*. Nemo dixit duos deos, licet Deum et Deum diceret; nemo non unam imaginem Patris et Filii adnuntiauit; et ideo unum Deum nouit dicere in confessione fides catholica: non tamen ut per confessionem unius Dei Filius negetur esse quod Deus est, quia sicut Pater Deus est, ita et Filius Deus est. Nam si non sicut Pater Deus est, ita et Filius Deus est, quomodo illis una imago est, secundum Moysen? uel quomodo, secundum Paulum, in forma Dei Christus est aequalis existens Deo?

9. (I, 8) Sed et Iohannes cum Verbum Deum adserit in principio apud Deum esse, non extra Deum esse, per hanc Verbi Dei a Deo inseparabilitatem idem mihi uidetur significare, quod in significantia imaginis et formae est. Nam si per unam imaginem eandemque formam Patris et Filii inseparabilitas ostenditur, cur non cum Iohannes Dei et Dei inseparabilitatem adnuntiat, per hoc quod ait: *Et Verbum erat apud Deum* et *hoc erat in principio apud Deum*, unam imaginem eandemque formam Patris et Filii significasse credatur? Plane hic sensus uideatur ambiguus, si non idem euangelista hoc ipsum paululum infra apertius prosecutus est, dicens: *Et uidimus gloriam eius, gloriam quasi unigeniti a Patre*: sicut et una imago eademque forma, ita et gloria non alia est Filii, quam quae Patris est. Interea, qui Christum de adoptione filium dicis, quomodo intellegis gloriam eius quasi unigeniti a Patre? Quod si plures esse Dei filios de adoptione profiteris, quod si et Christus adoptiuus est, quomodo unigenitus a

Genesis says above. So too did John relate that *In the beginning was the Word, and the Word was with God, and the Word was God.*[57] Neither one said two gods, though he might say God and God; both related that the appearance of the Father and the Son was one. Likewise, the catholic faith knew to say "one" in its confession,[58] but not so that by this confession it might be denied that the Son of the one God is God;[59] just as the Father is God, so too is the Son God. For if the Father is not God in the same way that the Son is also God, how do they have a single appearance, in accordance with Moses? Or how, in accordance with Paul, does Christ in the form of God exist as an equal to God?

9. (I, 8) When John asserts that God as the Word was in the beginning with God, not that it was apart from God, he also seems to me to indicate the same inseparability of the Word of God from God that their appearance and form indicate.[60] The inseparability of the Father and Son is demonstrated through their single appearance and same form; why then, when John relates the inseparability of God and God (through saying *and the Word was with God* and *This was in the beginning with God*),[61] should we not believe that he is indicating that the Father and Son have a single appearance and the same form?

Of course, the meaning would seem ambiguous here if the same Evangelist did not follow up on this more clearly a little further on: *And we saw his glory, glory that belonged to the only begotten of the Father.*[62] Just as their appearance is singular and their form is the same, so too is the Son's glory none other than the Father's glory. Meanwhile, you who say that Christ is the Son by adoption, how do you understand his *glory that belonged to the only begotten of the Father*?[63] If you profess that there are many sons of God by adoption, and if Christ was also adopted, how is he the only begotten of the Father, since he cannot be only begotten given that other sons also exist through adoption? But if he is truly the only begotten of the Father in

---

57. John 1:1. See Hilary of Poitiers, *Trin.* 4.18.
58. In the Nicene Creed, which in Latin begins "Credimus in unum Deum."
59. See Gregory of Elvira, *Fid.* 5–7.
60. See Athanasius, *Apol. sec.* 3.5; *Decr.* 17; Hilary of Poitiers, *Trin.* 8.48.
61. John 1:1–2.
62. John 1:14. See Hilary of Poitiers, *Trin.* 9.39. Earlier in his *De Trinitate*, Hilary gives an extended discussion of John 17 (which does not appear in Faustinus's *De Trinitate*) and the nature of Christ's glory (3.11–17; Beckwith 2008, 135–40).
63. See Athanasius, *Dion.* 23.

Patre est, cum non sit unigenitus, existentibus quoque aliis per adoptionem filiis? Quod si uere unigenitus a Patre est ideo quia ipse solus de ipso uere Patre generatur, quomodo adoptiuus adseritur, cum adoptiuus inter plures adoptiuos proprietatem unigeniti a patre habere non possit? Sed etsi adoptiui sunt, de nullo tamen eorum dictum esse: *Et uidimus gloriam eius, gloriam quasi unigeniti a Patre.* Sed de Christo solo dictum est: *Et uidimus gloriam eius, gloriam quasi unigeniti a Patre*: non ergo adoptiuus est, de quo hoc dicitur quod do adoptiuis dici non potest. Et merito una illi image cum Patre est, quia ipse solus unigentus a Patre est. Quid ergo mirum, si in Filii imagine Patris imago signatur? Ideo et ipse Saluator dicebat: *Qui me uidit, uidit et Patrem*: non hoc ut Sabellius dico, quasi se ipsum Patrem dicat esse, qui sit et Filius. Confiteor enim Patrem esse, qui genuit; Filium vero esse, qui natus est. Sed cum dicit: *Qui me uidit, uidit et Patrem,* sicut Patris et Filii non unam ostendit esse personam, ita unam ostendit esse deitatem, cum in Patris et Filii substantia nulla diuersitas inuenitur.

10. (I, 9) Iterum in hoc quoque loco dicam: Si creatura est Filius, quomodo qui uidet Filium, uidet et Patrem? Nemo enim in uisione creaturae Patrem uidet: de inspectione enim creaturae creator uideri potest; Pater autem non uidetur nisi de inspectione Filii. Si ergo Christus creatura est et non uere Filius, non potest in creaturae visione Pater uideri; et quomodo ait: *Qui me uidit, uidit et Patrem,* nisi quia uere Filius de Deo Patre natus est? Et ideo cum uideris Filium, necesse est ut et Patrem uideas. Sine Filio enim Pater non est, sicut nec Filius sine Patre. Inde etiam subdidit: *Ego in Patre et Pater in me,* non utique per quandam passiuam confusionem,

that he alone was truly begotten from that Father, how can you assert that he was adopted? One who is adopted among many adopted sons cannot have the particular quality of being the only begotten of a father. But even if they were adopted, *And we saw his glory, glory that belonged to the only begotten of the Father* was nevertheless not said about any of them. It says, *And we saw his glory, glory that belonged to the only begotten of the Father* about Christ alone. Therefore he was not adopted, since what is said about him cannot be said about adopted sons, and his appearance is deservedly one with the Father, because he alone is the only begotten of the Father.[64] Why is it surprising, then, if the appearance of the Father is indicated by the appearance of the Son? This is also why the Savior himself said, *He who has seen me has seen my Father as well.*[65] I do not take this like Sabellius does, as though he were saying that he himself was the Father who begat him, but instead as though he were saying that he truly was the Son, who was born. But when he says, *He who has seen me has seen my Father as well*, he also demonstrates that there is one deity, since no difference is found in the substance of the Father and the Son, just as he demonstrates that the person of the Father is not that of the Son.[66]

10. (I, 9) Again, on this point I would also say: If the Son is something created, how does he who sees the Son see the Father as well? Certainly no one sees a father by seeing something created. While a creator may be apparent when considering something created, a father is only apparent when considering a son.[67] Therefore if Christ is something created and not truly the Son, and if a father cannot become apparent by considering something created, how can he say, *He who has seen me has seen my Father as well*,[68] unless it is because the Son was truly born from God the Father? Therefore, when you see the Son, it is necessary that you also see the Father. For without the Son there is no Father, just as there is no Son without the Father. Thus he also puts below, *I am in the Father and the*

---

64. See Hilary of Poitiers, *Trin.* 8.49; 9.69. Prestige (1952, 285–86) describes Hilary's argument as "Athanasian."

65. John 14:9. See below, §§10, 36.

66. See Lucifer of Caligari, *Mor. esse Dei fil.* 10.

67. In other words, when one sees something created, the existence of a creator is implied; when one sees a son, the existence of a father is implied. See Phoebadius of Agen, *Ar.* 25.3; Hilary of Poitiers, *Syn.* 22, which Weedman (2007a, 506–7) argues derives from Basil of Ancyra; *Trin.* 7.5, 35–36 (with Weedman 2007b, 143–44).

68. John 14:9. See above, §9; below, 36; Phoebadius of Agen, *Ar.* 25.1–4.

sed quia consequens est ut ubi Pater est, illic esse cognoscatur et Filius; et ubi Filius est, illic etiam Patrem exstare cognoscas. Est et alius sensus dicti istius: *Qui me uidit, uidit et Patrem*: non qui corporeis oculis in corpore uidisset Iesum, uidisse Patrem refertur: alioquin absurda est increpatio Domini ad Philippum dicentis: *Tanto tempore uobiscum sum, et non me nosti, Philippe?* Secundum corpus enim non solus Philippus uidebat Iesum, sed et omnes Iudaei, qui ei aduersabantur: nec tamen per hoc quod uidebant secundum corpus Iesum, Patrem quoque uidisse credendi sunt. Quid ergo est: *Qui me uidit, uidit et Patrem*? Intende cordis aciem et uide, secundum fidei spiritalis obtutus, Christum Filium Dei non creaturam esse sed creatorem; intende eum uere esse Deum sine initio sempiternum; et secundum hoc quod Deus est, inuisibilem inaestimabilem incorruptibilem indemutabilem et per omnia talem, qualis est et Pater eius qui eum genuit: et ita uidens Filium, Patrem quoque te uidisse non dubium est.

*Father in me,*⁶⁹ certainly not in some mixed-up confusion, but because it follows that wherever there is a father, it is understood that a son is there too; and wherever there is a son, you also understand that a father exists too.⁷⁰

There is another meaning of that remark, *He who has seen me, has seen my Father as well.* It does not mean that he who had seen Jesus in body with his own body's eyes had seen the Father. Otherwise, the Lord's rebuke to Philip, *I have been with you for so long, and you do not know me, Philip?,* is absurd.⁷¹ For it was not Philip alone who saw Jesus according to his body, but all the Jews who turned against him.⁷² Nevertheless, you should not believe that they also saw the Father in the same way that they saw Jesus, according to his body. Why, then, is it, *He who has seen me has seen my Father as well?* Look with your heart⁷³ and see, in accordance with the consideration of the spiritual faith, that Christ, the Son of God, is not something created but a creator; regard him to truly be God, eternal without beginning; and in accordance with this (that he is God) regard him invisible, inestimable, incorruptible, immutable, and in all things of the same quality as his Father who begat him.⁷⁴ When you see the Son in this way, there is no doubt that you have also seen the Father.

---

69. John 14:10. See below, §§11, 13–14, 36; Phoebadius of Agen, *Ar.* 25.3–4.

70. Or with reference to the specific Father and Son under discussion, i.e., "but because it follows that wherever the Father is, the Son is understood to be there too; and wherever the Son is, you also understand that the Father exists there too." Faustinus will return to the theme of the necessary existence of a father given a son, and a son given a father, in §49 below. See Athanasius, *Apol. sec.* 1.16, 19, 33; Hilary of Poitiers, *Syn.* 64; *Trin.* 7.31; 10.6.

71. John 14:9. See Hilary of Poitiers, *Trin.* 7.36. This is one of many passages where Hilary takes up John 14:9; see Beckwith 2008, 112.

72. See above, §1.

73. See Ambrose, *Spir.* 1.8.93: "sed unitatem habet plenitudinis, quo aciem nostri cordis illuminet pro nostrae possibilitate virtutis."

74. Long lists of the qualities of God are not uncommon in dogmatic literature (and see 1 Tim 1:17); in addition to §§11, 14, 22 below, see, e.g., Lucifer of Caligari, *Mor. esse Dei Fil.* 10: "incommutabilis, inconvertibilis, inaestimabilis, inenarrabilis, aeternus, perfectus"; Phoebadius of Agen, *Fid.* 8: "omnipotens, invisibilis, inconvertabilis, inmutabilis, perfectus, semper idem, aeturnus" (PL 20:45); Hilary of Poitiers, *Trin.* 4.12: "solum infectum, solum sempiternum, solum sine initio, solum verum, solum immortalitatem habentem, solum optimum, solum potentem, omnium creatorem, ordinatorem, et dispositorem, inconvertibilem, immutabilitem"; Ambrosiaster, *Quaest. Vet. Nov. Test.* 1.2.1: "invisibilis, inaestimabilis, infinitus, perfectus, nul-

11. (I, 10) Hoc sensu accipe et illud quod ait: *Ego in Patre et Pater in me.* Pater cum enim sit perfectus, perfectum Filium genuit; et cum sit inuisibilis inconprehensibilis inaestimabilis qui eum genuit: et ideo ait: *Ego in Patre et Pater in me.* Cum enim omnia quae sunt paternae uirtutis et deitatis, habentur in Filio, Pater in Filio est et Filius in Patre. Et ideo praemisit: *Si me sciretis, et Patrem meum sciretis*: et hic ostenditur quod eadem sit Patris et Filii substantia eo quod sit una utriusque cognitio. Sed creaturae et creatoris non est una cognitio, quia non et una substantia est. Patris autem et Filii una cognitio est: ergo non est Filius creatura, sed creator est, sicuti et Pater creator est; et Deus est, sicuti et Pater Deus est: non tamen per haec duos deos dicimus. Hic est ubi, impie haeretici, diabolico furore quasi in stultitiam istius confessionis inardescis, cum Deum et Deum audis, nec tamen duos deos dicimus. Inflatus enim de littera saeculari, in hac quaestione insanabiliter aegrotas, et putas te debere constringere ut duos deos dicamus, cum Deum et Deum confitemur. Noli, infelix, aduersus Christum Dominum totius creaturae Aristotelis artificis litium argumenta colligere, qui te Christianum qualitercumque profiteris, nec aduersus piam confes-

11. (I, 10) Also understand this meaning when he says, *I am in the Father and the Father in me.*[75] For the Father, since he is perfect, begat a perfect Son; and since he is the invisible, incomprehensible, inestimable God,[76] and the true light, his Son too was born with the qualities of the one who begat him. This is why he says, *I am in the Father and the Father in me.* For when all the things that are of the Father's power and deity are held in the Son, the Father is in the Son and the Son in the Father. This is why he first said, *If you knew me, you would know my Father as well.*[77] Here it is shown that the substance of the Father and the Son is the same, because the two are understood the same way, whereas understanding a created being is not the same as understanding a creator, because their substance is likewise not the same. Yet the Father and Son *are* understood the same way. Thus the Son is not a created being, but a creator, just as the Father is also a creator; he is God, just as the Father is also God.

Yet, in these arguments we are not saying that there are two gods. Here is where, impious heretic, you grow inflamed with a diabolic fury when you hear God and God, as though you were inflamed against the foolishness of that confession; but we nevertheless do not say two gods. Puffed up by secular literature,[78] you grow incurably sick concerning this question, and you think that you ought to treat us as though we were saying two gods when we acknowledge God and God. You unhappy one, who would profess himself in some way to be Christian, do not gather together against the Lord Christ the contentious arguments of ingenious Aristotle on every created being.[79] You should not approach the pious confession of the inde-

---

lius egens, aeturnus, inmortalis omni modo"; Ambrose, *Fid.* 4.2.22: "si sempiternum si omnipotentem si inaestimabilem si incomprehensibilem" (and see also 5.19.227). None of these examples perfectly matches the list of qualities that Faustinus provides (or each other).

75. John 14:10. See above, §10; below, §§13–14, 36; Gregory of Elvira, *Fid.* 53–55; Hilary of Poitiers, *Trin.* 7.38; 8.52. Gregory relies heavily here on the Greek term *homoousios*, while Hilary emphasizes the obscurity of the meaning of this passage (see Beckwith 2008, 128).

76. See above, §10; below, §22.

77. John 14:7.

78. See Tertullian, *Marc.* 5.19.7, and for the sentiment in the fourth century, most famously, Jerome, *Ep.* 22.30.

79. The reference to Aristotle here (and especially at §27 below) is quite interesting. Arian use of Aristotle's *Categories* in particular (or handbooks describing it or Porphyry's *Isagoge*, more likely) seems to date to the 350s at the earliest (see Turcescu

sionem inenarrabilis de Deo sacramenti ut calculo calumniator aduenias. Inspice potius diuinos libros et de diuina fide diuinis utere sermonibus. Legisti utique: *Et in lumine tuo uidebimus lumen.* Quae hic distantia luminis a lumine est? Posuisset enim et distantiam, si fuisset, ne quis luminis a lumine nullam distantiam crederet. Quod si nulla distantia est, non ergo duo lumina sed unum lumen est, cum in lumine Patris Filii lumen agnoscitur. Hoc lumen est de quo et Danihel loquitur dicens: *Et lumen cum ipso est*: non enim de aliqua creatura hoc dicitur, sed de splendore ipsius Dei existentis sempiterni luminis. Si Pater sempiternum lumen est, sine dubio et Filius sempiternum, quomodo in Patris sempiterno lumine lumen Filii, quod non est sempiternum, uidetur? Sed in laudibus Dei non est haec falsa

scribable sacred mystery concerning God like a charlatan with a counting stone,[80] as one who deceives by using his education in earthly reasoning. Instead, look into the divine books, and concerning the divine faith, make use of divine sayings.

Surely you have read, *And in your light we shall see the light*.[81] What is the difference here between the light and the light? For [David] would have also established a difference between the light and the light, if there had been one, so that no one would believe that there was no difference. But if there is no difference, there are therefore not two lights but one light, since the light of the Son is recognized in the light of the Father. This is the light that Daniel speaks of when he says, *And the light is with him*.[82] For this is not said about another created being, but about the splendor of that very God who exists as eternal light. If the Father is the eternal light, without a doubt the Son is also the eternal light. Truly, if one denies that the Son is the eternal light of God, how is the light of the Son, which is not eternal, seen in the eternal light of the Father? But what the saints

---

2005, 28–30). Faustinus definitely implies that whoever sent his arguments to Flacilla was using Aristotelian philosophy in some way, though it is not entirely clear how. There is no condemnation or even mention of Aristotle in many of the earlier Latin works on the Trinity (Hilary of Poitier's *De Trinitate*, Phoebadius of Agen's *Contra Arianos*, Gregory of Elvira's *De fide*, and Ambrose's *De fide*), and Marius Victorinus is surely not the inspiration for Faustinus's distaste here, as he was a Nicene Christian who had translated works of Aristotle into Latin and argued against Arian Christians by using Aristotle (see, in general, Cooper 2016). This dearth of material to draw from perhaps explains why Faustinus does not offer more specific condemnations of Aristotelian philosophy in this treatise. In the East, on the other hand, Gregory of Nyssa (*Eun.* 1.1.6; 7.1; 12.5) strongly criticizes Eunomius for relying on Aristotle. Gregory of Nyssa was writing against Eunomius in the 370s, shortly before Faustinus wrote his *De Trinitate* while also in the East, and if Eunomius was a prominent Eastern Arian who made use of Aristotle, he was surely not the only one (see Elders 1996). The language here is very reminiscent of the criticisms leveled by Julian of Eclanum against Augustine (whom he calls a "Punic Aristotle") and by Augustine against Julian of Eclanum: see Lössl 2011, 113–14.

80. In other words, someone who deceives another by using mathematics. This possibly is a reference to disreputable accounting or money-changing practices (see, e.g., Cicero, *Rosc. com.* 1–7; Suetonius, *Galba* 9.1; Ausonius, *Ep.* 15), but more probably a general reference to anyone who philosophizes or relies on sciences such as mathematics instead of faith.

81. Ps 36:9 LXX. See Gregory of Elvira, *Fid.* 58–59; Ambrose, *Fid.* 1.7.49; Hilary of Poitiers, *Trin.* 7.29.

82. Dan 2:22.

dictio sanctorum: *Et in lumine tuo uidebimus lumen*. Ergo et Filii lumen sempiternum est, quod non distat a Patris lumine sempiterno: et ideo licet lumen est, quia in Patre et Filio nulla discretio est, nulla separatio luminis est, quomodo nec imaginis secundum Moysen, nec formae secundum apostolum Paulum.

12. (I, 11) Sacramentum autem inseparabilis unitatis secundum hoc quod uterque, id est, Pater et Filius aequaliter et indiuise, neque secundum portionem, Deus unus, et pluralitatis secundum hoc quod unus pater est et unus filius, etiam de hoc capitulo manifestatur quod legimus in Euangelio, ipso Saluatore dicente: *Ego et pater unum sumus*. "Sumus" enim pluralitatem significat personarum, quia hic pater et hic filius; "unum" autem unam eamdemque in Patre et Filio substantiam deitatemque consignat, ut uere Pater et Filius unus Deus sit, cum ambo, id est, Pater et Filius unum sunt secundum deitatem, non unus secundum personas. *Ego et pater unum sumus*: hac una uoce et Sabellius excluditur et Arius confutatur. Sabellius enim ipsum dicit Patrem, qui sit et Filius, hoc modo, tamquam si unus habeat duo nomina, et interpretatur "unum" ideo dictum, ut unius personae singularitas crederetur. Contra uero Arrius, respiciens ad hoc quod ait "sumus," in hoc sermone pluralitatem intellegens, introduxit impiam pluralitatem deorum, credens unum sempiternum Deum, et alium qui esse coeperit deus; unum omnipotentem et alium qui non sit omnipotens. Sed, o caecitas in utrisque! Habent ante oculos quod pie uideant, et incautis offensionibus impie litigare contendunt: saltem commodent sibi sensus suos, et piae fidei perspicient veritatem. Sabellius

said among the praises of God is not false: *And in your light we shall see the light.* Thus the light of the Son is also eternal, because it does not stand apart from the eternal light of the Father. This is why, although the light is the Son and the Father is the light, there is nevertheless a single light of the Father and Son, because in the Father and Son there is no difference, there is no separation of light—nor a separation of appearance, according to Moses,[83] nor a separation of form, according to the apostle Paul.[84]

12. (I, 11) Furthermore, the sacred mystery of their inseparable unity in accordance with the fact that both the Father and the Son are one God, equally and indivisibly, and not in parts, and of their plurality in accordance with the fact that there is one Father and one Son, is also clear in this passage that we read in the gospel, where the Savior himself says, *I and the Father are one.*[85] For *are* signifies the plurality of persons, because here is the Father and here is the Son; but *one* indicates that the substance and deity are one and the same in the Father and Son, so that the Father and Son are truly one God when both, that is, the Father and the Son, are one according to their deity, not one according to their persons. *I and the Father are one*: with this one expression, Sabellius is shut out and Arius is confounded.[86] For Sabellius describes the Father, who is also the Son in some way, just as if the one had two names, and he interprets *one* for this reason as something said so that the singularity of one person should be believed. On the other hand, since he looks back to this passage that says *are* and understands a plurality in this assertion, Arius has introduced an impious plurality of gods, believing in one eternal God and another who began to be a god, one omnipotent and another who is not omnipotent.

The blindness in both! They have before their eyes that which they might piously see, and they impiously exert themselves to argue with offensive recklessness. They should at least accommodate their own understandings to one another and perceive the truth of the pious faith.

---

83. See above, §7.
84. See above, §5.
85. John 10:30. See below, §§13–15, 36; Origen, *Cels.* 8.12; Phoebadius of Agen, *Ar.* 25.1–4; Gregory of Elvira, *Fid.* 12, 24; Hilary of Poitiers, *Trin.* 7.5; 8.36; Ambrose, *Fid.* 1.1.9 (drawing on Tertullian, *Prax.* 22; Novatian, *Trin.* 27).
86. It was a common Nicene rhetorical tactic, as here, to set Arius as an archetypical theologian splitting God into separate beings in opposition to Sabellius or Photinus as archetypical theologians denying any difference between them: see, e.g., Phoebadius of Agen, *Ar.* 14.1; Williams 2006.

admiratione virtutum quas Christus operabatur, Christum Deum uerum esse credit, et non qui aliquando coeperit, sed qui semper fuerit et possit omnia: credat hoc Arrius, et non blasphemet in Christum, quem filium confitetur. Item Arrius negat Christum esse Patrem: neget hoc et Sabellius, et pie praedicet quod Christus uere Deus est, non existens Pater sed Filius. Adhuc apertius dicam: Sabellius uincat Arrium, quod Christus uerus Deus est; et Arrius uincat Sabellium, quod Christus sub confessione ueri Dei uerus et Filius est: et mihi catholico ambo uicerunt, immo et mecum ambo uincunt impietatis errorem, cum mecum intellexerint sacrae fidei ueritatem, quae et pluralitatem personarum et unitatem deitatis intellegit in hac pronuntiatione Domini dicentis: *Ego et Pater unum sumus.* Sed hanc diuinam pronuntiationem et hanc piam divinae pronuntiationis intelligentiam Arrii sectatores, cum quaerunt subuertere, alio modo interpretantur, et dicunt: Vnum sunt quidem, sed non substantia non deitate non potestate sed voluntate: id est, quia unam eamdemque habeant voluntatem, ideo ait: *Ego et Pater unum sumus.* Dicite, o haeretici impii, si qui substantiuum Verbum Dei est et qui linguae sermonem dedit, nescit loqui et ignorauit altum sensum uestrum propriis et conpetentibus sermonibus explicare, et inefficax fuit dicere: Ego et pater unum volumus, et non substantiae ac deitatis uolebat intellegi.

13. (I, 12) Sed nunc, quaeso, regina, memineris quae capitula ex persona haereticorum scribere dignata es. Ipsi haeretici aiunt: *Qui me misit Pater, ipse mihi praeceptum dedit, quid dicam et quid loquar,* et: *Descendi de caelo non ut faciam uoluntatem meam, sed uoluntatem eius qui me misit Patris.* Hoc artificium haereticorum est, ut alibi negent quod alibi confitentur, ut cum se uident praesentium quaestionum absolutionibus

Sabellius, in admiration of the miracles that Christ worked, believed that Christ truly was God, who always was and had mastery over all things, and was not someone who began at some time. Let Arius believe this and not blaspheme against Christ, whom he confesses is the Son. Likewise, Arius denies that Christ is the Father; let Sabellius also deny this, and piously proclaim that Christ truly is God, not existing as the Father but as the Son. Here I would simply say: Sabellius would conquer Arius, because Christ is truly God, and Arius would conquer Sabellius, because Christ is also the true Son of God under the confession of the true God.[87] With me, the catholic, they have both conquered—that is to say, they both conquer the error of impiety along with me when they both understand along with me the truth of the sacred faith, which understands both a plurality of persons and the unity of the deity in this proclamation of the Lord: *I and the Father are one.*[88]

But when they seek to subvert matters, Arian sectarians interpret this divine proclamation and this pious understanding of the divine proclamation another way, and they say, "They are indeed one, but not in substance, nor in deity, nor in power, but in will; that is, because they have one and the same will, he says, *I and the Father are one.*"[89] Tell us, O impious heretics, whether he who is the self-existent Word of God and who conveyed this expression did not know how to speak, was ignorant of how to explain your other meaning in proper and suitable wording, and was incapable of saying, "I and the Father will one thing," if he wished at this point for a unity of will, and not of substance and deity, to be understood.

13. (I, 12) But now, Empress, I ask you to recall those chapters you deemed worthy to relate that are characteristic of the heretics. These heretics say, *The Father who sent me commanded me as to what I should say and what I should speak,*[90] and *I descended from heaven not that I might do my will, but the will of my Father who sent me.*[91] This is the artifice of the heretics, that they might deny in one place what they affirm in another, so

---

87. See Hilary of Poitiers, *Trin.* 1.26; 7.4.
88. The military metaphor pervasive in this passage recalls §§1–3 above; see also Jerome, *Lucif.* 28.
89. See Hilary of Poitiers, *Trin.* 8.5; 9.70. According to Hilary, in support of this interpretation, Arians would cite Acts 4:32; 1 Cor 3:8; and John 17:20–21 to prove that multiple souls may be united into one "soul" when they are united by one will.
90. John 12:49.
91. John 6:38. See Hilary of Poitiers, *Trin.* 8.5; 9.70.

uehementer adstringi, serpentino lubrico semper eludant. Certe dicitis, o haeretici, praeceptum dedisse Filio Patrem, quid dicat, quid loquatur: et quomodo, quasi nesciat loqui, uos uerba eius emendatis, immo iam Patris, quia Filius quod dicit, quod loquitur, secundum praeceptum quod dedit ei Pater, et dicit et loquitur? Iamne intellegitis quia, cum profano spiritu aduersus Filii deitatem exercere uestram contenditis amentiam, etiam in Patrem prorumpitis insanientes? Clamat Filius: *Ego et Pater unum sumus*; et uos quasi grammatici, ueluti inefficaciam dominicae pronuntiationis suppositi uerbi demutatione supplentes, emendatis et dicitis: Hoc quod ait "sumus" "uolumus" intellegendum est, ut scilicet sic dictum sit: Ego et Pater unum uolumus. Sed reclamat Filius etiam contra uos, dicens illa quae dixit ad uestrae impietatis participes Iudaeos: *Quare loquelam meam non cognoscitis?* Habeant locum suum parabolae et allegoriae et aenigmata: hoc tamen loco apertissime et plene dictum est: *Ego et Pater unum sumus*; et quomodo unum sunt, alibi quoque declarat, cum dicit: *Credite mihi quia ego in Patre et Pater in me*; et ne uideretur ipse de se usurpare quod non erat, ut ueritatem dictionis ostendat, praemisit dicens: *Non creditis quia ego in Patre et Pater in me? Verba quae ego loquor uobis, a me ipso non loquor: Pater autem in me manens ipse loquitur, et opera quae ego facio, ipse facit.* Sed et alibi: *Sicut docuit me Pater, haec loquor; et qui me misit mecum est; non reliquit me solum, quia ego quae placita sunt ei, facio semper.* Non quia Filius ignoraret quid sibi loquendum erat (quid est

that when they see themselves vigorously held in check by answers to the questions they present, they might always escape with a snake-like slipperiness.[92] Heretics, certainly you say that the Father commanded his Son as to what he should say, what he should speak.[93] So why are you correcting his words (or rather, now, his Father's words, given that whatever the Son says and speaks is according to the command that his Father gave him) as if he does not know how to speak? Don't you understand that when you struggle to work your madness against the deity of the Son with your profane spirit, you also burst forth raging against the Father? The Son cries, *I and the Father are one*,[94] and you, as though you were grammarians supplying a deficiency in the Lord's proclamation with the perversion of a falsely substituted word, correct him and say, "This part that says 'are' should be understood as 'will,' so that it says, of course, 'I and the Father will one thing.'" But the Son still cries back against you, saying what he said to the Jewish participants in your impiety, *Why do you not understand what I am saying?*[95] Let the parables, allegories, and enigmas have their proper place; in this place, it is most clearly and plainly written, *I and the Father are one*.

How they are one he declares elsewhere when he says, *Believe me, that I am in the Father and the Father in me*.[96] So that it would not look like he was claiming for himself something that he was not, he put this first to demonstrate the truth of what he said: *You do not believe that I am in the Father and the Father in me? The words that I speak to you I do not speak by my own self, but my Father, remaining in me, speaks, and the works that I do, he does*.[97] In still another place, he also says, *Just as my Father taught me, I say these things, and he who sent me is with me; he did not leave me alone, because I always do the things that are pleasing to him*.[98] He says,

---

92. See below, §§14, 26. Much the same point is made by Hilary concerning John 14:28; 10:30; and 14:10 (see Beckwith 2008, 192–93). Hilary was concerned that his opponents misunderstood the scriptural passages they adduced because they had taken them out of context; Faustinus attributes a much more underhanded motive to his enemies.
93. See Hilary of Poitiers, *Trin.* 6.7.
94. John 10:30. See above, §12; below, §§14–15, 36.
95. See above, §1.
96. John 10:38. See above, §§10–11; below, §§14, 36.
97. John 14:10.
98. John 8:28–29.

enim quod Dei sapientia ignoret?), sed ut duritiam indomitae fidei tuae ad piam diuinae unitatis intellegentiam Patris quoque auctoritate molliret, ait: *Pater in me manens ipse loquitur*; uel illud: *Sicut docuit me Pater, haec loquor.* Sicut autem opera Filii opera Patris sunt, eo quod, faciente Filio, Pater in ipso manens loquitur non aliud quam quod loquitur Filius, quia nec Filius aliud loquitur quam quod loquitur Pater in ipso manens. Eadem ergo Patris et Filii loquela est, sicut eadem et operatio; et ideo dicebat: *Alioquin propter opera ipsa credite*: quae utique similiter faciebat ut Pater, ut postremo uel auctoritate operum crederetur quia Filius in Patre est et Pater in Filio est.

14. (I, 13) Hoc autem quomodo intellegendum est quod ait: *Ego in Patre et Pater in me*, iam supra expositum est. Sed et nunc breuius dicam. Secundum indifferentiam substantiae audiendum est: *Ego in Patre et Pater in me*; sed et illud quod ait: *Ego et Pater unum sumus*, secundum indifferentiam substantiae unum sunt Pater et Filius. Nolo ergo, impie haeretice, ut indifferentiam substantiae Patris et Filii adimas, et inportune unitatem uoluntatis interseras, quam alibi impie negas dicendo: Scriptum est: *Descendi de caelo non ut faciam uoluntatem meam, sed uoluntatem eius qui me misit Patris*. Qui in hoc capitulo ignorans dictionis eius sacramentum, tam impie negas Patris et Filii unam esse uoluntatem, quomodo tibi credam quia sinceriter confiteris quod una eademque uoluntas Patris et Filii significatur in hoc quod pronuntiauit Dominus dicens: *Ego et Pater unum sumus*? Tu si uere credis quod Pater et Filius unum sunt uolun-

The Father, remaining in me, speaks, or, *Just as my Father taught me, I say these things*, not because the Son was ignorant as to what he should have said (for what is there that the Wisdom of God is ignorant of?) but so that he might also soften the stubbornness of your uncouth faith towards the pious understanding of divine unity by the Father's authority. Moreover, the works of the Son are likewise the works of the Father; this is why when the Son is acting, the Father acts, remaining in the Son. Thus the things that the Son says, the Father says, and he says nothing other than what the Son says, remaining in him, because the Son also does not say anything other than what the Father says, remaining in him.[99] Therefore the speech of the Father and the Son is the same, just as their work is also the same. This is why he says, *Otherwise, believe on account of the works themselves*,[100] works that he surely did similarly to the Father, so that later, at least on the authority of his works, one might believe that the Son is in the Father and the Father is in the Son.

14. (I, 13) Now the way that this should be understood—when he says, *I am in the Father and the Father in me*[101]—was already explained above.[102] But I will briefly discuss it now as well.[103] Concerning the lack of difference in their substance, one should hear, *I am in the Father and the Father in me*, and he also says, *I and the Father are one*.[104] Concerning the lack of difference in their substance, the Father and the Son are one. Do not, impious heretic, also insolently add in that there is unity in their will (which you elsewhere impiously deny by saying, "It is written: *I descended from heaven not that I might do my will, but the will of my Father who sent me*"[105]) so that you might dismiss the lack of difference in substance between the Father and Son. You who would so impiously deny that there is unity in the will of the Father and Son, being ignorant in regards to that statement as to the sacred mystery of what he said, how should I believe that you sincerely confess that the will of the Father and Son is indicated as one and the same when the Lord proclaimed, *I and the Father are one?*[106]

---

99. See Hilary of Poitiers, *Trin.* 7.40–41.
100. John 14:12.
101. John 14:10.
102. See above, §§10–11, 13; see also §36 below.
103. See Hilary of Poitiers, *Trin.* 8.10.
104. John 10:30. See above, §§12–13; below, §§15, 36.
105. John 6:38. See above, §13.
106. See Hilary of Poitiers, *Trin.* 9.70.

tate, non uideo quomodo negare possis quia et substantia et diuinitate et potestate unum sunt. Quare enim non una substantia sit, una diuinitas et potestas, quibus una uoluntas est? Si enim ex aequo illis uoluntas est, ex aequo et diuinitas est. Si non ex aequo diuinitas, nec ex aequo uoluntas. Dei enim uoluntas et cuiuslibet, non tamen Dei, uoluntas pariare non potest, quia alia est uis uoluntatis eius qui Deus est, et alia uis uoluntatis eius qui Deus non est. Voluntas Dei naturaliter bona est, perfecta est, indemutabilis est, semper eadem existens et sine initio existens et sine fine perseuerans. Voluntas uero eius qui non est Deus, eo quod habeat initium, sicut et ipse qui non est Deus, potest et nutare, potest et uerti, sicuti et ipse qui non est Deus; ac per hoc nec uere bona, quia non naturaliter bona, nec uere perfecta est, quae potest uerti et minui, ita ut quod hodie uoluit, crastino nolit, uel quod hodie noluit, crastino uelit.

15. (I, 14) Dicam exemplo apertius: angelus iste qui nunc diabolus est, antequam fieret diabolus, bonam habuit uoluntatem; sed ubi factus est diabolus, proprii arbitrii agitatione amisit bonam uoluntatem: ideo scilicet, quia ex factura subsistit, et non naturaliter Deus est. Hoc et de omni creatura rationabili sentiendum est: etsi enim quidam eorum non declinauerunt neque declinant a bona uoluntate, tamen in natura habent posse declinare, quia creaturae sunt et non Deus. Hoc enim quod non declinant, ex disciplinae perpetua obseruatione obtinent, non ex naturae indemutabilis ueritate. Deus autem, sicut ipse solus sine initio bonus et perfectus et inconuertibilis est, sine initio quoque habens bonam et perfectam et inconuertibilem uoluntatem, non institutione neque ex profectu obseruationis habet bonam et perfectam et inconuertibilem uoluntatem, sed ex naturae indemutabilis ueritate, qua et bonus et perfectus et inconuertibilis Deus est. Viderit, si qua fortassis est haeresis quae hunc sensum respuat;

If you truly believe that the Father and Son are one in their will, I do not see how you can deny that they are also one in their substance, divinity, and power. Why would there not be one substance, one divinity and power, for whom there is one will? For if their will is equal, their divinity is also equal. If their divinity is not equal, their will is not equal either. For the will of God and the will of whomever else other than God cannot be made equal, because there is one force of will for one who is God and another force of will for one who is not God. The will of God is naturally good, it is perfect, it is immutable, it always exists as the same will, it exists without beginning, and it persists without end.[107] Truly, the will of one who is not God, because it has a beginning (like one who is not God), can sway and be changed (like one who is not God). Because of this, the will of one who is not God is also not truly good, because it is not good by nature, nor is this will truly perfect, as it can be changed and diminished in such a way that what it wants today, it does not want tonight, or what it does not want today, it does want tonight.

15. (I, 14) I shall speak more clearly using an example. That angel who is now the devil[108] had a good will before he became the devil, but when he became the devil, he parted with his good will by using his own judgment—because, of course, he exists as something made, and is not by nature God.[109] We should think this way about every created being regarding its reason: for even if some of them did not turn away and do not turn away from their good will, they nevertheless have in their nature the capacity to turn away, because they are created beings and not God. For this—that they do not turn away—they maintain from the constant observation of what they have learned, not from the truth of their immutable nature.[110] But God, just as he alone is without beginning, good and perfect and unchanging, has also without beginning a good and perfect and unchanging will. He has this good and perfect and unchanging will not from instruction or by profiting from what he has observed, but from the truth of his immutable nature, by which God is also good and perfect and unchanging.[111] It shall be seen whether perhaps there is some heresy that

---

107. See above, §§10, 11; below, §22.
108. Satan.
109. This is a fairly inventive example on Faustinus's part. See Tertullian, *Marc.* 2.10; Cyril of Jerusalem, *Catech. myst.* 2.4.
110. See Hilary of Poitiers, *Trin.* 1.2.
111. See Ambrose, *Trin.* 2.8.65; 5.16.194.

tu tamen praecipue ad hoc, Arriane, consentis, qui et ipsum Filium Dei, quem totius creaturae Dominum confiteris, conuertibilem et mutabilem dicis, quod eum a Deo factum de nihilo praedicas, non tamen de Deo uere natum. Si haec tibi sententia est, quod omnis creatura uertibilis est et mutabilis, Christum autem dicis esse creaturam, ergo et ipse, secundum te, ex conditione creaturae conuertibilis et mutabilis existens, non habet inconuertibilem et indemutabilem uoluntatem. Et quomodo interpretaris quod Pater et Filius unum sunt uoluntate, cum Patris et Filii, secundum te, diuersae sunt uoluntates et contrariae? Quia scilicet una est indemutabilis et inconuertibilis, alia uero mutabilis et conuertibilis est, deprehenderis et detegeris, haeretici fraudulente, quomodo conaris simplices animas circumuenire et capere. Constrictus enim et coarctatus testimonio domincae pronuntiationis dicentis: *Ego et Pater unum sumus*, ut de hac uoce qualitercumque euoles, quae claris sermonibus in Patre et Filio unitatem deitatis ostendit, subcubuisti necessitate, non arbitrio, ad hoc ut uel ad momentum in praesenti capitulo summis labiis et, ut ita dixerim, superficie sola uerborum, unitatem uoluntatis interseras, quo expressius et uiuacius et medullitus unitatem deitatis excluderes. Tollis enim sensum "unitate substantiae," qui facile creditor ex ipsa simplicitate uerborum, et interpretaris sensum "unitate uoluntatis," ut, quia supra dicta ratio eius non facile apud omnes intellegitur, interim simplicem decipias auditorem, cum illud agis ne unitatem diuinitatis intellegat. Nam et unitatem uoluntatis in Patre et Filio fides catholica sincerissime et uerissime credit, non labiis tantum sed et toto corde, quae et unitatem substantiae et diuinitatis agnoscit. Sicut enim indemutabilis et inconuertibilis substantiae est cum Patre Filius, ita et indemutabilis et inconuertibilis uoluntatis est cum Patre Filius. Atque ideo una uoluntas est Patris et Filii, sicuti et una uirtus et una imago: magis

spits back at this sense; but you in particular, Arian, agree on this point, you who say that the very Son of God, whom you confess is the Lord of every created being, is changeable and mutable, because you proclaim that he was made by God from nothing, but was not truly born from God.

But if this is your understanding, that every created being is changeable and mutable, and if moreover you say that Christ is a created being, then according to you, he also does not have an unchanging and immutable will because he exists as changeable and mutable due to his condition of being a created being. How would you explain that the Father and Son are one in their will when, according to you, the wills of the Father and of the Son are different and contrary? Naturally, since one will is immutable and unchanging but another is mutable and changeable, you are checked and uncovered, you fraudulent heretic, in your attempt to encircle and capture simple souls. For you are constrained and confined by the testimony of the Lord's pronouncement when he says, *I and the Father are one*.[112] However you fly away from this statement, which demonstrates in clear words the unity of the divinity between the Father and the Son, you are overcome by necessity, not by sound judgment, to this: briefly, with just lip service on the verse in question and, so to speak, on the surface meaning of the words alone, you insert a unity of their will by which you expressly, vigorously, and thoroughly exclude the unity of their divinity. For you take away the meaning of "with a unity of substance," which is easily believed from the very simplicity of the words, and interpret the meaning of "with a unity of will." When you act to prevent the simple listener from understanding the unity of their divinity, you say this so that you might deceive him for awhile, because not everyone easily understands the reason for going beyond what was said. Now, the catholic faith most sincerely and most truly believes in the unity of the will in the Father and Son, not just paying lip service but with its whole heart, which well knows both the unity of their substance and of their divinity. For just as the Son is of an immutable and unchangeable substance with the Father, so too is the Son of an immutable and unchangeable will with the Father.[113] This is why there is one will of the Father and of the Son, just as there is also one power and one appearance.

I would say further that the Son himself is the will of the Father. For just as there is one appearance of the Father and the Son according to Moses,[114]

---

112. John 10:30. See above, §§12–14; below, §36.
113. See Athanasius, *Apol. sec.* 3.66.
114. See above, §7.

enim dixerim quod ipse Filius uoluntas est Patris. Sicut enim Patris et Filii una image cum sit secundum Moysen, tamen et ipse Filius *imago Dei inuisibilis* scribitur ab apostolo, ita et una uoluntas cum sit Patris et Filii, pie definitur quod uoluntas Patris est Filius. Sicut est Dei inuisibilis imago, similiter et de uirtute intellege. Fides enim catholica dicit unam uirtutem esse Patris et Filii; et tamen scribit apostolus Christum Dei esse uirtutem et Dei sapientiam. Pie ergo dictum est quod Filius uoluntas est Patris, sicut idem ipse est et sapientia Dei. Et tamen si adhuc mouet hic sensus, intende ad ea quae dicimus. Certe Dei sapientia Christus est: quid autem est Dei uoluntas quam Dei sapientia? Non enim in Deo aliud uoluntas est et aliud sapientia. In hominibus quidem potest esse uoluntas, non tamen haec ipsa et sapientia, quia uoluntas hominis eruditione et meditatione et profectu ad sapientiam sibi possibilem peruenit. Dei autem uoluntas non eruditione non meditatione non profectu peruenit ad sapientiam, sed ipsa nihil indigens, naturaliter substantiua sapientia est. Vnde et Christus Dei sapientia existens, Dei quoque et uoluntas est, quia in Deo non aliud uoluntas et aliud sapientia.

16. (II, 1) Quod non sit ex nihilo factus sed uerus sit Filius de ipso Patre uere et sine initio genitus.

Dauid uno lapidis ictu Goliae frontem percutiens magni corporis fortem strauit inimicum. Sed nostrae non est uirtutis de uno lapide uincere,

the Son himself is furthermore also recorded as the *appearance of the invisible God* by the Apostle.[115] Thus it is pious to define the Son as the will of the Father when there is one will of the Father and of the Son.[116] Just as the appearance of God is invisible, think of his power in a similar fashion.[117] For the catholic faith says that there is a single power of the Father and of the Son, and furthermore, the Apostle writes that Christ is the Power of God and the Wisdom of God. Thus it is piously said that the Son is the will of the Father, just as this same one is also the Wisdom of God.

Nevertheless, if this still disturbs your sense of understanding, consider what we are saying. Certainly Christ is the Wisdom of God—and what is the will of God but the Wisdom of God?[118] For there is no will in God in one respect and wisdom in another.[119] Certainly among men there can be a will, but this itself is not also wisdom, since the will of a man comes to potential wisdom for himself through learning, preparation, and improvement. But the will of God does not come to potential wisdom through learning, preparation, and improvement, but itself, since it lacks nothing, is substantive wisdom by nature. Thus Christ both exists as the Wisdom of God and also is the will of God, since in God there is no will in one respect and wisdom in another.

16. (II, 1) That the Son was not made from nothing but is the true Son from the true Father, and was begotten without beginning.

David, striking the forehead of Goliath with one blow of a stone, laid low the hostile strength of his huge body.[120] But it is not within our power to

---

115. Col 1:15. See Hilary of Poitiers, *Trin.* 2.8. Faustinus ignores the rest of the passage, which identifies Christ as "the firstborn over all creation" and was a popular text among homoiousians. See Beckwith 2008, 18, 60, 112.

116. See 1 Cor 1:24; Athanasius, *Apol. sec.* 2.2; Gregory of Nyssa, *Eun.* 2.218. Augustine (*Trin.* 15.20.38) explicitly rejects such a position, instead arguing that the Son is the "will of the will" just as he is "substance of the substance" and "wisdom of the wisdom" of the Father.

117. Faustinus here draws a direct correlation between God's will (*voluntas*) and power (*virtus*), that is, what he wishes to accomplish and his ability to accomplish.

118. Here Faustinus switches to a direct correlation of God's will (*voluntas*) and wisdom (*sapientia*), that is, what he wishes to accomplish and what is wise to accomplish.

119. See Athanasius, *Apol. sec.* 2.38.

120. See 1 Sam 17:50. David and Goliath was a popular theme in late antique

duplici, ut opinor, ex causa: quia nec nos tales uires habemus, quales habuit et Dauid; et isti nimis frontem praeferunt inpudentiae impietatibus obduratam, unde iam licet multos lapides non in uacuum miserimus, tamen adhuc in Dei gratia repetendum nobis est, et inpudens frons eorum, illa quae est sine signo Domini, crebris testimoniorum lapidibus elidenda est, ut, etsi non caro eorum effundit cruorem multis effossa uulneribus, tamen uel pudor suffusione sanguinis erubescat, si etiam ex iis quae illorum scripseras opprimantur. Haec uerba ais esse haereticorum: Ex nihilo—inquit—Deus sibi Filium fecit. Si fecit eum ex nihilo, creatura est et non filius. Et quid est quod filium dicis, quem creaturam esse confirmas, cum dicis eum factum esse ex nihilo? Non ergo potes et filium eum dicere et creaturam: filius enim ex natiuitate consistit, creatura uero ex factura. Quid tibi contraria profiteris? unum elige de duobus: dic aut filium uere filium aut creaturam uere creaturam. Si ita filium dicis ut uere filium dicas,

be victorious by using a single stone for two reasons, as I judge it: because we do not have such powers as David had and because those men show that their foreheads are too hardened by the impieties of their shamelessness. Even though we may have already fired off many stones (and without missing), this is why we must still attack again in the grace of God, and this is why their shameless foreheads, which are without the sign of the Lord, must be crushed by numerous stones of testimonies.[121] Even if they pour out their gore without a care after they are pierced by many wounds, their shame might still nevertheless grow red by the spreading blood[122] if they are also overcome in the material that you had written about.

You say that these are the words of the heretics: "From nothing," he says, "God made a Son for himself."[123] If he made him from nothing, he is a created being and not the Son. How can you call him the Son, whom you assert is a created being, when you say that he was made from nothing? You cannot call him the Son and a created being this way, for a son exists from birth but a created being from its fabrication. Why do you bring up things contrary to yourself? Pick one of the two: call him either the Son, truly as the Son, or a created being, truly as a created being. If you call him

---

literature and society at large, both among Christians and Jews, forming the basis for a variety of metaphors. For a few examples, see, e.g., Jerome, *Ep.* 70.2; Ambrose, *Exp. Luc.* 10.12–14; Augustine, *Ennarat. Ps.* 144; Prudentius, *Psych.* 291–304; numerous statements in the Talmud (see Hirsch 1904); and in art, a fresco on the third-century Dura-Europos church (Kraeling and Welles 1967, 69–71); a synagogue mosaic floor (Ilan 1995); and a silver plate from the early seventh century (Leader 2000, 407–8, 413–15). Ambrose, like Faustinus, identifies Goliath with heresy.

121. See above, §§1–3, for militant imagery, and below, §§17, 18, 24, 26, where Faustinus returns to this metaphor. The sign of the Lord may refer to the Christian practice of marking one's forehead with a finger (in the sign of a cross?) as a general apotropaic symbol (see Tertullian, *Cor.* 3.4), which naturally would be considered ineffective if a heretic were the one making the sign. This passage, however, probably refers to the mark made by a priest on the forehead of a catechumen when he received baptism (which may have been a cross; see Augustine, *Faust.* 12.30). Perhaps Faustinus believed that heretical baptism was invalid; on the other hand, it might signify that Faustinus believed that heretical baptism was valid but ineffective unless the individual in question joined the proper communion group: Jerome (*Lucif.* 2–4) and Augustine (*Agon.* 30.32) both believed that the Luciferians did not rebaptize.

122. In other words, the red blood suggested by the David and Goliath metaphor might be matched by redness on their blushing faces.

123. Faustinus switches from the plural "heretics" to the singular "he says," which probably reflects the specific beliefs of whoever penned these Arian tracts for Flacilla.

negasti eum esse creaturam. Et quomodo eum de nihilo factum esse dicis, quem uere filium confiteris? Si autem dicis eum uere esse creaturam, cur eum filium nominas, cum in eo istius nominis abneges ueritatem?

17. (II, 2) Sed de uiuis lapidibus diuinae uocis percutiamus frontis eius inpudentiam. Tu dicis eum esse creaturam; ego dico eum esse filium: quis inter nos de professionis ueritate pronuntiet? Puto quod libenter habeas ut ille iudicet, a quo tu, renuentibus nobis, factum dicis Christum ex nihilo. Audiamus ergo quid de caelis ipse pronuntiet: *Hic est Filius meus dilectus, in quo mihi bene conplacui.* Numquid dixit: Hic est quem ego feci ex nihilo? Et uide quia hoc tunc primum dixit, quando Iesus ut homo accessit ad baptismum; et, puto, non alia ratione quam quia poterat credi non esse Filius Dei, qui corporeus uidebatur, et inter ceteros homines ipse quoque ut homo peccator ueniebat ad baptismum, cum peccata propria non haberet. Ne ergo, cum sacramentum baptismatis in homini adsumpto consummat Iesus, non uere Dei Filius crederetur, clamat de caelo Pater: *Hic est Filius meus dilectus.* Intellexerat quidem et Iohannes suum illum esse Dominum quando et uenienti ad baptismum ait: *Ego debeo a te baptizari, et tu uenis ad me?* Sed ne forte apud aliquos Iohannis testimonium non tam magnum uideretur, ut uinceret fidem carnis et humilitatis in Christo, et omnia omnino quae per carnem eius agebantur, ipse quo nemo maior, ipse quo nemo melior cognitor, dat testimonium de caelis dicens: *Hic est Filius meus dilectus, in quo bene conplacui.* Inquantum enim mani-

the Son in such a way that you truly call him the Son, you deny that he is a created being. How can you say that he was made from nothing, whom you assert is truly the Son? But if you say that he is truly a created being, why do you name him the Son, since you deny him the truth of his name?[124]

17. (II, 2) Let us strike the shamelessness of his forehead with the living stones of the divine voice.[125] You say that he is a created being; I say that he is the Son. Which of us makes his pronouncement from the truth of his profession? I reckon that you would gladly have [the Father] himself judge, whom you say made Christ from nothing (we disagree). So let us hear what he himself pronounces from heaven: *This is my beloved Son, in whom I am well pleased.*[126] Did he ever say, "This is whom I made from nothing"? See how he first said this when Jesus came up as a man to baptism, and, I think, with no other reason than because it had been possible to disbelieve that he was the Son of God who appeared corporally and who himself also came among the rest of men like a sinful man to baptism, even though he did not have his own sins. Thus, when Jesus fulfills the sacrament of baptism in the adopted form of a man, lest he not truly be believed to be the Son of God, the Father cries from heaven, *This is my beloved Son.* Certainly John [the Baptist] had also understood that the Son was his Lord since he says of him, when he was coming to baptism, *I ought to be baptized by you, and you come to me?*[127] But just in case John's testimony does not seem significant enough to overcome their belief in the flesh and the humility of Christ and that everything is done everywhere through his flesh, [the Father] himself— whom no one is greater than, whom no one knows better than—he himself gives testimony from heaven when he says, *This is my beloved Son, in whom I am well pleased.* For as much as the faith was clear concerning the flesh of the Savior, the faith should also have been clear concerning the divinity of

---

124. In the fourth century, Christian theologians frequently connected the names of things and their natures; see Toom 2010; DelCogliano 2010, esp. 182–84, on the role homoiousians in the mid-fourth century played in making the meaning of *Father* and *Son* a central point of Trinitarian debate. Faustinus's points about name(s) are much simpler and less philosophically inclined than Hilary's; see Weedman 2007b, 136–39.

125. See above, §16; below, §§18, 24, 26.

126. Matt 3:17. See Hilary of Poitiers, *Trin.* 6.23; Athanasius, *Apol. sec.* 2.23; Ambrose, *Fid.* 1.13.83.

127. Matt 3:14. This passage is rarely discussed in patristic texts in the context of Nicene-Arian polemic. If it is not an independent development on Faustinus's part, perhaps he had heard the suggestion that Matt 3:14 could be used this way personally or it appeared in some form in the letter sent to Flacilla.

festa fides erat circa carnem Saluatoris, intantum et manifesta fides esse debuit circa deitatem Saluatoris: tunc enim et uerus Deus est, si sit et uerus Filius. Carnem quidem eius, uel potius hominem dicam, nemo ambigebat, quia nec ambigi poterat. Sed illud quod in homini erat et natum cum homine, quia uideri per naturam non poterat, ne esset incertum, uoce et quasi digito Patris ostenditur dicentis: *His est Filius meus dilectus, in quo bene conplacui*: et interea pari auctoritate fides utriusque substantiae, id est, Dei et hominis, commendatur in Christo. Hominis enim in se fidem Dei Filius ipse significabat per conceptionem et partum Virginis, per infantiae uagitum, per cunas et inuolumenta, per ipsa matris ubera, per ipsa materni lactis alimenta, per incrementa corporeae aetatis, per hoc ipsum quod uenit ut baptizaretur. Vides quomodo interim usque ad baptismum expressit in se hominis ueritatem, tanto pressius hoc agens, quanto et difficilius credit poterat Deum in hominem fieri. Et ne forte ad hoc coactum putes et non sponte Filium Dei filium quoque factum esse hominis, audi apostolum dicentem de eo: *Qui cum in forma Dei esset constitutus, non rapinam arbitratus est esse se aequalem Deo, sed semetipsum exinaniuit, formam serui accipiens*. Si ergo semetipsum exinaniuit formam serui accipiens, non coactus est, sed sponte factus factus est filius hominis, existens in forma Dei Deo aequalis. Habes igitur Filium exprimentem in se fidem hominis.

18. (II, 3) Item uideamus fidem in eo diuinitatis expressam; et licet sufficienter supra de fide eius diuinitatis expressum est, et adhuc sint alia

the Savior: if he is truly the Son, then he is also truly God. Certainly no one is unsure about his flesh, or I should rather say, that he was a man, since no one could be unsure.[128] But so that it would not be unclear as to what was in the man and born with the man, since it could not have been seen by its nature, a voice indicates it like the Father's finger by saying, *This is my beloved Son, in whom I am well pleased.*

Meanwhile, faith in Christ is validated by the equal authority of both substances, that is, in him as God and in him as a man.[129] For the Son indicated faith in his human self through his conception and birth from the Virgin, through the crying of his infancy,[130] his cradle and swaddling clothes, the very breasts of his mother, the very nourishment of his mother's milk, his bodily growth over time, and when he came to be baptized. You see how in these times up to his baptism he expressed in himself the truth of his human self. The more accurately he did this, the more difficult it was to believe that he could have become God in a man.[131] In case you happen to think that the Son of God was forced to do this and was not made the son of a man by his own accord, listen to the Apostle, who says about him, *he who, though he was constituted in the form of God, did not regard equality with God as a boon, but diminished himself by taking the form of a servant.*[132] Thus if he diminished himself by taking the form of a servant, he was not compelled, but of his own accord was made the son of a man, who existed in the form of God, equal to God. So, you have the Son expressing in himself faith in his human self.

18. (II, 3) Likewise, let us see how faith in his divine self is expressed; and although enough was expressed above concerning faith in his divine

---

128. Cf. John 1:14.

129. How to describe the unity (or disunity) of the divine and human persons of the Son became a central point of conflict in the fifth century, but the phrase "utriusque substantiae" had good authority in the West in Tertullian, *Prax.* 27; Ambrose, *Hymn.* 4.15 (however, in *Incarn.* 5.35 Ambrose uses *naturae* in the same phrasing); and later, Augustine, *Trin.* 13.17.22. Hilary (*Trin.* 9.14) only describes the *persona* of the Son as two *naturae* (perhaps owing in part to the theological discussions he had during his Eastern exile; see above, p. 48 n. 108).

130. See Hilary of Poitiers, *Trin.* 2.24: "et per conceptionem partum vagitum cunas omnes naturae nostrae contumelias transcucurrit."

131. I.e., the more closely he resembled a man, the more difficult it was to believe he was God.

132. Phil 2:6–7. See above, §3; below, §§20, 23, 32, 34, 36–38. Edwards (1999, 231) implies that the emphasis on Christ's willingness is unique to Faustinus.

quoque multo copiosiora quibus fides in Christo diuinitatis appareat, tamen illa nunc taceo: sufficit enim mihi si fidem in Christo diuinitatis solus interim Pater ostendat dicens: *Hic est Filius meus dilectus, in quo bene conplacui.* Quid ais, haeretice? credis sine dubio Christo, quod se filium hominis fecerit. Quid censes de Patre? estne ueridicus apud te, cum Christum Filium suum esse testatur? Si non credis Patri, cum Christum Filium suum esse testatur, iam maioris apud te auctoritatis est Christus, cui de fide in se hominis credis; et minus idoneus Pater est, cui de Filii testatione non credis. Et quomodo Patrem maiorem Deum uindicas, cuius uocem quasi minimi depretias? uel quomodo Christum Deum minorem adseris, cui tantum credis quantum nec ei, quem maiorem praedicas? Magnus iste honor tuus est quem Patri defers, ut ei non credas de suo Filio profitenti. Qui tamen iterum et alibi profitetur esse illum suum Filium, quando cum apostolis Petro et Iacobo et Iohanne Dominus ascendit in montem et refulsit facies eius ut sol. Percutiat iterum diuinum testimonium tuae frontis inpudentiam: *Et ecce*—inquit—*nubes lucida inobrumbrauit eos, et ecce uox de nube dicens: Hic est Filius meus dilectus, in quo bene conplacui: ipsum audite.* Certe Moyses et Helias pariter uidebantur cum eo loquentes, quos utique de adoptione factos esse filios Dei negare non potes: et quomodo de solo Christo uox diuina testatur dicens: *Hic est Filius meus dilectus in qua bene conplacui: ipsum audite?* Si enim et Christus de adoptione filius est, cum staret inter duos filios adoptiuos, dixisset utique: Et hic Filius meus est, ne Christus solus filius esse crederetur. At cum dicit: Hic est Filius meus dilectus, adoptionis filios separauit, ut proprietas uerae natiuitatls in Christo solo Filio crederetur. Sed non sufficit ut Christum

self, there still might be other, much richer instances where faith in the divinity of Christ may also be apparent. I nevertheless say nothing about those for now, as it is enough for me if the Father alone demonstrates faith in the divinity in Christ when he says, *This is my beloved Son, in whom I am well pleased.*[133] What do you say, heretic? Without a doubt you believe in Christ, in that he made himself the son of a man. How do you rate the Father? Is he untruthful when he testifies that Christ is his own Son? If you do not believe the Father, when he testifies that Christ is his own Son, Christ—whom you believe concerning faith in his human self—is now a greater authority for you, and the Father—whom you do not believe concerning his testimony about the Son—is less suitable. Now, how can you affirm that the Father as God is the greater, when you value his voice as little as possible? Or how can you assert that Christ as God is the lesser, when the more you believe in him, the less you believe in the one whom you profess is greater? This is your great honor that you confer on the Father: you do not believe in what he professes concerning his own Son.

Moreover, he professes again elsewhere that this is his own Son, when along with the apostles Peter, James, and John, the Lord ascended the mount and his face shone like the sun.[134] Once again, divine testimony strikes the shamelessness of your forehead:[135] *And lo,* he says, *a bright cloud cast a shadow over them, and lo, a voice, speaking from the cloud: This is my beloved Son, in whom I am well pleased. Listen to him.*[136] Certainly Moses and Elijah, both of whom you cannot deny were made sons of God through adoption, were seen speaking together with him; so why does the divine voice testify about Christ alone when it says, *This is my beloved Son, in whom I am well pleased. Listen to him*?[137] For if Christ was also a son through adoption, then when he was standing with the two adopted sons, he assuredly would have said, "And this is my Son," so that no one would believe that Christ was his only son. But when he says, *This is my beloved Son,* he separates him from the adopted sons, so that the particular quality of Christ's true birth as his only Son would be believed. It is not enough to

---

133. Matt 3:17. In other words, Faustinus will focus on the passage at hand as proof of Christ's divinity rather than turning to other scriptural examples; see above, §13.
134. See Matt 17:2.
135. See above, §§16, 17; below, §§24, 26.
136. Matt 17:5.
137. See Hilary of Poitiers, *Trin.* 6.24; Ambrose, *Fid.* 1.13.81.

tantummodo suum Filium esse profiteretur; addidit enim quod uero filio debebatur, dicens: *Ipsum audite*. Magnam, immo et parem sibi auctoritatem ostendit in Filio cum ita audiendus est Filius, ut audiendus et Pater est: *Ipsum*—inquit—*audite*. Quicquid ergo iam dixerit Christus, audiendus est. Et uideamus si nusquam se dicit esse Filium Dei, si nusquam se Deum patrem habere profitetur. Ipsius uox est: *Ommis plantatio quam non plantauit Pater meus, eradicabitur.* Et iterum: *Domum Patris mei fecistis domum negotiationis.* Alibi quoque: *Et tu credis in Filio?* Numquam praesumeret dicere: *Pater meus*, et: *Patris mei*, et: Tu credis in Filio Dei?, nisi esset confidentia naturae, quae uindicat uocabulum ueritatis in Patre, de conscientia propriae natiuitatas. Quid enim insolenter ille loqueretur, qui semetipsum humiliauit, factus oboediens usque ad mortem et mortem crucis?

19. (II, 4) Sunt et alia testimonia plurima; sed nos nunc non librum scribimus ut omnia prosequamur, sed causa breuitatis paucis testimoniis summas claudimus, ut uox illa obruatur, quae negat Christum uerum esse Filium Dei. Sane dicit se Christus filium esse quoque hominis, cum ait: *Et uidebitis filium hominis*, et: *Quem me dicunt esse filium hominis?* Hoc est enim sacramentum fidei in Christo, ut cum illum Filium Dei esse credideris, credas quoque et filium hominis esse eum factum. Illud enim quod Filius Dei est, naturaliter possidet; hoc autem quod filius hominis factus est, qua beneficus nobis praestitit: et ideo qui Christum. Filium Dei esse non credit, impius est; sed et qui Christum filium hominis esse factum confiteri dedignatur, ingratus est. Tu tamen, haeretice, credis quod Christus filius hominis factus est, et cum hoc ipsum de se Saluator dicat, non

just profess that Christ is his Son, for he adds what is owed to his true Son when he says, *Listen to him*. He demonstrates in the Son the great, no, an even equal authority to his own, when the Son must thus be listened to in the way that the Father also must be listened to.

Listen—he says—*to him*. Thus whatever Christ now says must be listened to. So let us see if he ever says that he is the Son of God, if ever he professes to have God as his Father.[138] He states, *Everything planted that my Father did not plant will be destroyed*.[139] And again, *You have made the house of my Father a house of business*.[140] Also, elsewhere, *And do you believe in the Son?*[141] He would never presume to say *my father* and *of my Father* and *Do you believe in the Son of God?* unless he was confident from the knowledge of his own birth that his nature justifies the truthful term "Father." Why would he speak arrogantly, given that he humbled himself and was made obedient up to his death, even death by crucifixion?[142]

19. (II, 4). There are many other testimonies, but we are not writing a book now, where we would follow up on everything.[143] For the sake of brevity, we are summing up the highlights with a few testimonies to overwhelm that voice which denies that Christ is the true Son of God. Certainly, Christ says that he was also the son of a man when he says, *And you will see the Son of Man*[144] and *Who do they say is the Son of Man?*[145] For this is the sacred mystery of faith in Christ: while you believe that he is the Son of God, you also believe that he was made the son of a man as well. For his being the Son of God, he possesses by nature; but his being made the son of a man is how he offered himself for our benefit. Therefore, whoever does not believe that Christ is the Son of God is impious, but beyond this, whoever scoffs at confessing that Christ was made the son of a man is without grace. Yet you, heretic, you believe that Christ was made the son of a man, and when he says about himself that he is the Savior, you do not

---

138. See Hilary of Poitiers, *Trin.* 6.25.
139. Matt 15:13.
140. John 2:16.
141. John 9:35 reads, "Do you believe in the Son of Man," but Faustinus renders it "the Son of God" in the following sentence, as it appeared in some early manuscripts: see, e.g., Steegen 2010, 541–43.
142. See Phil 2:7.
143. See above, §§3, 8; below, §48.
144. Mark 14:62.
145. Matt 16:13. See Hilary of Poitiers, *Trin.* 6.25.

abnuis. At uero cum dixerit Pater: *Hic est Filius meus*, et cum dixerit Filius: *Pater meus*, tu ut cor Pharaonis obduras et non credis. Superest inpudentiae tuae ut quasi melancholicus non uera perspiciens, Patrem et Filium dicas esse mentitos. Non—inquit—nego Filium; sed nego uerum Filium: ergo et Petrus ideo beatitudinis uocem meruit, quia Christum uerum Filium esse non credidit licet Filium Dei uiui sit confessus. Magnum reuera confessae fidei sacramentum est in Petri conscientia, ut cum labiis dicat: *Tu es Christus, Filius Dei uiui*, in corde tamen habeat quod non sit uerus Filius Dei uiui. Ego homo sum: uerba audio, uerba intellego, interpretationem tacitam cordis audire non possum. Christum Filium dixit Dei uiui: nisi et adoptiuum adiecerit, ego aliud nihil intellego quam quod et loquitur. Viderit si Christus, qua Dominus et Deus, cor adspicit: mihi tamen qui auribus tantum audio, debuit etiam per uocem fieri cordis eius manifesta confessio, propter quem et Petrus interrogatur: non enim sibi soli Petrus interrogatus est, sed et omnibus nobis, ut cum ille de Christo bene confitetur, et nos similiter. disceremus pari confessione ad beatitudinem peruenire. Et interea uideamus si digne Petrus beatitudinis praeconium consequitur, credens in corde quod non sit uerus filius sed adoptiuus; si

deny it. But whenever the Father says *This is my Son*[146] and whenever the Son says *My Father*,[147] you harden like the heart of Pharaoh and do not believe them.[148] All that is left for your shamelessness, as though you were filled with bile[149] and did not perceive what is true, is to say that the Father and Son are liars.

He says: "I do not deny the Son, but I deny the true Son. This is why Peter was also thus worthy of being termed 'blessed,' since he did not believe that Christ was the true Son, even though he did confess that he was the Son of the living God." Great indeed is the sacred mystery of the faith confessed in Peter's conscience, that when he said with his lips, *You are Christ, the Son of the living God*,[150] he maintained in his heart that he was not the true Son of the living God!

I am a man: I hear the words, I understand the words; I cannot hear the silent intention of his heart. He said that Christ is the Son of the living God: unless he were to add in "adopted," I understand nothing but what he said. He will see if Christ, as Lord and God, examines the heart. But to me, who hears with ears alone (and for whose sake Peter was asked), the confession of his heart ought to have been made clear through his voice as well, for Peter was not asked for himself alone, but for all of us, so that when he made a good confession concerning Christ, we also might likewise learn to attain blessedness by the same confession.

Meanwhile, let us see if Peter was worthy of obtaining his commendation of being called blessed by believing in his heart that Christ was not the true Son but adopted—let us see whether this revelation is worthy of the

---

146. Matt 3:17.
147. Matt 17:5. See Hilary of Poitiers, *Trin.* 6.26.
148. See Exod 7:13; Faustinus and Marcellinus, *Lib. prec.* 6.
149. "Melancholy" as a translation for *melancholicus* does not quite fit the tone that Faustinus implies here and elsewhere, where he presents Arians as excessively angry rather than depressed, nor does the passage make much sense if the Arian in question calls the Father and Son a pair of liars because he was depressed (although the 1721 translator [p. 29] does offer "melancholy mad"). In ancient theories concerning the four humors of the body, *melancholicus* referred to an excess of black bile, thought to lead to either excess depression or excess anger/impetuousness; clearly the latter is meant here. The Roman (and medieval) conception of the humors is most fully expressed by Galen; see Grant 2000, 1–12 (for Galen and ancient medicine in general), 14–18 (for Galen's explanation of the humors), and 19–36 (for Galen's discussion of black bile).
150. Matt 16:16. See Hilary of Poitiers, *Trin.* 6.36; Ambrose, *Fid.* 2.15.129.

digna haec Patris reuelatio est, et non potius carnis et sanguinis. Plurimi certe adoptione sunt filii Dei: et non solum Hieremias, qui adhuc cum esset in uulua matris, sanctificatus est; neque solus Iohannes Baptista, qui in utero matris infans exsultauit in spiritu; sed neque solus Helias, qui mortem adhuc usque non passus est, uel quilibet ex numero prophetarum, ex quibus unus, ut in Euangelio relatum est, putabatur Christus: sed ad hoc nomen adoptionis meretrices et publicani, quamuis emendatione, uenerunt. Et ne quis me putet blasphemare, audiat in Euangelio dici: *Meretrices et publicant praecedunt uos in regno caelorum*, ubi non nisi filii adoptionis sunt. Cum ergo nec blasphemis nec turpibus adoptionis gratia denegetur, si corrigant, hoc pro magno sacramento Pater Petro reuelauit quod scilicet Filius quidem Dei uiui est, sed adoptione potius et non natiuitate, et tantum nomine, non etiam et nominis ueritate? Plane qui hoc credit, non beatus est ille sed miserrimus omnium hominum, habens non solum intellegentiam carnis et sanguinis, uerum etiam et spiritum diaboli. Sed quaeso, regina, sentias quod multa in hoc loco dici poterant, quae ego ad consequentia festinans, praetereo, credens quod, data occasione, quasi una de sapientissimis, plus possis sentire quam loquimur, secundum sententiam Salomonis: *Da sapienti occasionem et sapientior erit.*

20. (II, 5). Haec uestra, Arriani, doctrina est, haec uestra interpretatio singularis, hoc secretum fidei uestrae mysterium: Adoptione—inquit—Christus filius est, et non uerus filius. Interrogemus et Iohannem: potest et hic uerum didicisse, siue quia interfuit cum Petri laudata confessio est, siue ex peculiari dilectione Saluatoris, qua ita erat ei proximus, ut etiam supra pectus eius recumberet. Videamus quid haerens pectori eius hauserit: *Deum nemo uidit umquam, nisi unigenitus Filius, qui est in*

Father, and not rather of flesh and blood. Certainly very many men are the sons of God by adoption, and not only Jeremiah, who was sanctified while still in his mother's womb;[151] and not only John the Baptist, who leapt with joy in the Spirit as an infant within his mother;[152] and not only Elijah, who has not suffered death even up to the present;[153] nor whosoever you please from the number of the prophets, one of whom, as was related in the gospel, was reckoned to be Christ.[154] Yet prostitutes and tax collectors, with a great deal of correction, came to be called adopted. In case anyone thinks that I am blaspheming, let him listen to the gospel, which says, *The prostitutes and tax collectors go before you into the kingdom of heaven,*[155] where they are none other than adopted children. Given, then, that the grace of adoption is not denied on account of blasphemies or disgraces, if they are corrected, did the Father reveal this to Peter as the great sacred mystery—that although Christ is indeed the Son of the living God, it is instead by adoption and not by birth, and only by name, yet not with the truth of the name as well? Clearly, he who believes this is not blessed but is the most wretched of all men, and has not only the sense of flesh and blood but even the spirit of the devil, too! But I ask, Empress,[156] that you understand how many things may be said on this point that I am passing over in my haste. I believe that given the opportunity, you, as one of the wisest of women, may understand more than we are saying, in accordance with the sentiment of Solomon: *Give the wise man an opportunity and he will become wiser.*[157]

20. (II, 5) This is your doctrine, Arians, this is your peculiar interpretation, this is the secret mystery of your faith: "Christ is the Son by adoption," he says, "and not the true Son." Let us ask John. It is possible that he had also learned the truth, whether because he was present when Peter's confession was praised or from the Savior's particular love (John was so close to him that he even reclined on his breast).[158] Let us see what John gleaned from clinging to his breast: *No one has ever seen God, except*

---

151. See Jer 1:5; Athanasius, *Apol. sec.* 3.33.
152. See Luke 1:44.
153. See 2 Kgs 2:11; Sir 48:13–15. See Pseudo-Athanasius, *Ep.* 51.6.
154. See Matt 16:14.
155. Matt 21:31.
156. On the use of the term *regina*, see above, p. 163 n. 240.
157. Prov 9:9; see above, §1.
158. See John 13:23.

sinu Patris. Nulla creatura uidet Deum, secundum hoc quod Deus est; et ideo ait: *Deum nemo uidit umquam.* Sed sequitur et dicit: *nisi unigenitus Filius*: ergo unigenitus Filius non est creatura, qui Deum uidet, quem nulla uidit creatura. Et ne forte unum eum de adoptionis: filiis crederes, amputauit occasionem sensus impii, cum eum dixit non solum Filium, sed etiam unigenitum Filium. Hoc nomen non habet socios: et licet dicantur alii filii, adoptione tamen, non natura sunt filii. Sed Christus solus unigenitus Filius est, quia solus uerus Filius est, non adoptione sed natura, non nuncupatione tantum sed et genere: solus—inquam—uerus Filius est, qui etiam in sinu Patris est. Filii adoptiui in sinu Abrahae sunt: qui autem uerus Filius est, et unigenitus Filius est, in sinu Patris est. Intellege tamen et in hoc inseparabilem paternae substantiae Filium, quod in sinu Patris esse dicitur. Item legimus: *Sic enim dilexit Deus mundum ita ut Filium suum unigenitum daret, ut omnis, qui credit in eum, non pereat sed habeat uitam aeternam.* Non uideo quomodo dilectio Dei commendetur ad mundum, si non uerus et unigenitus est Filius, quem dedit pro mundi redemptione. Mundus sine dubio creatura est: si et Christus creatura est, quid contulit mundo, dans pro creatura creaturam? Omnis creatura seruili condicione censetur: si Christus creatura est, seruus est: et quomodo redemit ad libertatem, cum seruus nullo iure possit conferre libertatem? Et tamen Abraham, ut commendaret dilectionem quam habebat ad Deum, proprium et uerum unigenitum et dilectissimum filium obtulit in holocaustum, cum hoc ipsum Deus ad probandam cunctis eius in se

the only begotten Son, who is in his Father's bosom.[159] No created being sees God, given what God is,[160] and this is why he says, *No one has ever seen God.* But he follows this by saying, *except the only begotten Son.* Thus the only begotten Son is not a created being, as he sees God, whom no created being has seen. Lest by chance you should believe that he is one of the adopted sons, John cut off the opportunity for your impious understanding when he said that he was not only the Son, but also the only begotten Son. This title is not shared by partners. Although other sons may be spoken of, they nevertheless are sons by adoption, not by nature. Christ alone is the only begotten Son, since he alone is the true Son, not by adoption but by nature, not by pronouncement alone but by origin as well.[161] He alone, I say, is the true Son, who is also in his Father's bosom. The adopted sons are in Abraham's bosom, but he who is the true Son, and the only begotten Son, is in his Father's bosom.[162] Moreover, also understand in this that the Son cannot be separated from the Father's substance, since he is said to be in his Father's bosom.

We likewise read, *For God so loved the world that he gave his only begotten Son, so that all who believe in him might not perish but might have eternal life.*[163] I do not see how the love of God is conveyed to the world if it is not his true and only begotten Son whom he gave for the redemption of the world. The world, without doubt, is a created thing; if Christ is also a created being, what does the Father provide to the world in giving something created for something created?[164] Everything created is distinguished by its servile condition. If Christ is a created being, he is a servant: how can he redeem anything to liberty, when a servant has no right to confer liberty?[165] Moreover, Abraham, to convey the love which he had for God, offered up his own true, only begotten, and most-beloved son as a burnt offering, when God had ordered that he do this to prove to everyone

---

159. John 1:18. See Hilary of Poitiers, *Trin.* 6.39.
160. See above, §10.
161. See Hilary of Poitiers, *Trin.* 6.40.
162. See Luke 16:22.
163. John 3:16.
164. See Athanasius, *Apol. sec.* 2.67.
165. But see above, §5, in which Faustinus discusses Christ "taking the form of a servant," "forma serui accipiens." *Servus* and *servilis* are here used more in the sense of "slave," though they are translated here as "servant" to match other scriptural references. See above, §§3, 17; below, §§23, 32, 34, 36–38.

dilectionem, fiere praecepisset. Et tu dicis, impie, quia Deus uolens commendare dilectionem suam mundo, non habuit uerum filium quem daret, sed usus est necessitate, more sterilium, ut, quia uerum de se genitum filium non habuit per naturam, uel ex nihilo factum daret?

21. (II, 6) Dic, impie: Ergo maiori uirtute dilectionem commendauit Abraham, proprium et unigenitum filium offerens quam Deus, qui non proprium neque uere unigenitum dedit? Et est quod uelit Deus magnopere commendare: et inferius commendat quam commendauit homo. Et ille Deus, quem maiorem praedicas, minor est homine in commendanda dilectione: minus enim commendauit dilectionem, si non uerum et unigenitum filium dedit pro mundi dilectione. Et Abraham plus commendauit, qui proprium et unigenitum obtulit. Sed absit haec impietas, ut uel in dilectione commendanda minor sit Deus, qui est per omnia inaestimabilis: uerum enim et unigenitum Filium dedit, diligens mundum. Hoc etiam Paulus, uas electionis, exsequitur, uolens Dei in nos commendare dilectionem, dicens: *Qui suo Filio non pepercit, sed pro nobis omnibus tradidit illum.* Cum dicit: suo Filio, proprietatem ueritatis expressit in nomine. Et uide tamen quo sermone usus est, dicens: *Qui suo Filio non pepercit.* Legisti utique dicentem Deum ad Abraham, cum filium pro Dei dilectione uellet occidere: *Ne inicias manum tuam in puerum, ne facias illi quicquam: nunc enim cognoui quia times Deum tuum et non pepercisti filio tuo dilecto propter me.* Dicit et Paulus: *Qui Filio suo non pepercit, sed pro nobis omnibus tradidit eum*: dicit apostolus ex Dei uoce quomodo commendaret dilectionem: improprie usus fuerat uerbis diuinis, si non et hic de uero filio loqueretur. Et tamen quis fidelium nesciat in patre Abraham

his love for him.[166] Are you saying, impious one, that since God wished to convey his own love to the world and did not have a true son whom he might give, he instead appealed to necessity like a eunuch,[167] so that, since he did not have by nature a son truly begotten from himself, he instead gave something made from nothing?

21. (II, 6) Speak, impious one: in offering his own, his only begotten, son, did Abraham convey his love with greater force than God, who did not give his own or truly only begotten son? This above all is what God wishes to convey, yet he conveys it in a lesser manner than a man conveys it? That very God, whom you proclaim is greater, is less than a man in conveying his love: for he conveyed less love if he did not give his true and only begotten son for his love of the world, and Abraham, who offered up his own and only begotten son, conveyed more. But let this impiety begone, that God who is inestimable in all things just be lesser in conveying his love. For he gave his true and only begotten Son in love for the world. Paul, the chosen vessel,[168] follows up on this because he wants to convey God's love for us, and says, *He who did not spare his own Son, but handed him over for all of us*.[169] When he says, *his own Son*, he demonstrates the particular quality of truth in the name. Furthermore, look at the wording he uses when he says, *He who did not spare his own Son*. You have read elsewhere that God said to Abraham, when he wished to kill his son for his love of God, *Do not put your hand to the boy, do not do anything to him: for now I know, since you fear your God and did not spare your own beloved son for me*.[170] Paul says, *He who did not spare his own Son, but handed him over for all of us*. The Apostle describes how God conveyed his love using God's own language; he used divine language improperly if he was not speaking here about the true Son as well.[171]

Furthermore, who among the faithful does not know that the representation of the truth to come had its precedent in Abraham the father

---

166. See Gen 22.
167. Eunuchs, however powerful they might become politically, were traditionally reviled figures.
168. See Acts 9:15.
169. Rom 8:32. See Hilary of Poitiers, *Trin.* 6.44–45.
170. Gen 22:12.
171. In keeping with contemporary practices, Faustinus makes these linguistic connections between the Old Testament and New Testament without any concern over the fact that the former was composed in Hebrew, the latter in Greek, and the *De Trinitate* in Latin.

et filio eius Isaac imaginem praecessisse futurae ueritatis? In Deo Patre et Christo unigenito Filio eius sacramentum praecedentis figurae monstrauit et apostolus, consignans ipsis sermonibus ueritatem, quibus et primum figura signata est, dicens: Qui Filio suo non pepercit, sed pro nobis omnibus tradidit eum. Si ergo figura erat in Abraham, cum offerret filium; ueritas autem in Deo Patre, cum tradidit Filium: quid ais, doctor impietatis? ubi maior uis uersari debet: in figura an in ueritate? Sine dubio in ueritate. Et quomodo tu minorem exhibes ueritatem, pleniorem uero figuram? Plenior enim est figura, ubi uerus filius offertur; et minor est ueritas, ubi, secundum te, non uerus filius traditur. Sed plane maior est ueritas et minor est figura. Hoc si uis probari, crede uerum unigenitum Filium Dei; et intelleges quod multo plus quam Abraham, gessit Deus, dans Filium suum unigenitum pro mundi dilectione, secundum Euangelium; uel cum, secundum Paulum, *suo Filio non pepercit sed pro nobis omnibus tradidit eum*. Abraham enim, licet filium suum obtulerit, tamen pro Dei dilectione obtulit, cui quicquid obtuleris, non aequas ad quod dignus est; et obtulit filium, quem posteaquam per naturam habere non potuit, per Deum tamen contra naturam adeptus est: obtulit ergo Deo quod ei contra spem naturae Deus dederat, et obtulit filium.

22. (II, 7) Facit ad causam, si dixero se minorem et sine illa condicione praesenti quandoque mortalitatis lege moriturum. Contra examina

and Isaac his son?[172] The Apostle indicated the sacred mystery of the prefiguration regarding God the Father and Christ his only begotten Son by signaling the truth with the very words in which the figure was first signaled: he said, *He who did not spare his own Son, but handed him over for all of us.*[173] Thus if the figure was in Abraham, when he was offering his son, but the truth was in God the Father, when he handed over *his* Son, what do you say, scholar of impiety? What greater force ought to be considered, the figure or the truth? Without a doubt, the truth! For the figure is more fulfilled when the true Son is offered, and the truth is lesser when (as according to you) the true Son is not handed over. But clearly the truth is greater and the figure is lesser. If you want proof, believe in the true only begotten Son of God, and you will understand how much more than Abraham God did when he gave his only begotten Son for his love of the world,[174] according to the gospel, or when, according to Paul, *he did not spare his own Son but handed him over for all of us*. For Abraham, though he offered his own son, nevertheless offered him for his love of God, and whatever you might offer to God, you would not equal what is owed. Abraham offered his son, too, whom he obtained against the natural way of things through God, though he could not have had one in the natural way of things afterwards.[175] Thus he offered to God that which God had given to him against natural hope, and he offered his son.

22. (II, 7) It will help my case if I call [Abraham] inferior even apart from the circumstance at hand, given that [Isaac] was bound to die at

---

172. See Tertullian, *Marc.* 3.18; Origen, *Hom. Gen.* 8.9; Ambrose, *Abr.* 1.8; Gregory of Nazianzus, *Or.* 45.22; and later, Augustine, *Trin.* 2.6.11. The connections between the two figures were powerful enough that even some midrash authors conceive of Isaac bearing wood "like a cross": see Sherwood 2004, 837, citing Genesis Rabbah 56.3, Pesiqta Rabbati 31, and Midrash Sheqalim Tov 61. The argument is typical of one strand of late antique exegesis concerning the Old Testament, in which elements from the Old Testament are said to have prefigured elements in the New Testament or even events in the present. See, in general, Kannengiesser 2004, 238–42, with extensive bibliography.

173. In other words, the phrase "you did not spare your own son" (non pepercisti filio tuo) from the account of Abraham and Isaac in Genesis prefigured the same phrasing in Romans (suo Filio non pepercit).

174. See John 3:16.

175. See Gen 21:1–7.

quid Deus praestiterit: Filium suum praestitit unigenitum, quem non sero ex alicuius adeptus est gratia, sed semper habet sine initio ex proprietate naturae natum de se, qualis et ipse Pater est qui eum genuit, inuisibilem inaestimabilem sempiternum inpassibilem et inmortalem et omnipotentem, sicut et ipse Pater est, et postremo per omnia, secundum hoc quod Deus est, aequalem ei qui eum genuit. Vides qualem dedit Filium Pater. Ecce iam Deus inaestimabiliter superior inuenitur in Filio: et nunc considera quod hunc talem unigenitum Filium pro mundi dilectione praestiterit; et expende nunc quidnam sit mundus: utique creatura est; similiter et Deus quid sit expende: utique creator est. Et nunc iam conpara quem dilexerit Abraham et quem dilexerit Deus: Abraham quidem dilexit Deum. Sed recense quanta Deus Abrahae praestiterit, et inuenies quod Abraham multo minus Deo dilectionis debitum reddidit quam debebat, licet reddiderit quantum reddere potuit. Deus autem mundum diligit pro nulla sibi ab eo data gratia. Vides quia multum commendabilior est dilectio Dei, quae non ex debito praestatur, quam illa Abrahae, quae praestatur ex debito. Sed uide adhuc supereminentiam dilectionis, qua Deus diligit mundum, non solum sibi, qui eum condidit, nullo merito iustitiae commendatum, uerum etiam peccatorem et aduersum se impium. Mundum ergo dilexit Deus peccatis et impietatibus reum, non quia peccata et impietates dilexerit mundi: sed dilexit mundum, ut de peccatis et impietatibus mundus ipse liberetur. Et audi apostolum per haec mire commendantem Dei dilectionem, cum scribit ad Romanos: *Vt quid enim Christus, cum adhuc infirmi essemus, secundum tempus pro impiis mortuus est? uix enim pro iusto quis moritur. Nam pro bono forsitan quis audeat mori. Commendat autem suam caritatem Detis in nobis: quoniam, si cum adhuc peccatores essemus, Christus pro nobis mortuus est, multo magis iustificati nunc in sanguine ipsius, salui erimus ab ira per ipsum.*

some point in accordance with the law of mortality.[176] Against these considerations is what God offered: he offered his only begotten Son, whom he did not obtain later through the grace of anyone, but whom he always had, born from him, without a beginning, from his particular nature, of the same quality as the Father himself who begat him, invisible, inestimable, eternal, without suffering, both immortal and omnipotent, just as the Father is as well, and finally, equal in all things to the one who begat him, in accordance with what God is.[177] You see what sort of Son the Father gave. Look, now God is inestimably found superior in his Son.

Now consider that he offered such an only begotten Son as this for his love of the world. Ponder too, now, what this world is: it is a created thing, of course. Likewise, ponder too what God is: he is the creator, of course. *Now* compare what Abraham loved and what God loved: certainly, Abraham loved God. But calculate how much God offered to Abraham, and you will find that Abraham returned his debt of love to God by much less than he owed, though he returned as much as he could return. Yet God loves the world not for the thanks given to him by it. You see how much more commendable the love of God is, which is not offered up for a debt, than that of Abraham, which is offered up for a debt.

Consider, though, the preeminence of the love with which God loves the world, and not only love for the man dedicated to him because he formed it, without deserving justice, but the sinner and the impious one opposed to him too. Thus God loved the world that was guilty of sins and impieties, but not because he loved the sins and impieties of the world: he instead loved the world so that this world might be freed from its sins and impieties. Listen to the Apostle on these matters. He marvelously conveys this love of God when he writes to the Romans, *Why did Christ, while we were still weak, die for the impious at the right time? Certainly it is rare that anyone die for the just. But for a good man, perhaps someone would dare to die. Nevertheless, God conveys his love to us, since if Christ died for us while we were still sinners, then with all the more justification in his blood will we be safe from [God's] wrath through him.*[178]

---

176. In other words, regardless of how Isaac died, the fact that he was going to die at some point from being mortal makes him a lesser sacrifice than the immortal Christ.

177. See above, §§10, 11, 14.

178. Rom 5:6–9. The word for "love" in this passage is *caritatem*, "dearness, love," as opposed to the word for "love" that Faustinus has been using, *dilectio*.

23. (II, 8) Intellego quidem quod hoc testimonium discuti desiderat: sed nunc quod facit ad causam breuiter pandimus. Mundum habitatores mundi interpretatus apostolus ostendit, quod pro impiis et peccatoribus mortuus est Christus, ut suam caritatem commendaret in nobis, qui sumus in mundo: et moritur—inquit—Christus pro impiis et peccatoribus, quandoquidem uix pro iusto quis moritur, licet forsitan pro bono quis audeat mori. Iamne intellegis quam inenarrabiliter praecellat dilectio Dei, ubi est ueritatis expressio, et quam minor sit dilectio Abrahae, ubi figura signata est? Non hoc dico quasi non multum dilexerit Abraham: immo tantum dilexit Deum quantum et potuit, quantum nemo ex natis mulierum supergredi potest. Sed licet multum dilexerit Deum, et de toto corde et de totis uiribus animae suae dilexerit, tamen inenarrabili supereminentia diuinae dilectionis in infinitum superatur. Quis enim possit explicare dilectionem quam Deus mundo praestitit, dans unigenitum Filium suum ita ut homo nasceretur qui Deus est, et haberet, secundum carnem, humanam sortem initium natiuitatis, qui sine initio de Patre natus est; et ille aequalis Deo in forma Dei semper existens, accepta forma seruili minor fieret non solum Patre, uerum etiam angelis, immo et hominibus, nescio si non et multum infra, uermi quoque conparatus; et postremo, ut secundum naturam sus-

23. (II, 8) Of course I understand that this testimony calls for discussion; but for now, we are just briefly unfolding what helps our case. After explaining that the world means the inhabitants of the world, the Apostle shows that Christ died on behalf of the impious and the sinners so that he might convey his own love for us who are in the world. Christ dies, he says, on behalf of the impious and the sinners, though indeed it is rare that anyone die for the just, though perhaps for a good man someone would dare to die.[179] Do you now understand how indescribably superior God's love is, where the truth is expressed, and how much lesser is Abraham's love, where the figure was signaled? I do not say this as though Abraham did not have much love; no, rather, he loved God as much as he could, so much that no man (of those born of women) could surpass him.[180] But although he loved God very much, and loved him with his whole heart and all the powers of his soul, he nevertheless is overcome by the indescribable supremacy of God's boundless love. For who could explain the love that God offered to the world when he gave his only begotten Son so that a man was born who was God, and so that he had, in the flesh, humanity from the beginning at his birth,[181] a man who was born without a beginning from the Father. Forever existing equal to God in the form of God and having taken the form of a servant,[182] he became lesser not only than the Father, but even lesser than the angels, and what's more, even lesser than men.[183] I do not know whether or not he was even much lower, comparable even to a worm.[184] Finally, in accordance with the nature of the human soul that

---

179. See Rom 5:6–7. The syntax, which differs slightly from what Faustinus provides in §22 above, has been retained in the translation.

180. See Matt 11:11. The parenthetical is meant to avoid suggesting that the Son, whom Faustinus has been arguing was truly a man, would in any way be able to love less than Abraham.

181. In other words, he was fully human the moment he was born; he did not later come to his humanity.

182. See above, §§3, 17, 20; below, §§32, 34, 36–38.

183. See Phil 2:6–7; Heb 2:7. Ambrose (*Fid.* 2.8.64), by contrast, argues that while Christ made himself lesser than the angels, the angels still served Christ, and that to use this text to diminish Christ vis-à-vis the Father also diminishes him vis-à-vis the angels, a clearly untenable position.

184. See Ps 21:6 LXX. At *Lib. prec.* 12 and 13, Faustinus and Marcellinus call Arius's followers worms. Ambrose (*Fid.* 2.61) explicitly states that Christ was speaking in this psalm.

ceptae humanae animae, usque ad mortem tristitiam pateretur, qui totus gaudium est, non solum Abrahae, qui *diem eius cupiens uidere, uidit et gauisus est,* sed et omnium sanctorum? Praestitit ergo mundo unigenitum Filium suum, ut qui uera uita est, pendens in ligno secundum carnem, mortem crucis pateretur, occultata interim sempiterna et inuiolabili diuinitate eius, quae illi una cum Patre est. Vide dilectionem, ut pro mundi salute Dominus maiestatis crucifigatur in terra, qui se Filium Dei credentibus uitam aeternam praestat in caelis. O te beatissimum, patriarcha Abraham, cuius maxima dilectio in Deum non nisi inexplicabilis diuinae dilectionis inundatione submergitur: et nescio si non hoc tantum pro respectu tuae dilectionis et fidei Deus impio praestitit mundo. Tibi enim et semini tuo promiserat Deus, ut heres esses mundi per iustitiam fidei, sicut docet apostolus Paulus.

24. (II, 9) Sed satis tardo, si hunc locum uoluero plenius exsequi: ad te conuertar, haeretice, conmonens ut intendas quomodo Deus diligens mundum, dedit unigenitum Filium suum, uel—ut ait apostolus—quomodo *suo Filio non pepercit, sed pro nobis omnibus tradidit eum.* Si sacramentum istius ineffabilis diuinae dilectionis agnosceres, numquam aduersus Filium Dei impias conponeres quaestiones, quas qui piae mentis est, per illa quae supra diximus, intellegit absolutas. Sed adhuc reliquam partem propositi testimonii uideamus, ut tuae frontis inpudentia multo pressius obteratur. Nam cum dixisset: *Sic enim dilexit Deus mundum ita ut Filium suum unigenitum daret,* prosequitur et dicit: *ut omnis qui credit in eum, non pereat sed habeat uitam aeternam.* Iterum dicam: Si creatura est unigenitus Filius, quomodo qui credit in eum, non perit sed habebit uitam aeternam, cum credere in creaturam sit diuinitatis offensio? Respice ad apostolum Paulum, considera quae opprobria, quas obscenitates de

he had taken up, he suffered sorrow up to death[185]—he who is every joy, not only of Abraham, who *was longing to see his day, saw it, and rejoiced*,[186] but of all the saints as well.[187]

Thus he offered to the world his only begotten Son, so that he who is the true life might suffer death by crucifixion, hanging on the wood in the flesh, with his eternal and inviolable divinity meanwhile hidden—the divinity which for him is one with the Father. See his love, that the Lord of Majesty be crucified on Earth for the welfare of the world, the Lord who offers eternal life in heaven to those believing in him as the Son of God. O most blessed are you, patriarch Abraham, whose greatest love for God is not submersed except by an inundation of divine love! I do not know whether or not God offers this much to the impious world out of respect for your love and faith, for God had promised to you and your offspring that *you be heir to the world through the justice of your faith*,[188] just as the apostle Paul teaches.

24. (II, 9) I would be thoroughly delayed if I turned to follow up this point more fully. Let me swing back to you, heretic, reminding you that you are considering how God, because he loved the world, gave his only begotten Son, or—as the Apostle says—how *He did not spare his own Son, but handed him over for all of us*.[189] If you understood the sacred mystery of that indescribable love, you would never put together impious questions against the Son of God, questions that a piously minded man understands are resolved by the things we said above. But still, let us see the rest of the testimony put forth, so that the impudence of your forehead might be more forcibly crushed.[190] For after he had said, *For God so loved the world that he gave his only begotten Son*, he followed up on it by saying, *so that all who believe in him might not perish but might have eternal life*.[191] Again, I would say: if the only begotten Son is a created being, how can one who believes in him not perish, but have eternal life, since it is an offense to divinity to believe in a created being? Look back to the apostle Paul, consider what disgraces, what obscenities he refers to concerning these men

---

185. See Matt 26:38.
186. John 8:56.
187. See Hilary of Poitiers, *Trin.* 11.15; Ambrose, *Fid.* 2.8.16.
188. Rom 4:13.
189. Rom 8:32. See Hilary of Poitiers, *Trin.* 6.45.
190. See above, §§16, 17, 18; below, §26.
191. John 3:16. See Hilary of Poitiers, *Trin.* 6.40.

his referat qui, ut ipse ait, *conmutauerunt ueritatem Dei in mendacio, et coluerunt et seruierunt creaturae potius quam creatori.* Tu si sic credis et sic colis et seruis unigenito Filio Dei, ut eum dicas esse creaturam, illa te mala miser exspectant, quibus illi puniuntur qui conmutauerunt ueritatem Dei in mendacio, et coluerunt et seruierunt creaturae potius quam creatori. Adoptione—inquit—Christus Filius Dei est, et non uerus filius. Omnia leguntur Euangelia, et nusquam scriptum est quod Christus adoptione est filius et non uerus filius. Et bene quod Iohannes, ille Iohannes recubans supra pectus Domini, causas scripti Euangelii referens posuit, et dixit: *Multa quidem et alia signa fecit Iesus coram discipulis suis, quae non sunt scripta in hoc libro: haec autem scripta sunt, ut credatis quoniam Iesus est Christus Filius Dei, et ut credentes uitam aeternam habeatis in nomine eius.* Est ne opus adhuc apertius explanare? *Multa*—inquit—*et alia signa fecit Iesus*; et licet non sint omnia scripta, quia nec scribi poterant infinita rerum copia, tamen haec ipsa ideo scripta sunt, ut credamus *quod Iesus est Christus Filius Dei*; et, ut fidem singulorum prouocaret, ostendit et praemium dicens: *ut credentes uitam aeternam habeatis in nomine eius.* Si uere adoptione esset filius Dei et non natura, si sola nuncupatione et non etiam quod in nuncupationis intellegentia est, nusquam magis hoc ipsum explanasset quam in ultimo scriptionis, ne fides in ambiguo derelicta, uitam aeternam perderet per credulitatis incertum. Sed euangelista, qui ad hoc positus est, ut, habens gratiam Sancti Spiritus, illa maxime lucidius panderet, quae ad uitae aeternae praemia pertinerent, non in ambiguo clausit Euangelium, sed manifestissime expressit ideo scripta Euangelia, *ut credatis*—inquit—*quoniam Iesus est Christus Filius Dei, et ut credentes uitam aeternam habeatis in nomine eius.* Etiamne hic suspicio est creaturae in Filio Dei, ubi qui crediderit quod Filius Dei est Christus, aeternam uitam possidet, et non aliter quam in nomine eius? qui utique non est creatura sed creator, et non adoptione filius sed uerus Filius Dei: in nomine

who, as he says, *have entirely transformed the truth of God into falsehood, and worshiped and served a created being rather than the creator.*[192] If you believe and worship this way and serve the only begotten Son of God in such a way that you say that he is a created being, then, wretch, those evils await you by which those who *have entirely transformed the truth of God into falsehood and worshiped and served a created being rather than the creator* are punished.

By adoption, [the Arian] says, Christ is the Son of God and not the true Son. All the gospels are gathered together, and it is nowhere written that Christ is the Son by adoption and not the true Son. John, the one who reclined on the breast of the Lord, presented his reasons for writing a gospel well, and said, *Indeed, Jesus also made many other signs before his disciples, which are not written in this book, but these things are written so that you believe that Jesus is Christ the Son of God, and so that in believing, you might have eternal life in his name.*[193] Is there still a need to more openly explain this? He says, *And Jesus made many other signs*, and although they are not all written down, since they could not have all been written down due to the infinite abundance of material, these specific things nevertheless were written down so that we believe *that Jesus is Christ the Son of God*. So that he might appeal to the faith of each individual, he also pointed out the reward when he said, *so that in believing, you might have eternal life in his name*. If he were truly the Son of God by adoption and not by nature, if by proclamation alone and not also by what is understood in the proclamation, John would have explained this in no other place than at the end of his composition, so that the faith, abandoned to ambiguity, would not be deprived of eternal life because his confidence was uncertain. But the Evangelist, who was appointed to make what pertains to the rewards of eternal life known much more clearly because he had the grace of the Holy Spirit, ended his gospel not in ambiguity but most plainly expressed that his gospel was written for this reason: *so that you believe*, he says, *that Jesus is Christ the Son of God, and so that in believing, you might have eternal life in his name.* Is there still any suspicion that the Son of God is a created being, when whoever believes that the Son of God is Christ might possess eternal life, and in no other way than in his name? He is assuredly not a created being but the creator, and the Son not by adoption but the true Son

---

192. Rom 1:25. See Gregory of Elvira, *Fid.* 2; Ambrose, *Fid.* 1.16.10.
193. John 20:30–31. See Hilary of Poitiers, *Trin.* 6.41.

enim creaturae ne quidem uitam temporalem potest quis adsequi, nisi si aliquis eam non auferendo praestare dicatur.

25. (II, 10) De nihilo—inquit—fecit sibi Deus Filium. Praetereo multa testimonia: loquatur Iohannes Christi Domini dilectione perspicuus. Scribens epistulam ait: *Omnis qui diligit Patrem, diligit eum qui ex eo natus est:* numquid ait: Diligit eum quem Deus fecit ex nihilo? Sed nec Patrem omnino nominasset, nisi scisset de eo natum Filium. Et fac nunc quia ita intellegendum est, ut tu, haeretice, interpretaris: quod scilicet ab eo factus sit ex nihilo quem ex Patre natum dicit Iohannes; et quaero numquid, secundum te, solus Christus factus est ex nihilo. Nonne, ut taceam de aliis, etiam mundus ipse ex nihilo factus est? Ergo et mundus a nobis diligendus est, si diligendus est Pater. Sed clamat idem Iohannes: *Nolite diligere mundum.* Numquidnam tam leuis est Iohannes, ut ipse sibi contraria praedicaret? Absit haec impietas, ut dicatur Iohannes repugnantia sibi loquitur, qui in Sancto Spiritu loquebatur. Scit distantiam facti et nati in ipso iam principio Euangelii sui, sicut supra expositum est, cum de ipso capitulo tractaretur: et ideo non ut facturam intellegit eum, quem dicit ex Patre natum, quia nec singulariter poneret, si hoc quod ex Patre natum est, facturam uoluisset intellegi, sciens multos factos esse ex nihilo; sed singulariter ponens, de solo uero Filio posuit dicens quod ex Patre natus est, quia uere ipse solus ex Patre natus est, ceteri autem omnes facti sunt ut a conditore. Noli ergo facere uim diuinis sermonibus: quid inseris quod ille non loquitur? quid doces quod ille non docuit? Si Christianus es et si apud te uerus doctor est Iohannes, crede quod docuit. Ex Patre—inquit—natus

of God, for no one can obtain even a temporal life in the name of a created being, unless they are said to offer life by not taking it away.

25. (II, 10) From nothing—he says—God made the Son for himself. I am passing over many testimonies; let John speak, as he is preeminent in being loved by Christ the Lord.[194] Writing a letter, he says, *Everyone who loves the Father loves the one who was born from him.*[195] Does he say, "loves the one that God made from nothing"? Yet he would not have called him the Father at all unless he had known that the Son was born from him. Now, heretic, make it so that we must understand it the way you interpret it: "Of course he made him from nothing, whom John says was born from the Father." I ask if, according to you, Christ alone was made from nothing. To skip over some things: was not the world itself also made from nothing? Then we should also love the world, if we should love the Father. But the same John cries out, *Do not love the world.*[196] Is John so fickle that he proclaims things contradictory to himself?

Let this impiety begone, that John, who spoke in the Holy Spirit, allegedly said self-contradictory things.[197] He understands the difference between "made" and "born" right away in the very beginning of his gospel, as was explained above when that chapter was treated.[198] For that same reason, when he says that Christ was born from the Father, he understands that Christ is not something made, because he would not specifically put it this way if he wanted us to understand that the one born from the Father was something made, since he knew that many things are made from nothing. But when he specifically put it this way, he put it this way about the true Son alone when he said that he was born from the Father, because he alone truly was born from the Father while all the rest were made as though by a craftsman.

Do not do violence to the words of God. Why do you insert something he does not say? Why do you teach what he did not teach? If you are a Christian, and if John is a true teacher to you, believe what he taught.

---

194. See John 19:26; 21:20.
195. 1 John 1:5. See Hilary of Poitiers, *Trin.* 6.42.
196. 1 John 2:15.
197. Lactantius (*Inst. div.* 1.22) softly criticizes Aristotle because he "secum ipse dissideat, ac repugnantia sibi et dicat et sentiat," but unlike Faustinus (*Trin.* 11, 27), who completely rejects Aristotle, Lactantius argues that Aristotle's acceptance of a single God is broadly correct.
198. Above, §§3–4.

est: hoc si credideris, diligis Patrem, et diligendo Patrem, diligis Filium, qui ex eo natus est. Quod si non credideris quia ex Patre natus est, neque Patrem diligis neque eum qui ex eo natus est: non autem diligis hoc modo, cum in Patre negas esse quod Patris est, id est, generare, et in Filio negas esse quod Filii est, id est, nasci. Et audi nunc quale tibi beatus Iohannes nomen inposuit, dicens: *Hic est antichristus, qui negat Patrem et Filium.* Tu quidem falso Christiani cognomen tibi inponis; sed a ueridico Iohanne pro sectae tuae merito antichristus uocitaris. Mentior si non tu in Patris uocabulo intellegis creatorem, si non in Filii nomine adseris creaturam. Iohannes Patrem et Filium nuncupat, et tu in his nominibus creatorem et creaturam interpretaris. Merito ergo uocaris antichristus, qui negas Patrem et Filium sub interpretatione impia.

26. (II, 11) Sed adhuc audi, o quisquis ille es insolens et contumax in Filium et de Patris persona gloriaris, et intellege quia Patrem habere non potes, si non confitearis et Filium. Idem prosequitur Iohannes: *Qui negat Filium, neque Patrem habet: qui confitetur Filium, et Filium et Patrem habet.* Vides ubique Iohannem ipsa nomina ponere, ut nihil aliud intellegatur quam quod est in natura nominum: et tamen, si adhuc frons inpudentiae tuae potest ictus lapidum sustinere, et si tanta obstinatio duritiae tuae est, ut cum audis Patrem et Filium, non tamen uerum Patrem neque uerum Filium credas: ecce idem Iohannes qui est dilectus a Domino, uicem reddens dominicae dilectioni, fortiori lapide iam non tantum frontem, sed ipsum caput serpentinum tuae conquassat impietatis, scribens in ultimo epistulae suae: *Scimus quia Filius Dei uenit,* et incarnatus est propter nos

From the Father, he says, he was born. If you believe this, you love the Father, and by loving the Father, you love the Son, who was born from him. But if you do not believe that he was born from the Father, you love neither the Father nor the one who was born from him. Furthermore, you do not love them when you deny the existence of the quality of a father in the Father, that is, to generate, and you deny the existence of the quality of a son in the Son, that is, to be born.[199] Hear now what sort of name the blessed John imposes on you when he says, *This man is antichrist, who denies the Father and the Son.*[200] You indeed falsely put the surname of Christian onto yourself, but you are termed antichrist by the truth-telling John as your sect deserves.[201] I am a liar if you do not understand that there is a "creator" in the word "Father," if you do not assert that there is a "created being" in the name "Son." John calls them "Father" and "Son," and in these names you interpret "creator" and "created being." Thus you are deservedly termed antichrist, you who deny the Father and Son in your impious interpretation.

26. (II, 11) Keep listening, whoever you are, you who are insolent and obstinate against the Son and you who take such pride concerning the person of the Father, and understand that you cannot have the Father if you do not also acknowledge the Son. The same John follows: *He who denies the Son also does not have the Father; he who acknowledges the Son has both the Son and the Father.*[202] You see where John places these names, so that only what is in the nature of the names is understood. Furthermore, if the forehead of your shamelessness can still sustain the blows of the stones,[203] and if your stubborn obstinacy is such that when you hear "Father and Son" you do not, nevertheless, truly believe in the Father or truly believe in the Son, look: the same John who was beloved by God,[204] in repayment for the Lord's love, smashes with a harder stone here not so much your brow, but that very snake-like[205] head of your impiety, when he writes at the end of his letter, *We know that the Son of God has come*, and

---

199. See above, §8.
200. 1 John 2:22. See Ambrose, *Fid.* 2.15.135.
201. See John 19:35. Note that Faustinus here uses the word *secta* rather than *haeresis*.
202. 1 John 2:23. See Hilary of Poitiers, *Trin.* 6.42.
203. See below in this section, and above, §§16, 17, 18, 24.
204. See John 19:26; 21:20; and above, §20.
205. See above, §13.

et passus est et resurgens de mortuis adsumpsit nos, *et dedit nobis intellectum bonum, ut cognoscamus ipsum uerum et simus in ipso uero Filio eius Iesu Christo. Hic est Deus uerus et uita aeterna et resurrectio nostra in ipso.* Explicari non potest quantos aduersum te sermonum lapides et saxa congessit sub uno hoc testimonio. *Scimus*—inquit—*quia Filius Dei uenit.* Habes unam de Filio confessionem, et paululum infra post sacramenta incarnationis et passionis eius et resurrectionis, quae utique propter nos in se exercuit, subsequitur dicens: *et dedit nobis intellectum bonum:* sine dubio quia ipse dator bonus est, dat intellectum bonum. Non impie intellegimus, si hunc intellectum bonum dixerimus esse Spiritum Sanctum, qui et dicitur Spiritus intellegentiae, in quo cognoscimus ipsum uerum. Sine Spiritu enim Sancto non potest ueritas cognosci: habes enim testimonium in Euangelio, ubi et Dominus ipsum Sanctum Spiritum pollicetur, et de ipso ait quod: *Ipse mihi testimonium perhibebit:* utique per apostolos uel per quoslibet Filii Dei praedicatores, dans eis intellegentiam, tamquam Spiritus intellegentiae uerum cognoscendi. Vnde et apostolus Paulus scribens ad Corinthios, ait: *Nos autem non spiritum huius mundi accepimus, sed Spiritum qui ex Deo est, ut sciamus quae a Deo donata sunt nobis.* Dedit ergo intellectum bonum, id est, Spiritum Sanctum, ut cognoscamus ipsum uerum.

27. (II, 12) Adhuc si non intellegis de tot supra editis dictionibus, uel ex consequentibus animaduerte omnes suspiciones impiae interpretationis exclusas: *Vt simus*—inquit—*in ipso uero Filio eius Iesu Christo.* Et adhuc amplius piam fidem densat, dicens: *Hic est uerus Deus;* et nondum tacuit, sed cumulat et exaggerat, ut impius sensus sophisticis confidens

was incarnated for us, and suffered, and rising from the dead he received us, *and he gave to us good understanding, so that we might know that he is true and that we might be in his true Son, Jesus Christ. This is the true God and eternal life and our resurrection in him.*[206]

It cannot be explained how many stones and rocks of sayings against you he has gathered under this one testimony. *We know,* he says, *that the Son of God has come.* You have one confession concerning the Son, and a little later after the holy mysteries of the incarnation, passion, and resurrection, which Christ surely worked in himself for us, John follows by saying, *and he gave to us good understanding.* Without a doubt, since the giver himself is good, he gives good understanding. We would not understand impiously if we were to say that this good understanding is the Holy Spirit, who is also called the Spirit of understanding,[207] in whom we know the truth itself. Without the Holy Spirit, the truth cannot be understood, for you have testimony in the gospel, too, when the Lord announces the Holy Spirit and says about him, *He shall bring forth testimony of me*[208] (surely through the apostles or any of those who praise him, by giving them understanding as the Spirit of understanding so they would know what was truth). Thus the apostle Paul, when he writes to the Corinthians, also says, *Yet we do not receive the spirit of this world, but the Spirit who is from God, so that we might understand what is given to us by God.*[209] In sum, he gave good understanding—that is, the Holy Spirit—so that we might know the truth itself.[210]

27. (II, 12) If you still do not understand from the many sayings adduced above, direct your mind to how all the suggestions of your impious interpretation are excluded by what follows: *So that we might be,* he says, *in his true Son, Jesus Christ.*[211] He solidifies the pious faith still more fully when he says, *This is the true God.*[212] He was still not silent, but heaps and piles up more, so that your impious view, which relies on sophistic arguments,

---

206. 1 John 5:20. The noncanonical interpolation in the Vetus Latina also appears in Hilary of Poitiers, *Trin.* 6.42, with some variations: "Quia scimus quod Filius Dei venit, et incarnatus est propter nos, et passus est, et resurrexit a mortuis assumpsit nos."
207. See Isa 11:2.
208. John 15:26.
209. 1 Cor 2:12.
210. See 1 John 5:20.
211. 1 John 5:20. See Hilary of Poitiers, *Trin.* 6.43.
212. 1 John 5:20.

argumentationibus obruatur: subsequens enim ait: *Et uita aeterna et resurrectio nostra in ipso.* Vbi nunc sunt illa impia uestra sophismata quae Aristotelis episcopi uestri magisterio didicistis dicentes: Filius est, sed non est uerus filius; Deus est, sed non est uerus Deus? Ecce uno testimonio tot modis filii uerum nomen expressum est, immo quia et uerus Deus est. Quomodo enim non uerus Deus est, qui uerus est Filius? quandoquidem non solum de ueri Filii nomine Deus uerus probatur, sed etiam per hoc, quod uita aeterna est. Vita enim aeterna non habet initium neque finem: ergo uerus Deus est Christus, non habens initium neque finem, existens ipse uita aeterna, quae est sine initio et fine. Sed et cum resurrectio nostra est, potestas in eo uerae diuinitatis agnoscitur, cum mortem per uirtutem resurrectionis excludit, exemplo sui quem adsumpsit hominis, in quo et de uirgine nasci dignatus est, in quo et nos iam resurreximus, habituri unusquisque nostrum specialem resurrectionem pro merito uerae fidei ac uitae, siue ad refrigerium siue ad ustionem. Vide, miser, ne adhuc non credas uerum esse Filium, et incipias habere resurrectionem ad poenam perpetuam gehennae in tenebris exterioribus, ubi fletus oculorum est et stridor dentium, si tamen non adhuc aliquid tetrius manet impios in Filium.

28. (II, 13) Satis, ut opinor, licet pauculis testimoniis conprobatum est quod sit uerus Filius Dei, natus de Patre, non factus ex nihilo. Sed adhuc, quaeso, exhibe infatigabilem patientiam, ut hoc ipsum de ueteris Scripturae uel uno testimonio conprobemus. Dicis, haeretice, ex nihilo factum Filium, cum hoc nusquam legeris; negas illud quod scriptum est quia ex Patre natus est. Dic mihi cuius uerba sunt: *Ex utero ante Luciferum genui te.* Si ambigis, respice ad initium psalmi eius, et lege scriptum: *Dixit Domi-*

is overwhelmed. For subsequently he says, *and eternal life and our resurrection in him.*[213] Where now are those impious sophistries of yours, which you learned from the teaching of your bishop Aristotle,[214] that say, "He is the Son, but he is not the true Son; he is God, but he is not the true God"? Look, in one testimony the true name of the Son is expressed in so many ways, because he is indeed also the true God. For how is he not the true God who is the true Son, seeing as he is not only proven to be the true God from the name of the true Son, but also through this: he is eternal life. Indeed, eternal life has neither a beginning nor an end. Thus Christ is the true God, as he has neither a beginning nor an end, and exists himself as eternal life, which is without beginning and end. But when he is our resurrection, the power of true divinity is also recognized in him, since he excludes death by virtue[215] of his resurrection, in the pattern of the human form that he assumed, in which he also deemed it worthy to be born from a virgin. We now have been resurrected in this pattern, and each of us will have a particular resurrection of our own in accordance with the worthiness of our true faith and life, whether to comfort or to the flames. See to it, wretch, that you do not continue to disbelieve that he is the true Son and undertake your resurrection to perpetual punishment in hell, in the outer shadows where there are weeping eyes and the gnashing of teeth[216]—if something still fouler yet does not await those who are impious against the Son.

28. (II, 13) This is enough, in my opinion, though in very few testimonies, to prove that he is the true Son of God, born from the Father, not made from nothing. But still, I ask you to offer up your tireless patience[217] so that we may prove this from just one attestation in the Old Testament. You, heretic, say that the Son was made from nothing, though you read this nowhere. You deny that which is written, that he was born from the Father.[218] Tell me whose words these are: *From the womb I have begotten you before the morning star.*[219] If you are unsure, look back to the

---

213. 1 John 5:20. Faustinus cleverly breaks this passage into several parts so that he might in turn rhetorically pile it up.

214. I.e., the Arians rely on classical philosophy. See Epiphanius, *Pan.* 69.71.1, and see above, §11.

215. The Latin term *virtus* here has added connotations of "power" and "miracle."

216. See Matt 8:12.

217. See above, §3; below, §30.

218. See 1 John 5:1.

219. Ps 109:3 LXX. See Hilary of Poitiers, *Trin.* 6.16; Ambrose, *Fid.* 1.14.89. In the background throughout the following discussion is the fact that Lucifer of Cagliari

nus Domino meo: Sede ad dexteram meam, donec ponam inimicos tuos scabellum pedum tuorum. Hoc testimonio ipse Saluator usus est, cum uult se Dominum credi, loquens ad eos qui illum solum in hominem putabant natum ex semine Dauid, non etiam et Deum qua Dei Filium. Sed et Paulus apostolus hoc ipsum credens quod et olim Spiritus Sanctus in Dauid locutus est et postea Saluator exposuit, ait in epistula sua: *Ad quem autem angelorum dixit aliquando: Sede ad dexteram meam?*, hoc explanans quia nemo de angelis talis est, qualis est Filius: omnes enim angeli facti sunt, solus autem Filius natus est, cui et dicit: *Sede ad dexteram meam*, quia et solus ipse est *unigenitus Filius qui est in sinu Patris*. Non autem nunc expositio totius psalmi necessaria est, sed illud solum probandum fuit quia Dominus Pater dicit Filio Domino meo: *Sede ad dexteram meam*, ut et illud quod in sequenti dicitur, non alius quam Pater dixisse credatur, id est: *Ex utero ante Luciferum genui te*. Nonne etiam hoc testimonio uerissimo probatum est sepultam uocem impiam esse dicentium quod ex nihilo fecerit Deus Filium? Quomodo enim ex nihilo, cum ipse Pater clamat: *Ex utero ante Luciferum genui te*? Et uide ne putes nos intellegere quod Deus membrorum partiumue conpositione subsistat. Absit haec impietas. Deus enim, quodcumque illud est, simplex est: totus idem est secundum substantiam, non pars et pars, non membrum et membrum; sed, ut diximus, simplex nescio quid, quod sit integrum et perfectum et inaestimabile tamen et inexplicabile. Licet ergo talis est, ut non membris partibusue subsistat, tamen Scriptura diuina, cum uult nobis Dei fabricatoris ueram intellegentiam commendare ex his quae nouimus, loquitur dicens opera manuum eius esse caelos, uel unamquamque creaturam, quia apud homines uere et proprie opus uel fabrica intellegitur quod efficitur

beginning of his psalm, and read what is written: *The Lord said to my Lord, Sit at my right hand, until I place your enemies as a footstool for your feet*.[220] The Savior himself used this testimony when he wished for it to be believed that he was the Lord and spoke to those who thought that he was born only as a man, from the seed of David, but not also as God, as the Son of God.[221] Paul the apostle also believed in what the Holy Spirit said through David long ago and what the Savior later set forth, and said in his letter, *But to which of the angels did he ever say, Sit at my right hand?*,[222] explaining that none of the angels is such as the Son is. For all the angels were made, but the Son alone was born, to whom he also says, *Sit at my right hand*, since he alone is also the *only begotten Son, who is in his Father's bosom*. However, an exposition of the whole psalm is unnecessary right now, just that point which was to be proven: that the Lord, the Father, says to my Lord, the Son, *Sit at my right hand*, so that none but the Father is believed to have said what is said next, that is, *From the womb I have begotten you before the morning star*.[223] Does even this most truthful testimony not prove that their impious saying, that God made the Son from nothing, is buried? For how do you get "from nothing" when the Father himself cries, *From the womb I have begotten you before the morning star*? See to it that you do not think that we suppose that God exists in a combination of limbs or parts. Let this impiety begone! For God, whatever he is,[224] is simple. He is all the same in his substance, not part and part, not limb and limb, but like we said, something simple (I know not what) that is whole, perfect, and inestimable, but also inexplicable. Thus although God does not exist with limbs or parts, divine scripture, when it wishes to convey to us true understanding of God as a fabricator, nevertheless speaks in the things that we know when it says that the heavens (or whatever is created) are the works of his hands,[225] since among men it is truly and rightly understood that "work," or "fabrication," is that

---

took his name from "the morning star." In the fourth century, Lucifer was not a common term for Satan.

220. Ps 109:1 LXX.
221. See Matt 22:41–46.
222. Heb 1:13.
223. See Hilary of Poitiers, *Trin.* 12.8–12; Ambrose, *Fid.* 4.8.88.
224. Literally, "whatever that is." The neuter (rather than masculine or feminine) suggests how indescribable the substance of the Trinity is.
225. See Ps 101:25 LXX.

manibus: denique cum uisum est arte aliquid fabricatum, ad manus refertur artificis. Et similiter autem inter nos uolentes filii designare naturam, uteri facimus mentionem: nemo enim de ueris filiis non de utero nascitur. Et Deus ergo uolens ex se natum Filium demonstrare, dixit quod eum ex utero genuerit, ne tu, haeretice, calumniareris ex nihilo. Sed sicut, cum Deus manibus fecisse dicitur, ut Deo dignum intellegendum est, ita et cum ex utero genuit, non contra quam Deo dignum est opinemur. Illud tamen certissime confitendum est, quod uerus est conditor in significatione operis manuum, et uerus est Pater in significatione uteri gignentis, etsi nihil in se membrorum habeat.

29. (II, 14) Sed quia soletis dicere, o Arriani: In Deo id ipsum est facere, quod et generare, opportune et hanc uestram peruersitatem de praesenti occasione conuincam. Multa sunt nempe opera manuum, sed unus est unigenitus Filius uentris: non ergo id ipsum est facere quod et generare: et omnia quidem per Verbum et in sapientia facta sunt: Verbum autem siue sapientia non per aliquem, sed ex Deo nata est: unde non id ipsum est facere, quod et generare. Nisi enim esset distantia inter facere et generare, nihil prohibebat ut diceret: Manus meae generauerunt te, et: Caeli uentris mei sunt opera. Sed sicut dictio multam habet differentiam, ita et res quas dictio determinat. *Ex utero*—inquit—*ante Luciferum genui te.* Hoc autem dicit Pater ad Filium, non quod Filius ignoret, sed ut nos scire possimus proprietatem Patris ad Filium, uel Filii ad Patrem: ideo ita scriptum est, sicut et ipse unigenitus Filius existens sapientia ait: *Ante omnes autem colles genuit me.* Vnde et hoc in loco ante Luciferum genitus esse dicitur. In Luciferi uocabulo omnis ubi ubi lucidior creatura signatur:

which is effected by hands; and lastly, when something appears to be artfully fabricated, it is associated with the hands of its maker. Now, in a like manner, again among us, when we wish to indicate the nature of a son we make mention of a womb, for no one who is a true son is not born from a womb. God, thus wishing to demonstrate that the Son was born from him, said that he was begotten from a womb, so that you, heretic, would not falsely allege that he was born from nothing. Just as when God is said to have made something with his hands, it should be understood in a way worthy of God, we should also, when he has begotten from a womb, judge that this is nothing other than what is worthy of God. It most certainly must be confessed that he is truly a craftsman in what is signified by the work of his hands, and that he is truly the Father in what is signified by the begetting of the womb, even if he himself has no limbs.[226]

29. (II, 14) Since you are accustomed to say, O Arian, "For God, 'to make' is the same thing as 'to beget,'" I should also take this opportunity to refute this perversity of yours on the present occasion.[227] Certainly the works of his hands are many, but there is only one only begotten Son of the womb; thus "to make" is not the same thing as "to beget." All things indeed are made through the Word and in his Wisdom,[228] but the Word, or Wisdom, was not made by anything but was born from God; thus "to make" is not the same thing as "to beget." For unless there were a distinction between making and begetting, nothing would prohibit him from saying "My hands begat you" and "The heavens are the works of my womb." But just as the wording carries great distinction, so too do the matters that the wording defines. *From the womb*, he says, *I have begotten you before the morning star.*[229] Now, the Father says this to the Son not because the Son did not know it, but so that we might learn for ourselves the proper place of the Father in respect to the Son, or of the Son in respect to the Father. This is why it is written this way, just as the only begotten Son himself, existing as Wisdom, says, *But before all the hills, he begat me.*[230] Thus, in this place, too, he is said to have been begotten before the morning star. The phrase "morning star" signifies every more luminous created thing, wherever it

---

226. *Limb* should be taken here (and above) as synecdoche for any body part.
227. See Arius, *Ep. Eus.* 5 (= Epiphanius, *Pan.* 69.6.4; Theodoret, *Hist. eccl.* 1.5.2); Athanasius, *Apol. sec.* 2.58.
228. See John 1:3, Ps 103:24 LXX.
229. Ps 109:3 LXX.
230. Prov 8:25.

unde cum dicitur ex utero ante Luciferum genitus, hoc specialiter docetur, quod uere ex Patre sit natus, et non factus; quod autem ait: ante Luciferum, ante omnem creaturam significat, secundum quod dictum est: *Et ipse est ante omnes.*

30. (III, 1) Quod Dei Filius sit omnipotens et indemutabilis, et quod una sit omnipotentia Patris et Filii, sicuti et una deitas; et de sacramento incarnationis Filii, uel potius suscepti ab eo hominis.

Percutiamus et aliam eorum blasphemiam, per quam, ut scribis, dicunt quod non sit omnipotens Filius. Et hoc breuiter faciam, ne longius extendens laborem legenti tribuam. Dicant quomodo non est omnipotens, per quem, ut ipsi quoque confitentur, omnia facta sunt; dent unum opus Patris quod non fecerit et Filius, ut probent non esse omnipotentem Filium: at cum nullum sit opus, quod non et Patris existat et Filii, sine dubio omnipotens est et Filius, faciens quaecumque facit omnipotens Pater. Sufficit, si hoc ipsum etiam diuinis testimoniis adprobemus. Apud prophetam Zachariam legimus: *O, o, fugite a terra Aquilonis, dicit Dominus, quoniam a quattuor uentis caeli colligam uos, dicit Dominus; in Sion resaluamini, qui inhabitatis filiam Babylonis, quoniam haec dicit Dominus omnipotens: Post honorem misit me super gentes quae exspoliauerunt uos, quoniam qui tangit uos, sicut qui tangit pupillam oculi ipsius: quoniam ecce ego infero manum meam super eos; et erunt spolia, qui spoliauerunt illos: et scietis quia Dominus omnipotens misit me. Si intendas huic capitulo, inuenies*

is; thus when he is said to be begotten from the womb before the morning star, it is specifically taught that he was truly born from the Father, and not made, because although he says *before the morning star,* he means "before every created being," just as it was written, *And he is prior to all.*[231]

30. (III, 1) That the Son of God is omnipotent and immutable, and that there is one omnipotence of the Father and the Son, just as there is one deity; and on the sacred mystery of the incarnation of the Son, or rather, his assumption of humanity.

Let us strike yet another blasphemy of theirs, in which, as you write, they say that the Son is not omnipotent.[232] I will do this briefly, so that I do not make reading a chore by going on too long.[233] They say that in some way he is not omnipotent, through whom, as they themselves also admit, all things were made. Let them provide one work of the Father that the Son did not also do, so that they might prove that the Son is not omnipotent. But since there is no such work that does not exist as both the Father's and the Son's, the Son is without a doubt also omnipotent, as he makes whatever the omnipotent Father makes. It will suffice if we also prove this with divine testimonies.[234] In the prophet Zechariah, we read, *O, o, flee from the north, the Lord says, since I shall collect you from the four winds of heaven; in Zion you will be made safe again, you who live in the daughter of Babylon, since the omnipotent Lord says these things: after the honor*[235] *he sent me over the nations that despoiled you, since he who touches you is like one who touches the apple of his eye, since lo, I bear my hand over them; those who plundered you will be plunder, and you will know that the omnipotent Lord sent me.*[236] If you turned to this chapter, you would find that the omnipo-

---

231. Col 1:17. See Hilary of Poitiers, *Trin.* 11.8.
232. See Ambrose, *Fid.* 1.5.19.
233. See above, §§3, 28. Faustinus has just asked for patience above, but does so once more here; despite this, he is nowhere near completing the treatise.
234. See Ambrose, *Fid.* 2.4.35–36.
235. An obscure phrase; *gloriam* frequently appears in the place of *honorem* in early Latin texts of Zechariah (including the Vulgate). The Septuagint offers ὀπίσω δόξης, which suggests that the speaker is coming in the footsteps of the nebulous honor rather than just temporally later than or even in pursuit of the honor/glory. But there are at least eight radically different interpretations of this phrase (for which see Wolters 2000, 95–96).
236. Zech 2:6–9 LXX. The LXX passage differs quite significantly from the modern

quod Filius omnipotens a Patre omnipotente sit missus, ut positis in captiuitate subueniat. Considera enim prophetam dicere: *Haec dicit Dominus omnipotens;* et audiamus, propheta referente, quid dicit Dominus omnipotens: *Post honorem*—inquit—*misit me super gentes:* sine dubio Filius est, qui post honorem missum esse se dicit super gentes, quem propheta dicit Dominum omnipotentem. Hic ergo Filius existens Dominus omnipotens ait in ultimo testimonii: *et scietis quia Dominus omnipotens misit me.* Ergo omnipotens Filius, ut supra dictum est, ab omnipotente missus est Patre. Sed et apostolus Iohannes in Apocalypsi haec dicit: *Amen, testis fidelis, initium creaturae Dei, qui est et qui erat et qui uenturus est Dominus Deus omnipotens.* Sed et Salomon inter cetera ait de sapientia, quae utique Christus Filius Dei est: *Splendor est enim lucis aeternae, et speculum sine macula Dei maiestatis, et imago bonitatis illius: et cum sit una, omnia potest.* Quomodo non omnipotens est, cum possit omnia? Nam et supra de eadem sapientia dixerat: *Omnem habens uirtutem:* ergo omnipotens est, omnem habens uirtutem. Sed adhuc ipse Salomon ait de eadem sapientia: *Et permanens in semetipsa, omnia innouat.*

31. (III, 2) Agnosce omnipotentiam eius, cum omnia innouat; agnosce interea et quod indemutabilis est, cum in semetipsa permanet omnia innouans: id est, licet omnia innouet, ipsa tamen indemutabilis perseuerat, quod non nisi Dei omnipotentis est. Sed quia uere indemutabilis est Filius

tent Son was sent by the omnipotent Father so that he might come to help those placed in captivity. Consider how the prophet says, *The omnipotent Lord says these things,* and we should hear (as the prophet recounts) that he says the Lord is omnipotent. *After the honor,* he says, *he sent me over the nations.* Without a doubt it is the Son who says that he was sent after the honor over the nations, whom the prophet says is the omnipotent Lord. The Son, then, existing as the omnipotent Lord, says in his last testimony, *and you will know that the omnipotent Lord sent me.* Thus the omnipotent Son, as was said above, was sent by the omnipotent Father. Yet the apostle John also says these things in Revelation: *the amen, the faithful witness, the beginning of the creation of God, who is, who was, and who is to come, Lord God omnipotent.*[237] Solomon too, among other things he says concerning Wisdom, which is surely Christ the Son of God, says, *For it* [Wisdom] *is the splendor of eternal light, the untarnished mirror of the majesty of God, and the image of his goodness: and although it is alone, it does all things.*[238] How is it not omnipotent, since it can do all things? For even earlier, concerning the same Wisdom, he had said, *having every power.*[239] Therefore, it is omnipotent, *having every power.* Solomon also says about the same Wisdom, *and remaining in itself, it restores all things.*[240]

31. (III, 2) Recognize Wisdom's omnipotence, when it restores all things; recognize too, meanwhile, that it is immutable, since it remains in itself, restoring all things. That is, although it restores all things, it itself nevertheless persists immutable, since it belongs only to the omnipotent

---

text of Zechariah. In the Vulgate, this passage reads, "o o fugite de terra aquilonis dicit Dominus quoniam in quattuor ventos caeli dispersi vos dicit Dominus, o Sion fuge quae habitas apud filiam Babylonis, quia haec dicit Dominus exercituum post gloriam misit me ad gentes quae spoliaverunt vos qui enim tetigerit vos tangit pupillam oculi eius quia ecce ego levo manum meam super eos et erunt praedae his qui serviebant sibi et cognoscetis quia Dominus exercituum misit me."

237. Rev 3:14. See Athanasius, *Apol. sec.* 3.4.
238. Wis 7:26–27. There is a significant manuscript variant here that adds "dominus omnipotens nomen est ei item ipse est qui redimit illos dominus omnipotens nomen est illi item in machabaeorum nondum enim omnipotentis et Omnia possidentis dei iudicium," that is, "*The Lord omnipotent is the name for him who himself redeemed them.* The omnipotent Lord is the name for him again in Maccabees: *for you have not yet escaped judgment of omnipotent God, who possesses all things.*" 2 Macc 7:35 reads in the NRSV: "You have not yet escaped the judgment of the almighty, all-seeing God."
239. Wis 7:23.
240. Wis 7:27. See Gregory of Elvira, *Fid.* 2.

et conditor omnium, etiam his psalmorum uersibus adprobatur: *In initio terram tu fundasti, Domine, et opera manuum tuarum sunt caeli: ipsi peribunt, tu autem permanebis; et omnes sicut uestimentum ueterascent, et sicut opertorium mutabis eos et mutabuntur: tu autem ipse es et anni tui non deficient.* Hoc de Filio Dei scriptum interpretatus est Paulus, scribens ad Hebraeos. Habes ergo per haec capitula et omnipotentem Filium et indemutabilem et omnium conditorem, sicut et omnium artificem, dicente Salomone: *Omnium enim artifex docuit me sapientia.* Sed ne duos omnipotentes intellegas, praecauendum est: licet enim et Pater sit omnipotens et Filius, tamen unus est omnipotens, sicut et unus est Deus: quia Patris et Filii eadem omnipotentia est, sicut et eadem deitas, secundum quod supra pro uiribus et pro condicione temporis coartantis expressum est. Sed et nunc inferius explanabitur testimonio Esaiae prophetae: *Fatigata est Aegyptus et negotiatio Aethiopum, et Sabain uiri excelsi ad te transibunt et tui erunt serui et post te sequentur alligati uinculis et adorabunt te et in te deprecabuntur, quoniam in te est Deus, et non est Deus praeter te. Tu enim es Deus, et nesciebamus, Deus Israhel Saluator. Erubescent et confundentur omnes qui aduersantur ei, et ibunt cum confusione.* Intende quia ad Filium dicitur: *Et tui erunt serui et post te sequentur alligati uinculis et adorabunt te et in te deprecabuntur.* Ergo et hinc Deus uerus ostenditur Filius, cum adoratur. Dei enim est adorari, siquidem et alibi docet apostolus de Filio Dei esse scriptum: *Et adorent eum omnes angeli Dei:* scilicet quia uere Deum et Dominum. Sed in praesenti testimonio Esaiae, sicut ipse Deus est, sic etiam in ipso Deus est: ait enim: *Quoniam in te est Deus, et non est Deus praeter te.* Et cum dixerit in Deo Deum esse, subsequitur et dicit: *Tu enim es Deus, et nesciebamus, Deus Israhel Saluator.* Ergo cum Deus in Deo est, et non est Deus praeter eum in quo Deus est, et ipse est Deus Israhel

God. Now, that the Son is truly immutable and the craftsman of all things is also demonstrated in these verses of Psalms: *In the beginning you established the Earth, Lord, and the heavens are the works of your hands. They will perish, but you will remain, and all will grow old like clothing, and you will change them like a garment and they will be changed; but you yourself are, and your years shall not come to an end.*[241] Paul interpreted this as being written about the Son of God when he wrote to the Hebrews.[242] Thus you have in these verses the Son being omnipotent, immutable, and the craftsman of all things, just as he also fashions all things, which Solomon says: *For Wisdom, who fashions all things, taught me.*[243] But lest you deduce that there are two omnipotences, you must beware: although the Father is omnipotent and the Son is omnipotent, there is nevertheless only one omnipotence, just as also there is only one God, since the omnipotence of the Father and that of the Son is the same, just as their deity is the same, as I expressed above (given my abilities and that my time was constrained).[244] Still, now it will also be explained below from the testimony of the prophet Isaiah: *Egypt is exhausted; the merchandise of the Ethiopians and the tall men of Saba will come over to you, and they will be your servants and follow after you bound by chains; they will adore you and pray to you, since God is in you, and there is no God besides you. For you are God, and we did not know, God, savior of Israel. All who oppose him will blush and be confounded, and they will go into confusion.*[245] Pay attention to what is said about the Son: *and they will be your servants and follow after you bound by chains; they will adore you and will pray to you.* Thus the Son here is also shown to be the true God, since he is adored: adoration belongs to God, since indeed the Apostle also teaches elsewhere that it is written about the Son of God, *and let all the angels of God adore him,*[246] obviously because he is God and the Lord. Now, in the testimony of Isaiah at hand, just as he himself is God, so too is God in him, for he says, *since God is in you, and there is no God besides you.* When he says that God is in God, he continues by saying, *for you are God, and we did not know, God, savior of Israel.* Thus since God is in God, and since there is no God beyond the one in whom

---

241. Ps 102:26–28 (101:26–28 MT). See Athanasius, *Apol. sec.* 1.36.
242. See Heb 1:10–12.
243. Wis 7:21. See Hilary of Poitiers, *Trin.* 4.38; Ambrose, *Fid.* 1.3.20.
244. See above, §§7, 9, and esp. 12.
245. Isa 45:14–16 LXX. See Gregory of Elvira, *Fid.* 71–72; Ambrose, *Fid.* 1.3.20–21.
246. Heb 1:6.

Saluator, ostenditur unitas diuinitatis in Patre et Filio, sicut et omnipotentiae, et quicquid omnino diuinae substantiae est: hoc solo differens a Patre Filius, quod ille Pater est et hic Filius: id est, quod ille genuit et hic natus est; non tamen, quia natus est, minus habet aliquid quam quod in Deo Patre est, *imago Dei inuisibilis* existens, et *splendor gloriae et character substantiae eius*. Hoc qui de Filio Dei non credunt, Esaiae sententiam sustinebunt dicentis: *Erubescent et confundentur omnes qui aduersantur ei, et ibunt cum confusione*. Sed et Ieremias de Filii deitate exprimit dicens: *Hic Deus noster et non debutabitur alius absque eo: qui inuenit omnem uiam prudentiae et dedit eam Iacob puero suo et Israhel dilecto sibi; post haec in terra uisus est et cum hominibus conuersatus est*. Non utique Pater Deus, sed Filius factus homo in terra uisus est et cum hominibus conuersatus est, naturam in se hominis sine peccato exercens propter nostram salutem, de quo et legimus: *Et Verbum caro factum est et habitauit in nobis: et uidimus gloriam eius, gloriam quasi unigeniti a Patre.*

32. (III, 3) Si ergo Verbum caro factum est et habitauit in nobis, natus ex uirgine nobiscum Deus, quo nunc, haeretice, proficis, si infirmitates adsumptae carnis obicias, si animae humanae, quam cum carne susceperat, utiles nobis aestus describas, cum constet eum, secundum quod Deus est et Dei Filius, esse per omnia ut Patrem inpassibilem? Ideo enim et illa quae sunt deitatis eius praemisimus, ut iam si quid humilitatis et infirmitatis in Christo legitur, non deitas eius uiolata credatur, sed naturae suscepti hominis, et disciplinae quam tradebat, exsecutio probetur. Vanum est enim uoluisse ut hominem nasci, licet ex uirgine tamen hominem, nec infirmam hominis in se designare naturam. Vanum est praecepta dare,

God is, and since he is God, the savior of Israel, the unity of the divinity in the Father and the Son is demonstrated, and so is the unity of their omnipotence, and whatever at all there is of divine substance. In this alone does the Son differ from the Father: the one is the Father and the other is the Son, that is, the one begat and the one was born.[247] However, he does not have anything less than what is in God the Father because he was born, as he exists *as the image of the invisible God*[248] and *the splendor of his glory and the character of his substance.*[249] Those who do not believe this about the Son of God will suffer the sentence of Isaiah, who says, *All who oppose him will blush and be confounded, and they will go into confusion.* Yet Jeremiah also describes the deity of the Son when he says, *This is our God, and none shall be considered other than him. He has found every path of knowledge and given it to his servant Jacob and to his beloved Israel. After these things he was seen on Earth and conversed with men.*[250] Certainly it was not God the Father, but the Son, who was made into a man and was seen on Earth, who conversed with men and worked the nature of man into himself without sin for our salvation, and about whom we also read, *And the Word was made flesh and also lived among us; and we saw his glory, glory as belongs to the only begotten of the Father.*[251]

32. (III, 3) If, then, the Word was made flesh and lived among us, born from a virgin as God with us, how now, heretic, does it help you to ignore the weaknesses of the flesh that he assumed, if you describe the passions of the human soul (which he had taken along with the flesh) as stirrings that are useful for us, given that it stands that he is in all respects without passion, just like the Father, in accordance with what God and the Son of God are?[252] This is why we first brought up those matters that pertain to his deity, so that now, if any lowness or weakness is attributed to Christ, one does not believe that his deity was violated, but rather the human nature that he assumed, and to demonstrate his enactment of the way of life that he taught. For it is meaningless to have wanted him to

---

247. See Athanasius, *Apol. sec.* 3.11.
248. Col 1:15.
249. Heb 1:3.
250. Bar 3:36–38. See Hilary of Poitiers, *Trin.* 4.42; Gregory of Elvira, *Fid.* 7; Ambrose, *Fid.* 1.3.28.
251. John 1:14.
252. See Ambrose, *Incarn.* 5.39. Passion here refers neither to romantic love nor to suffering, but rather to changeable nature of human emotions.

quibus homines uiuerent, et ipsum iam, quia semel homo esse dignatus est, sine praeceptorum obseruatione cucurrisse. Ille si non hominis infirmitatem factus homo exercere uoluisset, quis crederet quod homo factus fuerat ex originis nostrae matrice, licet sine uiri conplexu? Quandoquidem hodieque non desint qui negent eum nostram gestasse corpulentiam, etiam posteaquam infirmitates carnis exercuit. Ille si factus homo non seruasset quam docere uenerat disciplinam, non bonum magisterii dedisset exemplum. Quis enim discipulorum seruare conaretur quod non magister ipse seruauit, factus ut homo, cum hodie iam quicumque seruat, ipsius exemplo releuatur ut seruet? Vides quia et infirmitates pati debuit, ut homo natus probaretur, et factus homo obseruare quodcumque docuisset, ut ceteros inuitaret, magis autem dixerim ut ceteros subleuaret: iam enim caro nostra didicit in eius carne releuari. Si enim infirmitates hominis pati noluisset, ut quid et de uirgine in hominem natus est? et si nolebat obseruare praecepta, quia Dominus, ut quid et formam serui acceperat, quae praeceptis et oboedientiae obnoxia est? Atquin totum sacramentum a Deo adsumpti hominis hoc est, ut quod in Adam non est de inoboedientia seruatum, in Christo homine de oboedientia seruaretur. Hoc ipsum apostolus Paulus inter cetera quae diuine tractat, adserit: *Sicut enim per inoboedientiam unius hominis peccatores constituti sunt multi, ita et per unius obauditionem iusti constituuntur multi.* Sicut enim per unius hominis contemptum peccatores constituti sunt multi, ita et per sacramentum obauditionis in Christo, quam non ex infirmitate sed ex bonitate deitatis praestat in salutarem hominis disciplinam, saluantur multi.

33. (III, 4) Videamus nunc et sacramentum passionis. Totus Adam peccauerat; totus Adam expulsus de paradiso fuerat: totum expulsum suscipere debuit, qui totum saluare uenerat. Non autem uidebatur totum

be born a man (though from a virgin, nevertheless a man) if he did not to represent the weak nature of man in himself. It is meaningless to give commands by which men should live if he himself, who once deemed it worthy to be a man, went about without observing these commands. If he, made a man, did not wish to take on the weakness of man, who would believe that he had been made a man from the motherly source of our own origin (though without the embrace of a man)?[253] Especially since today there is no shortage of people who deny that he bore our bodily nature, even after he took on the weaknesses of the flesh. If he had not observed the way of life that he had come to teach, though he was made a man, he would not have given a good example of his teaching. For what student would attempt to be observant of something the teacher himself (who was made as a man) was not observant of, seeing as today whoever is observant is elevated by his example to observance? You see that he also ought to suffer weaknesses to prove that he was born a man, and when made a man, to observe whatever he had taught so that he might stimulate others, or rather, now, I should say, so that he might assist others, for now our flesh has learned to be supported in his flesh. If he had not wished to suffer the weaknesses of man, why was he born into humanity from a virgin? If he did not wish to observe his own commands, since he is the Lord, why did he also assume the form of a servant, which is obedient and subject to commands?[254] Yet this is the sacred mystery of the humanity assumed by God: that which Adam did not observe in disobedience was observed by the man Christ in obedience. The apostle Paul, among other things that he divinely discusses, asserts this very thing: *For just as many are made sinners through the disobedience of one man, so too are many made just through the heedfulness of one.*[255] For just as many are made sinners through one man's contempt, so too are many saved through the sacred mystery of Christ's heedfulness, which he performed for the salutary teaching of man not in weakness but in the goodness of his deity.

33. (III, 4) Let us also look now to the sacred mystery of his passion. Adam in his totality had sinned; Adam in his totality had been expelled from paradise; he who had come to save all ought to have assumed all of

---

253. A typical qualification, since Christ had to be born from her if he were to be fully human, but she had to remain a virgin in bearing him. See, e.g., Hilary of Poitiers, *Trin.* 3.19; Ambrose, *Fid.* 3.14.114; Augustine, *Trin.* 4.14.19; 8.5.7; 13.18.23.

254. See above, §§3, 17, 20, 23; below, §§34, 36–38.

255. Rom 5:19.

expulsum in se suscepisse, nisi illum suscepisset per substantiam carnis et animae eius: hoc enim totus homo est per naturam. Hoc autem tunc probari potuit, si ipsas infirmitates carnis eius et animae sustineret, licet sine uitio peccatorum, ut uere non aliam substantiam carnis et animae suscepisse putaretur: ut, cum in se hominem ab infirmitatibus et passionibus liberat, etiam hos, qui secundum uestigia eius sectantur, liberatos esse crederemus. Sed patrocinetur huic sensui gentium doctor apostolus uiuacius et ut mysticus scribens: *Sicut enim in Adam omnes moriuntur, ita et in Christo omnes uiuificantur.* Sed naturam suscepti in eo hominis melius describat Esaias: *Domine, quis credidit auditui nostro? et brachium Domini cui reuelatum est? Adnuntiauimus coram ipso sicut puer, sicut radix in terra sitienti: et non est species ei neque honor formae: et uidimus eum, et non habebat speciem neque decorem: sed species eius sine honore, deficiens praeter ceteros homines: homo in plaga positus, et sciens ferre infirmitatem, quia auersa est facies eius: depretiatus est nec aestimatus est. Hic peccata nostra fert et pro nobis dolet: et aestimauimus eum in dolore esse et in plaga et in malo: ipse autem uulneratus est propter iniquitates nostras et infirmatus est propter peccata nostra: doctrina pacis nostrae super eum: plaga eius nos sanati sumus. Omnes sicut oues errauimus: homo a uia sua errauit, et Dominus tradidit eum pro peccatis nostris: et ipse, propter quod male tractatus est, non aperuit os. Sicut ouis ad occisionem adductus est et sicut agnus coram tondente se, sic non aperuit os suum: in humilitate iudicium eius sublatum est. Generationem eius quis enarrabit? quia aufertur a terra uita eius: ab iniquitatibus plebis meae adductus est ad mortem; et dabo malos pro sepultura eius et ipsos diuites pro morte eius: quia iniquitatem non fecit, neque dolum in ore suo locutus est.*

what was expelled.²⁵⁶ However, it would not seem like he assumed all of what was expelled unless he assumed for himself the substance of flesh and soul—for this is all man is, by nature. But if he assumed those weaknesses of his flesh and soul (albeit without the offense of the sins) to be reckoned to have truly assumed no other substance than that of the flesh and soul, then this can be proven: since he frees the humanity in himself from weaknesses and passions, we may believe that those who follow in his footsteps are freed too.²⁵⁷ But let the Apostle, teacher of the gentiles, be the defender of this interpretation, when he writes vigorously and mystically, *For just as all die in Adam, so too are all revived in Christ.*²⁵⁸ Yet Isaiah described the nature of man that he assumed better: *Lord, who has believed our message? And to whom is the arm of the Lord revealed? We have called out in his presence like a boy, like a root in the dry earth. And he has neither beauty nor a charming appearance, and we saw him, and he had neither beauty nor elegance. And his look is without charm, lacking more so than the rest of men, a man pressed by affliction and fully knowing weakness because his face was turned away. He was unappreciated and was not esteemed. He carries our sins and grieves for us, and we judged him to be in pain and in affliction and in misfortune. Yet he was wounded on account of our iniquities and was weakened on account of our sins. The chastisement of our peace was upon him, by his affliction we are healed. We all stray like sheep; man strayed from his path, and the Lord handed him over for our sins. And that one, though he was wickedly treated, did not open his mouth. Just like a sheep he was led to the slaughter, and just like a lamb before one who shears it he did not open his mouth. In his humiliation, judgment was taken away. Who will explain his generation, since his life is withdrawn from the world? He was led to death by the iniquities of my people, and I will trade the wicked for his grave and the rich for his death, since he did not commit an iniquity, and neither did he deceive with his mouth.*²⁵⁹

---

256. See Pseudo-Athanasius, *Apoll.* 1.17; Origen, *Dial.* 6; Hilary of Poitiers, *Trin.* 10.20; Gregory of Nazianzus, *Ep.* 10.7; 30.5. Phoebadius (*Ar.* 26.1–2) makes this point using Phil 2:6–7, one of the most commonly cited passages in Faustinus's *De Trinitate* (see §§3, 17, 20, 23, 32, 34, 36–38); that Faustinus did not use this passage here perhaps suggests that Faustinus was not working with a copy of Phoebadius's *Contra Arianos*.

257. In other words, Christ took the liability to sin but did not himself sin, thus serving as an example for the rest of humankind that while they are liable to sin, they need not do so (but, tellingly, this freedom only comes through Christ).

258. 1 Cor 15:22.

259. Isa 53:1–9 LXX.

34. (III, 5) Sufficit hoc testimonio probatum quod omnem in se hominis naturam peregit, sine peccato tamen suo, licet peccata nostra portaret. Sed ne homo tantummodo crederetur, interposuit et dixit: *Generationem eius quis enarrabit?:* illam utique qua de Deo Patre generatus est, quae sine initio est: et ideo de ea ait: *Generationem eius quis enarrabit?*, non quasi ignorabilem sed quasi inexplicabilem dicens. Omnes enim catholici scimus quia de Deo Patre natus est, sed inenarrabiliter: et ideo ait: *Generationem eius quis enarrabit?* Hanc autem generationem, qua de uirgine secundum carnem nascitur, refert Euangelium, eius quoque tempora describens. Diurnae autem eius generationis initium, ut diximus, inuestigari non potest, sicut nec diuinitatis, quae illi una cum Patre est: et ideo ait: *Generationem eius quis enarrabit?* Si ergo in sacramento fidei hoc accepimus, ut Christum et Deum credamus et hominem: Deum quidem, qua de Deo sine initio natum, hominem autem, qua de uirgine in temporibus natum: non calumniemur diuinitati eius, cum pro nostra medela quae sunt hominis exsequitur, habens in se acceptam hominis naturam: quia nec homo negandus est, cum propriae diuinitatis naturalem exerit potestatem, accepta in se forma seruili. Si ergo et orat Patrem et si nihil ab se facere se dicit, nisi quod Patrem uiderit facientem, ut nihil nunc aliud dicam, certe humanae extollentiae modum, qua magister, inponit: ut tanto magis discat homo Deo deferre, quanto detulit et uerus Filius, qui causam subiectionis propriam non habebat, qui et formam orandi dederat, ut non tam fieri nostram uoluntatem rogaremus, sed *uoluntatem Patris qui est in caelis*. Et ideo, ut quod docuerat inpleret, ait: *Non ueni meam uoluntatem facere, sed uoluntatem eius, qui me misit*. Sed et quod minor factus est, quod crescit,

34. (III, 5) This testimony is enough to prove that he carried in himself all the nature of man, but without his own sin, even though he bore our sins. Lest someone believe that he was only a man, Isaiah interjected and said, *Who will explain his generation?*[260]—that generation, certainly, which is without a beginning, in which he was generated from God the Father. This is why he says, *Who will explain his generation?*—not as though speaking in ignorance but as though describing something inexplicable. For all catholics understand that he was born from God the Father, but indescribably so. This is why he says, *Who will explain his generation?* Furthermore, the gospel refers to this generation, in which he was born from a virgin in the flesh, when describing his life, too.[261] But the beginning of his divine generation, as we have said, cannot be analyzed, just as his divinity cannot (which for him is one with the Father's). This is why he says, *Who will explain his generation?* If, therefore, we accept in the sacred mystery of faith that we believe that Christ is God and a man (God, of course, in that he was born from God without a beginning, but a man in that he was born from a virgin into our times), let us not slight his divinity, though he does what a man does having assumed the nature of man for himself for our healing, because his humanity must not be denied, since he exercises the natural power of his own divinity in taking the form of a servant for himself.[262] Thus if he prays to the Father and says that that he does nothing apart from him but what he sees the Father doing[263] (I will say nothing else for now), he assuredly imposes a limit on human pride in his role as a teacher, so that man might learn to defer to God as much as the true Son also deferred to him. He did this even though there was no particular reason for his subjection,[264] and also gave us a way of praying[265] so that we do not ask that our will be done but the *will of the Father who is in heaven.*[266] Therefore, so that he might fulfill what he taught,[267] he says, *I have come not that I might do my will, but the will of him who sent*

---

260. Isa 53:8 LXX. See Phoebadius of Agen, *Ar.* 9.4–9; Hilary of Poitiers, *Trin.* 2.9.
261. See Luke 2.
262. See above, §§3, 17, 20, 23, 32; below, §§36–38.
263. See Mark 1:35; Luke 22:41–42; John 5:19; 17:1.
264. That is, because the Son is God, his subjection serves purely as an example to humankind.
265. See Matt 6:9.
266. Matt 7:21; John 6:38.
267. See Matt 23:3.

quod proficit, quod esurit, quod sitit, quod laborat, quod flet, quod dolet, quod tristis est, postremo quod moritur: ad naturam adsumpti hominis referendum est, quam pro sacramento nostrae salutis mystice exercuit, sub illa intellegentia qua supra in testimonio Esaiae relatum est. Sub hoc fidei sacramento non solum illa capitula soluuntur de quibus interrogare dignata es, sed et omnes quaestiones quas contra Filii diuinitatem coaptant impii haeretici.

35. (IV, 1) De hoc quod ait Filius: *Pater maior me est.*

Accipe nunc et has quaestiones, quas ex diuersa parte proposueras fortiores, specialiter absolutas. Dicunt—inquis—haeretici ad depretiandam Filii perpetuam et perfectam in omnibus deitatem: *Pater maior me est.* Sed requirendum est quando hoc dixit Filius: nonne quando inpletum est in eo quod scriptum est: *Minorasti eum paulo minus ab angelis, gloria et honore coronasti eum*? Quomodo minoratus est, exponat apostolus Paulus tertii caeli conscius: *Paulo minus*—inquit—*ab angelis minoratum uidemus Iesum propter passionem mortis; gloria et honore coronatum, ut gratia Dei pro omnibus gustaret mortem.* Pro omnibus, ait, non: Pro se: ergo qui pro omnibus gustauit mortem, quid mirum si pro omnibus et minoratus est? Pro omnibus autem gustauit mortem, non pro se eo quod, omnibus in peccati reatu positis, ipse homo factus nullo proprio peccato tenebatur obnoxius. Et uide quomodo hoc ipsum, quod minoratus est propter passionem mortis et quod gratia Dei pro omnibus gustauit mortem, ad

*me.*²⁶⁸ Now, that he was made lesser, that he grows, that he develops, that he hungers, that he thirsts, that he works, that he cries, that he suffers, that he is sad, and finally, that he dies²⁶⁹—this has to refer to the nature of man that he assumed, which he worked for the sacred mystery of our salvation in the interpretation which was related above in the testimony of Isaiah. In this sacred mystery of faith, not only are those chapters that you deemed worthy to ask me about resolved, but all the questions that the impious heretics have compiled against the divinity of the Son, too.

35. (IV, 1) On that which the Son says: *The Father is greater than me.*²⁷⁰

Now accept that the following queries are specifically resolved, too, which you proposed as being the other party's more forceful ones. You relate that the heretics say, to depreciate the eternal and perfect deity of the Son in all ways, *The Father is greater than me.*²⁷¹ But one must ask: when did the Son say this? Was it not when that which was written was fulfilled in him: *You have made him a little lesser than the angels, you have crowned him with glory and honor?*²⁷² Let the apostle Paul, who knew about the third heaven,²⁷³ explain how he was made lesser: *We see Jesus,* he says, *made a little*²⁷⁴ *lesser than the angels on account of his suffering death, crowned with glory and honor so that he might taste death by the grace of God for all.*²⁷⁵ *For all,* he says, not for himself. What wonder is it if he who tasted death for all was also made lesser for all? Though he tasted death for all, yet not for himself, because the one who was made a man and tasted death

---

268. John 6:38.
269. For these attributes, see Luke 2:52; Matt 4:2; John 19:28; Luke 22:43; 19:41; John 11:35, 33; Matt 26:38; 27:50; see also Hilary of Poitiers, *Trin.* 3.10.
270. John 14:28.
271. See Phoebadius of Agen, *Ar.* 13.4–14.3; Hilary of Poitiers, *Trin.* 7.6; 9.51; Ambrose, *Fid.* 2.8.59. This was a common Arian prooftext; among others, Palladius appealed to it at the Council of Aquileia in 381. See Hanson 1988, 110. Palladius and others used this text to argue that Christ had human flesh, but his mind and soul were completely divine; at Aquileia, Ambrose argued instead that Christ had to have had a human soul in order for his flesh to speak. In the *De fide*, Ambrose offers an exegesis of this passage much closer to Faustinus's.
272. Ps 8:5. See Ambrose, *Fid.* 2.8.63.
273. See 2 Cor 12:2. On the concept of a third level of heaven, see Torbus 2008.
274. There is a slight play on words here between Paul and "a little," *paulo.*
275. Heb 2:9.

decorem operis interpretatur sapientissimus Paulus ita subsequens: *Decebat enim eum propter quem omnia et per quem omnia, multis filiis in gloriam adductis, ducem salutis eorum per passiones consummare.* Vides quam pulchrum quamue decorum nostrae salutis sacramentum in eo quod Filius est minoratus, ostenditur. Quomodo ergo ad obfuscandam diuinitatem eius inproperas quod exsequitur ad decorem? *Pater maior me est:* hoc tunc dixit posteaquam *Verbum caro factum est et habitauit in nobis.*

36. (IV, 2) Et uide ne demutabilem credas, quasi desierit esse Verbum, posteaquam caro factum est; sed manens semper Verbum Deus, et caro quoque factum est. Etsi enim dixit: *Et Verbum caro factum est,* pressius loqui uoluit, ne quis in eo non ueram carnem crederet. Siquidem et post tam pressam locutionem non desunt qui dicant carnem illum habuisse putatiuam. Vt autem manifestum sit Verbum carnem factum non demutatione diuinae substantiae sed susceptione carnis humanae, intende quid sequitur: *Et habitauit in nobis.* Non ergo interceptum est Verbum demutatione, quod per carnem adsumptam habitauit in nobis: habitatio enim probat perseuerantiam Verbi. Hoc ideo interposui, ne quis Filium Dei demutabilem credat, cum legit: *Et Verbum caro factum est.* Dicit ergo Filius: *Pater maior me est,* posteaquam Verbum caro factum est et suscepit officium ministrantis: *uenit enim non ministrari sed ministrare. Pater maior me est:* quid ais, ueritas? quomodo dicis Patrem te esse maiorem?

for all those placed in the condition of sin was held liable by no sin of his own. Look how the most wise Paul thus concludes about him, because he was made lesser on account of his suffering death and because he tasted death for all by the grace of God, in the following: *For it was fitting that he, because of whom all things are and through whom all things are, was perfected as the leader of salvation through his sufferings for the many sons that are brought to glory.*[276] You see how lovely or how fitting the sacred mystery of our salvation is, in that it is revealed how the Son became lesser. How then do you cast this as a reproach to obfuscate his divinity, when it results in his glory?[277] *The Father is greater than me;*[278] he says this after *The Word was made flesh and also lived among us.*[279]

36. (IV, 2) See to it that you do not think of him as being changeable, as if he ceased to be the Word when he became flesh. God, while always remaining the Word, was also made flesh, too. For even though he said, *And the Word was made flesh,*[280] he wanted to speak more precisely so that no one would believe that his flesh was not true—since indeed it is not hard to find those who even after such precise wording say that his was an imaginary flesh.[281] Now, so that it be clear that the Word was made flesh not by a change in his divine substance but by his assuming human flesh, turn to what follows: *And he lived among us.*[282] The Word that lived among us in the flesh that it assumed, then, was not interrupted by some change, for its habitation proves the constancy of the Word. I have brought this up so that no one believe that the Son of God is changeable when he reads, *And the Word was made flesh.* Thus the Son says *The Father is greater than me*[283] after the Word was made flesh and undertook the duty of ministering: *For he comes not to be ministered but to minister.*[284] *The Father is greater than me.* What do you say, truth? How can you say that the Father

---

276. Heb 2:10.
277. There is a play on words throughout between *decor, decorus,* meaning "comely," and *decus, decorum,* meaning "glory."
278. John 14:28.
279. John 1:14.
280. John 1:14.
281. That is, docetism; see Kelly 1978, 141 (for the origins of the belief), 280 (for the belief in the fourth century).
282. John 1:14. See Hilary of Poitiers, *Trin.* 9.66; 10.26; Ambrose, *Fid.* 2.8.65; *Incarn.* 6.55.
283. John 14:28.
284. Matt 20:28.

Certe una tibi et Patri imago est secundum Moysen, eademque forma secundum apostolum Paulum, qui me etiam docuit quod sis *splendor gloriae et character substantiae eius.* Sed et tu ipse docuisti dicens: *Qui me uidit, uidit Patrem,* et *Ego in Patre et Pater in me,* et *Ego et Pater unum sumus.* Sed et quaecumque facit Pater, facis et tu similiter: tua enim uerba sunt: *Quaecumque enim ille facit, haec et Filius facit similiter,* et *Sicut Pater suscitat mortuos et uiuificat, sic et Filius quos uult uiuificat,* et *Vt honorificent Filium sicut honorificant Patrem.* Cum ergo eadem tibi imago est, eadem forma eademque substantia, eadem naturae unitas, eadem potestas, eadem libertas uoluntatis, idem honor, et omnia omnino quae Patris sunt, tua sunt, quia et quae tua sunt, Patris sunt: quomodo ergo dicis: *Pater maior me est,* cum in omnibus quae sunt deitatis, talis es qualis et Pater? Loquatur apostolus Paulus, in quo Christus loquebatur, secundum quod ipse ait: *An experimentum quaeritis qui in me loquitur Christi?* quid dicit apostolus? *Qui cum in forma Dei esset constitutus, non rapinam arbitratus est esse se aequalem Deo.* Ergo secundum hoc, quod in forma Dei est et quod aequalis est Deo, non est maior Pater. Et quomodo maior est

is greater than you? Certainly the appearance of the Father is also the same as yours, according to Moses,[285] and your form is the same, according to the apostle Paul,[286] who also taught me that you are *the splendor of glory and the imprinting of his substance*.[287] You yourself even taught this when you said, *He who has seen me, has seen the Father*,[288] and *I am in the Father and the Father in me*,[289] and *I and the Father are one*.[290] Yet whatever the Father does, you also do likewise; your words are, *For whatever he does, the Son also likewise does*,[291] and *Just as the Father raises the dead and makes them live, so too does the Son make those live whom he wishes*,[292] and *Let them honor the Son just as they honor the Father*.[293] Thus, because your appearance is the same, and your form the same and your substance the same, your unity of nature the same, your power the same, your freedom of will the same, your honor the same, so too is everything which is the Father's completely yours, because everything which is yours is also the Father's.[294] How then do you say, *The Father is greater than me*, since in all things that pertain to your deity, you are of such a kind and such a sort as the Father? Let the apostle Paul speak, in whom Christ spoke when he said, *Would you seek to test Christ who speaks in me?*[295] What does the Apostle say? *He who, though he was constituted in the form of God, did not regard equality with God as a boon*.[296] Thus, in this respect, that he is in the

---

285. See Gen 1:26; see also above, §7.
286. See Phil 2:6; see also above, §15.
287. Heb 1:3.
288. John 14:9. See above, §§9–10.
289. John 14:10. See above, §§10–11, 13–14.
290. John 10:30. See above, §§12–15; Origen, *Hom. Gen.* 1.13; Hilary of Poitiers, *Trin.* 7.16; 9.23; *C. Const.* 17; Ambrose, *Fid.* 2.8.69.
291. John 5:19. Phoebadius (*Ar.* 15.1) also make the point briefly; the passage is more fully explored in Hilary of Poitiers, *Trin.* 7.18–19; Ambrose, *Fid.* 2.8.69; 4.4.39–40; 5.2.34.
292. John 5:21.
293. John 5:23.
294. These points have been made piecemeal throughout the *De Trinitate*; here they are finally summarized to provide evidence against what surely must have been one of the most popular passages for Arians to cite and one of the most difficult passages for Nicene Christians to explain. Phoebadius (*Ar.* 12.3–5) likewise provides a list of passages in John wherein the Father and Son are said to be equal, but with some variations: in order, he cites John 5:23; 1:18; 17:10; 5:19; 6:38; 8:29; 14:10.
295. 2 Cor 13:3.
296. Phil 2:6. This passage is more fully discussed immediately below, in §37.

Pater, subsequentia demonstrant: *Sed semetipsum*—inquit—*exinaniuit, formam serui accipiens.*

37. (IV, 3) Vide ne et hic interceptionem diuinitatis intellegas, cum audis quod semetipsum exinaniuerit: intende enim ad hoc quod sequitur: *formam serui accipiens.* Manere ergo in suo statu ostenditur, qui formam serui dicitur accepisse. Sed quamuis maneat et perseueret in eo status diuinus, tamen semetipsum exinaniuit, scilicet per occultationem diuinitatis, *formam serui accipiens, in similitudine hominum factus, et habitu inuentus ut homo: humiliauit seipsum factus oboediens usque ad mortem, mortem autem crucis.* Iam talis si dicat: *Pater maior me est,* non inpugnat aequalitatem diuinitatis, sed designat sacramentum susceptae humilitatis per hoc quod semetipsum exinaniuit formam serui accipiens. Iam talis si dicat: *Qui misit me Pater, mandatum mihi dedit quid dicam et quid loquar,* et *Descendi de caelo non ut faciam uoluntatem meam sed uoluntatem eius qui me misit,* ostendit quod semetipsum exinaniuit, formam serui accipiens, in similitudine hominum factus et habitu inuentus ut homo: humiliauit seipsum factus oboediens usque ad mortem: et tamen quae est in his diminutio eius diuinitatis, si ad amputandam in hominibus arrogantiam, ipse non sibi arrogans loqueretur? Mentior si non hoc ipsum testimonium ideo posuit apostolus Paulus, ut ad humilitatem, Saluatoris exemplo, singulos prouocaret. Hoc ita inuenies, si eandem epistulam quam scribit ad Philippenses, intentius legeris. Sed et si haeretici nolunt ob sacramentum exinaniti Dei per acceptionem formae seruilis esse dictum: *Pater maior me est,* dicamus et nos Patrem maiorem de solo sacramento generationis: et hunc enim pium sensum nonnulli catholici prosecuti sunt dicentes Patrem et Filium

form of God and that he is equal to God, the Father is not greater. The following demonstrates how the Father is greater: *but diminished himself,* he says, *by taking the form of a servant.*[297]

37. (IV, 3) See to it that you do not gather from this that there is also an interruption of his divinity here when you hear that he has diminished himself; turn your mind to that which follows: *taking the form of a servant.*[298] Thus it is shown that the one who is said to have taken the form of a servant remained in his own state. But as much as the divine state should remain steady and be constant, he nevertheless did diminish himself, of course, in concealing his divinity, *taking the form of a servant, made in the likeness of men, and in his appearance having come like a man. He lowered himself, obedient up to death, even death on the cross.*[299] Now if such a person should say, *The Father is greater than me,*[300] he does not contest the equality of their divinity but points out the holy mystery of the low status that he assumed, in which he diminished himself by taking the form of a servant. Now if such a person should say, *The Father who sent me commanded me as to what I should say and what I should speak,*[301] and *I descended from heaven not that I might do my will, but the will of my Father who sent me,*[302] he shows that he diminished himself by taking the form of a servant in that he was made in the likeness of men and was found to be like a man in his appearance; he lowered himself in that he was made obedient up to death. Moreover, what lessening of his divinity is there if he does not speak arrogantly about himself so as to cut off arrogance among men? I am a liar if the apostle Paul does not place this very testimony so that that he might provoke individuals to humility by the example of the Savior. You will find it so, if you attentively read the same letter he writes to the Philippians.

Now, even if the heretics do not wish for *The Father is greater than me* to be said about the holy mystery of God lowering himself by accepting a servant's form, let us also say that the Father is greater by the sacred mystery of his generation alone. For some catholics follow this pious interpretation when they say that the Father and the Son are of the same

---

297. Phil 2:7. See above, §§3, 17, 20, 23, 32, 34; below, §§37–38.
298. Phil 2:7. See above, §§3, 17, 20, 23, 32, 34, 36; below, §38; and for this argument in particular, Hilary of Poitiers, *Trin.* 8.45; 9.14; 10.25; 11.48.
299. Phil 2:7–8.
300. John 14:28.
301. John 12:49.
302. John 6:38.

eiusdem esse substantiae, et ideo secundum substantiam alterum altero non esse maiorem. Qualis enim Deus Pater est, talis et Deus Filius est: nihil enim minus ex se genuit quam ipse est: perfectus enim existens perfectum genuit, et plenitudo existens plenitudinem genuit. Etsi ergo qua Deus, Deo aequalis est Filius, tamen qua filius, minor dicitur Patre: id est, quia filius de patre sit; Pater autem genuit Filium; et ideo non dixit: Deus maior me est, sed *Pater maior me est*.

38. (V, 1) Quod in Actibus apostolorum legitur: *Certissime itaque sciat omnis domus Israhel quia et Dominum illum et Christum Deus fecit hunc Iesum, quem uos crucifixistis.*

Inter cetera haereticorum, ut scilicet Filius Dei factura credatur, etiam hoc ex persona diuersae partis posuisti, quod legimus in Actibus apostolorum, beato Petro dicente: *Certissime itaque sciat omnis domus Israhel quia et Dominum illum et Christum Deus fecit hunc Iesum, quem uos crucifixistis.* Sed huius quoque quaestionis absolutio manifesta est secundum superiorem expositionem, in qua diximus Filium Dei etiam filium hominis factum. Qui, etsi pati non potest, quia Filius Dei est Verbum et sapientia Dei existens, quia secundum hoc semper inpassibilis perseuerat sicut et Pater eius: tamen per hoc quod homo factus est, natus de Maria uirgine, passibilis est: quippe qui et mortem sustinuit, et mortem crucis, manens in se semper quia Deus inuiolabilis, etiam cum in homine et uersatur et crucifigitur. Hunc ergo Iesum, qui est secundum carnem, Dominum illum et Christum fecit Deus. Nam secundum hoc quod est unigenitus Filius Dei, qui est Verbum et sapientia Dei, non est aliqua factura neque exspectans promotiones, quippe existens in omnibus Deus perfectus, sicut et Pater

substance, and this is why in respect to substance the one is not greater than the other.[303] For just as God is the Father, so too is God the Son: he begat nothing less from himself than he himself is; existing as perfect, he begat what is perfect, and existing as complete, he begat what is complete. Thus even if as God, the Son is equal to God, nevertheless as the Son, he is said to be less than the Father—that is, because the Son is from the Father, but the Father begat the Son, and this is why he did not say "God is greater than me" but instead *The Father is greater than me*.

38. (V, 1) That which is read in the Acts of the Apostles: *Thus certainly all the house of Israel knows that God made him Lord and Christ, whom you have crucified.*[304]

Among the remaining matters of the heretics, you also have offered this, acting like someone from the opposing faction making it plainly credible that the Son of God is something made. We read in the Acts of the Apostles, with blessed Peter speaking, *Thus certainly all the house of Israel knows that God made him Lord and Christ, whom you have crucified*.[305] But the resolution of this question is also obvious along the lines of the explanation above, where we said that the Son of God was also made the son of a man. Even if it is not possible for him to suffer, since the Son of God exists as the Word and the Wisdom of God and because in accordance with this he is at all times incapable of suffering, just as his Father also is,[306] nevertheless, in that he was made a man when he was born from the Virgin Mary, he is capable of suffering. Of course, he even underwent death, and death on the cross, while always remaining in himself, since God is inviolable even when he is turned into a man and crucified. God made Jesus, who exists in the flesh, Lord and Christ. For in that he is the only begotten Son of God, who is the Word and

---

303. See Athanasius, *Apol. sec.* 1.58; Hilary of Poitiers, *Trin.* 9.56.
304. Acts 2:36.
305. See Athanasius, *Apol. sec.* 1.58; Ambrose, *Fid.* 1.15.95.
306. See Athanasius, *Apol. sec.* 2.11–12; Ambrose, *Fid.* 1.15.95. The Arian points—which Faustinus very swiftly moves past—are that the passage says "God *made* him Lord and Christ" and that, by suffering, Christ showed that he was different from/subordinate to the Father, who cannot suffer. To address the former, Faustinus gestures to his points above in §19; for the latter, Faustinus offers little more than these declarative sentences. Hilary, on the other hand, grappled with these points extensively; see Hilary of Poitiers, *Trin.* 10, in general, and Weedman 2007b, 166–73.

eius. Hic autem Iesus secundum carnem Christus factus est, quando primum forma illa seruilis quam acceperat de Adae peccato, liberata est. Adam enim de dominio in seruitutem recidit ex commissione peccati: *omnis* enim *qui facit peccatum seruus est.* Saluator autem reuocauit multo firmius, immo et incorruptibilius in adsumpto homine dominium, cum in eo ipsum peccatum, quod per Adam fuerat causa abiectae seruitutis, absterserit. Sed factus est iterum uere Dominus, cum in illum populi credentes, se eius dominio subdiderunt. Prouocatus enim per hortamenta sacrae Scripturae dicentis: *Seruite Domino in timore,* unusquisque iam cognoscens in Christo salutare dominium, ait: *Nonne Deo subdita est anima mea?* Huius enim seruum fieri summi decoris est, et quasi quaedam supereminens mundo nobilitas. Ideo et apostolus ad gloriam suam scribit: *Paulus seruus Iesu Christi.* Vides quomodo sit factus Dominus, quando illum et is, qui persecutus fuerat, suum Dominum pro summa sui gloria confitetur.

39. (V, 2) Factus est autem Iesus secundum carnem non solum Dominus sed et Christus. In Christi autem nomine regis et sacerdotis sacramenta uersantur. Legimus in ueteri Scriptura sacerdotes et reges apud Israhelitas olei unctione consignatos: atque ideo christi uocabantur. Christus enim quod Graece dicitur, hoc apud Latinos unctus siue linitus est interpretatus. Sed Saluator noster uere Christus secundum carnem factus est, existens

the Wisdom of God, he is not some created thing and he does not await promotion, as he obviously exists as the perfect God in all things, just as his Father also does. This Jesus, then, who exists in the flesh, was made Christ when the servant's form[307] that he took up from the sin of Adam was first freed: Adam fell away from the Lord into servitude when he committed a sin, *For everyone who commits a sin is a servant*,[308] but the Savior renewed a much stronger, no, a much more incorruptible kingdom within the humanity that he assumed when he wiped away that very sin within it that had been the cause of abject servitude for Adam.[309] Now in turn, he was truly made the Lord when the people who believed in him subjected themselves to his rule. Summoned now by the urgings of sacred scripture, which says, *Serve the Lord in fear*,[310] everyone who now knows Christ's salutary kingdom says, *Isn't my soul subject to God?*[311] For to become his servant is the highest honor, and is like some nobility towering over the world. This is why the Apostle also writes for his own glory, *Paul, a servant of Jesus Christ*.[312] You see how he was made the Lord when even that one, who had been his persecutor, confesses that him being his Lord is his highest glory.

39. (V, 2) Moreover, Jesus was made (in the flesh) not only Lord but also Christ. Now, the holy mysteries of the king and priest are wrapped up in the name of Christ. We read in the Old Testament that priests and kings among the Israelites were marked by being anointed with oil, and for this reason they were called *christs*, for *christ* in Greek is translated into Latin as *anointed* or *smeared*.[313] Our Savior was truly made Christ in the flesh,

---

307. See above, §§3, 17, 20, 23, 32, 34, 36–37.
308. John 8:34.
309. Just as Hilary dedicated most of *Trin.* 10 to the question of Christ's incarnation, which Faustinus handles briefly above, he dedicated most of book 11 to the question of God's plan of salvation, which Faustinus here also treats very cursorily and only as it relates to another point. On Hilary's arguments, see Weedman 2007b, 174–79. That Faustinus treats these two topics consecutively, just as Hilary does, suggests that he at least had Hilary in mind when composing these sections even if he did not have the time or inclination to dedicate the same attention to these questions.
310. Ps 2:11.
311. Ps 61:2 LXX.
312. Rom 1:1.
313. See Exod 30:30; Lev 8:12; 1 Sam 10:1; 2 Sam 12:7. The words in question are the Greek χριστός and Latin *unctus* and *linitus*, respectively. See Athanasius, *Apol. sec.* 1.46; Cyril of Jerusalem, *Catech. myst.* 10. This is the only instance in which Faustinus

uerus rex, uerus et sacerdos: utrumque idem ipse, ne quid in Saluatore minus haberetur. Audi itaque ipsum regem factum, cum dicit: *Ego autem constitutus sum rex ab eo super Sion montem sanctum eius.* Audi quod etiam sacerdos sit de Patris testimonio dicentis: *Tu es sacerdos in aeternum secundum ordinem Melchisedech.* Aaron primus in lege ex unctione chrismatis factus est sacerdos: et non dixit: secundum ordinem Aaron, ne et Saluatoris sacerdotium successione haberi posse crederetur. Illud enim sacerdotium quod fuit in Aaron, successione constabat: sacerdotium uero Saluatoris non in alteram successione transfertur, eo quod ipse sacerdos iugiter perseueret, secundum quod scriptum est: *Tu es sacerdos in aeternum secundum ordinem Melchisedech.* Est ergo Saluator secundum carnem et rex et sacerdos, sed non corporaliter unctus sed spiritaliter. Illi enim apud Israhelitas reges et sacerdotes, olei unctione corporaliter uncti, reges erant et sacerdotes: non utramque unus, sed singuli quique eorum aut rex erat aut sacerdos: soli enim Christo perfectio in omnibus et plenitudo debetur, qui et legem uenerat adinplere. Sed licet non utrumque singuli eorum essent, tamen regali aut sacerdotali oleo uncti corporaliter, christi uocabantur. Saluator autem, qui uere Christus est, Spiritu Sancto unctus est, ut adinpleretur quod de eo scriptum est: *Propter ea unxit te Deus, Deus tuus oleum laetitiae prae consortibus tuis.* In hoc enim plus quam consortes ipsius nominis unctus est, cum est unctus oleo laetitiae, quo non aliud significatur quam Spiritus Sanctus.

40. (V, 3) Hoc uerum esse ab ipso Saluatore cognoscimus. Nam cum accepisset et aperuisset librum Esaiae et legisset: *Spiritus Domini super me propter quod unxit me,* adinpletam tunc dixit prophetiam in auribus auditorum. Sed et Petrus princeps apostolorum illud chrisma unde Saluator Christus ostenditur, docuit esse Spiritum Sanctum, id ipsum et uirtutem Dei, quando in Actibus apostolorum ad fidelissimum et misericordem, qui erat tunc centurio, loquebatur. Nam inter cetera ait: *Incipiens a Gali-*

existing as the true king and the true priest. The same one was both, lest anything be considered inferior in respect to the Savior. Hear that he was made king when he says, *But I am set as king by him over his holy mountain, Zion*.[314] Hear that he is also a priest in the Father's testimony, who says, *You are a priest for eternity in the order of Melchizedek*.[315] Aaron was made the first priest by law by the application of ointment, yet the Father did not say "in the order of Aaron," lest someone believe that the priesthood of the Savior could be held by succession too. For that priesthood which was Aaron's was sustained by succession, but the Savior's priesthood is not transferred by succession to anyone else because he remains a priest perpetually, as was written: *You are a priest for eternity in the order of Melchizedek*.

The Savior, then, is both king and priest in the flesh, yet anointed not physically but spiritually. For those kings and priests among the Israelites who were anointed physically by an anointing of oil were kings and priests. No one was both; each one of them was either a king or a priest. For perfection in all things and completeness belongs to Christ alone, who also came to fulfill the law. Now, although none of those individuals were both, they were still called christs, as they were physically anointed with kingly or priestly oil. But the Savior, who is truly Christ, was anointed by the Holy Spirit to fulfill what was written about him: *Therefore God, your God, has anointed you with the oil of gladness, beyond your fellows*.[316] For he was anointed more so than those who shared his name[317] when he was anointed with the oil of gladness, which means nothing other than the Holy Spirit.

40. (V, 3) We recognize that this is true from the Savior himself. For when he had taken and opened the book of Isaiah and read, *The Spirit of the Lord is over me, because he has anointed me*,[318] he said that the prophecy was then fulfilled in the ears of those listening. Peter, the leader of the

---

attempts to discuss anything related to the Greek language; even the word *homoousios* is absent from his writings (but does appear in Lucifer of Caligari [*Mor. esse Dei fil.* 4] and Gregory of Elvira [*Fid.* 1]).

314. Ps 2:6. See Athanasius, *Apol. sec.* 2.9.
315. Ps 110:4 LXX.
316. Ps 44:8 LXX. See Athanasius, *Apol. sec.* 1.47; Cyril of Jerusalem, *Catech. myst.* 3.
317. That is, "christs."
318. Isa 61:1; Jesus reads the passage aloud at Luke 4:16–20.

laea post baptismum quod praedicauii Iohannes, Iesum Nazaraeum, quem unxit Deus Spiritu Sancto et uirtute, hic circuiuit faciens uirtutes et magnalia, atque omnes liberans obsessos a diabolo. Vides quia et Petrus dixit hunc Iesum secundum carnem unctum esse Spiritu Sancto et uirtute. Vnde et uere ipse Iesus secundum carnem factus est Christus, qui unctione Sancti Spiritus et rex factus est et sacerdos in aeternum. Haec autem ideo prosecutus sum, ut liquido appareat Iesum Filium Dei non secundum quod est Verbum et sapientia Dei, crucifixum uel factum esse Dominum et Christum, sed secundum hoc quod adsumpsit de Maria, quamuis per adsumpti hominis passionem et unigenitum Filium Dei passum esse dicamus: non quia uere ipse unigenitus Filius, qua est Verbum et sapientia Dei, passus est, sed quia quicquid in adsumptum hominem eius iniuriae uel passionis illatum est, id totum ad ipsum unigenitum inpassibilem Deum quadam ratione reuocatur. Vnde et apostolus Paulus scribens ad Corinthios ait: *Si enim cognouissent*—scilicet principes huius saeculi—, *numquam Dominum maiestatis crucifixissent.* Si ista manifesta sunt, apparet iam quomodo dictum sit: *Certissime itaque sciat omnis domus Israhel quia et Dominum illum et Christum Deus fecit hunc* scilicet *Iesum, quem uos crucifixistis:* quem et idem Petrus supra uirum nominauit dicens: *Viri Israhelitae, audite uerba haec: Iesum Nazarenum, uirum a Deo probatum in uobis uirtutibus et prodigiis et signis:* hunc scilicet Iesum Christum, quem et Paulus hominem dixit scribens ad Timotheum: *Vnus Deus, unus et mediator Dei et hominum, homo Iesus Christus:* qui et dicebat in Euangelio: *Nunc autem quaeritis me occidere, hominem qui ueritatem locutus sum uobis.*

41. (V, 4) Non pro impio Photino haec loquimur, qui nudum uult esse hominem sine Dei Verbi incarnatione, sed contra Arrium antichristum

apostles, also taught that the ointment that shows Christ is the Savior is the Holy Spirit, the very power of God, when in the Acts of the Apostles he spoke to a very faithful and compassionate man who was a centurion at the time. For among other things, he says, *beginning from Galilee after the baptism which John proclaimed, Jesus of Nazareth, whom God anointed with the Holy Spirit and his power, went around performing miracles and great works, and freeing all who were possessed by the devil.*[319] You see that Peter too said that Jesus in the flesh was anointed by the Holy Spirit and his power. Thus even Jesus in the flesh was truly made Christ, as he was made king and priest for eternity by the anointing of the Holy Spirit. Now, I have pursued these things to make it plainly seen that Jesus, Son of God, was neither crucified nor made Lord and Christ as the Word and the Wisdom of God, but rather in the form that he assumed from Mary. We do say, however, that when the humanity that he assumed suffered, the only begotten Son of God suffered—and not because that only begotten Son, insofar as he is the Word and the Wisdom of God, truly suffered, but because whatever injury and suffering was inflicted on his assumed humanity is completely, by some reasoning, in reference to the only begotten God who is incapable of suffering. This is why the apostle Paul, when he writes to the Corinthians, also says, *For if they had understood*—namely, "the rulers of this age"—*they never would have crucified the Lord of Majesty.*[320] If these things are obvious, it is now clear why it is written, *Thus certainly all the house of Israel knows that God made him*—"Jesus," namely—*Lord and Christ, whom you have crucified,*[321] whom Peter also called a man earlier on when he said, *Men of Israel, hear these words: Jesus of Nazareth, a man proven by God among you by these powers, portents, and signs.*[322] Of course, Paul also calls this Jesus Christ a man when he writes to Timothy, *There is one God, and one mediator of God and men, the man Jesus Christ.*[323] He [Christ] also said in the gospel, *Now, then, you seek to kill me, a man who has told you the truth.*[324]

---

319. Acts 10:37–38. See Athanasius, *Apol. sec.* 2.12. Miracles play a significant role in Hilary's understanding of Christ as divine (see *Trin.* 3.5–8, 18–21; Beckwith 2008, 132–35), but not Faustinus's.
320. 1 Cor 2:8.
321. Acts 2:36.
322. Acts 2:22.
323. 1 Tim 2:5. See Ambrose, *Fid.* 3.2.8.
324. John 8:40.

recitamus, qui uult ipsum unigenitum Filium, qui est Verbum et sapientia Dei, qua Deum et non qua hominem crucifixum, et ipum factum esse Dominum et Christum. Sed etsi durissima obstinatione contendunt, dicentes de ipso Deo Verbo scriptum esse quod Deus illum fecerit et Dominum et Christum, nec sic pertimescimus fiducia ueritatis, ne forte per hoc quod scriptum est, Verbum Dei factura credatur. Fac enim Verbum Dei factum esse Dominum et Christum: quid hoc praeiudicat eius substantiae, qua semper est Verbum Dei? Intende enim quia non substantiam Verbi Dei dixit esse factam, sed hoc ipsum Verbum, quod semper est Filius Dei, factum esse Dominum et Christum. Non enim id ipsum est hoc quod omnino non erat fieri, et id quod erat aliquid fieri. Nam et Deus fit aliquotiens adiutor et protector; non tamen quia factus est adiutor et protector, iam etiam hoc quod Deus est, factus esse credendus est. Nam et Moyses, posteaquam diuinum sensit auxilium ac protectionem, de Deo qui contra Pharaonem et adiuuerat et protexerat, dixit: *Adiutor et protector factus est mihi in salutem;* et multa simillima testimonia inuenies, quae ego, ne multum adhuc prolongem, praetereo. Si ergo, cum Deus sit adiutor et protector, non hoc quod Deus est, fieri creditur, sed hoc ipsum quod adiutor et protector esse dignatur: quid est quod, cum Verbum Dei factum esse Dominum et Christum dicunt, putemus Dei Verbi substantiam factam? Numquid, quia legimus: *Et Verbum caro factum est,* ideo ipsum quoque Verbum factum esse credendum est? Sed manifestissime expressum est non tam Verbum esse factum quod erat in principio apud

41. (V, 4) We do not say these things on behalf of the impious Photinus, who wishes for the man to be bare, without the incarnation of God the Word,[325] but to denounce the antichrist Arius, who wishes for the only begotten Son, who is the Word and the Wisdom of God, to be crucified as God and as the one made Lord and Christ and not as a man.[326] Yet even if they fight with the firmest obstinacy and say that it is written about God the Word that God made him both Lord and Christ, we also, with confidence in the truth, are not terribly afraid that someone thus by chance might believe that the Word of God is a created being from what is written. For imagine that the Word of God was "made" Lord and Christ; how does this injure his substance, by which he is always the Word of God? Consider that he did not say that the substance of the Word of God was made, but that this very Word itself, which is always the Son of God, was made Lord and Christ. For "this which did not exist at all, was made" and "this which did exist, was in some respect made" are not the same thing.[327] Even God sometimes became a helper and protector; nevertheless, one must not believe that, even though he is God, he was "made" because he was made a helper and protector. For instance, after he sensed the divine aid and protection from God who both helped and protected him against Pharaoh, Moses said, *He is made my helper and protector for salvation.*[328] You will find many similar testimonies that I am passing over so that I do not go on much more here.[329] If, then, when God is a helper and protector, one should not believe that, because this is God, God is made, but rather that he found it worthy to be a helper and protector. Then why we should think that the substance of the Word of God is made when they say that the Word of God was made Lord and Christ? Because we read, *And the Word*

---

325. Photinus of Sirmium was a pupil of Marcellus of Ancyra, a radical Nicene theologian who was accused of Sabellianism (or monarchianism) by his opponents; he was also accused of teaching that the Son only began to exist when he was born in Bethlehem and, as here, that the Son was entirely human, in both flesh and soul, and that human was then filled with the Word. Faustinus ignores this connection to the Sabellian beliefs he criticizes elsewhere in the tract. See Socrates, *Hist. eccl.* 2.18; Kelly 1978, 241–43. Hilary, throughout book 10 of his *De Trinitate*, deals with Photinian and other related beliefs concerning the person of Christ: see Weedman 2007b, 169–70.
326. See Hilary of Poitiers, *Trin.* 7.7; Ambrose, *Fid.* 1.1.6.
327. See Athanasius, *Apol. sec.* 2.45.
328. Exod 18:4.
329. See above, §§3, 28, 30.

Deum, sed ipsum Verbum quod semper erat, postea factum esse carnem, ut factura non tam in Verbo sit, quam in hoc quod caro factum est. Ita ergo et cum dicitur Verbum Dei factum esse Dominum et Christum, non tam substantiam Verbi Dei factam esse intellegendum est, sed quia Dominus et Christus factum est hoc ipsum Verbum, quod semper Deus erat.

42. (V, 5) Fit autem Dominus eorum, qui se eidem mancipant proposito seruiendi. Et da mihi ueniam, beatissime Mathaee, si dixero quod nondum tibi Christus Deus erat Dominus, quando adhuc teloneo seruiebas. Sed et apostolis uniuersis tunc primum Dominus factus est, quando derelictis omnibus, eidem seruire maluerunt. Ipsarum quoque gentium tunc Dominus factus est, quando idolorum uana superstitione derelicta, ipsae gentes se eius dominio tradiderunt: inquantum enim quis peccati seruus est uel mammonae, in tantum Dei seruus esse non potest. Cum ergo peccato et mammonae quis abrenuntiauerit, faciens iustitiam habendique cupiditatem respuens, tunc Iesus Dominus eius efficitur. Eadem quoque ratione eum etiam Christum fieri intellegitur: siquidem, ut supra dictum est, reges et sacerdotes Christi uocabulo taxabantur. Factus est ergo Saluator rex eorum, qui regno mortis ulterius non tenentur adstricti, in quorum mortali corpore cessauit regnare peccatum, posteaquam per diuina magisteria didicerunt, docentibus apostolis: *Non ergo regnet peccatum in uestro mortali corpore.* Sed et cum fungitur pro nobis sacerdotis officio, Christus uerissime factus est, maxime defensor et aduocatus pro nobis semper adsistens, interpellans quoque Patrem, qua solus purissimus sacerdos, ut, expiata labe delinquentiae, diuina eius propitiatione seruemur. Per haec ergo, quod Iesus factus est et Christus et Dominus, non tam substantiae eius diuinae aliquid confertur, quam nobis prospectum est, quibus regni eius et sacerdotii ac dominii potestas uelut munus salutare conlatum est.

was made flesh,³³⁰ must we really believe that the Word was also made? Now, it is expressed very clearly not so much that the Word which *was in the beginning with God*³³¹ was made, but rather that the Word, which always existed, was afterward made flesh: the creation is not so much in the Word, but in that which was made flesh. So, then, when the Word of God is said to have been made Lord and Christ, it must be understood not so much that the substance of the Word of God was made, but that this very Word, which was always God, was made Lord and Christ.

42. (V, 5) Moreover, he is made the Lord of those who deliver themselves to him intent on serving him. Indulge me, most blessed Matthew, if I say that Christ, our God, was not yet your Lord while you still served in the customs house.³³² No, he was first made Lord to all the apostles when they left all their things behind and chose to serve him. He was made Lord of all the gentiles when they left behind the empty superstition of idols and handed themselves over to his kingdom. For however much someone is a servant of sin or Mammon, so much is he incapable of being a servant of God.³³³ Therefore, Jesus is made his Lord whenever someone renounces sin and Mammon, creates justice, and spits on the desire to possess. By this same reasoning, he is understood to be made Christ as well—if indeed, as was said above, kings and priests shall be classified under the term "christ." Thus the Savior was made the king of those who are no longer bound by the kingdom of death, and in whose mortal bodies sin has ceased to reign after they have learned the divine instruction that the apostles teach, *Thus do not let sin reign in your mortal body*.³³⁴ But when he performs the office of the priest on our behalf, he is most truly made Christ. He always stands as the greatest defender and advocate on our behalf, and as an intercessor with the Father, too, in his role as the only completely pure priest, so that we might be saved by his divine propitiation after the disgrace of our fault is atoned for.³³⁵

Therefore, in these matters—that Jesus was made both Christ and

---

330. John 1:14.
331. John 1:3.
332. See Matt 9:9; Mark 2:14.
333. See John 8:34; Matt 6:24.
334. Rom 6:12.
335. In other words, just as priests must be pure in order to administer sacraments such as penance, Christ is the purest priest of all, and thus only he is capable of administering penance to all men for all sins, including the sin of Adam (which Faustinus discussed above, at §§32–33, 38).

Non uidetur absurdum si et illud similiter intellegas, quod ait: *Ego autem constitutus sum rex ab eo supra Sion montem sanctum eius:* etsi enim constitutus esse rex dicitur, tamen cum additur *supra Sion montem sanctum eius*, ostenditur quod non de illo regno eius dicat, quod habuit etiam ante quam constitueretur rex supra Sion montem sanctum eius. Rex enim est ante omnia aeua aeuorum, continens potestate sua omnem, quam condidit, creaturam: unde et omnipotens adprobatur, quod possit omnia continere quae facta sunt.

43. (VI, 1) De hoc quod ait Salomon: *Dominus creauit me initium uiarum suarum in opera sua.*

Tangamus et illam in ultimo quaestionem, quam inter ceteras addidisti: *Dominus*—inquit—*creauit me initium uiarum suarum in opera sua*. Dicit haereticus: Vides creaturam esse sapientiam, quae utique, interprete Paulo apostolo, Christus est. Ergo Christus—inquit —, qui est sapientia, non est uerus Filius, sed, creatura existens, adoptione factus est Filius. Hoc uenenum Arrianorum est. Sed o quam caeca est impietas ad id uidere quod pium est! Iam semel quia, ut scriptum est, *oderunt sapientiam et uerbum Domini non adsumpserunt,* nihil in illa sincerissimi decoris adspiciunt: sicut et lippientibus oculis nulla est uisio ueritatis, quandoquidem aliter eorum renuntiat adspectus, quam in fide rerum est; sed et cui saporem proprium redundans sui fellis amaritudo uitiauit, si dulcia mella degustet, ut amaram dulcedinem mellis infamat, non recognoscens malum propriae amaritudinis. Sed, o miser haeretice, quid potes ueri luminis uidere, cum caecutias uel ambules in uiis tenebrarum, omnia quae sunt impietatis excogitans? Clamet licet uir ille spiritalis suauissimo experimento diuinae epulationis inuitans: *Gustate et uidete quam suauis est Dominus,* sed tibi,

Lord—it is not so much that anything was brought into his divine substance as it is that he was provided for us, us to whom the power of his kingdom, priesthood, and lordship was brought like a saving gift. For it does not seem absurd if you likewise understand it when he says, *But I am set as king by him over his holy mountain, Zion*.[336] Even if he is said to have been set as king, when *over his holy mountain, Zion* is also added, it shows that he is not speaking about his kingdom that he had even before he was set as king *over his holy mountain, Zion*. For he is king before all the ages of ages, and holds in his power every created being that he formed. This also proves that he is omnipotent, because he is able to preserve all things that are made.

43. (VI, 1) Concerning what Solomon says: *The Lord created me as the beginning of his ways for his works*.[337]

Let us now touch upon that question that you added among the others at the end. *The Lord*—he says—*created me as the beginning of his ways for his works*. The heretic says: You see that Wisdom is a created being, which certainly, as the apostle Paul explains, is Christ.[338] Thus Christ—he says—who is Wisdom, is not the true Son, but exists as a created being and was made the Son by adoption. This is the poison of the Arians. But O, how blind impiety is, to see something pious in this! Now already, because (as is written) *they hate Wisdom and do not accept the Word of God*,[339] they see nothing in Wisdom of its most genuine beauty, just as bleary eyes do not see reality in their vision, since their sight indeed reports something other than what is real. This is also like someone misled by the bitterness of his own gall when it washes over him with its own flavor, so that when he tastes sweet honey, he denigrates the pungent sweetness of the honey and does not recognize the badness in his own bitterness.[340] But, O wretched heretic, what can you see of the true light when you are blind or walking

---

336. Ps 2:6. See Athanasius, *Apol. sec.* 2.52.
337. Prov 8:22.
338. See Athanasius, *Apol. sec.* 2.1; Hilary of Poitiers, *Trin.* 12 in general, and esp. 12.35; see also Weedman 2007b, 180, 188–95; Beckwith 2008, 202–7.
339. See Bar 3, particularly 3:10–13, 20.
340. There is a play on words here, as *amaritudo* and *amarus* generally mean "bitterness" and "bitter," often associated with gall, or "sourness" and "sour," but can also more generally reflect "pungency" and "pungent." Thus Faustinus describes the *amaritudino*, or "bitterness," of the bile, and the *amaram dulcedinem* of the honey, its "pungent sweetness" or, rather, its "bitter sweetness." See Jerome, *Ep.* 15.4, and above, p. 18.

si gustaueris, nihil suaue sentitur in Domino, eo quod, sicut scriptum est, *uenenum aspidum sub labiis tuis est,* eo quod *os tuum maledictione et amaritudine plenum est.* Denique cum infinita et ipse Salomon de Dei sapientia praedicauerit, et ita diuine de ea fuerit prosecutus, ut non aliud in illa crederetur, quam quod in natura Dei est: in illis omnibus haereticus caecutiens hoc solum uidere se credidit, per quod probaret eam esse creaturam. Sed scriptum est—inquit—: *Dominus creauit me initium uiarum suarum in opera sua.* Sed nos non ibimus longius, neque de aliis libris Salominis, quae sunt pro sempiterna Dei sapientia, proferemus. Sufficit nunc si de hoc ipso loco, unde testimonium protulit, pars diuersa supereretur.

44. (VI, 2) Ais, haeretice, scriptum: *Dominus creauit me initium uiarum suarum in opera sua:* sed intende quia haec ipsa sapientia nihilominus ait: *Ante omnes autem colles genuit me.* Quomodo ergo haec ipsa sapientia in eodem loco et creatam se esse dicit et genitam? Et prius est ut uideamus quid primum sit: utrum quod genita an quod creata est. Sed licet primum dixerit: *Dominus creauit me initium uiarum suarum in opera sua,* tamen, ne se creaturam putares, recurrit ad illud quod prius est, in sequenti dicens: *Ante omnes autem colles genuit me.* Vide enim ne putes postea genitam, quia primum praemiserit se creatam. Etsi enim in ordine

in shadowy paths, devising everything that pertains to impiety? Let that spiritual man cry out, inviting you with the proven sweetness of a divine feast to *taste and see how sweet the Lord is*.[341] But if you taste, you perceive nothing sweet in the Lord, because (as is written) *there is a poisonous snake on your lips*, because *your mouth is filled with cursing and bitterness*.[342]

Finally, Solomon also has made endless declarations about the Wisdom of God and has described it so divinely that no one would believe anything about it other than what they believe about the nature of God; but in all these matters, the heretic, blind to this, believes that he alone sees how to prove it is a created being. Now, it is written—he says—*The Lord created me as the beginning of his ways for his works*. We will not go on long, nor will we bring out things from the other books of Solomon on behalf of the eternal Wisdom of God. It is enough for now if the opposite party is overcome from the same place from which he brought out this testimony.

44. (VI, 2) You say, heretic, that it is written, *The Lord created me as the beginning of his ways for his works*.[343] But consider that this same Wisdom nevertheless says, *But before all the hills, he begat me*. How then can this same Wisdom, in this exact same place, say that it is both a created being and begotten? First things first—let us see what is first and whether it is that "begotten" or that "created." Now, although it first said, *The Lord created me as the beginning of his ways for his works*, it nevertheless runs back to what was first, so that you do not reckon that it is something created, saying in the following, *But before all the hills, he begat me*.[344] See to it that

---

341. Ps 33:9 LXX.

342. Ps 13:3 LXX. It is worth noting how much invective Faustinus opens with rather than immediately treating the verse in question. Hanson (1988, 559–60) calls Prov 8:22 the Arian trump card: an explicit statement that the Father *created* the Son. For earlier interpretations of this verse, see Simonetti 1965, 9–87; see also Beckwith 2008, 202–7.

343. Prov 8:22.

344. Prov 8:25. See Athanasius, *Apol. sec.* 2.2, 44, 56, 60, 80 (though almost the entire second oration concerns itself with this passage). While Faustinus follows Athanasius's reasoning (particularly at 2.60), Eusebius and Basil of Caesarea, among others, argued that this passage was a rarity and occurred in a book filled with parables and mystical language (and was originally written in Hebrew anyway), and therefore should not be weighted as heavily as numerous other, clearer passages affirming that the Son is not a created being. On the relative influences of Eusebius of Caesarea's and Athanasius's interpretations of this passage, see DelCogliano 2010. Basil (*Eun.* 1.2.20) himself refers to the passage only once.

sermonum primum positum est quod creata est, deinde autem quod genita: tamen sensus hoc indicat, quod primum est genita quam creata, ut sit sensus ita sapientiae dicentis: *Dominus creauit me initium uiarum suarum in opera sua:* sed ne quis me putet per hoc esse creaturam, aut tunc primum esse coepisse quando creauit me initium uiarum suarum in opera sua, subsequor et dico: *Ante omnes autem colles genuit me:* ut scias prius me genitam quam creatam. Cum enim dicit: *Ante omnes autem colles genuit me,* facit illud esse postea quod creata est, ut praecedat et sit anterius illud quod genita est. Si ergo sic creata est, ut ante fuerit genita, sensus impietatis exclusus est, qua ideo eam dixerat creatam, ut tunc primum substitisse sapientia crederetur, quando et retulit se creatam a Domino initium uiarum suarum in opera sua. Ecce enim sensus manifestat etiam antequam crearetur, sapientiam substitisse, quippe quae prius est genita quam creata.

45. (VI, 3) Sed magis commendabitur hic sensus catholicus, si et ipsa uerba, prout nobis possibile est, discutiantur, quibus uel genitam se refert sapientia uel creatam. *Dominus*—inquit—*creauit me initium uiarum suarum in opera sua.* Intende quia cum dixerit: *Dominus creauit me,* non tacuit, ne uere creatura putaretur, sed prosequitur explanans quid sit creata et ob quam causam sit creata. Ait enim: *Creauit me initium uiarum suarum:* et cum sequitur: *in opera sua,* palam est quod ostendit et causas cur creata sit initium uiarum Domini. Non ergo sapientia, quasi quae non esset, creata est ad hoc ut esset: sed cum semper substantialiter fuerit, tunc creata est secundum dispensationem initium uiarum Domini, et in opera Domini creata est. Initium ergo uiarum Domini creata est, et in opera Domini creata est sapientia: non tamen, quia substantialiter ante non erat, ideo creata est sapientia. At uero cum dicit se ante omnes colles genitam, non propter aliquam rem dicit se esse genitam; sed existens semper Patris sempiterna progenies, ob quasdam causas creatam se dicit initium uiarum

you do not think that the begetting happened later because it put down that it was created first. For even if it first put that it was created in the order of the verses, and then that it was begotten, the meaning nevertheless indicates that it was first begotten rather than created. The meaning of Wisdom when it speaks is this:

> *The Lord created me as the beginning of his ways for his works*, but so that no one thinks that I am a created being because of this, or to have first begun to exist when he created me as the beginning of his ways for his works, I will follow up on this and say, *But before all the hills, he begat me*, so that you will know that I was begotten first rather than created.

For when it says, *But before all the hills, he begat me*, it makes that which was created that which was later, so that which was begotten is the earlier antecedent. If, then, it was created in such a way that it was begotten first, the interpretation of impiety—which had said that Wisdom was created to make it believable that Wisdom first existed at the point when it says that it was created by the Lord as the beginning of his ways for his works—is shut out. Look, the meaning also makes it obvious that it existed as Wisdom before it was created, since surely that which was begotten is prior to that which was created.

45. (VI, 3) This catholic way of understanding will be more agreeable if we also discuss, as much as we can, those statements in which Wisdom refers to itself as either only begotten or created. *The Lord*—it says—*created me as the beginning of his ways for his works*.[345] Consider how when it said, *The Lord created me*, it did not remain silent, in case it was actually reckoned to be a created being, but follows up by explaining why it was created and for what reason it was created. For it says, *He created me as the beginning of his ways*; when it continues *for his works*, it is clear that it is presenting the reasons why it was created as the beginning of the ways of the Lord. Wisdom was not created at that point so that it would exist, as if it were something that did not exist; although it had always existed, it was created at that point in its dispensation as the beginning of the ways of the Lord, and was created for the works of the Lord.[346] Wisdom, then, was created as the beginning of the ways of the Lord, and it was created for the works of the Lord, but Wisdom was not created because it did not exist

---

345. Prov 8:22.
346. See Hilary of Poitiers, *Trin.* 12.45; Gregory of Elvira, *Fid.* 2; Athanasius, *Apol. sec.* 2.45.

Domini, id est, in opera Domini. Ergo et ex hoc manifestum est non esse creaturam sapientiam, quae in aliud creata est, id est, in opera Domini, cum ipsa sit genita, non in opera, sed de Patre existens, ut diximus, sempiterna progenies.

46. (VI, 4) Sed et hoc intendendum est, quod aliud est dicere creari sapientiam, et aliud est dicere quod sit creatura. Quamuis enim legatur creata esse sapientia, nusquam tamen legitur quod sit creatura. Non enim omne quod creatum est, iam et creatura dicendum est, licet omnis creatura creata sit: sicut nec omne quod factum est, iam factura adseueranda est, licet omnis factura facta sit. Si uidetur obscurum, exemplo dilucidabo. Legimus quendam gratulari ac dicere ad Deum: *Ego autem cantabo uirtutem tuam et exaltabo mane misericordiam tuam, quia factus es susceptor meus et refugium meum in die tribulationis meae.* Ecce Deus factus est susceptor et refugium: non tamen Deus factura est; et hoc est quod dixi: Non omne quod factum est, iam factura dicendum est. Deus enim non existens factura, qui semper est, factus est susceptor et refugium in die tribulationis homini, ut quod factus est susceptor et refugium in die tribulationis homini, uideatur contulisse quod factus est; non tamen quia susceptor et refugium homini factus est, etiam Deus quoque factura esse credendus est, cuius diuina substantia sempiterna est. Similiter et sapientia si creata dicatur, non tamen creatura est, quae semper est: sed cum existat semper, creatur ad aliquid ut prosit, non ut creatura dicatur quasi facta quae non fuit. Erat enim inseparabilis a Deo Dei sapientia: et haec ipsa existens Dei sempiterna progenies, creata est initium uiarum Domini.

47. (VI, 5) Sed adhuc apertius edisseram. Certe sapientia Dei ipsa est, quae et Verbum Dei esse scribitur, ut in superioribus ostensum est. Et

before this. Truly, when it says that it was begotten before all the hills, it does not say that it was "begotten" for the sake of anything. Instead, since it exists as the eternal progeny of the Father, it says that it was "created" for particular reasons—that is, as the beginning of the ways of the Lord and for the works of the Lord. Here, too, it is clear that Wisdom is not a created being, as it was created for something, that is, for the works of the Lord, while it was begotten not for works, but exists from the Father as his eternal progeny, as we said.

46. (VI, 4)[347] Now, consider this, too: it is one thing to say that Wisdom is created and another to say that it is a created being. For however often one reads that Wisdom is created, one nevertheless nowhere reads that it is a created being. Not everything that is created should also be called a created being, then, though every created being is created—just as not everything that is made should then be declared to be something manufactured, though everything manufactured was made. If this seems obscure, I will clear things up with an example. We read that someone was grateful and said to God, *But I will sing your virtue and I will exalt your mercy in the morning, because you are made my guardian and my refuge in the day of my distress.*[348] Look—God is made a guardian and a refuge, but God is not something manufactured. This is what I said: not everything that is made should then be called something manufactured. For God, who always exists and does not exist as something manufactured, was made a guardian and refuge for a man in a day of distress, so something that was made a guardian and refuge for a man in a day of distress might seem to have referred to something made. But just because he was made a guardian and refuge for a man, one should not believe that God is also something manufactured, as his divine substance is eternal. Likewise his Wisdom, if it is called "created," is also nevertheless not a created being, as it always exists. But although it always exists, it is created for something so that it might be beneficial, and not so that it might be called a created being, like something made which had not existed. For the Wisdom of God was inseparable from God, and this same Wisdom, as it exists as the eternal progeny of God, was created as the beginning of the ways of the Lord.

47. (VI, 5) I will explain this even more plainly. Certainly, the Wisdom of God is that which is also described as being the Word of God, as was

---

347. The terminology concerning creating/making in the following sections is very specific and has been retained despite the resulting awkwardness in English.

348. Ps 58:17 LXX.

numquid, quia de Verbo Dei scriptum est: *Et Verbum caro factum est*, iam et Verbum facturam esse adseueramus, quasi tunc primum esse coeperit, cum caro factum est? Sed bene, quia apertissime demonstratum est per Verbum omnia facta, et in ultimis temporibus hoc ipsum Verbum carnem factum. Non ergo factura est Verbum Dei, licet factum caro esse dicatur: ita et sapientia, licet dicatur creata esse initium uiarum Domini et in opera, non tamen creatura est, quam constat ante omnem esse creaturam, quandoquidem omnia in sapientia facta sint. Addo et hoc quia non omne quod creari dicitur, quasi fiat in substantia intellegendum est. Denique quidam uir uidens cor suum esse quibusdam sordibus infectum, precem fundit ad Dominum dicens: *Cor mundum crea in me, Deus:* non utique cordis substantiam in se fieri precabatur, sed ut hoc ipsum cor in eo existens, quod ei erat sordidum, crearet mundum. Non ergo omne quod creari dicitur, iam statim et secundum substantiam fieri intellegendum est: quandoquidem cor quod erat, id ipsum ut mundum crearetur a Domino precabatur. Ergo et sapientia cum creari dicitur, non tam substantia eius, quasi quae non erat, facta est, sed ipsa existens, ut saepius dictum est, creata est initium uiarum Domini in opera eius. Ergo quod creata est sapientia, ad mysterium uel rerum creandarum uel humanae dispensationis intellege, quam cum Dei sapientia dignanter adsumit, creata dicitur: quod uero se genitam dicit, ut nihil in illa minus diuinitatis agnoscas, quam habet ille qui genuit. Valde enim impium est credere quod aliquando Deus sine sua fuerit sapientia. Vnde et quia uere genita est a Deo sapientia, id existens

shown in the preceding passages.[349] Because it is written about the Word of God, *And the Word was made flesh*,[350] should we really now assert that the Word is also something manufactured, as though it first began to exist right when it was made flesh? Ah, good—because it was very plainly demonstrated that all things are made through the Word, yet in very recent times this same Word was made flesh. The Word of God is not, therefore, something manufactured, though it is said that it was made flesh; so too Wisdom, though it is said that it was created as the beginning of the ways of the Lord and for his works, is nevertheless not a created being. Instead, it clearly stands that it existed before every created being, since indeed all things are made in Wisdom.[351]

I add this, too: not everything that is called "created" should be understood as though it were made in regards to its substance. In short, a certain man, when he saw that his heart was stained with a certain uncleanliness, poured out a prayer to the Lord and said, *Create a clean heart within me, God*.[352] Surely he was not praying that the substance of a heart be made within him, but that the same heart that existed within him be created clean for him, as it was unclean. Thus, not everything that is called "created" should then be immediately understood as also created with regards to its substance, seeing as he was praying that the same heart that existed be created clean by the Lord. So, too, when Wisdom is called "created," it is not so much its substance that was made as though it did not exist, but that same Wisdom, already existing (as has been said repeatedly),[353] was created as the beginning of the ways of the Lord for his works. Understand, then, that Wisdom was created for the divine mystery either of the things that were to be created or of the direction of humanity, as the Wisdom of God is called "created" when it deigns to undertake these things. But truly, it says that it is begotten so that you do not recognize any less divinity in it than the one who begat it has. For it is exceedingly impious to believe that God was at any time without his own Wisdom.[354] So, because Wisdom

---

349. Above, §2. See Athanasius, *Apol. sec.* 1.62; Ambrose, *Fid.* 3.5.35.
350. John 1:14.
351. See Ps 103:24 LXX.
352. Ps 50:12 LXX. See Athanasius, *Apol. sec.* 2.46.
353. There is a slight play on words here between Wisdom, *sapientia*, and repeatedly, *saepius*.
354. See Athanasius, *Apol. sec.* 1.19; Gregory of Elvira, *Fid.* 2; Ambrose, *Fid.* 1.13.79.

secundum substantiam quod est genitor, sapientia autem ipsa Christus est: ergo Christus, qui est sapientia, non est adoptione filius, sed uerus Filius, existens Dei progenies, et non factura.

48. (VII, 1) De Spiritu Sancto.

Vniuersas quas de Patre et Filio scripseras quaestiones, prout Dei gratia praestitit, arbitror absolutas: si tamen hoc apud te uerum est, tua religiosa prudentia iudicabit, quamuis fatear et coartatione temporis et rei festinatione et ipso arido angusti mei sermonis eloquio, summas earum me potius tetigisse, quam plenitudinem prosecutum: quia non ut librum, sicut praedixi, scribere coeperam, sed ut quasi cuiusdam adbreuiationis de fide quaedam taxatio signaretur, ne ad hoc me de tua mira beneuolentia prouocatum infidelem crederes, si tacerem. Sed nunc de Sancto Spiritu, etsi breuiter, confitendum est, ne si non aliquid de eo specialiter dixerimus, credamur similiter blasphemare, sicuti et illi qui dicunt illum esse creaturam: quorum tamen miramur insaniam, quod impie sentiant de eo quem Sanctum Spiritum confitentur. Si enim Spiritus sanctus est, quomodo creatura est? Non enim sic sanctus est, ut ceteri qui ad sancti uocabulum fide et Deo placita conuersatione atque ipsius Sancti Spiritus sanctificatione uenerunt: sed ipse naturaliter semper sanctus est ita ut alios sanctificet, non tamen ut ipse, quasi ut qui ante non habuerit, extrinsecus acceperit sanctitatem: hoc nomen sancti ita possidet, ut possidet Pater et Filius: possidet autem non ipse aut Pater existens aut Filius, sed Spiritus Dei. Sic autem Spiritus Dei dicitur, non ut angelus Dei neque ut homo Dei,

was truly begotten by God and exists in regards to substance as the same thing that its progenitor is, Wisdom itself is, moreover, Christ.[355] Therefore Christ, who is Wisdom, is not the Son by adoption, but the true Son, as he exists as the progeny of God and not something manufactured.

48. (VII, 1) On the Holy Spirit.

In my opinion, all the questions about which you had written concerning the Father and Son are resolved to the extent that the grace of God has helped me, but your religious understanding will judge whether this is true for you. I must confess, though, that I have touched on the highlights of these matters rather than followed through in their entirety due to the constraint of time, my haste in the matter, and that meager articulation of my paltry speech.[356] I had begun to write something not like a book, as I said before, but instead as though you had called for some abstract or summary about the faith,[357] so that you would not think that if I were silent when called forth by your extraordinary benevolence that I was faithless in this matter. Now, something must be confessed, even if briefly, about the Holy Spirit, for fear that if we have not said anything particular about it, we will likewise be believed to be blasphemers like those who say that it is a created being too.[358] However, we marvel at their insanity, that they think impiously about what they confess is the Holy Spirit.[359] For if it is the Holy Spirit, how is it a created being? It is not holy in the same way as the rest who come to the term "holy" by faith, a way of life that is pleasing to God, and sanctification from that very Holy Spirit. Rather, it itself is naturally always holy so that it might sanctify others, not so that it might receive sanctity from without as though it did not previously have it. Thus, it carries the name "holy" just as the Father and Son carry it. Yet it carries it not because it exists as either the Father or the Son, but rather as the

---

355. See 1 Cor 1:24.
356. *Angustus* as a descriptive term for Faustinus's speech can mean "paltry, low, base," as translated here, but also suggests once more that Faustinus is constrained by time and space, as the more usual meaning of the term is "narrow, tight, constrained." See above, §1; below, §51.
357. See above, §§3, 8, 19.
358. So-called Pneumatomachians or Macedonians, who argued that the Holy Spirit was either created or was in some way subordinate to the Father; see Kelly 1978, 259–60.
359. See Ambrose, *Spir.* 1.5.63.

quorum natura a diuina substantia inaestimabiliter discreta est: sed sic est Spiritus Dei, ut sit eiusdem substantiae cum Patre et Filio, quia et una sanctitas est Patris et Filii et Spiritus Sancti: quandoquidem idem Spiritus Sanctus usque adeo uere et naturaliter sanctus est, ut hoc ei naturaliter et uerum sit uocabulum. Intende enim ad uerba Saluatoris dicentis: *Euntes ergo nunc docete omnes gentes, baptizantes eos in nomine Patris et Filii et Spiritus Sancti.* Sicut enim uerum uocabulum Patris est et uerum uocabulum Filii est, ita et uerum est uocabulum Spiritus Sancti. Et quomodo uerum uocabulum Patris dicatur, scire poterimus, si animaduertamus quomodo uerus Deus dicitur.

49. (VII, 2) Multi dicuntur dii sed non sunt uere dii: et taceo nunc de Satana ac daemoniis eorumque similibus, qui usurpatione impia dii uocantur. Dicti sunt quidem et homines dii secundum hoc testimonium: *Ego dixi: Dii estis et filii Excelsi omnes:* sed quam uere sint dii, subsequentia manifestant, quae ita se habent: *Vos autem sicut homines moriemini, et sicut unus de principibus cadetis.* Si ergo ubi ubi quilibet sancti dii uocantur, hoc illis pie et cum iustitia uiuentibus ex Dei gratia prouenit, maxime cum in eis Sanctus Spiritus inhabitet; de quo quidem uocabulo excidunt, si non ambulare in uiis Domini perseuerent: nemo ergo de creaturis uerus Deus est, quia nemo naturaliter Deus est. Solus autem Deus naturaliter uerus Deus est, hoc ipsum existens sine initio et fine. Per hanc nunc ueri Dei intellegentiam intellegamus et uerum uocabulum Patris. Apud homines enim exinde pater quis dicitur, ex quo genuit filium: sed licet ex se genuerit filium, tamen non proprie uerus est pater, cui accessit hoc uocabulum, et hoc ipsum a Deo praestitum: qui quidem et tam diu pater dicitur, quam diu eius uiuit et filius. Sicut enim, nato ex se filio, uocabulum patris adeptus est,

Spirit of God. Furthermore, it is called the Spirit of God, not the "angel of God" or the "man of God," as their nature is inestimably different than the divine substance[360]—but the Spirit of God is such that it shares in the same substance as the Father and the Son, because there is one holiness of the Father, the Son, and the Holy Spirit. This same Holy Spirit is so truly and naturally holy that this is naturally and truly its name. For instance, consider the words of the Savior, who says, *Thus go now, teach all the nations, baptizing them in the name of the Father and the Son and the Holy Spirit.*[361] Just as the term "Father" is true, and the term "Son" is true, so too is the term "Holy Spirit" true. We will try to understand why the term "Father" is called true by turning our attention to why he is called the true God.

49. (VII, 2) Many are called gods but are not truly gods (I am remaining silent for now concerning Satan, demons, and similar beings, who are called gods in an impious appropriation of the term). There are even some men called gods, as in this testimony: *I have said: You are gods and all sons of the highest.*[362] But the subsequent text clarifies in what respect they are actually gods, as it defines them this way: *But you shall die like men, and you will fall like one of your rulers.*[363] If, then, whenever any holy men whatsoever are called gods, it comes about for them because they live piously and with righteousness from the grace of God, especially when the Holy Spirit lives within them. Some forfeit this name if they do not continue to walk in the paths of the Lord. Thus, no created being is the true God, because no one is naturally God. God alone, on the other hand, is naturally the true God, because he exists as such without beginning or end. In this understanding the true God, we may now also understand the truth of the term "Father." For among men, one is called a "father" from the time when he begets a son.[364] But although he begat a son from himself, he is nevertheless not properly the "true Father" to whom this term applies, that term

---

360. See Ambrose, *Spir.* 3.4.28.
361. Matt 28:19. See Pseudo-Athanasius, *Trin.* 10; a letter issued by Basil of Ancyra from the Synod of Ancyra in 357, in Epiphanius, *Pan.* 73.3–4; Gregory of Elvira, *Fid.* 10; Hilary of Poitiers, *Syn.* 11. Homoian Arians such as Valens and Ursacius used this passage to emphasize the separation of the three persons just as homoousian and homoiousian theologians such as Basil of Ancyra, Hilary, and Faustinus used the passage to emphasize the unity and equality of the three. See Weedman 2007a, 501.
362. Ps 81:6 LXX. See Athanasius, *Apol. sec.* 1.9; Hilary of Poitiers, *Trin.* 6.18; 7.10; Gregory of Elvira, *Fid.* 2.
363. Ps 81:7 LXX.
364. See Athanasius, *Apol. sec.* 1.21–22; *Ep. Serap.* 4.6.

ita et morte filii uocabulum patris amittit. Deus autem solus proprie uerus Pater est, qui sine initio et fine Pater est. Non enim aliquando coepit esse quod pater est, sed semper Pater est, semper habens Filium ex se genitum, sicut et semper uerus Deus est, sine initio et fine perseuerans. Ergo sicut uocabulum ueri Dei solus obtinet Deus, ita et uocabulum ueri Patris ipse solus obtinet, qui sine initio et fine solus Pater uocatur. Ita intellegamus et uerum uocabulum Filii Dei. Apud homines enim qui filius est, coepit esse quod filius est, et morte patris amittit hoc uocabulum. Frequenter autem et de filii uocabulo transit in uocabulum patris, cum genuerit filium: non est ergo proprium et uerum uocabulum filii in creatura, quia et esse coepit filius et potest hoc uocabulum non habere uel patris occasu uel cum idem ipse transfertur in uocabulum patris, etiam antequam condicio mortis obueniat. Solus autem Filius Dei uerus est filius, existens hoc sine initio, sine fine, semper habens Patrem, et numquam ipse, uti est genitus, generans, accipit uocabulum patris. Vnde et proprium et uerum uocabulum filii in solo Filio Dei est, habens hoc naturaliter, sicut et naturaliter uerus Deus est. Si ergo cognouimus quomodo proprium et uerum uocabulum Patris est, et quomodo proprium et uerum uocabulum Filii est, sequitur ut ita intellegamus quomodo proprium et uerum uocabulum est Spiritus Sancti, scilicet cum hoc ipsum est naturaliter Spiritus Sanctus, sine initio, sine fine: numquam enim ex aequa nominis auctoritate cum Patris et Filii ueris uocabulis Sancti Spiritus uocabulum iungeretur, si non et Sancti Spiritus proprium uerumque uocabulum probaretur.

50. (VII, 3) Si ergo hoc ei proprium et uerum et naturaliter, sine initio et fine uocabulum est, non est igitur creatura Spiritus Sanctus, qui ita proprium et uerum uocabulum Sancti Spiritus habet, sicut nulla potest habere creatura. Sed et cum praecipit Dominus ut gentes in nomine Patris et Filii et Spiritus Sancti baptizentur, apertissimum est Spiritum Sanctum non esse creaturam, uel ex ipsa societate quae illi una cum Patre et Filio est,

given by God. Indeed, he is called a father just as long as his son also lives. For just as he adopts the term "father" when his son is born, so too does he give up the term "father" when his son dies. But God alone is properly the true Father, who is the Father without beginning or end. For he did not begin to be a father at some time, but is always the Father, as he always has the Son begotten from himself, just as he is also always the true God, as he continues without beginning or end. Therefore, just as God alone retains the term "true God," so too does he alone enjoy the term "true Father," as he alone is called the Father without beginning or end.

This is how we should understand the true meaning of "Son of God." For among men, anyone who is a "son" began to be what a "son" is, and he gives up this term when his father dies. Moreover, he often switches from being termed a "son" to being termed a "father" after he begets a son.[365] The term "son" is thus not proper and true for a created being, both because he began to be a son and because he cannot keep this name, either when his father dies or when he himself switches to using the term "father" even before his father's death. The Son of God alone is the true Son, as he exists as such without beginning, without end, always has the Father, and is never termed a "father" by begetting as he was begotten. This is why the term "son" is proper and true for the Son of God alone, as he has it by nature, just as he is the true God by nature. If, then, we have understood how the term "Father" is proper and true, and how the term "Son" is proper and true, it follows that we thus understand how the term "Holy Spirit" is proper and true, since clearly this thing is the Holy Spirit by nature, without beginning and without end. For the term "Holy Spirit" would never be joined with equal authority in its name to the true terms of "Father" and "Son" unless the term "Holy Spirit" were also proven proper and true.

50. (VII, 3) Therefore, if this term is proper and true and natural for it, without beginning and end, then the Holy Spirit is not a created being, as it thus bears the proper and true term "Holy Spirit" as no created being could. Now, when the Lord ordered the nations to be baptized in the name of the Father and the Son and the Holy Spirit, it is also very clear that the

---

365. Though, of course, he would also remain a son; *patria potestas* was alive and well in late antiquity, though it became more common for fathers to formally emancipate their sons compared to earlier Roman periods (see Arjava 1998, esp. 161). On late antique Christian reticence toward identifying the father-son relationship with the Father-Son relationship, see Nathan 2000, 146–47.

uel quod numquam praeciperet Dominus ut in creaturae nomine aliquis baptizaretur: multum enim diuinae potentiae derogaret, si cum confessione diuini nominis par quoque creaturae confessio poneretur. Et bene quod unum nomen posuit dicens: *In nomine Patris et Filii et Spiritus Sancti*, ut una principalis auctoritas crederetur indiuisibilis et perfectae Trinitatis. Quomodo enim Spiritus Sanctus a principali auctoritate discretus esse credatur, quando de ipso scriptum legimus in quinquagesimo Psalmo: *Et spiritu principali confirma me*? Ergo et per hoc ostenditur quod una est principalitas Patris et Filii et Spiritus Sancti, siquidem et in omni condicione Patri et Filio consors inuenitur. Accipe interim uel unum testimonium: *Verbo Domini caeli firmati sunt, et spiritu oris eius omnis uirtus eorum*. Et per hoc ostenditur Spiritus Sanctus non esse creatura, siquidem et ipse cum Patre et Filio conditor adprobatur. Dicam plane et Deum et Dominum Spiritum Sanctum, doctus a maioribus ecclesiasticis uiris, qui et ipsi per testimonia Scripturarum diuinarum prius a uiris apostolicis eruditi, suis posteris tradiderunt. Exsequerer et ego singula illa quaeque testimonia, nisi apud animam fidelem de his quoque quae supra breuiter intimata sunt, Sancti Spiritus diuinitas eluceret: maxime quia et nunc mihi non tam disputatio de Sancto Spiritu proposita est, quam ut de diuino eius nomine pia confessio signaretur. Hoc tamen ad compendium probandae diuinitatis eius subdam, quod etiam per hoc ipsum Deus probatur Spiritus Sanctus, per quod ostenditur non esse creatura. Omne enim quod est, aut diuinitas aut creatura est: sed Spiritus Sanctus hoc ipsum existens, sine initio et fine, non est creatura: ergo Spiritus Sanctus res est diuinitatis, qua

Holy Spirit is not a created being, either because of its association in unity with the Father and the Son or because the Lord would never order that anyone be baptized in the name of a created being. It would greatly detract from his divine power if confessing a created being is established as equal to confessing the divine name. He did well to put down a single "name" when he said, *In the name of the Father and the Son and the Holy Spirit*,[366] so that one would believe in a single ruling authority of the indivisible and perfect Trinity.[367] For how can one believe that the Holy Spirit is separate from this ruling authority when we read what is written about it in the fiftieth Psalm: *And strengthen me with your ruling Spirit?*[368] Here, too, it is shown that there is a single ruling authority of the Father and the Son and the Holy Spirit, seeing as in every situation the Holy Spirit is found as a companion to the Father and the Son. For the time being, take just one testimony: *The heavens were made firm by the Word of the Lord, and all their strength by the breath [Spirit] of his mouth.*[369] It is also shown here that the Holy Spirit is not a created being, seeing as it is also proven to be a maker along with the Father and Son. I will openly call the Holy Spirit both God and Lord as I have learned from the past members of the church, who themselves were first instructed about the testimonies of divine scripture by apostolic men and handed down their instruction to posterity. I would also follow up on each individual testimony, except the divinity of the Holy Spirit is clear to the faithful soul out of those matters which were briefly related above—especially because a dispute about the Holy Spirit was not set before me so much as a pious confession about its divine name was called for. Nevertheless, I will supply this as a short way of proving its divinity: here too, where it is shown that the Holy Spirit is not a created being, it is proven to be God. For all that is, is either divinity or a created being. Now, the Holy Spirit, existing as such without beginning or end, is

---

366. Matt 28:19. In other words, the passage does *not* read, "In the *names* of the Father and the Son and the Holy Spirit." Hilary (*Trin.* 2.1–3) takes this passage to make a point similar to Faustinus's discussion of the nature of fathers and sons at §8 above and at the beginning of this section. On Hilary's use of this passage as regards the word *name*, see Toom 2010, 458–59.

367. This marks the first time that the word *Trinitas* appears in the *De Trinitate*.

368. Ps 50:14 LXX; the LXX reads *potenti*, not *principali*, for "ruling."

369. Ps 32:6 LXX. In Latin, *spiritus* can mean spirit or breath. There is an understood correlation here between *verbum* and *spiritus*, i.e., the "Word of the Lord" and the "Spirit/breath of his mouth." See Athanasius, *Ep. Serap.* 1.31; 3.5; Ambrose, *Spir.* 2.5.35.

incorruptibilis et indemutabilis et sempiternus Spiritus Dei. Vna est ergo diuinitas Patris et Filii et Spiritus Sancti, sicut et una sanctitas eiusdem perfectae et inseparabilis Trinitatis.

51. (VII, 4) Sed hic finem faciamus: inquantum enim quis intentior ad sacras Scripturas de fide loqui uoluerit, intantum non deerit quod loquatur. Hoc autem non ambigo, quod si quis forte eloquens haec ipsa legerit, delinquentiam incompti sermonis inueniet: non tamen, si fidelis est, piae confessionis errorem, quam quidem in nobis ex Dei gratia praestitam cupimus usque ad mortem, auxilio eius qui praestitit, uindicare sine labe communionis haereticorum atque praeuaricatorum, quia et Deo teste metuimus eorum damnationis participes inueniri. Viderit si quis putat se de eorum societate reum non posse fieri, habens fiduciam propriae conscientiae, qua integram fidem uindicat ita, ut numquam ipse eius fidei praeuaricator exstiterit: tamen ego in causa Dei cautius timere conpellor, siquidem et de ipsis cautum legimus: *Haereticum hominem post unam correptionem deuita, sciens quoniam peruersus est huiusmodi, et peccat et est a semetipso damnatus.* Sed et de poena praeuaricatorum legimus, dicente Esaia: *Et ueniet omnis caro in conspectu meo adorare in Hierusalem, dicit Dominus Deus. Et procedent sancti, et uidebunt membra hominum, qui praeuaricati sunt in me. Vermis eorum non morietur et ignis eorum non exstinguetur: et erunt in uisionem omni carni.* Sed et apostolus ait: *Nolite iugum ducere cum infidelibus,* quia et alibi idem apostolus post descriptionem malorum: *Non solum*—inquit—*qui faciunt ea, sed etiam qui consentiunt facientibus ea.* Et multa sunt alia testimonia diuina, quibus supradictorum consortium prohibetur. Sed ego haec ideo ipsa,

not a created being; thus the Holy Spirit is a thing of divinity, and as such it is the incorruptible, unchangeable, and eternal Spirit of God. Thus there is one divinity of the Father, the Son, and the Holy Spirit, just as there is one holiness of the same perfect and inseparable Trinity.[370]

51. (VII, 4) We should put an end to things here. For the more someone considers the sacred scriptures and wishes to speak about the faith, the more he finds to talk about. I do not hesitate on this point, though: if someone eloquent happens to read these things, he will find fault with this inelegant discourse.[371] But if he is faithful, he will not find an error of faith. Indeed, the faith was bestowed on us by the grace of God, and we long to defend it to the death with the help of the one who bestowed it and without the disgrace of communion with heretics and prevaricators, because with God as our witness we are afraid to be found partners in their damnation.[372] Let whoever thinks that he cannot be made guilty by association with them see to himself, trusting in his own conscience that he is defending the intact faith in such a way that he himself never stands out as a prevaricator concerning the faith. But I am compelled by fear to greater caution in the cause of God, seeing as we read a warning about them: *Shun a heretical man after a single reproach, knowing indeed that a man of such character is ruined, and sins and condemns himself.*[373] We also read about the punishment of prevaricators when Isaiah says, *And everybody will come into my sight to worship me in Jerusalem, says the Lord God, and the saints will go forth and see the limbs of men who have prevaricated about me. Their worm shall not die and their fire shall not go out, and they will be in everybody's view.*[374] Still, the Apostle too says, *Do not bear your yoke with the unbelievers,*[375] because elsewhere the same Apostle, after a description of evils, also says, *Not only those who do these things, but those too who agree with the ones doing them.*[376] There are many other divine testimonies in which fellowship with the aforementioned men is forbid-

---

370. See Hilary of Poitiers, *Trin.* 8.26; Ambrose, *Spir.* 3.16.109.
371. See above, §§1, 48.
372. Here, at the very end of the treatise, Faustinus veers into the territory covered by the *Libellus precum*.
373. Titus 3:10–11.
374. Isa 66:23–24. Isaiah traditionally reads "in satietatem visionis," "abhorrent in appearance" or "loathsome" to all flesh.
375. 2 Cor 6:14.
376. Rom 1:32.

licet breuiter, intimaui, ne nos de uana superstitione credat aliquis nolle communicare cum talibus, quos perspicit per diuinam sententiam reprobari. Diuinitas te incolumem ac beatam in fide sui nominis etiam in regno caelorum praestet cum tuis omnibus affectibus inueniri.

den. But I made these things known, albeit briefly, so that no one would believe that we do not hold communion with such men, whom he sees are condemned by divine judgment, from vain superstition.[377]

May the Divinity grant that you be found unharmed and blessed in the faith of his name and also in the kingdom of heaven with all you hold dear.

---

377. See Salzman 1987.

Pseudo-Athanasius, *Epistula* 50

1. Domino dilectissimo fratri Lucifero episcopo et confessori Athanasius in Domino salutem.

2. Deo favente corpore valentes misimus etiam nunc charissimum nostrum Eutychetem diaconem, ut tua quoque religiosa sanctitas, quod est nobis optandum et desiderabile, de tua incolumitate tuorumque omnium certiores nos efficere dignetur. Vobis namque confessoribus ac servis Dei viventibus credimus statum catholicae ecclesiae renovari, et, quod haeretici conscindere tentaverunt, hoc Dominum nostrum Iesum Christum per vos ad integrum restituere. (1037D)

3. Quamquam enim praecursores antichristi per potentiam huius mundi omnia egerint, ut exstinguerent lucernam veritatis, tamen divinitas per vestram confessionem clariorem eius lucem ostendit, ut neminem latere possit eorum fallacia. (1038C) Ante hac vel simulare poterant, nunc antichristi nominantur. Quis enim non exsecretur, qui eorum communionem tamquam maculam, ac virus anguis non fugiat? Omnis ubique ecclesia luget, omnis civitas gemit, senes episcopi in exsilio laborant, et haeretici dissimulant, qui, dum negant Christum, publicanos se effecerunt sedentes in ecclesiis, et exigentes vectigalia. O novum genus hominum, et persecutionis, quod adinvenit diabolus, ut ipsis ministris ad malefaciendum, et his tanta crudelitate uteretur!

Pseudo-Athanasius, *Epistle* 50

1. To his Lordship, the most beloved brother Lucifer, bishop and confessor, Athanasius sends greetings in the Lord.

2. Being well in body by God's favor, we have sent our dearest deacon Eutyches[1] so that your pious holiness might find it worthy to assure us that you and all those with you are safe, something hoped for and desirable to us. For we believe that the condition of the catholic church is renewed while you confessors and servants of God are still alive, and that through you, our Lord Jesus Christ is restoring in full that which the heretics have tried to tear apart.[2]

3. For although the forerunners of antichrist have tried everything through the power of this world to extinguish the lamp of truth, the divinity, through your confession, has shown its light all the more clearly,[3] so that their deceit cannot escape anyone's notice. Before this, they could dissemble; now they are called antichrists.[4] Who would not curse them? Who would not flee their blighted communion like he would the venom of a snake? Every church everywhere mourns, every city groans, old bishops toil in exile and heretics dissemble—heretics who, while they deny Christ, have made themselves tax collectors who sit in churches and draw revenues.[5] What a new breed of men and persecution the devil has invented, so that he might use these ministers for evildoing—and with such cruelty!

---

1. Otherwise unknown. It was not uncommon for bishops to send deacons, priests, or monks to one another to ascertain how local matters stood. See, e.g., Jerome, *Ep.* 89, 102.1 (= Augustine, *Ep.* 68.1).

2. This paragraph and the following establish that these letters were to be understood as being written during the Arian persecutions of the 350s.

3. See Matt 5:15–16; Pseudo-Athanasius, *Ep.* 51.5. There is an understood play on words between *lucerna* ("lamp"), *lux* ("light"), and the name *Lucifer* ("light-bringer").

4. In other words, Lucifer's writings have exposed heretics claiming to be orthodox for what they are.

5. Faustinus and Marcellinus frequently complain about bishops who sacrifice

4. Sed et si haec tanta agunt, et superbias et blasphemias extenderunt, confessio tamen, et religio, et sapientia vestra non modicum, sed maximum solatium et magna consolatio est fraternitati. (1038D) Pervenit enim ad nos scripsisse sanctitatem tuam Augusto Constantio, et magis magisque miramur, quia in medio tamquam scorpionum habitans, animi tamen libertate uteris, ut vel monendo, vel docendo, vel emendando errantes ad lumen veritatis adducas. Rogo igitur, rogant mecum etiam omnes confessores, ut digneris nobis exemplum destinare, ut non tantum auditu, sed etiam ex litteris perspicere possint omnes animae tuae virtutem, fideique fiduciam et libertatem.

5. Salutant sanctitatem tuam qui mecum sunt; saluto omnes qui tecum sunt. Divinitas te incolumem, vegetum, memoremque nostri semper tueatur, domine dilectissime ac vere homo Dei.

6. His acceptis litteris, beatus Lucifer misit libros quos ad Constantium scripserat; quos cum legisset Athanasius, hanc infra epistolam misit.

4. But even if they do such things as these, and have spread their arrogance and blasphemies, your confession, religious devotion, and wisdom nevertheless are the greatest comfort (not a modest one) and a great consolation for the brotherhood. For we know that Your Holiness has written to Emperor Constantius,[6] and we marvel all the more that while living as though in the midst of scorpions, you nevertheless employ your spirit's forthrightness[7] so that by warning, teaching, or correcting, you may bring sinners to the light of truth. I ask, then, and all the confessors ask with me, that you find it worthy to send us a copy so that everyone might be able to perceive your virtue, faith, fidelity, and forthrightness not only by hearing about it but also through your writings.

5. Those who are with me send their greetings to Your Holiness; I send greetings to all those who are with you. May the divinity keep you safe, lively, and always mindful of us, our most beloved Lordship and true man of God.

6. When he received this letter,[8] blessed Lucifer sent the books that he had written to Constantius. After Athanasius had read those, he sent the following letter.

---

orthodoxy in order to acquire material goods; see, e.g., *Lib. prec.* 16–17, 49, 61, 117, and esp. 121.

6. It is not clear which of Lucifer's five tracts addressed to Constantius is meant here, or whether the request for a "copy" is more general in nature; there seem to be references to both *Moriendum esse pro Filio Dei* and *Pro Sancto Athanasio* in the following letter. All five tracts are available in PL 13:767–1038 and CCSL 8, but only one (*Moriendum esse pro Dei Filio*) has been translated (Flower 2016, 141–86). Concerning their quality, Barnes (1993, 6) writes that the "violent and often hysterical diatribes of Lucifer contain distressingly little of real historical value." Hanson (1988, 508n4) likewise writes, "We have already had occasion to form no very high opinion of the subtlety of thought or elegance of the language of Lucifer of Calaris.... Almost everybody who writes about Lucifer finds him an intolerable bore and bigot."

7. *Libertas* here has the force of the Greek παρρησία, the "freedom of speech" that some could exercise before powerful men by virtue of their virtuous and moral behavior; the concept had a long pedigree in antiquity. See Rapp 2005, 267–73.

8. The authors of these supposed letters must also have composed this explanatory note.

Pseudo-Athanasius, *Epistula* 51

1. Domino gloriosissimo ac merito desiderantissimo coepiscopo Lucifero Athanasius in Domino salutem. (1039B)

2. Et si credo pervenisse etiam ad sanctitatem tuam de persecutione, quam etiam nunc adversus fraternitatem facere conati sunt inimici Christi, quaerentes sanguinem nostrum, possunt tamen etiam charissimi nostri referre religioni tuae: in tantum enim rabiem suam per milites extendere ausi sunt, ut non solum civitatis clericos effugarent, sed etiam ad eremitas exirent, et funestas suas manus adversus μονάζοντας immitterent. Inde factum est ut etiam ego me longius abducerem, ne etiam qui nos susceperunt, negotium ab eisdem paterentur. Cui etenim parcent Ariani, qui nec animis suis pepercerunt? Quando autem possunt recedere a suis nefandis actibus, dum permanent negando Dominum Christum, unicum Filium Dei? (1039C)

3. Haec est radix eorum pravitatis, hoc suo arenoso fundamento aedificant perversas suas vias, sicut scriptum invenimus in tertio decimo psalmo: *Dixit insipiens in corde suo: Non est Deus* (Ps 13:1). Et mox sequitur: Corrupti sunt, et abominabiles facti sunt in operibus suis (Ps 13:1). Inde Iudaei negantes Filium Dei digni fuerunt audire: *Vae, gens peccatrix, populus plenus delictis, semen malignum, filii sine lege. Unde sine lege?*

Pseudo-Athanasius, *Epistle* 51

1. To his Lordship, the most glorious and deservedly most missed fellow bishop Lucifer, Athanasius sends greetings in the Lord.

2. Even though I believe that news of it has come to Your Holiness, our dearest ones might still be able to report to Your Reverence on the persecution that the enemies of Christ, who were out for our blood, just now attempted to effect against our brotherhood. For they dared to spread their madness using soldiers[1] to such a degree that not only did they drive the clergy away from the city, but they even went out to the hermits and set their deadly hands against those living the solitary life.[2] Accordingly, it came to pass that I even secluded myself for fear that they would trouble those who supported me.[3] For whom do the Arians spare when they have not spared their own souls? How can they pull back from their unholy actions while they persist in denying the Lord Christ, the only Son of God?

3. This is the root of their depravity. They build their perverse ways on this sandy foundation, just as we find written in the thirteenth Psalm: *The fool has said in his heart, There is no God.*[4] And there soon follows: *They are corrupt, and have been made abominable in their works.* Thus the Jews, who deny God, deserved to hear this: *Alas, race of sinners, people full of offenses, seed of evils, sons without law. Why without law? Obviously because you*

---

1. Misuse of government agents, especially the military, is a common allegation used frequently by Faustinus and Marcellinus: see *Lib. prec.* 80, 96.

2. An interesting use of a Greek word (μονάζοντας) in a document otherwise composed in Latin; the word also appears (albeit in the Latin form *monazontes*) in Egeria, *Itinerarium Egeriae* 24.1; 25.2, 7, 12, and much later in Cassian, *Collationes* 18.5, as a synonym for the more common *monachi*.

3. Interestingly, Athanasius's tract *Apologia de fuga sua*, which he wrote as a justification for going into hiding during Constantius's persecutions under the bishop George of Cappadocia, ignores this point and focuses almost entirely on biblical examples of saints and Christ fleeing persecution.

4. Ps 13:1 LXX.

Quippe quia dereliquistis Dominum (Isa 1:4). Inde beatissimus Paulus cum coepisset non tantum credere in Filium Dei, verum etiam praedicare deitatem ipsius, scribebat: *In nullo mihi mali conscius sum* (1 Cor 4:4).

4. Ita iuxta vestram confessionem etiam nos optamus tenentes apostolicam traditionem vivere iuxta divinae legis mandata, ut possimus vobiscum inveniri in choro illo, in quo nunc exsultant patriarchae, prophetae, apostoli, ac martyres. Licet igitur Ariana insania cum extranea potentia ita se movebat, ut non liceret nec fratres, quantum illi saeviebant, libere aerem videre, tamen iuxta orationes tuas Deo favente, et si cum labore et periculo, videre potui fratrem, qui solet tam necessaria quam epistolas tam sanctitatis tuae quam aliorum destinare. (1040B) Accepimus itaque epistolas et libros religiosissimae ac sapientissimae animae tuae, in quibus perspeximus imaginem apostolicam, fiduciam propheticam, magisterium veritatis, doctrinam verae fidei, viam coelestem, martyrii gloriam, triumphos adversus haeresem Arianam, traditionem integram patrum nostrorum, regulam rectam ecclesiastici ordinis.

5. O vere Lucifer, qui iuxta nomen lumen veritatis ferens, posuisti super candelabrum ut luceat omnibus. Quis enim, exceptis Arianis, non pervidet ex tua doctrina veram quidem fidem, maculam autem Arianorum? (1040C) Valde et admirabiliter, ut est lumen a tenebris, ita separasti

have forsaken the Lord.[5] Thus the most blessed Paul, when he began not only to believe in the Son of God but also to proclaim his divinity, wrote, *In no way am I conscious of my own evil.*[6]

4. Thus in accordance with your confession, we, too, by remaining loyal to the apostolic tradition, chose to live in accordance with the commands of the divine law, so that we may be found with you in that choir where the patriarchs, prophets, apostles, and martyrs now rejoice.[7] Consequently, although the Arian insanity promoted itself with help from an outside force[8] so much that (this is how fierce those men were) the brethren could not freely see the air, with God's favor and in accordance with your prayers, I nevertheless have been able to see a brother who customarily brought both essential news and letters from both Your Holiness and from others, even though it took hard work and danger. And so we have received your most pious and wisest soul's letters and books, in which we have observed an apostolic likeness,[9] prophetic accuracy,[10] instruction in the truth, the doctrine of true faith, the heavenly path,[11] the glory of martyrdom, triumphs against the Arian heresy, the undiminished tradition of our fathers, and the fitting rule of our ecclesiastic order.

5. Truly, Lucifer, you who bring the light of truth in accordance with your name,[12] you have placed it on a lamp stand so that it might shine over everyone.[13] For who (except the Arians) would not perceive in your doctrine the true faith and the blight of the Arians? You have vehemently

---

5. Isa 1:4. The comparison between heretics and Jews is not made explicit in any of our other Luciferian writings, but Jerome (*Lucif.* 2, 9, 15) suggests that Luciferians commonly drew this equivalency. See Faustinus, *Trin.* 1.

6. 1 Cor 4:4.

7. See below, §7.

8. That is, the patronage of Constantius.

9. See Athanasius, *Ep.* 7.3.

10. The phrase also appears in Evagrius of Antioch's Latin version of Athanasius's *Vit. Ant.* 15; see Jerome, *Vir. ill.* 125. It is worth noting that in 388 Evagrius of Antioch became the successor to Paulinus of Antioch, who had been ordained by Lucifer while the Council of Alexandria was ongoing and who was firmly supported by Western Nicene Christians. See above, pp. 11–14.

11. A common enough phrase derived from John 14:6; for a roughly contemporaneous use around 396, see Victricius of Rouen, *Laude sanct.* 6.2; Clark 1999, 365–66. The phrase is used again below in §6.

12. As noted above (Pseudo-Athanasius, *Ep.* 50.3), *Lucifer* literally means "light-bringer."

13. See Matt 5:15–16; Pseudo-Athanasius, *Ep.* 50.3.

veritatem a calliditate et hypocrisi haereticorum, defendisti catholicam Ecclesiam, probasti nihil esse, sed tantum phantasiam Arianorum verba, docuisti calcandos esse frendores diabolicos. (1041A)

6. Quam bona et iocunda hortamenta tua ad martyrium, quam desideratissimam ostendisti mortem esse pro Christo Filio Dei, quam futuri saeculi et vitae coelestis amorem manifestasti! Videris esse verum templum Salvatoris, qui in te habitans haec ipse per te loquitur, ipse qui tantam gratiam praebuit sermonibus tuis, quippe qui ante eras apud omnes amabilis; nunc tamen tantus est amor affectionis tuae in animis omnium collocatus, ut Heliam te temporibus nostris nominent: et non mirum; si enim, qui Deo placere videntur, filii Dei nominantur, tanto magis participes prophetarum confessores, et maxime te appellare dignum est. Crede mihi, Lucifer, non tu solus haec locutus es, sed Spiritus sanctus tecum. Unde haec tanta memoria Scripturarum, unde sensus et intellectus earumdem integer? unde talis ordo sermonis compositus? unde tanta hortamenta in viam coelestem? (1041B) unde fiducia contra diabolum et probationes adversus haereticos, nisi Spiritus sanctus collocatus esset in te?

7. Gaude igitur in eo te esse iam pervidens, in quo etiam praedecessores tui nunc sunt martyres, hoc est in choro angelorum. Gaudemus etiam nos habentes et exemplum virtutis, et patientiae, et libertatis. Nam de his,

and admirably separated the truth from the duplicity and hypocrisy of the Arians like light from the shadows, you have defended the catholic church, you have proven that the words of the Arians are nothing but a great illusion, and you have taught that their diabolic gnashing of teeth must be avoided.

6. How good and pleasing are your exhortations to martyrdom, how exceedingly desirable you have shown death for Christ, the Son of God, to be,[14] how you have demonstrated love of the coming age[15] and the heavenly life! You seem like a true temple of the Savior, who lives in you and himself says these things through you, who himself offers so much grace in your discourses. Certainly everyone loved you before, but now there is so much affectionate love for you nestled in everyone's souls that they call you the Elijah of our times[16]—and no wonder, for if those who seem to please God are called the sons of God,[17] then all the more worthy is it to call confessors the companions of the prophets, and especially you. Believe me, Lucifer, you did not say these things alone, but the Holy Spirit with you. Where did your great recollection of the scriptures come from? Where did this complete perception and understanding of them come from?[18] Where did such well-composed lines of discussion come from? Where did such encouragements toward the heavenly path come from?[19] Where did your confidence against the devil and your proofs against heretics come from, unless the Holy Spirit had nestled in you?

7. Rejoice, then, at seeing that you are already there where your predecessors the martyrs are now too, that is, in the choir of angels.[20] We too rejoice at having the example of your virtue, patience, and forthright-

---

14. Probably a specific reference to Lucifer's *Moriendum esse pro Filio Dei*.

15. I.e., following Christ's return. For other Luciferian examples of the common distinction between this age and the age to come, see, e.g., Faustinus and Marcellinus, *Lib. prec.* 7, 22, 57, 85, 98, 102, 119.

16. High praise indeed! Jesus compares John the Baptist to Elijah or identifies the two (Matt 11:14; see Mark 6:15, Luke 9:8), and Jesus's disciples thought that he might be Elijah (Mark 8:28; John 1:21). In late antiquity, Theodoret compared Simeon Stylites to Elijah (*Hist. rel.* 7), and Shenoute's biographer Besa refers to the monk as a "new Elijah" (*Sin. Vit. Boh.* 7, 18; CSCO 129:3.30–31; 7.20). See Faustinus and Marcellinus, *Lib. prec.* 69, 111.

17. See 1 John 3.

18. See Faustinus and Marcellinus, *Lib. prec.* 90, on Lucifer's command of Scripture.

19. See above, §4.

20. See above, §4.

quae scripsisti de nomine meo, erubesco aliquid proferre, ne videar adulator; sed scio et credo ipsum Dominum, qui sancto et religioso animo tuo revelavit omnem notitiam, redditurum tibi etiam pro hoc labore praemium in regno coelorum. (1042A) Quia ergo talis es, precatorem te esse pro nobis per orationes Dominum petimus, ut iam inspicere dignetur, ut est misericors, ecclesiam catholicam, et eripiat omnes famulos suos de manibus persecutorum, quo etiam hi omnes, qui propter metum temporalem ceciderunt, levare se tandem possint, et reverti ad viam iustitiae, a qua seducti vagantur, nescientes in qua fovea sint miseri.

8. Specialiter autem ego peto, si aliquid minus a me dictum est, ignoscere digneris: a tanto enim fonte quod potuit imperitia mea vix haurire valuit. De fratribus autem nostris sin minus potui videre eosdem, iterum ignoscas peto. Est enim ipsa veritas testis optasse me et desiderasse hoc impetrare, et tantum habuisse dolorem quod non potui: nam nec lacrymae cessaverunt ab oculis, nec gemitus ab animo, quia nec fratres permittimur videre. Testis est autem Dominus, quia nec parentes quos habeo potui videre, ex quo persequuntur nos. Quid enim non faciunt Ariani? (1042B) itinera observant, curas agunt de proficiscentibus et exeuntibus de civitate, naves quaerunt, eremias gyrant, domos perturbant, concutiunt fratres, singulis negotia concinnant: sed Deo gratias; dum haec agunt, tanto magis et plus exsecrantur ab omnibus et cognoscuntur vere, ut dicit sanctitas tua, mancipia esse antichristi; et ipsi miseri, dum in odio habentur, durant in malignitate sua, donec morte avi sui Pharaonis et ipsi damnentur.

9. Salutant religionem tuam qui mecum sunt; dignare salutare qui tecum sunt. Divina Dei gratia incolumem te memorem nostri semper beatum

ness. Now, I am embarrassed to publicize anything that you have written about my name, lest I appear to be a flatterer. But I know and believe that the Lord himself, who has revealed all knowledge to your holy and pious soul, will yet give you a reward for this work in the kingdom of heaven. Thus, because you are such a man, we ask that you be an intercessor on our behalf through prayers to the Lord, so that he might then find it worthwhile (as he is merciful) to look after the catholic church and rescue all his servants from the hands of persecutors, and so that also all those who have fallen on account of momentary fear might be able to lift themselves back up and turn back to the path of justice, away from which they have been seduced and wandered, ignorant of what pit they are in as the wretches they are.[21]

8. I especially beg, however, that you find it worthwhile to forgive anything inferior I have said; my inexperience was scarcely capable of drawing from such a great well. Concerning our brethren, I beg you again to forgive that I have barely been able to see them. For the truth itself is my witness: I hoped and desired and tried to do this, and have had such sorrow that I have not been able to; tears have not stopped flowing from my eyes, nor wailing from my soul, because we have not been permitted to see the brethren. The Lord is my witness: because they persecute us, I have not been able to see my own parents. For what do the Arians not perpetrate? They watch the roads, they busy themselves about who enters and leaves the city, they search boats, they circle the deserts, they throw homes into disorder, they terrify the brethren, and they make trouble for every single person.[22] Still, thanks be to God—when they do these things, they are cursed more and more by everyone, and they are truly understood to be "servants of antichrist," as Your Holiness says.[23] These wretches, when they are hated, affirm their malice up till they are damned with the same kind of death as their ancestor, Pharaoh.[24]

9. Those with me greet Your Piety; find it worthy to greet those who are with you. May the divine grace of God keep you mindful of us and ever

---

21. See Ps 93:13 LXX.
22. A fascinating glimpse at how one Christian community might harass others.
23. See Lucifer of Cagliari, *Sanct. Ath.* 2, wherein Lucifer uses the phrase "servant [or 'slave'] of antichrist" in addressing Constantius in particular: "Ab apostolo iubeor animam ponere pro fratre [with reference to 1 John 3:16], et a te antichristi mancipio praecipitur mihi fratrem interimere."
24. See Faustinus and Marcellinus, *Lib. prec.* 6.

conservet, merito homo Dei, famule Christi, particeps apostolorum, solatium fraternitatis, magister veritatis, et in omnibus desiderantissime.

blessed, you who are worthily a man of God, servant of Christ, companion of the apostles, comfort of the brotherhood, teacher of truth, and in all respects most missed.

Bibliography

Allen, Pauline. 1990. "The Use of Heretics and Heresies in the Greek Church Historians: Studies in Socrates and Theodoret." Pages 265-90 in *Reading the Past in Late Antiquity*. Edited by Graeme Clark. Rushcutters Bay: Australian National University Press.

Ambrose. 1897. *De Abraham*. Edited by C. Schenkl. CSEL 32.1:501-638. Prague.

———. 1955. *De excessu fratris sui Satyri*. Edited by Otto Faller. CSEL 73:207-335. Vienna.

———. 1962. *De fide*. Edited by Otto Faller. CSEL 78:3-307. Vienna.

———. 1964. *De incarnationis dominicae sacramento*. Edited by Otto Faller. CSEL 79:225-81. Vienna.

———. 1964. *De Spiritu Sancto*. Edited by Otto Faller. CSEL 79:7-222. Vienna.

———. 1957. *Expositio Evangelii secundum Lucam*. Edited by M. Adriaen and P. A. Ballerini. CCSL 14:1-100. Turnhout: Brepols.

———. 1988. *Inni*. Edited by Manlio Simonetti. Biblioteca patristica 13. Florence: Nardini.

Ambrosiaster. 1908. *Quaestiones Veteris et Novi Testamenti*. Edited by Alexander Souter. CSEL 50. Vienna.

Ammianus Marcellinus. 1978. *Rerum gestarum libri qui supersunt*. Edited by Wolfgang Seyfarth with Liselotte Jacob-Karau and Ilsa Ulmann. 2 vols. Leipzig: Teubner.

Anderson, Øivind. 2001. "How Good Should an Orator Be?" Pages 3-16 in *The Orator in Action in Ancient Greece and Rome*. Edited by Cecil W. Wooten. Mnemosyne Supplements 225. Leiden: Brill.

Arjava, Antti. 1998. "Paternal Power in Late Antiquity." *JRS* 88:147-65.

Athanasius. 1935. *De decretis*. Edited by H.-G. Opitz. AW 2.1:1-40; 2.2:41-45. Berlin: de Gruyter.

———. 1935. *De sententia Dionysii*. Edited by H.-G. Opitz. AW 2.2:45-67. Berlin: de Gruyter.

———. 1935-1938. *Apologia de fuga sua*. Edited by H.-G. Opitz. AW 2.2:68-80, 2.3:81-86. Berlin: de Gruyter.

———. 1938-1940. *Apologia secunda*. Edited by H.-G. Opitz. AW 2.3:87-120; 2.4:121-60; 2.5:161-68. Berlin: de Gruyter.

———. 1940. *De Synodis Arimini et Seleuciae*. Edited by H.-G. Opitz. AW 2.6:231-40; 2.7:241-78. Berlin: de Gruyter.

———. 1940. *Epistula ad Serapionem*. Edited by H.-G. Opitz. AW 2.5:178-80. Berlin: de Gruyter.

———. 1940. *Epistula encyclica*. Edited by H.-G. Opitz. AW 2.5:169–77. Berlin: de Gruyter.

———. 1940. *Historia Arianorum*. Edited by H.-G. Opitz. AW 2.5:183–200; 2.6:201–30. Berlin: de Gruyter.

———. 1955. *S. Athanase, lettres festales et pastorales en copte*. Edited and translated by L.-Th. Lefort. CSCO 150. Leuven: Peeters.

———. 1996. *Epistula ad episcopos Aegypti et Libyae*. Edited by K. Metzler, D. Hansen, and K. Savvidis. AW 1.1:39–64. Berlin: de Gruyter.

———. 2000. *Epistula synodica ad Afros*. Edited by Hanns Christof Brennecke, Uta Heil, and Annette von Stockhausen. AW 2.8:322–39. Berlin: de Gruyter.

———. 2000. *Tomus ad Antiochenos*. Edited by Hanns Christof Brennecke, Uta Heil, and Annette von Stockhausen. AW 2.8:340–51. Berlin: de Gruyter.

Pseudo-Athanasius. 1957. *Eusebii Vercellensis quae supersunt*. Edited by Vincent Bulhart. CCSL 9. Turnhout: Brepols.

Augustine. 1891. *Contra Faustum*. Edited by Josef Zycha. CSEL 25.1:251–797. Prague.

———. 1900. *De agone Christiano*. Edited by Josef Zycha. CSEL 41:101–38. Prague.

———. 1910. *Scriptura contra Donatistas III*. Edited by M. Petschenig. CSEL 53:3–54. Vienna.

———. 1911. *Epistulae*. Edited by A. Goldbacher. CSEL 57. Vienna.

———. 1956. *Enarrationes in Psalmos*. Edited by E. Dekkers and J. Fraipont. 3 vols. CCSL 38–40. Turnhout: Brepols.

———. 1968. *De Trinitate*. Edited by W. J. Mountain and F. Glorie. CCSL 50. Turnhout: Brepols.

———. 1969. *De haeresibus*. Edited by M. P. J. van den Hout. CCSL 46:286–345. Turnhout: Brepols.

———. 1974. *Opus imperfectum contra Iulianum*. Edited by Michaela Zelzer. CSEL 85.1:3–506. Vienna.

———. 1992. *Confessions I: Introduction and Text*. Edited by James J. O'Donnell. Oxford: Clarendon.

Ausonius. 1921. *Epistles*. Edited and translated by Hugh G. Evelyn-White. LCL. Cambridge: Harvard University Press.

Ayres, Lewis. 2004. *Nicaea and Its Legacy: An Approach to Fourth-Century Trinitarian Theology*. Oxford: Oxford University Press.

———. 2014. *Augustine and the Trinity*. Cambridge: Cambridge University Press.

Bagnall, Roger S. 1993. *Egypt in Late Antiquity*. Princeton: Princeton University Press.

Bardy, G. 1929. "L'*Indiculus de Haeresibus* du Pseudo-Jérôme." *RevScRel* 19:385–405.

Barnes, T. D. 1992a. "The Capitulation of Liberius and Hilary of Poitiers." *Phoenix* 46:256–65.

———. 1992b. "Hilary of Poitiers on His Exile." *VC* 46:129–40.

———. 1993. *Athanasius and Constantius: Theology and Politics in the Constantinian Empire*. Cambridge: Harvard University Press.

Basil of Caesarea. 1926–1934. *Saint Basil: The Letters*. Edited and translated by Roy J. Deferrari. 4 vols. LCL. Cambridge: Harvard University Press.

Batiffol, P. 1920. "Les sources de l'*Altercatio Luciferiani et Orthodoxi* de St Jêrome." Pages 97–113 in *Miscellanea Geronimiana: Scritti varii pubblicati nel XV centena-*

rio dalla morte di San Girolamo. Edited by Vincenzo Vannutelli. Rome: Tipografia Poliglotta Vaticana.

Beatrice, Pier Franco. 2013. *The Transmission of Sin*. Translated by Adam Kamesar. Oxford: Oxford University Press.

Beckwith, C. L. 2005. "The Condemnation and Exile of Hilary of Poitiers at the Synod of Béziers (356 C.E.)." *JECS* 13:21–38.

———. 2008. *Hilary of Poitiers on the Trinity: From "De Fide" to "De Trinitate."* Oxford: Oxford University Press.

Besa. 1951. *Sinuthii vita Boairice*. Edited and translated by Hermann Wiesmann. CSCO 129. Leuven.

Binns, John. 1994. *Ascetics and Ambassadors of Christ: The Monasteries of Palestine, 314–631*. Oxford: Clarendon.

Blair-Dixon, Kate. 2007. "Memory and Authority in Sixth-Century Rome: The *Liber Pontificalis* and the *Collectio Avellana*." Pages 59–76 in *Religion, Dynasty, and Patronage in Early Christian Rome, 300–900*. Edited by Kate Cooper and Julia Hillner. Cambridge: Cambridge University Press.

Blumell, Lincoln H. 2012. *Lettered Christians: Christians, Letters, and Late Antique Oxyrhynchus*. Leiden: Brill.

Boersma, Gerald. 2016. *Augustine's Early Theology of Image: A Study in the Development of Pro-Nicene Theology*. Oxford: Oxford University Press.

Braun, R. 1977. *Deus Christianorum: Recherches sur le vocabulaire doctrinal de Tertullien*. Paris: Études Augustiniennes.

Brennecke, H. C. 1984. *Hilarius von Poitiers und die Bischofsopposition gegen Konstantius II*. Berlin: de Gruyter.

Brent, Allen. 1995. *Hippolytus and the Roman Church in the Third Century: Communities in Tension before the Emergence of a Monarch-Bishop*. Leiden: Brill.

Brumback, Richard Arwell, III. 2014. "*De Fide Orthodoxa* and Gregory of Elvira's Trinitarian Vision." PhD diss., Baylor University.

Buckley, Francis J. 1964. *Christ and the Church according to Gregory of Elvira*. Rome: Gregorian University Press.

Burns, Paul C. 1994. "Hilary of Poitiers' Road to Béziers: Politics or Religion?" *JECS* 2:273–89.

Cameron, Averil. 1991. *Christianity and the Rhetoric of Empire: The Development of Christian Discourse*. Sather Classical Lectures 55. Berkeley: University of California Press.

Canellis, Aline. 2001. "Arius et les Ariens vus par les Lucifériens dans le *Libellus Precum* de Faustin et Marcellin." StPatr 36:489–501.

———. 2003. *See* Jerome, *Dialogus contra Luciferianos*.

———. 2006. *See* Faustinus and Marcellinus, *Libellus precum*.

Capitula Sancti Augustini. 1978. Edited by F. Glorie. CCSL 85A:251–53. Turnhout: Brepols.

Carola, Joseph. 2005. *Augustine of Hippo: The Role of the Laity in Ecclesial Reconciliation*. Analecta Gregoriana 295. Rome: Editrice Pontificia Università Gregoriana.

Cassian, John. 1886. *Collationes*. Edited by Michael Petschenig. CCSL 13. Vienna: Geroldi.

Casson, Lionel. 1974. *Travel in the Ancient World*. London: Allen & Unwin.
Castelli, Elizabeth A. 2004. *Martyrdom and Memory: Early Christian Culture Making*. New York: Columbia University Press.
Cavallera, F. 1926. "Paul de Thèbes et Paul d'Oxyrhynque." *Revue d'ascétique et de mystique* 7:302–5.
Chadwick, Henry. 1976. *Priscillian of Avila: The Occult and the Charismatic in the Early Church*. Oxford: Clarendon.
Cicero. 1927. *Tusculan Disputations*. Edited and translated by J. E. King. LCL. Cambridge: Harvard University Press.
———. 1930. *Pro Q. Roscio comoedo*. Edited and translated by J. H. Freese. LCL. Cambridge: Harvard University Press.
Clark, Elizabeth A. 1992. *The Origenist Controversy: The Cultural Construction of an Early Christian Debate*. Princeton: Princeton University Press.
Clark, Gillian. 1999. "Victricius of Rouen: Praising the Saints." *JECS* 7:365–99.
de Clerq, Victor. 1954. *Ossius of Cordova: A Contribution to the History of the Constantinian Period*. Washington, DC: Catholic University of America Press.
Codoñer Merino, C. 1972. *El "Di viris illustribus" de Ildefonso de Toledo: Estudio y edición crítica*. Acta Salmanticensia, Filosofia y letras 65. Salamanca: Salamanca Universidad.
Coleman-Norton, P. R. 1966. *Roman State and Christian Church: A Collection of Legal Documents to A.D. 535*. 3 vols. London: SPCK.
Collectanea Antiariana Parisina. 1916. Edited by A. Feder. CSEL 65:43–205. Prague.
Conti, Marco. 1998. *The Life and Works of Potamius of Lisbon: A Biographical and Literary Study with English Translation and a Complete Commentary on the Extant Works of Potamius of Lisbon*. Instrumenta patristica 32. Turnhout: Brepols.
Cooper, Stephen A. 2016. "The Platonist Christianity of Marius Victorinus." *Religions* 7:122.
Corti, Giuseppe. 2004. *Lucifero di Cagliari: Una voca nel conflitto tra chiesa e impero alla meta del IV secolo*. Studia patristica Mediolanensia 24. Milan: Vita e Pensiero.
Crouzel, H. 1976. "Un 'résistant' toulousain à la politique pro-arienne de l'empereur Constance II: L'évêque Rhodanius." *BHE* 77:173–90.
Cyril of Jerusalem. 2004. *Catecheses mystagogicae*. Edited and translated by Auguste Piédagnel and Pierre Paris. SC 126. Paris: Cerf.
Damasus. 2015. *Damasus of Rome, The Epigraphic Poetry: Introduction, Texts, Translations, and Commentary*. Edited and translated by Dennis Trout. Oxford: Oxford University Press.
DelCogliano, Mark. 2010. *Basil of Caesarea's Anti-Eunomian Theory of Names: Christian Theology and Late-Antique Philosophy in the Fourth Century Trinitarian Controversy*. VCSup 103. Leiden: Brill.
Desmulliez, Janine. 2015. "Constantin et la christianisation de la Campanie." Pages 137–48 in *Constantino, ¿el primer emperador cristiano? Religión y política en el siglo IV*. Edited by Josep Vilella Masana. Barcelona: Publicacions i Edicions de la Universitat de Barcelona.
The Digest of Justinian. 1985. Translated by A. Watson with Latin text edited by T. Mommsen and P. Krüger. 4 vols. Philadelphia: University of Pennsylvania Press.

Doble, C. E. 1889. *Remarks and Collections of Thomas Hearne.* Vol. 3. Oxford: Clarendon.
Drake, H. A. 2015. "Speaking of Power: Christian Redefinition of the Imperial Role in the Fourth Century." Pages 291–308 in *Contested Monarchy: Integrating the Roman Empire in the Fourth Century A.D.* Edited by Johannes Wienand. Oxford: Oxford University Press.
Dunn, Geoffrey D. 2007. "Anastasius I and Innocent I: Reconsidering the Evidence of Jerome." *VC* 61:30–41.
Duval, Y.-M. 2001. "La place et l'importance du concile d'Alexandrie ou de 362 dans *l'Histoire de l'Église* de Rufin d'Aquilée (rôle d'Hilaire de Poitiers)." *REAug* 47:282–302.
Edwards, Mark J. 1999. *Galatians, Ephesians, Philippians.* ACCS New Testament 8. Downers Grove, IL: InterVarsity Press.
Egeria. 1994. *Itinerari Egeriae, sive, titulo prisco notati, Peregrinationis Aetheriae pars prior.* Edited by Clifford Weber. Bryn Mawr Latin Commentaries. Bryn Mawr, PA: Bryn Mawr College.
Elders, Leo J. 1996. "The Greek Christian Authors and Aristotle." Pages 111–42 in *Aristotle in Late Antiquity.* Edited by Lawrence P. Schrenk. Washington, DC: Catholic University of America Press.
Elm, Susanna. 1994. *Virgins of God: The Making of Asceticism in Late Antiquity.* Oxford: Clarendon.
Epiphanius. 1915. *Ancoratus.* Edited by Karl Holl. GCS 25:1–149. Leipzig: Hinrichs.
———. 1915–1933. *Panarion haereticorum.* Edited by K. Holl. Revised by J. Dummer. 3 vols. GCS 25:153–464; 31; 37. Berlin: Akademie.
Escribano, M. Victoria. 2005. "Heresy and Orthodoxy in Fourth-Century Hispania: Arianism and Priscillianism." Pages 121–49 in *Hispania in Late Antiquity: Current Perspectives.* Edited by Kim Bowes and Michael Kulikowski. Leiden: Brill.
Eusebius of Caesarea. 1902. *De laudibus Constantini.* Edited by I. A. Heikel. Eusebius Werke I. GCS 7:195–259. Leipzig: Hinrichs.
Eusebius of Vercelli. 1957. *Epistulae.* Edited by Vincent Bulhart. CCSL 9:103–10. Turnhout: Brepols.
Faustinus. 1721. *Faustinus the Presbyter, to the Empress Flacilla: Of the Trinity, Or, of the Faith against the Arians.* London: Phoenix.
———. 1967. *De Trinitate.* Edited by M. Simonetti. CCSL 69:295–353. Turnhout: Brepols.
Faustinus and Marcellinus. 2006. *Supplique aux empereurs: Libellus precum et lex augusta; Precede de Faustin, Confession de foi.* Edited and translated by Aline Canellis. SC 504:106–237. Paris: Cerf.
Fernández, G. 1993. "Constancio II, Osio de Córdoba y Potamio de Lisboa." Pages 311–16 in vol. 2 of *Actas del I Coloquio de Historia Antigua de Andalucia, Córdoba 1988.* Edited by Juan Francisco Rodríguez Neila. Cordoba: Cajasur.
Fernández Ubiña, José. 1997. "El *Libellus precum* y los conflictos religiosos en la Hispania de Teodosio." *Florentia iliberritana: Revista de estudios de antigüedad clásica* 8:103–23.

Ferrarini, A. 1981. "Tradizioni orali nella storia ecclesiastica di Socrate Scholastico." *Studia Patavina* 28:29–54.

Field, Lester L. 2004. *On the Communion of Damasus and Meletius: Fourth-Century Synodal Formulae in the "Codex Veronensis XL."* Studies and Texts 145. Toronto: Pontifical Institute of Mediaeval Studies.

Figus, Antonino. 1973. *L'enigma di Lucifero di Cagliari: A ricordo del XVI centenario della morte.* Cagliari: Fossataro.

Flower, Richard. 2013. *Emperors and Bishops in Late Roman Invective.* Cambridge: Cambridge University Press.

———. 2016. *Imperial Invectives against Constantius II.* Translated Texts for Historians 67. Liverpool: Liverpool University Press.

Fournier, Eric. 2006. "Exiled Bishops in the Christian Empire: Victims of Imperial Violence?" Pages 157–66 in *Violence in Late Antiquity: Perceptions and Practices.* Edited by H. A. Drake. Burlington, VT: Ashgate.

Galvão-Sobrinho, Carlos R. 2013. *Doctrine and Power.* Berkeley: University of California Press.

Garrett, James Leo, Jr. 1990. *Systematic Theology: Biblical, Historical, and Evangelical.* Vol. 1. Grand Rapids: Eerdmans.

Gennadius. 1896. *Hieronymus, Liber de viris inlustribus; Gennadius, Liber de viris inlustribus.* Edited by Ernest Cushing Richardson. Leipzig: Hinrichs.

Gesta episcoporum Neapolitanorum. 1878. Pages 398–466 in *MGH: Scriptores rerum Langobardicarum et Italicarum saec: VI–IX.* Edited by G. Waitz. Hanover.

Gilliard, Frank D. 1984. "Senatorial Bishops in the Fourth Century." *HTR* 1984:153–75.

Girardet, Klaus Martin. 1974. "Constance II, Athanase et l'édit d'Arles (353): A propos de la politique religieuse de l'empereur Constance II." Pages 63–92 in *Politique et théologie chez Athanase d'Alexandrie: Actes du colloque de Chantilly 23–25 septembre 1973.* Edited by Charles Kannengiesser. ThH 27. Paris: Beauchesne.

Gonis, Nikolaos. 2006. "Dionysius, Bishop of Oxyrhynchus, and His Date." *JJP* 36:63–65.

Grant, Mark. 2000. *Galen on Food and Diet.* London: Routledge.

Green, M. R. 1971. "The Supporters of the Antipope Ursinus." *JTS* 22:531–38.

Gregory of Elvira. 1967. *De arca Noe.* Edited by Vincent Bulhart. CCSL 69:147–55. Turnhout: Brepols.

———. 1967. *De fide.* Edited by Vincent Bulhart. CCSL 69:217–47. Turnhout: Brepols.

Gregory of Nazianzus. 1990. *Lettres.* Edited and translated by Pierre Maraval. SC 363. Paris: Cerf.

———. 2006. *Discours 27–31.* Edited and translated by P. Gallay. 2nd ed. SC 250. Paris: Cerf.

———. 2002. *Contra Eunomium libri I et II.* Edited by Werner Jaeger. Gregorii Nysseni Opera 1. Leiden: Brill.

Grelot, Pierre. 1971. "La traduction et l'interprétation de Ph 2, 6–7: Quelques éléments d'enquête patristique." *NRTh* 93:897–922, 1009–26.

Grig, Lucy. 2004. *Making Martyrs in Late Antiquity.* London: Duckworth.

Günther, Otto, ed. 1898. *Epistulae Imperatorum Pontificum Aliorum inde ab A. CCCLXVII usque ad A. DLIII datae Avellana quae dicitur Collectio*. 2 parts. CSEL 35. Prague.

Haehling, Raban von. 1978. *Die Religionszugehörigkeit der hohen Amtsträger des Römischen Reiches seit Constantins I: Alleinherrschaft bis zum Ende der Theodosianischen Dynastie (324-450 bzw. 455 n. Chr)*. Antiquitas 3. Bonn: Habelt.

Hanson, R. P. C. 1988. *The Search for the Christian Doctrine of God*. Edinburgh: T&T Clark.

Harries, Jill. 1999. *Law and Empire in Late Antiquity*. Cambridge: Cambridge University Press.

Harvey, Susan Ashbrook. 2006. *Scenting Salvation: Ancient Christianity and the Olfactory Imagination*. Berkeley: University of California Press.

Hefele, Charles Joseph. 1871. *A History of the Christian Councils from the Original Documents*. Vol. 1. Edinburgh: T&T Clark.

Pseudo-Hegemonius. 1957. *Adversus haereses*. Edited by A. Hoste. CCSL 9:325-29. Turnhout: Brepols.

Hilary of Poitiers. 1916. *Ad Constantium*. Edited by A. Feder. CSEL 65:181-87. Prague.

———. 1916. *Adversus Valentem et Ursacium*. Edited by A. Feder. CSEL 65:191-93. Prague.

Hirsch, Emil G. 1904. "Goliath." Pages 37-39 in vol. 6 of *The Jewish Encyclopedia*. Edited by Isaac Singer. 12 vols. New York: Funk & Wagnalls.

Holum, Kenneth G. 1982. *Theodosian Empresses: Women and Imperial Dominion in Late Antiquity*. Berkeley: University of California Press.

Honoré, Tony. 1998. *Law in the Crisis of Empire, 379-455 A.D.: The Theodosian Dynasty and Its Quaestors*. Oxford: Clarendon.

Humfress, Caroline. 2007. *Orthodoxy and the Courts in Late Antiquity*. Oxford: Oxford University Press.

Humphries, Mark. 1997. "In Nomine Patris: Constantine the Great and Constantius II in Christological Polemic." *Historia* 46:448-64.

Ilan, Z. 1995. "The Synagogue and Study House at Meroth." Pages 256-88 in *Ancient Synagogues: Historical Analysis and Archaeological Discovery*. Edited by Dan Urman and Paul V. M. Flesher. Leiden: Brill.

Isidore of Seville. 1911. *Etymologiae*. Edited by W. M. Lindsay. Oxford: Oxford University Press.

———. 1997. *El "De viris illustribus" de Isidoro de Sevilla: Estudio y edición crítica*. Edited by Carmen Codoñer. León: Gráficas Celarayn.

Jacobs, Andrew S. 2016. *Epiphanius of Cyprus: A Cultural Biography of Late Antiquity*. Christianity in Late Antiquity 2. Oakland: University of California Press.

Jerome. 1896. *Hieronymus, Liber de viris inlustribus; Gennadius, Liber de viris inlustribus*. Edited by Ernest Cushing Richardson. Leipzig: Hinrichs.

———. 1910. *Epistulae 1-70*. Edited by Isidore Hilberg. CSEL 54. Vienna.

———. 1956. *Die Chronik des Hieronymus*. Edited by R. Helm. GCS 47. Berlin: Akademie.

———. 1982. *Apologia contra Rufinum*. Edited by P. Lardet. CCSL 79:1-72. Turnhout: Brepols.

———. 1994. *Dialogue against the Luciferians*. NPNF 2/6:320–34.
———. 1996. *Epistulae 121–154*. Edited by Isidore Hilberg. CSEL 56.1. Repr., Vienna.
———. 2003. *Débat entre un Luciférien et un Orthodoxe*. Edited and translated by Aline Canellis. SC 473. Paris: Cerf.
———. 2007. *Jerome: Trois vies de moines: Paul, Malchus, Hilarion*. Edited and translated by P. LeClerc, E. M. Morales, and A. de Vogüé. SC 508:184–211. Paris: Cerf.
Kannengieser, Charles. 2004. *Handbook of Patristic Exegesis: The Bible in Ancient Christianity*. Leiden: Brill.
Kelly, J. N. D. 1975. *Jerome: His Life, Writings, and Controversies*. London: Duckworth.
———. 1978. *Early Christian Doctrines*. Rev. ed. San Francisco: HarperCollins.
Kelly, Kathleen Coyne. 2000. *Performing Virginity and Testing Chastity in the Middle Ages*. London: Routledge.
Kim, Young Richard. 2015. *Epiphanius of Cyprus: Imagining an Orthodox World*. Ann Arbor: University of Michigan Press.
Kraeling, Carl H., and C. Bradford Welles. 1967. *The Christian Building*. The Excavations at Dura-Europos 8.2. Monumenta archaeologica 5. New Haven: Yale University Press.
Krüger, Gustav. 1886. *Lucifer, Bischof von Calarius und das Schisma der Luciferianer*. Leipzig: Breitkopf und Härtel.
Lactantius. 1973. *Institutiones divinae*. Edited by Umberto Boella. Collezione Classiche della Filosofia cristiana 5. Florence: Sansoni.
Leader, Ruth E. 2000. "The David Plates Reconsidered: Transforming the Secular in Early Byzantium." *The Art Bulletin* 82:407–27.
Lequien, Michel. 1740. *Oriens christianus, in quatuor patriarchatus digestus: Quo exhibentur ecclesiae, partriarchae, caeterique praesules totius Orientis*. 4 vols. Paris.
Leroy-Molinghen, A. 1960. "La mort d'Arius." *Byzantion* 38:105–11.
Levine, Philip. 1955. "Historical Evidence for Calligraphic Activity in Vercelli from St. Eusebius to Atto." *Speculum* 30:561–81.
Leyerle, Blake. 2009. "Refuse, Filth and Excrement in the Homilies of John Chrysostom." *JLAnt* 2:337–56.
Libanius. 1921. *Libanii opera*. Vol. 10. Edited by R. Foerster. Leipzig: Teubner.
Lienhard, Joseph T. 1986. "Ps-Athanasius, Contra Sabellianos, and Basil of Caesarea, Contra Sabellianos et Arium et Anomoeos." *VC* 40:365–89.
———. 1989. "Basil of Caesarea, Marcellus of Ancyra, and 'Sabellius.'" *CH* 58:157–67.
———. 1999. *Contra Marcellum: Marcellus of Ancyra and Fourth-Century Theology*. Washington, DC: Catholic University of America Press.
Lim, Richard. 1995. *Public Disputation, Power, and Social Order in Late Antiquity*. TCH 23. Berkeley: University of California Press.
Livy. 1926. *History of Rome IV: Books 8–10*. Edited and translated by B. O. Foster. LCL. Cambridge: Harvard University Press.
Loseby, S. T. 2009. "Mediterranean Cities." Pages 139–55 in *A Companion to Late Antiquity*. Edited by Philip Rousseau. Chicester: Wiley-Blackwell.
Lössl, Josef. 2011. "The Bible and Aristotle in the Controversy between Augustine and Julian of Aeclanum." Pages 111–20 in *Interpreting the Bible and Aristotle in Late*

Antiquity: The Alexandrian Commentary Tradition between Rome and Baghdad. Edited by Josef Lössl and John W. Watt. Farnham, Surrey, UK: Ashgate.
Lucifer of Cagliari. 1978. *Luciferi Calaritani Opera quae Supersunt*. Edited by G. F. Diercks. CCSL 8. Turnhout: Brepols.
Lucretius. 1924. *On the Nature of Things*. Edited and translated by W. H. D. Rouse. Revised by Martin F. Smith. LCL. Cambridge: Harvard University Press.
Luiz Torres, Milton. 2008. "Christian Burial Practices at Ostia Antica." PhD diss., University of Texas at Austin.
Maier, H. O. 2005. "Heresy, Households, and the Disciplining of Diversity." Pages 213–33 in *Late Ancient Christianity: A People's History of Christianity*. Edited by Virginia Burrus. Vol. 2. Minneapolis: Fortress.
Marique, J. F.-M. 1963. "A Spanish Favorite of Theodosius the Great: Cynegius, Praefectus Praetorio." *CF* 17:43–65.
Martial. 1990. *Epigrammata*. Edited by D. R. Shackleton Bailey. Stuttgart: Teubner.
Martin, A. 1989. "Le fil d'Arius." *Revue d'histoire ecclésiastique* 84:297–333.
Matthews, John F. 1967. "A Pious Supporter of Theodosius I: Maternus Cynegius and His Family." *JTS* 18:438–46.
———. 2000. *Laying Down the Law in Late Antiquity: A Study of the Theodosian Code*. New Haven: Yale University Press.
———. 2010. "The Making of the Text." Pages 19–44 in *The Theodosian Code: Studies in the Imperial Law of Late Antiquity*. Edited by Jill Harries and Ian Wood. 2nd ed. London: Bristol Classical Press.
McLynn, Neil B. 1994. *Ambrose of Milan: Church and Court in a Christian Capital*. Berkeley: University of California Press.
Meslin, Michel. 1968. *Les Ariens d'Occident 335–430*. Patristica Sorbonensia 8. Paris: Seuil.
Muehlberger, Ellen. 2015. "The Legend of Arius' Death: Imagination, Space and Filth in Late Ancient Historiography." *Past & Present* 227:3–29.
Müller, Liguori G. 1956. "The 'De haeresibus' of Saint Augustine. A Translation with an Introduction and Commentary." PhD diss., Catholic University of America.
Nathan, Geoffrey S. 2000. *The Family in Late Antiquity: The Rise of Christianity and the Endurance of Tradition*. London: Routledge.
Novatian. 1972. *De Trinitate*. Edited by G. F. Diercks. CCSL 4:11–78. Turnhout: Brepols.
Ober, Josiah. 1989. *Mass and Elite in Democratic Athens: Rhetoric, Ideology, and the Power of People*. Princeton: Princeton University Press.
Olszaniec, S. 2013. *Prosopographical Studies on the Court Elite in the Roman Empire*. Translated by J. Wełniak and M. Stachowska-Wełniak. Toruń, Poland: Nicolaus Copernicus University Press.
Optatus. 1893. *De schismate Donatistarum*. Edited by Carolus Ziwsa. CSEL 26. Prague.
Origen. 1960. *Entretien d'Origène avec Héraclide*. Edited and translated by Jean Scherer. SC 67. Paris: Cerf.
———. 2001. *Contra Celsum*. Edited by M. Marcovich. VCSup 54. Leiden: Brill.
Ovid. 1924. *Tristia*. Edited and translated by A. L. Wheeler. Revised by G. P. Goold. LCL. Cambridge: Harvard University Press.

———. 1977. *Metamorphoses*. Edited by William S. Anderson. Leipzig: Teubner.
Papaconstantinou, A. 1996. "Sur les évêques byzantins d'Oxyrhynchos." *ZPE* 111:171–74.
Perez Mas, Javier. 2008. *La crisis luciferiana: Un intento de reconstrucción histórica.* SEAug 110. Rome: Institutum Patristicum Augustinianum.
Perrin, Michel-Yves. 2010. "The Limits of the Heresiological Ethos in Late Antiquity." Pages 201–27 in *Religious Diversity in Late Antiquity: An Introduction*. Edited by David M. Gwynn and Susanne Bangert. Leiden: Brill.
Phoebadius of Agen. 1999. *Contra Arianos: Streitschrift gegen die Arianer*. Edited by Jörg Ulrich. Fontes Christiani 38. Freiburg im Bresgau: Herder.
Pilsworth, Clare. 2000. "Dating the *Gesta martyrum*: A Manuscript-Based Approach." *EME* 9:309–24.
Possidius. 1919. *Vita Augustini*. Edited and translated by Herbert T. Weiskotten. Princeton: Princeton University Press.
Prestige, G. L. 1952. *God in Patristic Thought*. London: SPCK.
Prudentius. 1949. *Psychomachia*. Edited and translated by H. J. Thomson. LCL. Cambridge: Harvard University Press.
———. 1953. *Peristephanon*. Edited and translated by H. J. Thomson. LCL. Cambridge: Harvard University Press.
Quintilian. 2002. *The Orator's Education II: Books 3–5*. Edited and translated by Donald A. Russell. LCL. Cambridge: Harvard University Press.
Rapp, Claudia. 2005. *Holy Bishops in Late Antiquity; The Nature of Christian Leadership in an Age of Transition*. TCH 37. Berkeley: University of California Press.
Rebillard, Éric. 2009. *The Care of the Dead in Late Antiquity*. Ithaca, NY: Cornell University Press.
Ricciotti, Giuseppe. 1960. *Julian the Apostate: Roman Emperor (361–363)*. Translated by M. Joseph Costelloe. Milwaukee: Bruce.
Rossi, Giovanni Battista de, ed. 1871. "Epigrafe d'un sacro donario: In lettere d'argento sopra tabella di bronzo." *Bullettino di archeologia cristiana* 2/2:65–70.
Rougé, Jean. 1972. "La legislation de Théodose contre les hérétiques: Traduction de C. Th. XVI, 5, 6–24." Pages 635–49 in *Epektasis: Mélanges offerts au Cardinal Jean Daniélou*. Edited by Jacques Fontaine and Charles Kannengiesser. Paris: Beauchesne.
Rousseau, Philip. 1999. "Christian Culture and the Swine's Husks: Jerome, Augustine, and Paulinus." Pages 172–87 in *The Limits of Ancient Christianity: Essays on Late Antique Thought and Culture in Honor of R. A. Markus*. Edited by William E. Klingshirn and Mark Vessey. Ann Arbor: University of Michigan Press.
Rufinus. 1961. *Apologia ad Anastasium*. Edited by M. Simonetti. CCSL 20:19–28. Turnhout: Brepols.
———. 1999. *Die Kirchengeschichte*. Edited by E. Schwartz and T. Mommsen. GCS 2/6.2:951–1040. Berlin: Akademie.
Sághy, Marianne. 2000. "*Scinditur in partes populos*: Pope Damasus and the Martyrs of Rome." *EME* 9:273–87.

———. 2012. "*Renovatio memoriae:* Pope Damasus and the Martyrs of Rome." Pages 251–67 in *Rom in der Spätantike: Historische Erinnerung im städtischen Raum.* Edited by R. Berhwald and Ch. Witschel. Stuttgart: Steiner.
Saltet, L. 1906. "Fraudes littéraires des schismatiques lucifériens." *Bulletin de littérature ecclésiastique* 27:300–306.
Salzman, Michele R. 1987. "'Superstitio' in the Codex Theodosianus and the Persecution of Pagans." *VC* 41:172–88.
———. 2001. "Competing Claims to 'Nobilitas' in the Western Empire of the Fourth and Fifth Centuries." *JECS* 9:359–85.
Schor, Adam. 2009. "Performance and Social Strategy in the Letters of Theodoret." *JLAnt* 2:274–99.
Schwartz, Eduard. 1939. *Kyrillos von Scythopolis.* Leipzig: Hinrichs.
Shaw, Brent. 2003. "Judicial Nightmares and Christian Memory." *JECS* 11:533–63.
———. 2011. *Sacred Violence: Christians and Sectarian Hatred in the Age of Augustine.* Cambridge: Cambridge University Press.
Shephardson, Christine. 2014. *Controlling Contested Places: Late Antique Antioch and the Spatial Politics of Religious Controversy.* Berkeley: University of California Press.
Sherwood, Yvonne. 2004. "Binding-Unbinding: Divided Responses of Judaism, Christianity, and Islam to the 'Sacrifice' of Abraham's Beloved Son." *JAAR* 72:821–61.
Shuve, Karl. 2014. "The Episcopal Career of Gregory of Elvira." *Journal of Ecclesiastical History* 65:247–62.
Simonetti, Manlio. 1963a. "Appunti per una storia dello scisma luciferiana." Pages 67–81 in *Atti del convegno di studi religiosi sardi, Cagliari 24–26 maggio 1962.* Padua: Cedam.
———. 1963b. "Note su Faustino." *SacEr* 14:50–98.
———. 1965. *Studi sull'arianesimo.* Verba seniorum 5. Rome: Studium.
———. 1975. *La crisi arriana nel IV secolo.* SEAug 11. Rome: Institutum patristicum Augustinianum.
———. 1986. "Chapter II: Hilary of Poitiers and the Arian Crisis in the West." Pages 33–61 in *The Golden Age of Latin Patristic Literature from the Council of Nicaea to the Council of Chalcedon.* Vol. 4 of *Patrology.* Edited by A. di Berardino. Westminster: Newman.
———. 1998. "Lucifero di Cagliari nella controversia ariana." *Vetera Christianorum* 35:279–99.
Sirks, Adriaan J. Boudewijn. 2007. *The Theodosian Code: A Study.* Friedrichsdorf: Tortuga.
Smulders, Pieter. 1978. "Two Passages of Hilary's *Apologetica responsa* Rediscovered." *Bijdragen* 39:234–43.
———. 1988. "A Bold Move of Hilary of Poitiers: Est ergo erans." *VC* 42:121–31.
Socrates Scholasticus. 1995. *Sokrates Kirchengeschichte.* Edited by Günther Christian Hansen. GCS 2/1. Berlin: Akademie.
Sozomen. 1983. *Histoire ecclésiastique: Livres I–II.* Edited by Bernard Grillet and Guy Sabbah. Translated by André-Jean Festugière. SC 306. Paris: Cerf.

———. 1996. *Histoire ecclésiastique: Livres III–IV*. Edited by Bernard Grillet and Guy Sabbah. Translated by André-Jean Festugière. SC 418. Paris: Cerf.

———. 2005. *Histoire ecclésiastique: Livres V–VI*. Edited by Guy Sabbah. Translated by André-Jean Festugière and Bernard Grillet. SC 495. Paris: Cerf.

———. 2008. *Histoire ecclésiastique: Livres VII–IX*. Edited by Guy Sabbah and Laurent Angliviel de la Beaumelle. Translated by André-Jean Festugière and Bernard Grillet. SC 516. Paris: Cerf.

Steegen, Martijn. 2010. "To Worship to Johannine 'Son of Man': John 9,38 as Refocusing on the Father." *Bib* 91:534–54.

Stevenson, Walter. 2014. "Exiling Bishops: The Policy of Constantius II." *DOP* 68:7–27.

Strobel, Karl. 2007. "Strategy and Army Structure between Septimius Severus and Constantine the Great." Pages 267–85 in *A Companion to the Roman Army*. Edited by Paul Erdkamp. Malden, MA: Wiley-Blackwell.

Suetonius. 1914. *Lives of the Caesars II*. Edited and translated by J. C. Rolfe. LCL. Cambridge: Harvard University Press.

Sulpicius Severus. 1866. *Chronicon*. Edited by Karl Hahn. CSEL 1:3–105. Vienna.

Tertullian. 1890. *De anima*. Edited by Augustus Reifferscheid and Georg Wissowa. CSEL 20:298–396. Prague.

———. 1906. *Adversus Marcionem*. Edited by Emil Kroymann. CSEL 47:290–650. Vienna.

———. 1906. *Adversus Praxeam*. Edited by Emil Kroymann. CSEL 47:227–89. Vienna.

———. 1966. *De corona militis*. Edited by J. Fontaine. Paris: Presses Universitaires de France.

Testini, P. 1979. "Indagini nell'area di S. Ippolito all'Isola Sacra: L'iscrizione del vescovo Heraclida." *Rendiconti della Pontificia Accademia Romana di Archeologia* 51–52:35–46.

Tetz, Martin. 1975. "Über nikäische Orthodoxie: Der sog. Tomus ad Antiochenos des Athanasios von Alexandrien." *ZNW* 66:194–222.

Theodoret. 1911. *Theodoret Kirchengeschichte*. Edited by Léon Parmentier. GCS 19. Leipzig: Hinrichs.

———. 2006. *Théodoret de Cyr, Histoire philothée 1–13 (Histoire des moines des Syries); Histoire religieuse*. Edited and translated by M. Pierre Canivet and Alice Leroy-Molinghen. SC 234. Paris: Cerf.

Theodosiani libri XVI cum constitutionibus Sirmondianis. 1905. Edited by Th. Mommsen and Paulus M. Meyer. Berlin.

Theodosius. 2006. *Supplique aux empereurs: Libellus precum et lex augusta; Precede de Faustin, Confession de foi*. Edited and translated by Aline Canellis. SC 504:236–43. Paris: Cerf.

Tilley, Maureen. 2001. "Theologies of Penance during the Donatist Controversy." StPatr 35:330–37.

———. 2007. "When Schism Becomes Heresy in Late Antiquity: Developing Doctrinal Deviance in the Wounded Body of Christ." *JECS* 15:1–21.

Toom, Tarmo. 2010. "Hilary of Poitiers' *De Trinitate* and the Name(s) of God." *VC* 64:456–79.

Torbus, Sławomir. 2008. "Le troisième ciel dans 2 Co 11, 30–12, 10." *Pallas* 78:353–59.

Trout, Dennis. 2015. *See* Damasus, *Epigrammata*.
Turcescu, Lucian. 2005. *Gregory of Nyssa and the Concept of Divine Persons*. Oxford: Oxford University Press.
Turner, E. G. 1952. "Roman Oxyrhynchus." *Journal of Egyptian History* 38:78–93.
———. 1975. "Oxyrhynchus and Rome." *HSCP* 79:1–24.
Urbano, Arthur P. 2013. *The Philosophical Life: Biography and the Crafting of Intellectual Identity in Late Antiquity*. Patristic Monograph Series 21. Washington, DC: Catholic University of America Press.
Van Dam, Raymond. 1992. *Leadership and Community in Late Antique Gaul*. Berkeley: University of California Press.
Victricius of Rouen. 1985. *De laude sanctorum*. Edited by J. Mulders. CCSL 64:67–93. Turnhout: Brepols.
Vincent of Lérins. 2008. *The Commonitory of Saint Vincent of Lerins/Adversus profanas omnium novitates haereticorum commonitorium*. Edited and translated by C. A. Heurtley. Sainte-Croix-du-Mont, France: Tradibooks.
Wallraff, Martin. 1997. *Der Kirchenhistoriker Sokrates: Untersuchungen zu Geschichtsdarstellung, Methode und Person*. Göttingen: Vandenhoeck & Ruprecht.
Weedman, Mark. 2007a. "Hilary and the Homoiousians: Using New Categories to Map the Trinitarian Controversy." *CH* 76:491–510.
———. 2007b. *The Trinitarian Theology of Hilary of Poitiers*. VCSup 89. Leiden: Brill.
Wiles, Maurice. 1996. *Archetypical Heresy: Arianism through the Centuries*. Oxford: Clarendon.
Williams, Daniel H. 1992. "The Anti-Arian Campaigns of Hilary of Poitiers and the 'Liber contra Auxentium.'" *CH* 61:7–22.
———. 1997. *Ambrose of Milan and the End of the Arian-Nicene Conflicts*. Oxford: Clarendon.
———. 2001. "Defining Orthodoxy in Hilary of Poitiers' *Commentarium in Matthaeum*." *JECS* 9:151–71.
———. 2006. "Monarchianism and Photinus of Sirmium as the Persistent Heretical Face of the Fourth Century." *HTR* 99:187–206.
Williams, Rowan. 2002. *Arius: Heresy and Tradition*. Rev. ed. Grand Rapids: Eerdmans.
Wilmart, A. 1908. "La tradition des opuscules dogmatiques de Foebadius, Gregorius Illiberitanus, Faustinus." *Sitzungsberichte der Kaiserlichen Akademie der Wissenschaften in Wien, Philosophisch-historische Klasse* 159:1–34.
Wolters, A. 2000. "Confessional Criticism and the Night Visions of Zechariah." Pages 90–117 in *Renewing Bible Criticism*. Edited by Craig Bartholomew, Colin Greene, and Karl Möller. Grand Rapids: Zondervan.
Wood, Jamie. 2012. "Playing the Fame Game: Bibliography, Celebrity, and Primacy in Late Antique Spain." *JECS* 20:613–40.
Zahn, T. 1867. *Marcellus von Ankyra: Ein Beitrag zur Geschichte der Theologie*. Gotha: Perthes.
Zanker, Paul. 1995. *The Mask of Socrates: The Image of the Intellectual in Antiquity*. Sather Classical Lectures 59. Berkeley: University of California Press.

Zosimus. 2000. *Histoire nouvelle*. Edited and translated by François Paschoud. 2nd ed. 3 vols. Paris: Les belles lettres.

Scripture Index

Hebrew Bible/Old Testament

Genesis
- 1:6–7 — 191
- 1:26 — 193, 195, 279
- 1:27 — 161, 185, 193–95
- 18:19–19:29 — 119
- 21:1–7 — 239
- 22:12 — 237–41

Exodus
- 7:13 — 67, 231
- 17:11–12 — 95
- 18:4 — 291
- 30:30 — 285

Leviticus
- 8:12 — 285

1 Samuel
- 2:25 — 105
- 10:1 — 285
- 17:50 — 219–21

2 Samuel
- 12:7 — 285

1 Kings
- 18:16–46 — 119
- 19:10–14 — 159

2 Kings
- 2:11 — 233
- 10:18–28 — 119
- 10:30 — 121

Psalms (LXX)
- 2:6 — 287, 295
- 2:11 — 285
- 8:5 — 8:5
- 13:1 — 321
- 13:3 — 73, 165, 167, 297
- 21:6 — 243
- 32:6 — 311
- 33:9 — 297
- 36:9 — 205–7
- 44:8 — 287
- 46:22 — 147
- 50:12 — 303
- 50:14 — 311
- 58:17 — 301
- 61:2 — 285
- 81:6 — 307
- 81:7 — 307
- 93:13 — 327
- 101:25 — 257
- 102:26–28 — 265
- 103:24 — 189, 191, 303
- 109:1 — 257
- 109:3 — 255–61
- 110:4 — 287

Proverbs
- 8:22 — 46, 47, 183, 295–301
- 8:25 — 259–61, 297–99
- 9:9 — 233
- 10:2 — 71

Isaiah (LXX)
- 1:4 — 323
- 11:2 — 253

Isaiah (LXX) (cont.)

45:14–16	265–67
53:1–9	271–73
61:1	287
66:23–24	313
66:24	73

Jeremiah

1:5	235
6:13–14	165
6:15	165

Daniel

2:22	205
3	157
6	157

Micah

6:10	71

Zechariah (LXX)

2:6–9	261–63

Apocryphal/Deuterocanonical Books

Wisdom

1:6	167
3:4	167
4:7	167
4:20–5:1	95
5:1	93
7:21	265
7:23	263
7:26–27	263
7:27	263

Sirach

48:13–15	233

Baruch

3:10–13	295
3:20	295
3:36–38	267

2 Maccabees

7:35	263
9:5	71
9:9	73

New Testament

Matthew

3:14	223
3:17	223–31
4:2	275
5:15–16	323
6:9	273
6:24	293
7:21	273
8:12	255
9:9	293
10:22	109
10:32	113
10:33	113
11:11	243
11:14	325
15:13	229
16:13	229
16:14	233
16:16	231
17:2	227
17:5	227, 231
20:28	277
21:31	233
22:41–46	257
23:3	273
23:10	135
26:38	245, 275
27:11–26	95
27:50	275
28:19	307, 311

Mark

1:35	273
2:14	293
6:15	325
8:28	325
14:62	229

General Index

Luke
- 1:44 — 233
- 2 — 273
- 2:7–13 — 167
- 2:52 — 275
- 4:16–20 — 287
- 9:8 — 325
- 10:38–42 — 157
- 12:16–19 — 99
- 12:20 — 99
- 12:43 — 99
- 16:19–26 — 99
- 16:22 — 235
- 19:41 — 275
- 22:41–42 — 273
- 22:43 — 275
- 23:43 — 179

John
- 1:1 — 46, 185–87, 197
- 1:1–1:2 — 197
- 1:2 — 187
- 1:3 — 187, 189, 293
- 1:14 — 197–99, 225, 267, 275–77, 291–93, 303
- 1:18 — 48–49, 233–35, 279
- 1:21 — 325
- 2:16 — 229
- 3:16 — 235, 239, 245
- 5:9 — 273
- 5:19 — 279
- 5:21 — 279
- 5:23 — 279
- 6:38 — 209–11, 213, 273–75, 279, 281
- 8:28–8:29 — 211–13
- 8:29 — 279
- 8:34 — 285, 293
- 8:40 — 289
- 8:56 — 245
- 9:35 — 229
- 10:30 — 207–9, 211–13, 217, 279
- 10:38 — 211–13
- 11:33 — 275
- 11:35 — 275
- 12:49 — 209–11, 281
- 13:23 — 233
- 14:6 — 323
- 14:7 — 203
- 14:9 — 199–201, 279
- 14:10 — 199–203, 211–13, 279
- 14:12 — 213
- 14:27 — 111, 165
- 14:28 — 46, 47, 211, 275–83
- 15:26 — 253
- 17:1 — 273
- 17:3 — 47
- 17:10 — 279
- 17:20–21 — 209
- 18:28–40 — 95
- 19:25 — 251
- 19:26 — 249
- 19:28 — 275
- 19:35 — 251
- 20:30–31 — 247
- 21:20 — 249, 251

Acts
- 1:18 — 71
- 2:22 — 289
- 2:36 — 46, 47, 283, 289
- 4:32 — 209
- 9:15 — 109, 237
- 10:37–38 — 289
- 11:26 — 135
- 12:23 — 73
- 19:11 — 97
- 20:13–37 — 155
- 20:37–38 — 153
- 21:8–9 — 151

Romans
- 1:1 — 285
- 1:25 — 247
- 1:32 — 313
- 4:13 — 245
- 5:6–9 — 241–45
- 5:19 — 269
- 6:12 — 293
- 7:7 — 121
- 7:14 — 121

Romans (cont.)
8:8	109, 111, 135, 165
8:32	237–39, 245
12:11	69, 113, 133

1 Corinthians
1:24	183, 185, 219, 305
2:8	289
2:12	253
3:8	209
4:4	323
8:6	191
11:19	73
15:22	271

2 Corinthians
6:14	313
12:2	275
13:3	279

Galatians
1:8	109
2:18	109

Philippians
1:29	67
2:5–7	189
2:6	279–81
2:6–7	225, 243, 271
2:7	229, 281
3:20	139

Colossians
1:15	219, 267
1:16	191
1:16–17	189
1:17	261
2:5	105

1 Timothy
1:17	201
2:5	289
4:1	89
6:3	135

2 Timothy
4:1	97

Titus
3:10–11	313

Hebrews
1:3	267, 279
1:10–12	265
1:13	257
2:6	265
2:7	243
2:9	275–77
2:10	277
11:37	147
11:37–38	145

1 Peter
4:5	97
4:12–19	167

2 Peter
2:6	73

1 John
1:5	249
2:15	249
2:22	251
2:23	251
3:16	327
5:1	255
5:20	251–55

Revelation
1:5	69, 77, 95
3:14	263
17:14	69, 77, 95
19:16	69, 77, 95

General Index

Aaron, 287
Abraham, 235–45
Acacius of Caesarea, 157
Adam, 21, 269–71, 285, 293
adoption, 46–47, 49, 181–83, 185, 197–99, 223, 227, 231–35, 247, 295, 305
Adrianople, 30, 40, 117
adultery, 115, 151
Africa. *See* North Africa
Ahab, 119, 159
Alexander of Alexandria, 3–4, 6, 69
Alexander of Constantinople, 69, 73, 79
Alexandria, 3–4, 6, 9
    Council of, 8–15, 36, 67, 81, 83–85, 91, 107–9, 115, 323
altars, 32, 38, 69, 125, 145, 159
Ambrose of Milan, 18, 23, 25, 45, 48, 83, 93, 117, 221, 225, 275
angels, 109, 215, 243, 257, 265, 275, 307, 325
Anicius Auchenius Bassus. *See* Bassus
anointing, 285–89
anthropomorphites, 161, 257–59
antichrist, 251, 291, 317, 327
Antioch, 9–11, 30, 81, 161. *See also* Euzoïus of Antioch; Meletius of Antioch; Paulinus of Antioch
    Council of (341), 17
    "Luciferians" at, 11–14, 16
Antony (ascetic), 141
Apollinarianism, 16, 18, 21, 24, 61, 161, 171
Apollonius of Oxyrhynchus, 69, 149
apostasy, 69, 89, 91

appearance, 193–99, 207, 217–19, 271, 279, 281
Aquileia, Council of, 275
Arcadius, 25, 44, 52, 63, 89, 177
Arians, 1, 3–10, 14, 16, 18, 24. *See also* Arius
    and the *De Trinitate*, 43, 45–50, 52
    English, 55–57
    treatise of, sent to Flacilla, 43, 47, 177, 181, 205, 209, 221, 223
    and the *Libellus precum*, 26–28, 32, 37
Aristotle, 45, 50, 203–5, 249, 255. *See also* philosophy
Arius, 3–4, 10, 26–27, 36, 56, 67–75, 79, 89, 163, 171–73, 195, 207–9, 291. *See also* Arians
Arles, 4
    Council of, 6, 79, 99
army. *See* military
asceticism, 29, 34, 37, 85–87, 127, 137–47, 151. *See also* monasteries; virgins, dedicated; wealth
Asia Minor, 3, 4, 105, 153
assumption of humanity, 189, 223–35, 243–45, 267–85, 289–91
Asterius, 38, 131–33
Athanasius, 3, 6–8, 18–19, 36, 45, 48, 51, 57, 69, 79, 83, 87, 137, 141, 297, 317–29
Augusta (title), 44
Augustine of Hippo, 20, 21–22, 23, 25, 36, 51, 205, 225
Aurelius of Rome, 27, 29, 42, 127, 129, 133. *See also* Rome

Auxentius of Milan, 18, 81–83
baptism, 103, 221, 223–25, 289, 307, 311.
    See also rebaptism
Basil of Ancyra, 48, 307
Basil of Caesarea, 17–19, 48, 151, 297
Bassus, 31, 34, 133–35
begotten, as opposed to created, 46–50,
    59–61, 71, 181–83, 185, 195–99, 203,
    209, 215–17, 219–61, 267, 283, 289–
    91, 297–305, 307, 309–13
Besa, 325
Béziers, Council of, 7, 83
blindness (spiritual), 193, 207, 295–97
Bonosus of Trier, 27, 29, 125–27. See also
    Trier
book burning, 4
burial, 29, 36, 38, 131
Caecilian, 4
Caelestinus, 121
Capitula Sancti Augustini, 20
Catholic Church, 55, 65
catholicus (term), 65
christ (term), 285–89, 293
Chrysopolis, 4
churches (buildings), 9–10, 38, 69, 99–
    101, 115, 121–25, 131, 145, 149, 163,
    165, 317
Cicero, 31, 179
classical literature, 39, 50, 83, 203–5, 211.
    See also philosophy
Clementine, 31, 52, 93–97
clergy
    Christ as a cleric, 285–89, 293–95
    deacons, 3, 6, 9, 13, 17, 83, 85, 99, 129,
        141, 149, 157, 317
    episcopacy, 9, 15, 54, 95, 101, 103, 107,
        111–13, 117–19, 123, 145, 161
    leniency toward, 8–10, 13, 15, 28, 30,
        65–67, 75, 83, 107–9, 115, 127,
        129
    as messengers/legates, 6–7, 9, 29, 59,
        75–77, 79–81, 317, 323
    ordination, 9–10, 12–13, 28–29, 79,
        83, 85, 103, 107, 113, 115, 127, 131,
        133, 141–43, 151, 157, 323

clergy (cont.)
    presbyters, 1–3, 5, 25, 29, 38, 59, 93,
        121–33, 141, 149, 169
    reordination, 28–29, 103, 141, 145,
        147–49
Codex Theodosianus, 41–42
Collectio Avellana, 53–54
Commagene, 135
communion, 4, 9–10, 12–14, 18, 24, 28,
    36, 47, 48, 221, 313–15, 317
    and the *Libellus precum*, 69, 77, 79, 83,
        85, 87, 91–93, 99–107, 113, 121,
        127, 129–31, 139–41, 151–53, 157,
        159, 163, 173
Confessio fidei, 1–2, 14, 17, 24, 26, 53–55
confessor, 85, 107, 109, 115, 317, 319,
    325. See also martyrs
Constans, 5
Constantine, 3–5, 7, 28, 44, 67, 69, 79, 85
Constantine II, 5
Constantinople, 1, 4, 33, 40, 42–44, 48,
    52, 105, 155, 157
Constantius II, 5–8, 26–27, 31–32, 59,
    65, 73–83, 87, 89, 91, 105, 115, 127,
    135–37, 157, 163, 173, 319, 321, 323
Cordoba, 93, 123–25. See also Hosius of
    Cordoba
Council of Nicaea. See Nicaea, Council of
courtroom scenes. See trials
created, as opposed to begotten, 46–50,
    59–61, 71, 181–83, 185–203, 215–17,
    219–61, 283–305, 307–13
creeds, 6–9, 15, 18, 24, 46, 48, 59, 181. See
    also Nicene Creed; Sirmian Creed
    and the *Libellus precum*, 26–27, 37, 65,
        67, 79, 81, 83, 85, 89, 91, 107, 125,
        149, 157
cross/crucifixion, 221, 229, 239, 245,
    275–77, 281, 283, 289
Cynegius, 2, 40–42, 171, 175
Cyprus, 159
Cyril of Jerusalem, 157
Damasus of Rome, 12, 17–18, 25, 29,
    31–32, 36–37, 42, 54, 129–35, 143. See
    also Rome

Daniel, 157, 205
Dated Creed, 8
David, 50, 205, 219–21, 257
deacon. *See* clergy
decurions, 29, 35, 123–25
demons, 34, 87, 89, 127, 307
De Trinitate, 2–3, 14, 16, 26, 43–50, 57
   anonymous translation, 55–57
   authorship, 43, 44–45
   date, 44
   outline, 46–48
   sources, 48
   style, 48–50
   text and editions, 51–55
devil. *See* Satan/devil
Dialogus adversus Luciferianos. *See* Jerome
Diocletian, 85, 105
Dionysius of Milan, 6, 27, 81–83, 105
Dionysius of Oxyrhynchus, 141
docetism, 277
Donatists, 4, 16, 35–36, 131, 135, 145
Dorotheus of Oxyrhynchus, 149
Dura-Europos, 221
Eastern prefect. *See* Cynegius
Edict of Thessalonica, 42
Egypt, 3, 27, 29, 33, 69, 103, 137, 139–49, 265. *See also* Oxyrhynchus; Thebaid
Eleutheropolis, 27, 29–30, 32–33, 36, 79, 129, 135, 143, 149
Elijah, 39, 119, 159, 227, 233, 325
English Arianism, 55–57
Ephesius of Rome, 27, 29, 31–32, 34, 129, 133–35, 143, 151–55. *See also* Rome
Epictetus of Centumcellae, 85–87
Epiphanius of Salamis, 16, 19, 157–59
eternality, 46, 71, 175, 181–83, 185–91, 201, 205–207, 215, 241, 245, 247–49, 255, 265, 275, 301–3, 309–13
Eucharist, 125
Eunomius, 205
eunuch, 237
Eusebius of Caesarea, 10, 297
Eusebius of Vercelli, 6, 9–10, 13, 27, 51, 81–83, 91, 105, 107, 141, 159
Eutychius of Eleutheropolis, 157–59

Euzoïus of Antioch, 9, 157
Evagrius of Antioch, 323
exile, 4, 6–9, 11, 26–28, 32–33, 37, 67, 75, 77, 79–87, 89, 91, 95–97, 103, 105–7, 109, 115, 121, 127, 131, 133, 137, 141, 143, 173, 317
exorcism, 34, 87, 127, 287
famine, 30, 161
Father. *See* Trinity
Fausta, 44
Faustinus, 1–3, 24–25, 43–45, 51–53, 56–58, 129, 155, 169, 171, 177–81, 205
Faustus of Riez, 56
feast, divine, 177, 297
Felix of Rome, 85, 129. *See also* Rome
Flacilla, 2, 26, 40, 65
   and the *De Trinitate*, 43–49, 177, 195, 205, 209, 221, 223, 233, 305, 315
Florentius of Merida, 28, 36, 99–101, 125. *See also* Merida
Florentius of Ostia, 36, 38, 131–33
Forgery, 40
Fortunatus of Naples, 85
Gaius (Arian), 75
Galen, 231
Galla Placidia, 43
Gaul, 4, 6, 9, 33, 52, 83, 105
Gemellinus of Eleutheropolis, 157–59
generationism, 20
Gennadius of Marseille, 20–21, 43–44, 51–53
George of Cappadocia, 141, 145–49, 321
Germanicia, 133
Germinius, 37, 75, 85
Gesta episcoporum Neapolitanorum, 85, 113
Gesta martyrum, 38
gladiators, 67
Goliath, 50, 219–21
Gratian, 25, 40, 53, 63, 117, 161
Great Persecution, 4, 65, 69
Greece, 9
Greek language, 17–19, 48, 51, 54, 137, 237, 285–87
Gregory Nazianzus, 18, 47, 48

Gregory of Elvira, 19, 51, 173, 175, 195
  and the *Libellus precum*, 26, 28, 31–32, 42, 45, 48, 81, 83, 91–101, 105, 119, 121, 125, 127, 137–39, 147
Gregory of Nyssa, 83, 205
Hebrew language, 237, 297
Helena, 44
hell, 99, 255
Heraclida of Oxyrhynchus, 27, 29, 36, 42, 143–49, 151, 173, 175
heresy, 9–11, 13
  and the *Confessio fidei*, 59–61
  and the *De Trinitate*, 47, 55–57
  and the *Lex Augusta*, 40–41
  and the *Libellus precum*, 27, 30–31, 33–34, 36
  Luciferians accused of, 14–23
Hermione, 27, 29, 32–33, 149–57
Hilarius (deacon), 6, 83–85
Hilary of Poitiers, 6–7, 9, 17, 57
  and the *De Trinitate*, 45–46, 48, 193, 197, 199, 209, 283, 285, 291, 307, 311
  and the *Libellus precum*, 27, 36, 81, 83, 93, 105, 107, 109, 127, 135
Hippolytus, 143
Holy Spirit. *See* Trinity
homoios, 8, 47, 157, 307. *See also* Trinity
homoiousios, 8, 157, 219, 223, 307. *See also* Trinity
homoousios, 4–6, 8, 181, 287, 307. *See also* Trinity
Honorius, 177
Hosius of Cordoba, 4, 7, 28, 31–32, 36–37, 52, 91–99, 123, 139
households, 129, 153, 155, 157
human nature, 46, 47
humors, 231
Hydatius of Merida, 101, 125. *See also* Merida
Hyginus, 29, 35–36, 123–25
hypostasis. *See* Trinity
idols, 32, 89, 103, 125, 293
image. *See* appearance
imprisonment, 29, 35, 73, 111, 121, 123, 129

Indiculus de haeresibus, 19–22
Isaac, 235–45
Isaiah, 77, 265, 267, 271–75, 287, 313
Isidore of Seville, 51–53
Italy, 33, 139. *See also* Milan; Naples
Jehu, 28, 119–21
Jeremiah, 233, 267
Jerome, 2, 8–10, 12, 17–19, 21–22, 35, 39, 53, 65, 91, 109, 119, 129, 151, 179, 181
  Dialogus adversus Luciferianos, 2, 21, 51
John Maxentius, 20
John the Baptist, 157, 223, 233, 289, 325
Jovian, 26, 28, 107
Judaism, 35, 179, 201, 211, 221, 321, 323
judge, 31–32, 34, 63, 95, 97, 131–35, 139
Julian, 8, 26, 28, 87, 105–7, 133
Julian of Eclanum, 22, 205
Justina, 25, 44, 83
Justinian, 53
kingdom of Christ/heaven, 77, 87, 169, 233, 285, 295, 315, 327
Lactantius, 21, 249
laws, 30–31, 34–35, 40–43, 50, 53–54, 63–65, 73, 91–97, 105, 111, 119, 131–35, 145, 149, 157, 159, 163, 171–73, 287, 321–23. *See also Lex Augusta*
lay status, 9, 30, 38, 41, 103, 105, 109, 117–19, 131, 141, 147–49, 175
letters, 29, 33, 51, 105, 151, 155, 163, 317–29
Lex Augusta, 2, 19, 40–43, 53–54, 55, 171–75
Libellus precum, 2, 12, 17, 24–39, 40, 43, 47, 48, 65
  date, 25–26
  as a martyr narrative, 31, 37–38
  outline, 26–30
  parallel structure, 32–33
  as a petition, 30–31
  text and editions, 51–54, 55
Liberius of Merida, 99. *See also* Merida
Liberius of Rome, 6–8, 79–81, 83, 85, 105, 115, 129. *See also* Rome
Licinius, 4

Lisbon, 91, 125. *See also* Potamius of Lisbon
Lot, 39, 119
Luciferian (name), 1, 10–14, 15, 27, 29, 35, 133–35, 139
Lucifer of Cagliari, 6–7, 9–16, 21, 26–29, 33, 51, 73, 79–81, 83–85, 105, 113–15, 127, 133–39, 141, 159, 255–57, 317–29
Luciosus, 29, 35, 36, 123–25
Macarius, 27, 29, 36, 38
Macedonians. *See* Pneumatomachians
Magnentius, 5
Magnus Maximus, 25, 30, 42, 63
Majorinus, 4
Mammon, 293. *See also* wealth
Manichaeans, 21
Marcellinus, 1, 3, 25, 44–45, 52–53, 129, 155, 169, 171
Marcellus of Ancyra, 16, 18–19, 193, 291
Marius Victorinus, 45, 205
martyrs
 cult, 87, 127, 131–33, 141
 narrative tropes about, 31–33, 37–38
 and the *Libellus precum*, 25, 27–29, 36, 38, 79, 85–87, 89, 97, 107, 111–15, 119, 121–23, 127, 129, 167
 and Pseudo-Athanasius, *Ep.* 51, 323–25
Maternus Cynegius. *See* Cynegius
Maximian, 85
Maximus of Naples, 27, 28, 85, 113–15
Melchizedek, 287
Meletians, 69, 149
Meletius of Antioch, 9–10, 12–15, 17
Meletius of Lycopolis, 69
Merida, 32. *See also* Florentius of Merida; Hydatius of Merida; Liberius of Merida
midrash, 239
Milan, 6, 117
 Council of, 6–7, 75, 79–81, 83, 133
military, 6, 40, 46, 139, 145, 321. *See also* Adrianople; officials, government
 imagery, 179–81, 183, 209, 219–21
miracles, 32, 34, 87, 127, 137–39, 153, 209, 255, 289

mob violence, 29, 123–25, 141, 145, 175
modalism, 16
monasteries, 34, 147, 151, 321. *See also* asceticism; virgins, dedicated
Mopsuestia, 105
morning star (Lucifer), 255–61
Moses, 191, 195, 217, 227, 279, 291
Naples, 26, 32, 85–87, 113–15. *See also* Maximus of Naples; Zosimus of Naples
Nicaea, Council of, 3–4, 7, 15, 17, 59, 71, 73, 75
 in the *Libellus precum*, 25, 67
Nicene Creed, 1, 4–9, 14–15, 24, 33, 44, 59, 65, 67, 71, 73, 75, 79, 81, 109, 157, 197
Nicetas of Remesiana, 51
Noah, 28, 38–39, 119
nobility, 34, 149–53
North Africa, 3–4, 29, 117, 155
Novatians, 10, 42–43, 52, 131, 143
officials, government, 31–32, 34–35, 52, 93, 131, 145, 153
omnipotence, 46, 171, 173, 175, 209, 215, 219, 241, 261–67, 279, 295
Origen, 161
original sin, 21. *See also* sin
Osius. *See* Hosius of Cordoba
ousia. *See homoios*; *homoiousios*; *homoousios*; Trinity
Oxyrhynchus, 27, 29, 36, 79, 139–49. *See also* Heraclida of Oxyrhynchus
pagans, 8, 27, 31–32, 35, 37, 40, 87, 105–7, 119, 125, 131, 167, 181, 271, 293
Palestine, 29, 33, 149, 155, 159. *See also* Eleutheropolis
Palladius, 275
Pancratius, 6
patronage, 45, 50, 81, 179, 323
Paul (ascetic), 139–41
Paulinus of Antioch, 9–17, 56, 85, 107, 323. *See also* Antioch
Paulinus of Bordeaux, 56
Paulinus of Trier, 6, 27, 33, 79, 127. *See also* Trier

peaceful coexistence, 28, 30, 36–37, 109–13, 119, 121, 125, 163–65, 175
penance, 9, 105, 107, 119, 293
persecution
    under Constantine, 1, 4–5
    under Constantius II, 5–8, 27–28, 31–32
    in the *Lex Augusta*, 173
    in the *Libellus precum*, 26–39, 41, 65, 67, 75–87, 111, 121, 127, 129–35, 145–49, 155–61
    in Pseudo-Athanasius, *Ep.* 50, 317
    in Pseudo-Athanasius, *Ep.* 51, 321, 327
    as proof of virtue, 27, 37–38, 111, 167
Persia, 105, 107
person. *See* Trinity
Peter of Alexandria, 42
petitions, 1, 30–31, 40–41, 44, 171, 173. *See also Libellus precum*
philosophy, 135, 163, 203–5, 253–55. *See also* Aristotle; classical literature
Phoebadius of Agen, 45, 93, 271, 279
Photinus of Sirmium, 45, 171, 207, 291
Phrygia, 79, 83
Pneumatomachians, 47, 161–63, 305
Potamius of Lisbon, 28, 36, 91, 99. *See also* Lisbon
Praetextatus, 53
prefiguration, 39, 239, 243
prevaricators, 1, 9, 26–30, 32, 34–36, 45, 47, 50, 67, 85, 89–97, 101, 109, 113, 117–19, 121, 123, 127, 139–45, 151–61, 313
    as a term, 35
presbyter. *See* clergy
Priscillian, 123–25
Pseudo-Athanasius, 51, 137, 317–29
Pseudo-Hegemonius, 16
punishment, divine, 32, 36, 38, 69–73, 77, 89–91, 93, 97–103, 111–17, 121, 145, 165, 173, 315
purity, 28, 34, 38–39, 63, 69, 81, 91, 127, 133, 151, 153, 169
Quae gesta sunt inter Liberium et Felicem episcopos, 129, 135, 143

rebaptism, 23, 103, 221. *See also* baptism
rescripts. *See* laws
resurrection, 253, 255
Rhodanius of Toulouse, 7, 27, 83
Rimini, Council of, 8, 26–28, 59, 75–77, 79, 109, 163
Roman Empire, 1, 3, 5, 8, 30, 37, 40–41, 43–45, 63, 109, 127, 131, 155, 159–61, 167–69
Rome, 4, 6, 11, 27, 29–30, 36, 53–54, 93, 127–35, 139, 141, 143, 151–53, 155, 161, 173. *See also* Aurelius of Rome; Damasus of Rome; Ephesius of Rome; Felix of Rome; Liberius of Rome; Ursinus of Rome; Vigilius of Rome
Rufininus, 27, 85
Rufinus, 2, 10–15, 21–22
Sabellianism, 14, 16–19, 24, 45, 59, 125, 161, 171, 193, 195, 199, 207–9, 291
sacraments, 103, 129, 139, 141, 151, 155, 157, 159, 163, 293
sacrifice, 27, 32, 89, 125, 235, 241
sarcasm, 35, 65, 105, 117, 123, 145, 147, 155
Sardica, Council of, 99
Sardinia, 10–11, 15, 33, 79, 81, 117, 137. *See also* Lucifer of Cagliari
Satan/devil, 71, 73, 125, 129, 165, 215, 233, 257, 289, 307, 325
schism, 2, 10–14, 23, 42–43, 56–57
Seleucia-in-Isauria, Council of, 8, 27, 75, 77
servant/slave, 189, 225, 235, 243, 265, 269, 281, 285, 317, 327, 329
Severus, 27, 29, 36, 153–55
Shenoute, 325
sign of the Lord, 221
Simeon Stylites, 325
sin, 21, 39, 48, 173, 179, 223, 241, 243, 267, 269, 271–73, 277, 285, 293, 313, 319, 321
Sirmian Creed
    Second, 7, 46
    Fourth, 8, 37, 75
Sirmium, 7

slave/servant. *See* servant/slave
Socrates Scholasticus, 12–15
soldiers. *See* military
Son. *See* Trinity
Sozomen, 13, 15
Spain, 9, 27–29, 31–33, 36, 40, 44, 52, 91–101, 121–25, 139, 177
Spartans, epitaph for, 179
subordinationism, 16. *See also* Trinity
substance. *See* Trinity
superstition, 48, 171–73, 315
Talmud, 221
Taorgius, 133, 151
Taunacius Isfalangius, 123
Tertullian, 17, 20–22, 167
Thebaid, 9, 81, 135, 141. *See also* Egypt; Oxyrhynchus
Theodore of Oxyrhynchus, 29, 36, 141, 145–49
Theodoret of Cyrrhus, 15–16, 325
Theodosius I, 1–2, 19, 24–27, 30, 32, 37, 40–44, 59, 63, 89, 93, 117, 167–69, 171, 173, 177. *See also Lex Augusta*
Theodosius II, 52
Thermopylae, 179
traditor, 35
traducianism, 14, 19–22
trials, 29, 31–32, 34, 131–35
Trier, 29, 33, 79, 125–27, 139. *See also* Bonosus of Trier; Paulinus of Trier
Trinity, 3–5, 7–8, 16–17, 24, 45–50. *See also* adoption; appearance; begotten, as opposed to created; *Confessio fidei*; created, as opposed to begotten; *De Trinitate*; eternality; *homoios*; *homoiousios*; *homoousios*; omnipotence; subordinationism
 Eastern and Western terminology, 17–19, 59
 the Holy Spirit and, 24, 46, 47
Turbo of Eleutheropolis, 30, 32–33, 36, 155–59
Tyre, 12
Ulfilas, 157
Ursacius, 37, 75, 79, 83, 85

Ursinus of Rome, 18, 129–31
Valens, 26–28, 31, 40, 53, 65, 107, 117
Valens of Mursa, 6, 37, 75, 79, 83, 85
Valentinian I, 28, 53, 81, 91, 107, 117, 123
Valentinian II, 25, 40, 44, 63, 89
Vigilius of Rome, 53. *See also* Rome
Vigilius of Thapsus, 51
Vincentius, 27, 29, 93, 121–25
Virgin Mary, 157, 225, 255, 267, 269, 273, 283, 289
virgins, dedicated, 147, 149–51, 155–57. *See also* asceticism; monasteries
wealth, 30, 77, 91, 99, 103, 113, 163, 165–67, 271, 293. *See also* asceticism
will, 209–11, 213–19, 273–75, 281
Wisdom, 183, 185, 189, 213, 219, 263–65, 283, 289–91, 295–305
works, 213, 295–305
Zaragoza, Council of, 125
Zosimus of Naples, 26, 28, 36, 85, 113–17

www.ingramcontent.com/pod-product-compliance
Lightning Source LLC
Chambersburg PA
CBHW032149010526
44111CB00035B/1254